Thomas Vallaitis

Ultrafast Nonlinear Silicon Waveguides and Quantum Dot Semiconductor Optical Amplifiers

Characterization and Applications

Karlsruhe Series in Photonics & Communications, Vol. 7
Edited by Prof. J. Leuthold and Prof. W. Freude

Karlsruhe Institute of Technology,
Institute of Photonics and Quantum Electronics (IPQ)
Germany

Ultrafast Nonlinear Silicon Waveguides and Quantum Dot Semiconductor Optical Amplifiers

Characterization and Applications

by
Thomas Vallaitis

 Scientific Publishing

Dissertation, Karlsruher Institut für Technologie
Fakultät für Elektrotechnik und Informationstechnik, 2010

Impressum

Karlsruher Institut für Technologie (KIT)
KIT Scientific Publishing
Straße am Forum 2
D-76131 Karlsruhe
www.ksp.kit.edu

KIT – Universität des Landes Baden-Württemberg und nationales
Forschungszentrum in der Helmholtz-Gemeinschaft

KIT Scientific Publishing 2011
Print on Demand

ISSN: 1865-1100
ISBN: 978-3-86644-748-6

Ultrafast Nonlinear Silicon Waveguides and Quantum Dot Semiconductor Optical Amplifiers: Characterization and Applications

Zur Erlangung des akademischen Grades eines

DOKTOR-INGENIEURS

von der Fakultät für
Elektrotechnik und Informationstechnik
des Karlsruher Instituts für Technologie (KIT)

genehmigte

DISSERTATION

von

Dipl.-Phys. Thomas Vallaitis

geb. in: Böblingen

Tag der mündlichen Prüfung: 06.07.2010
Hauptreferent: Prof. Dr. sc. nat. Jürg Leuthold
Korreferenten: Prof. Dr.-Ing. Dr. h. c. Wolfgang Freude
                               Prof. Dr. rer. nat. Michael Siegel

Well done is better than well said.
– Benjamin Franklin (1706-1760)

Table of Contents

List of Figures

Abstract (German)

Die vorliegende Arbeit befasst sich mit den grundlegenden Eigenschaften von nichtlinearen Siliziumwellenleitern und optischen Quantenpunktverstärkern. Theoretische Betrachtungen werden dabei von einer detaillierten Charakterisierung der Stärke und Dynamik der linearen und nichtlinearen Prozesse ergänzt. Mit dem gewonnenen Verständnis werden vielversprechende Anwendungen für die optische Signalverarbeitung identifiziert und in Systemexperimenten erstmals auch demonstriert.

Das anhaltend schnelle Wachstum des Internet-Datenverkehrs stellt unsere Netze vor neue Herausforderungen - nicht nur für die übertragenen Datenraten, sondern vor allem auch für den Energieverbrauch und die Schadstoffemissionen. Um dieses Wachstum in Zukunft umweltverträglich zu gestalten, nimmt die voll-optische Signalverarbeitung eine wichtige Rolle ein. Voll-optische Vermittlungsknoten für zukünfige Übertragungsgeschwindigkeiten von mehr als 100 Gbit/s pro Wellenlänge beruhen auf zwei entscheidenden Komponenten: zum einen auf energieeffizienten linearen Verstärkern, zum anderen auf kompakten nichtlinearen Elementen.

Optische Quantenpunktverstärker sind vielversprechende nanophotonische Bauteile, die selbstorganisierte InAs Quantenpunkte als aktives Medium verwenden. Eine genaue Kontrolle der Wachstumsbedingungen ermöglicht, viele Eigenschaften wie z.B. das Gewinnspektrum gezielt zu wählen. Eine besondere Rolle spielt dabei die Zusammensetzung der umgebenden Schichten, die die Zusammensetzung der einzelnen Quantenpunkte maßgeblich beeinflusst.

Die Charakterisierung der Ladungsträgerdynamiken zeigt, dass die erhoffte schnelle Erholung der Amplitude immer von einer schwachen, aber unerwünscht langsamen Erholung der Phase begleitet wird. Während dies nichtlineare Anwendungen vor große Herausforderungen stellt, werden Anwendungen wie die lineare Verstärkung durch den kleinen dabei auftretenden Chirp begünstigt.

Systemexperimente mit amplituden- und phasenkodierten Signalen zeigen zum ersten Mal, dass quantenpunktbasierte Verstärker weniger Verzerrungen als herkömmliche Verstärker erzeugen. Mit ihrem erhöhten Eingangsleistungs-dynamikbereich stellen optische Quantenpunktverstärker daher vielversprechende

Bauteile für Zugangsnetze und Netze mit Modulationsverfahren höherer Ordnung darstellen.

Hybridintegration von Silizium-Wellenleitern mit organischen Materialien (engl. Silicon-Organic Hybrid, SOH) ist ein neuartiger Ansatz, um in einem Silizium-CMOS Prozess hochgradig nichtlineare passive Wellenleiter herzustellen. Dabei wird insbesondere die Wechselwirkung von hochkonzentriertem Licht mit einem nichtlinearen Mantelmaterial ausgenutzt, um die Bauteileigenschaften entscheidend zu verbessern. Die Charakterisierung der Ladungsträgerdynamiken zeigt dabei den entscheidenden Einfluss der gewählten Wellenleitergeometrie.

Wird nur die Nichtlinearität des Siliziumwellenleiterkerns ausgenutzt, so wird der erwünschte Kerr-Effekt von unerwünschter Zweiphotonenabsorption und einem langsamen Plasmaeffekt begleitet. Für hohe Lichtintensitäten leiden diese Wellenleiter unter Bitmustereffekten und sind daher für voll-optisches Schalten ungeeignet.

Wird ein erheblicher Anteil des Modus im Mantelmaterial geführt, so leistet die Kerr-Nichtlinearität des Mantelmaterials einen starken Beitrag und die unerwünschten Effekte des Siliziumwellenleiterkerns werden reduziert. Diese Wellenleiter sind einfach herzustellen und für voll-optisches Schalten ausreichend geeignet.

Wird in einer Schlitzwellenleitergeometrie der größte Teil des Modus auf ein sehr kleinen Querschnitt im Schlitz konzentriert, so dominieren die Eigenschaften des nichtlinearen Mantelmaterials. In diesen Wellenleitern ist der schnelle Kerr-Effekt nicht durch Zweiphotonenabsorption und den langsamen Plasmaeffekt begrenzt, was voll-optische Signalverarbeitung bis zu höchsten Geschwindigkeiten ermöglicht

Systemexperimente zur Wellenlängenkonversion zeigen, dass die verbesserten Eigenschaften der Hybridwellenleiter zum ersten Mal in der Siliziumphotonik volloptische Signalverarbeitung bei Geschwindigkeiten über 40 Gbit/s erlauben. Besonders die erfolgreiche Kreuzphasenmodulation (XPM) und die Vierwellenmischung (FWM) von phasenkodierten Signalen unterstreichen die mögliche Bedeutung von integrierten nichtlinearen Elementen für die Siliziumphotonik.

Preface

Novel integrated optical devices are key to the sustainability and growth of our information society. Compact and fast nonlinear devices and amplifiers are required to increase the network speed and simultaneously reduce the energy consumption.

Overall, the internet traffic will grow exponentially at a compound annual growth rate of 40 percent and increase by a factor of 5 from 2008 to 2013 [1]. In 2008, the internet is already responsible for 2 percent of the worldwide energy consumption, and the energy consumption is predicted to increase up to 15 percent of the worldwide energy consumption in 2020 [2]. While the exact values are debated [3], it is clear that a in information and communication technology a minimum reduction of the CO_2 emissions by 15 percent is needed until 2020 [4] in order to reduce global greenhouse gas emissions and to combat climate change.

A key parameter for quantifying the energy efficiency of a network is the energy required to transmit one bit. Depending on the available technology and the investigated scenario, the required energy per bit can be reduced by electronics [5] or optimized optics [6]. For bitrates up to 100 Gbit/s, the general opinion is that all-optical processing based on highly nonlinear fibers (HNLF) and periodically poled lithium niobate (PPLN) waveguides have larger footprint and power requirements than CMOS technologies [7]. While electronic devices build on a product development period of 40 years, optical devices still have a large potential for optimization. Indeed, optical signal processing is expected to become competitive for bitrates exceeding 100 Gbit/s [8].

To enable high-speed all-optical signal processing two key components are required: energy efficient amplifiers and compact nonlinear elements.

Amplifiers based on quantum dots promise unique properties, like high-speed operation, high gain, low noise figure, high energy efficiency, and large input power dynamic range (IPDR). Hybrid integration of silicon waveguides and highly nonlinear organic cladding materials is a promising approach to achieve record nonlinearities in very compact passive devices.

In this thesis, the suitability of quantum dot semiconductor optical amplifiers (QD SOA) and ultrafast nonlinear silicon-organic hybrid (SOH) waveguides for all-optical signal processing is investigated and possible applications are identified and demonstrated.

The thesis is structured as follows. In Chapter 1, the fundamental electromagnetic theory for linear and nonlinear waveguides is discussed and the heterodyne pump-probe measurement technique is introduced.

In Chapter 2, quantum dot semiconductor optical amplifiers are investigated. The influence of growth conditions on quantum dot formation is studied and the dynamics of QD SOA are characterized. Due to the slow phase recovery, linear amplification is identified as the main application, and a record-large IPDR of up to 30 dB is found both for amplitude-encoded and phase-encoded signals. This research has been published in several journal articles ([J1], [J2], [J6]–[J10]) and conference contributions ([C1], [C2], [C4], [C8], [C11], [C15], [C18], [C19], [C21], [C22], [C24], [C26], [C29]–[C34]).

In Chapter 3, the silicon-organic hybrid technology is introduced and basic designs of nonlinear waveguide are discussed. Experimentally, we find an optimum Kerr nonlinearity parameter of $\gamma \approx 100\,000\,(\mathrm{W\,km})^{-1}$. Unlike in monolithic silicon waveguides, the nonlinearity introduced by SOH technology does not suffer from two-photon absorption and slow free-carrier effects. In a series of experiments, the suitability of SOH waveguides for all-optical signal processing is demonstrated. This includes the first demonstration of cross-phase modulation at communication speeds and wavelengths and the first demonstrations of wavelength conversion of 42.7 Gbit/s 33% return-to-zero on-off keying (RZ-OOK). The suitability for advanced modulation formats is demonstrated by wavelength conversion of 56 Gbit/s non-return-to-zero differential quadrature phase-shift keying (NRZ-DQPSK) signals. Finally, we report on high-speed all-optical demultiplexing of time-multiplexed 170 Gbit/s down to a bitrate of 42.7 Gbit/s. These results have published in journal articles ([J3]–[J5]) and in several conference contributions ([C3], [C9], [C13], [C14], [C16], [C17], [C20], [C23], [C25], [C27], [C28]).

Chapter 4 summarizes the work and gives an outlook on future research.

Achievements of the Present Work

In this thesis, state of the art quantum dot semiconductor optical amplifiers (QD SOA) and nonlinear silicon-organic hybrid (SOH) waveguides have been investigated. By detailed characterization of steady-state and dynamic device properties, advantageous applications have been identified and proof-of-principle experiments have been demonstrated.

In the following, we give a concise overview of the main achievements.

Quantum Dot Fabrication: An extensive study of the influence of the growth parameters on quantum dot formation shows that shift of the ground state emission to the 1.3 µm wavelength region can be attributed to an increase in quantum dot size as well as to strain effects [J10].

Influence of Capping Layer: the growth of a capping layer strongly influences the composition of the quantum dot. Contrary to previous assumptions, if the composition analysis is corrected for wetting layer effects, a high indium concentration of up to 90% is found at the top of the quantum dot [J8].

QD SOA Dynamics: Heterodyne pump-probe spectroscopy is used to investigate amplitude and phase dynamics, with an emphasis on prospective system performance. Two characteristic time scales are found [C34]. The fast recovery process dominates the material gain response and shows a very small alpha-factor, i.e. a small chirp. The slow recovery process contributes only little to the gain dynamics but since the associated alpha-factor is large it dominates the phase response of the device and may significantly contribute to chirp [J7].

QD SOA Multi-Wavelength Capability: Steady-state cross-gain modulation is used to measure the homogeneous linewidth. At room temperature, a value of 16 meV is measured for a quantum dot ensemble with high dot density, which is in very good agreement with theoretical predictions. However, this corresponds to a linewidth of 22 nm or 60% of the total gain bandwidth, which effectively prevents multi-wavelength operation under gain saturation conditions.

Linear Amplification of Amplitude-Encoded Signals: For linear applications, quantum dot semiconductor optical amplifiers combine ultra-fast carrier dynamics with low distortions. In combination with the high gain, the moderate noise figure, and the relative temperature insensitivity, quantum dot semiconductor optical amplifiers fulfill all requirements for in-line amplifiers. For single-channel and multi-channel amplification of amplitude-shift keying signals, a large input power dynamic range is found, exceeding the performance of specially engineered linear optical amplifiers [C29]. For access networks, passive optical networks with quantum dot based range extenders might be a viable solution for providing cost efficient broadband internet access [C1][C12][C18][C19].

Linear Amplification of Phase-Encoded Signals: As inline amplifiers for phase-shift keying signals, clear advantages of quantum dot semiconductor optical amplifiers over bulk or quantum well semiconductor optical amplifiers are found. The alpha-factor in QD SOA is lower than in bulk SOA. As a consequence, in QD SOA the conversion of amplitude fluctuations to phase fluctuations is reduced and less phase errors are introduced [J1][C10].

SOH Waveguide Characterization: Geometry, nonlinearity, dispersion and two-photon absorption figure of merit of three basic silicon-organic hybrid waveguide designs are compared. Four-wave mixing and heterodyne pump-probe measurements [C23][C28] show that all designs achieve high nonlinearity parameters of $\gamma \approx 100\,000\,(\mathrm{W\,km})^{-1}$. The funasdamental limitation of two-photon absorption in silicon is overcome using silicon- organic hybrid integration, with a five-fold improvement for the figure of merit ($\mathrm{FOM_{TPA}}$). The value of $\mathrm{FOM_{TPA}} = 2.19$ measured for silicon-compatible nonlinear slot waveguides is the highest value published [J4].

Cross-Phase Modulation (XPM) in SOH Waveguides: Due to their large two-photon absorption figure of merit, slot waveguides have enabled the first proof-of-principle demonstration of cross-phase modulation at communication speeds and wavelengths on a silicon chip [C16].

Four-Wave Mixing (FWM) in SOH Waveguides: In slot waveguides, no slow patterning effects are found. This has enables error-free wavelength conversion of 42.7 Gbit/s 33% RZ-OOK signals [C17] and demultiplexing of data streams up to 170 Gbit/s using four-wave mixing [J5][C27].

Wavelength Conversion of Phase-Encoded Signals: SOH strip waveguides with cladding nonlinearity also show a large nonlinearity, yet are easy to fabricate. At 56 Gbit/s, this has enabled the fastest wavelength conversion experiment in silicon photonics, using four-wave mixing in a silicon-organic hybrid waveguide operated in transverse magnetic mode [C9].

1 Theoretical Background

To understand the linear and nonlinear optical phenomena present in semiconductor optical amplifiers and silicon waveguides, it is necessary to consider the electromagnetic theory in waveguides and dispersive media. Most of the concepts are standard knowledge and subject of a large number of textbooks. A good general overview of photonics can be found in the textbook by Saleh and Teich [9]. A comprehensive theory on linear waveguiding is developed in the books by Marcuse [10, 11] and Kawano and Kitoh [12]. A good introduction to nonlinear phenomena in bulk materials is presented in the book by Boyd [13]. Finally, for nonlinear effects in optial fibers, see the standard references by Agrawal [14, 15].

This chapter is structured as follows. In Section 1.1, the basic electromagnetic theory is introduced, beginning with Maxwell's equations. In Section 1.2, the propagation in linear waveguides is studied and the influence of dispersion, loss, and free carrier effects is discussed. In Section 1.3, the theory on third-order nonlinear interaction in waveguides is derived. Prominent effects are discussed, and the two-photon absorption figure of merit is derived. Section 1.4 describes wave propagation in an optical amplifier. Key parameters like gain and noise figure are introduced. Finally, to access all waveguide properties experimentally, the pump-probe spectroscopy is introduced in Section 1.5. Starting with a theoretical description of the heterodyne detection scheme, a direct measurement technique for the characteristic two-photon absorption figure of merit is developed.

1.1 Maxwell's Equations

The propagation of electromagnetic radiation in waveguides is governed by Maxwell's equations. In the absence of free charges and currents they take the form

$$\nabla \times \mathbf{H}(\mathbf{r},t) = \frac{\partial \mathbf{D}(\mathbf{r},t)}{\partial t}, \tag{1.1.1}$$

$$\nabla \times \mathbf{E}(\mathbf{r},t) = -\frac{\partial \mathbf{B}(\mathbf{r},t)}{\partial t}, \tag{1.1.2}$$

$$\nabla \cdot \mathbf{D}(\mathbf{r},t) = 0, \tag{1.1.3}$$

$$\nabla \cdot \mathbf{B}(\mathbf{r},t) = 0, \tag{1.1.4}$$

where $\mathbf{E}(\mathbf{r},t)$ and $\mathbf{H}(\mathbf{r},t)$ are the electric and magnetic field vectors, respectively. These vectors depend on the special coordinate $\mathbf{r}$ and the time t. We assume nonmagnetic media, to the magnetic flux density $\mathbf{B}(\mathbf{r},t)$ is

$$\mathbf{B}(\mathbf{r},t) = \mu_0 \mathbf{H}(\mathbf{r},t), \tag{1.1.5}$$

where $\mu_0 = 1.25664 \times 10^{-6}$ Vs/(Am) is the magnetic permeability of vacuum. The displacement field $\mathbf{D}(\mathbf{r},t)$ is

$$\mathbf{D}(\mathbf{r},t) = \varepsilon_0 \mathbf{E}(\mathbf{r},t) + \mathbf{P}(\mathbf{r},t), \tag{1.1.6}$$

where $\varepsilon_0 = 8.85419 \times 10^{-12}$ As/(Vm) is the electric permittivity of vacuum and $\mathbf{P}(\mathbf{r},t)$ denotes the electrical polarization.

If the optical frequency is far from all resonances in a medium, the spatially local response $\mathbf{P}(\mathbf{r},t)$ to a field $\mathbf{E}(\mathbf{r},t)$ can be phenomenologically described by a Volterra series,

$$\begin{aligned}
\mathbf{P}(\mathbf{r},t) = \varepsilon_0 &\int\limits_{-\infty}^{+\infty} \underline{\chi}^{(1)}(t-t')\mathbf{E}(\mathbf{r},t')\,\mathrm{d}t' \\
+\varepsilon_0 &\int\limits_{-\infty}^{+\infty}\!\!\int \underline{\chi}^{(2)}(t-t',t-t''):\mathbf{E}(\mathbf{r},t')\mathbf{E}(\mathbf{r},t'')\,\mathrm{d}t'\,\mathrm{d}t'' \\
+\varepsilon_0 &\int\limits_{-\infty}^{+\infty}\!\!\int\!\!\int \underline{\chi}^{(3)}(t-t',t-t'',t-t'''):\mathbf{E}(\mathbf{r},t')\mathbf{E}(\mathbf{r},t'')\mathbf{E}(\mathbf{r},t''')\,\mathrm{d}t'\,\mathrm{d}t''\,\mathrm{d}t''' \\
+\ldots &
\end{aligned} \tag{1.1.7}$$

where the influence functions $\underline{\chi}^{(n)}(t',t'',\ldots,t^{(n)})$ are tensors of rank $n+1$ and form the Volterra kernel of n-th order. To improve readability, the spatial dependence of $\underline{\chi}^{(n)}(t',t'',\ldots,t^{(n)})$ is omitted here.

Linear Polarization

The polarization

$$\mathbf{P}(\mathbf{r},t) = \mathbf{P}_{\mathrm{L}}(\mathbf{r},t) + \mathbf{P}_{\mathrm{NL}}(\mathbf{r},t). \tag{1.1.8}$$

can be split into a dominant contribution that depends linearly on the electric field,

$$\mathbf{P}_{\mathrm{L}}(\mathbf{r},t) = \varepsilon_0 \int\limits_{-\infty}^{+\infty} \underline{\chi}^{(1)}(t-t')\mathbf{E}(\mathbf{r},t')\,\mathrm{d}t', \tag{1.1.9}$$

and into further contributions, that depend on higher orders of the electric field

$$\mathbf{P}_{\mathrm{NL}}(\mathbf{r},t) = \varepsilon_0 \int\limits_{-\infty}^{+\infty}\int \underline{\chi}^{(2)}(t-t',t-t''):\mathbf{E}(\mathbf{r},t')\mathbf{E}(\mathbf{r},t'')\,dt'\,dt''$$

$$+\varepsilon_0 \int\limits_{-\infty}^{+\infty}\int\int \underline{\chi}^{(3)}(t-t',t-t'',t-t''') \vdots \mathbf{E}(\mathbf{r},t')\mathbf{E}(\mathbf{r},t'')\mathbf{E}(\mathbf{r},t''')\,dt'\,dt''\,dt''' \quad (1.1.10)$$

$$+\ldots$$

Although nonlinear polarization effects $\mathbf{P}_{\mathrm{NL}}$ are of particular interest, they can be treated as small perturbations to the linear polarization $\mathbf{P}_{\mathrm{L}}$ in all practical cases. In the following, linear waveguide theory will be discussed first, and consequences of nonlinear polarization terms will be included later.

After Fourier-transformation (A.21), the linear polarization becomes

$$\tilde{\mathbf{P}}(\mathbf{r},\omega) = \underline{\tilde{\chi}}^{(1)}(\omega)\tilde{\mathbf{E}}(\mathbf{r},\omega), \qquad (1.1.11)$$

where the Fourier transform of the first-order influence function $\underline{\tilde{\chi}}^{(1)}(\omega)$ is the linear optical susceptibility. Since the polarization response of the medium is causal, the components of $\underline{\chi}^{(n)}(t',t'',\ldots,t^{(n)})$ vanish for negative time arguments. As a consequence, real and imaginary part of the linear complex susceptibility $\underline{\tilde{\chi}}^{(1)}(\omega)$ are connected by the Kramers-Kronig relations and cannot be chosen independently for all $\omega \in \mathbb{R}$. However, if we only consider a small interval $\omega_1 < \omega < \omega_2$, we can freely choose real and imaginary part of $\underline{\tilde{\chi}}^{(1)}(\omega)$ independently.

Under the assumption that in the interval the susceptibility is constant $\underline{\tilde{\chi}}^{(1)}(\omega) = \underline{\tilde{\chi}}^{(1)} = \text{const.}$, the Fourier transformation of Eq. (1.1.11) simplifies the convolution in Eq. (1.1.9) to a simple multiplication with the optical susceptibility tensor $\underline{\tilde{\chi}}^{(1)}$, such that the displacement field in Eq. (1.1.6) becomes

$$\mathbf{D}(\mathbf{r},t) = \varepsilon_0 \left(\underline{\mathbf{1}} + \underline{\tilde{\chi}}^{(1)}\right)\mathbf{E}(\mathbf{r},t) = \varepsilon_0\underline{\varepsilon}_r\mathbf{E}(\mathbf{r},t), \qquad (1.1.12)$$

where $\underline{\mathbf{1}}$ denotes the unity tensor and $\underline{\varepsilon}_r$ is the dielectric permeability tensor. In the special case of isotropic media, the linear susceptibility tensor $\underline{\tilde{\chi}}^{(1)}$ can be replaced by scalar $\tilde{\chi}^{(1)}$, and the dielectric permeability tensor $\underline{\varepsilon}_r$ can be replaced by a scalar relative dielectric permeability $\varepsilon_r = 1 + \tilde{\chi}^{(1)}$. With the linear refractive index $n_0 = \sqrt{\varepsilon_r}$, the displacement field is given by

$$\mathbf{D}(\mathbf{r},t) = \varepsilon_0\varepsilon_r\mathbf{E}(\mathbf{r},t) = \varepsilon_0 n_0^2\mathbf{E}(\mathbf{r},t). \qquad (1.1.13)$$

Poynting Vector

The time dependent energy flux of the electromagnetic field is given by the Poynting vector

$$\mathbf{S}(\mathbf{r},t) = \mathbf{E}(\mathbf{r},t) \times \mathbf{H}(\mathbf{r},t). \tag{1.1.14}$$

In many cases the average energy flux is of interest. If the signals $\mathbf{E}(\mathbf{r},t)$ and $\mathbf{H}(\mathbf{r},t)$ are harmonic time signals with the angular frequency ω_c, and $\hat{\underline{\mathbf{E}}}(\mathbf{r},\omega_c)$ and $\hat{\underline{\mathbf{H}}}(\mathbf{r},\omega_c)$ are the complex amplitudes (A.38), the cross product of the complex amplitudes define a complex Poynting vector

$$\underline{\mathbf{S}}(\mathbf{r},\omega_c) = \frac{1}{2}\left(\hat{\mathbf{E}}(\mathbf{r},\omega_c) \times \hat{\underline{\mathbf{H}}}^*(\mathbf{r},\omega_c)\right). \tag{1.1.15}$$

The time averaged energy flux P through a surface D is then given by,

$$P(\omega_c) = \iint_D \mathrm{Re}\left[\underline{\mathbf{S}}(\mathbf{r},\omega_c)\right] \cdot \mathbf{n}\, ds, \tag{1.1.16}$$

where $\mathbf{n}$ is the normal to the surface D and ds is the associated surface element.

For a plane wave, where the approximation $|E(x,y,\omega_c)| = Z_0|H(x,y,\omega_c)|/n_0$ holds, the optical field intensity $I(x,y,\omega_c)$ is defined as

$$I(x,y,\omega_c) = \mathrm{Re}\left[\underline{\mathbf{S}}(x,y,\omega_c)\right] = \frac{1}{2}\frac{n_0}{Z_0}\left|\hat{E}(x,y,\omega_c)\right|^2. \tag{1.1.17}$$

1.2 Propagation in Linear Waveguides

We start with the curl of Eq. (1.1.1) and eliminate $\mathbf{B}$ and $\mathbf{D}$ in favor of $\mathbf{E}$ and $\mathbf{H}$, using Eqs. (1.1.2), (1.1.5), and (1.1.6),

$$\nabla \times \nabla \times \mathbf{E}(\mathbf{r},t) = -\frac{1}{c^2}\frac{\partial^2 \mathbf{E}(\mathbf{r},t)}{\partial t^2} - \mu_0\frac{\partial^2 \mathbf{P}(\mathbf{r},t)}{\partial t^2}, \tag{1.2.1}$$

where $c = (\varepsilon_0\mu_0)^{-1/2}$ is the speed of light in vacuum. If the nonlinear polarization $\mathbf{P}_{NL}$ is weak compared to the linear polarization $\mathbf{P}_L$, it can be treated as a small perturbation and be neglected for the moment.

In frequency domain, Eq. (1.2.1) for a linear waveguide becomes

$$\nabla \times \nabla \times \tilde{\mathbf{E}}(\mathbf{r},\omega) - \varepsilon(\omega)\frac{\omega^2}{c^2}\tilde{\mathbf{E}}(\mathbf{r},\omega) = 0. \tag{1.2.2}$$

With the propagation constant in vacuum $k_0 = \omega/c = 2\pi/\lambda$ and the vector identity $\nabla \times \nabla \times \mathbf{E} = \nabla(\nabla \cdot \mathbf{E}) - \nabla^2 \mathbf{E}$, we obtain from Eqs. (1.1.3) and (1.1.12)

$$\nabla^2 \tilde{\mathbf{E}}(\mathbf{r}, \omega) + \varepsilon(\omega) k_0^2 \tilde{\mathbf{E}}(\mathbf{r}, \omega) = 0. \tag{1.2.3}$$

Separation Ansatz

Eq. (1.2.3) can be solved by the method of separation of variables. If the signal consists of a carrier wave with a slowly varying envelope, the electric field $\tilde{\mathbf{E}}(\mathbf{r}, t)$ in the Fourier domain is an analytic function which can be written as the product of a transverse function $\mathcal{E}(x, y)$, an envelope function $\tilde{A}(z, \omega - \omega_c)$, a normalization constant $\mathcal{P}(\omega)^{-\frac{1}{2}}$, and a rapidly oscillating term $e^{-j\beta_{ref} z}$. The envelope $\tilde{A}(z, \omega - \omega_c)$ is a slowly varying function of z, and β_{ref} is an arbitrary propagation constant to be determined later,

$$\tilde{\underline{\mathbf{E}}}(\mathbf{r}, \omega - \omega_c) = \tilde{A}(z, \omega - \omega_c) \frac{\mathcal{E}(x, y, \omega_c)}{\sqrt{\mathcal{P}(\omega_c)}} e^{-j\beta_{ref} z}. \tag{1.2.4}$$

Analogously, the magnetic field is given by

$$\tilde{\underline{\mathbf{H}}}(\mathbf{r}, \omega - \omega_c) = \tilde{A}(z, \omega - \omega_c) \frac{\mathcal{H}(x, y, \omega_c)}{\sqrt{\mathcal{P}(\omega_c)}} e^{-j\beta_{ref} z}. \tag{1.2.5}$$

With the inverse Fourier transform (A.24) of the slowly varying envelope functions $F^{-1}\left\{\tilde{A}(z, \omega - \omega_c)\right\} = e^{j\omega_c t} A(z, t)$, the real-valued time domain ansatz for the electric field $\mathbf{E}(\mathbf{r}, t)$ and the magnetic field $\mathbf{H}(\mathbf{r}, t)$ is

$$\mathbf{E}(\mathbf{r}, t) = \frac{1}{2} \left\{ A(z, t) \frac{\mathcal{E}(x, y, \omega_c)}{\sqrt{\mathcal{P}(\omega_c)}} e^{j(\omega_c t - \beta_{ref} z)} + \text{c.c.} \right\}, \tag{1.2.6}$$

$$\mathbf{H}(\mathbf{r}, t) = \frac{1}{2} \left\{ A(z, t) \frac{\mathcal{H}(x, y, \omega_c)}{\sqrt{\mathcal{P}(\omega_c)}} e^{j(\omega_c t - \beta_{ref} z)} + \text{c.c.} \right\}, \tag{1.2.7}$$

where c.c. denotes the complex conjugate terms. The normalization constant is defined as

$$\mathcal{P}(\omega) = \frac{1}{2} \iint_{-\infty}^{+\infty} \text{Re}\left[\mathcal{E}(\omega) \times \mathcal{H}^*(\omega) \right] \cdot \mathbf{e}_z \, dx \, dy, \tag{1.2.8}$$

where $\mathbf{e}_z$ is the unit vector in z direction. This allows to normalize the transverse orthogonal field distributions $\mathcal{E}(x, y)$ and $\mathcal{H}(x, y)$ such that the guided-wave power is given by

$$P(z, t) = |A(z, t)|^2. \tag{1.2.9}$$

With the ansatz Eq. (1.2.4), the wave equation (1.2.3) reads

$$0 = \nabla^2 \left[\tilde{A}(z, \omega - \omega_c) \frac{\mathcal{E}(x, y, \omega_c)}{\sqrt{\mathcal{P}(\omega_c)}} e^{-j\beta_{ref} z} \right] + \varepsilon(\omega) k_0^2 \left[\tilde{A}(z, \omega - \omega_c) \frac{\mathcal{E}(x, y, \omega_c)}{\sqrt{\mathcal{P}(\omega_c)}} e^{-j\beta_{ref} z} \right],$$

(1.2.10)

$$0 = \left(\nabla^2 \mathcal{E}(x, y, \omega_c) \right) \tilde{A}(z, \omega - \omega_c)$$

$$+ \mathcal{E}(x, y, \omega_c) \left(\frac{\partial^2}{dz^2} - j2\beta_{ref} \frac{\partial}{dz} - \beta_{ref}^2 \right) \tilde{A}(z, \omega - \omega_c)$$

(1.2.11)

$$+ \varepsilon(\omega) k_0^2 \, \mathcal{E}(x, y, \omega_c) \, \tilde{A}(z, \omega - \omega_c).$$

For nonzero functions $\tilde{A}(z, \omega - \omega_c)$ and $\mathcal{E}(x, y)$, we can divide Eq. (1.2.11) by the product $\tilde{A}(z, \omega - \omega_c) \mathcal{E}(x, y, \omega_c)$,

$$0 = \frac{\nabla^2 \mathcal{E}(x, y, \omega_c)}{\mathcal{E}(x, y, \omega_c)} + \frac{1}{\tilde{A}(z, \omega - \omega_c)} \left(\frac{\partial^2}{dz^2} - j2\beta_{ref} \frac{\partial}{dz} \right) \tilde{A}(z, \omega - \omega_c) + \varepsilon(\omega) k_0^2 - \beta_{ref}^2.$$

(1.2.12)

Separation Constant

Since Eq. (1.2.12) should hold for all (x, y, z) we can separate the dependencies on (x, y) and z. As the sum of terms must be constant, we can define a separation constant $\beta'(\omega) \in \mathbb{C}$ [16],

$$\beta'^2 = \frac{\nabla^2 \mathcal{E}(x, y, \omega_c)}{\mathcal{E}(x, y, \omega_c)} + \varepsilon(\omega) k_0^2$$

$$= -\frac{1}{\tilde{A}(z, \omega - \omega_c)} \left(\frac{\partial^2}{dz^2} - j2\beta_{ref} \frac{\partial}{dz} \right) \tilde{A}(z, \omega - \omega_c) - \beta_{ref}^2.$$

(1.2.13)

Note that β'^2 could also be defined with a constant offset, as it would cancel again when performing the summation in Eq. (1.2.12). From Eq. (1.2.13) we can derive a set of coupled differential equations for the transverse field distribution $\mathcal{E}(x, y, \omega_c)$ and the envelope function $\tilde{A}(z, \omega - \omega_c)$,

$$\left[\nabla^2 + \varepsilon(\omega) k_0^2 \right] \mathcal{E}(x, y, \omega_c) = \beta'^2 \mathcal{E}(x, y, \omega_c),$$

(1.2.14)

$$\left(\frac{\partial^2}{dz^2} - j2\beta_{ref} \frac{\partial}{dz} \right) \tilde{A}(z, \omega - \omega_c) = -\left[\beta'^2 - \beta_{ref}^2 \right] \tilde{A}(z, \omega - \omega_c).$$

(1.2.15)

As a consequence of the separation ansatz Eq. (1.2.4), the value of β'^2 can be found by solving the eigenvalue problem of the transverse mode distribution in Eq. (1.2.14) without knowledge of the envelope function $\tilde{A}(z, \omega - \omega_c)$ in Eq. (1.2.15).

An analytic solution to this eigenvalue problem only possible for simple geometries like optical fibers or 2D slab waveguides [10-12]. For geometries with arbitrary cross-sections the problem is much harder [17]. A variety of numerical mode solvers exists, for example based on finite-difference [18], finite integration [19], finite-element [20], and mode-matching [21] techniques.

Slowly-Varying Envelope Approximation

As for most optical signals the change of the envelope is negligible on the order of one wavelength, in the slowly-varying envelope approximation (SVEA) higher order derivatives of the envelope are neglected,

$$\left|\frac{\partial}{\partial z}\tilde{A}\right| \ll \left|\beta_{\text{ref}}\tilde{A}\right| \quad \text{and} \quad \left|\frac{\partial^2}{\partial z^2}\tilde{A}\right| \ll \left|2\beta_{\text{ref}}\frac{\partial}{\partial z}\tilde{A}\right|. \tag{1.2.16}$$

With the ansatz in Eq. (1.2.4) and the slowly-varying envelope approximation, Eq. (1.2.15) simplifies to

$$-j2\beta_{\text{ref}}\frac{\partial \tilde{A}(z, \omega - \omega_c)}{\partial z} + \left[\beta'^2(\omega) - \beta_{\text{ref}}^2\right]\tilde{A}(z, \omega - \omega_c) = 0. \tag{1.2.17}$$

The error to Eq. (1.2.17) introduced by Eq. (1.2.16) can be minimized by choice of the arbitrary reference propagation constant,

$$\beta_{\text{ref}} \approx \beta'^2. \tag{1.2.18}$$

With Eq. (1.2.18) we can approximate

$$\beta'^2 - \beta_{\text{ref}}^2 = \left(\beta' + \beta_{\text{ref}}\right)\left(\beta' - \beta_{\text{ref}}\right) \approx 2\beta_{\text{ref}}(\beta' - \beta_{\text{ref}}), \tag{1.2.19}$$

which simplifies Eq. (1.2.17) even further,

$$\frac{\partial \tilde{A}(z, \omega - \omega_c)}{\partial z} + j\left[\beta'(\omega) - \beta_{\text{ref}}\right]\tilde{A}(z, \omega - \omega_c) = 0. \tag{1.2.20}$$

1.2.1 Dispersion

Assuming Eq. (1.2.14) has been solved, both eigenfunction $\mathcal{E}(x, y, \omega_c)$ and the eigenvalue

$$\beta^2(\omega) = \beta'^2(\omega) \tag{1.2.21}$$

are known. To evaluate the change of the signal envelope $\tilde{A}(z, \omega - \omega_c)$ in Eq. (1.2.20) for an unperturbed waveguide, the wave number $\beta(\omega)$ can be expanded in a Taylor series about the carrier frequency ω_c. When n_{eff} is the effective refractive index, the propagation constant is given by

$$\beta(\omega) = n_{\text{eff}}(\omega)\frac{\omega}{c} = \beta_0 + \beta_1\left(\omega - \omega_c\right) + \frac{1}{2}\beta_2\left(\omega - \omega_c\right)^2 + \dots$$

$$\beta_m = \frac{d^m \beta}{d\omega^m}\bigg|_{\omega = \omega_c} \qquad m = 0, 1, 2, \dots \tag{1.2.22}$$

The first-order term defines the group velocity v_g and group refractive index n_g, which describe the propagation of a wave packet along the z-direction,

$$\beta_1 = \frac{d\beta}{d\omega} = \frac{1}{c}\left(n_{\text{eff}} + \omega\frac{dn_{\text{eff}}}{d\omega}\right) = \frac{n_g}{c} = \frac{1}{v_g}. \tag{1.2.23}$$

The second-order term describes the group velocity dispersion (GVD) parameter, which is responsible for the spectral broadening of optical pulses,

$$\beta_2 = \frac{d\beta_1}{d\omega} = \frac{d}{d\omega}\left(\frac{1}{v_g}\right) = -\frac{1}{v_g^2}\frac{dv_g}{d\omega}. \tag{1.2.24}$$

Alternatively, this is often described by the dispersion coefficient D_2

$$D_2 = \frac{d\beta_1}{d\lambda} = -\frac{2\pi c}{\lambda^2}\beta_2 \approx -\frac{\lambda}{c}\frac{d^2 n_{\text{eff}}}{d\lambda^2}, \tag{1.2.25}$$

The third-order term defines the third order dispersion (TOD) parameter β_3,

$$\beta_3 = \frac{d^3 \beta}{d\omega^3} = \frac{d}{d\omega}\beta_2. \tag{1.2.26}$$

For bandwidth limited signals, the spectral width is often negligible compared to the carrier frequency, $\Delta\omega \ll \omega_c$. In practice, only for pulses shorter than 0.1 ps, the cubic and higher-order terms in Eq. (1.2.22) need to be taken into account [15].

1.2.2 Loss

Most effects in waveguides can be treated as small perturbations to the reference case of an unperturbed waveguide. The linear propagation loss can be treated as a small perturbation to the real-valued refractive index n_0. Through this complex-valued perturbation $\underline{\Delta n}$, also the refractive index can become complex,

$$\underline{n} = n' - jn'' = n_0 + \Delta n' - j\Delta n'' = n_0 + \underline{\Delta n}. \qquad (1.2.27)$$

The now complex dielectric permeability can be approximated as

$$\underline{\varepsilon}_r = \left(n_0 + \underline{\Delta n}\right)^2 \approx n_0^2 + 2n_0 \underline{\Delta n}. \qquad (1.2.28)$$

With the linear power loss coefficient α_0, the refractive index perturbation is

$$\underline{\Delta n} = -j\frac{\alpha_0}{2k_0}. \qquad (1.2.29)$$

The changed dielectric permeability causes a change of the propagation constant. From perturbation theory, the new propagation constant β is found [16]

$$\beta = \beta_0 + \Delta\beta = k_0(n_0 + \underline{\Delta n}) = \beta_0 - j\frac{\alpha_0}{2}. \qquad (1.2.30)$$

The evolution of the amplitude is described by Eq. (1.2.20).

Chosing the reference propagation constant as $\beta_{\text{ref}} = \beta_0$ leads to

$$\frac{\partial}{\partial z}\tilde{A}(z, \omega_c) = -\frac{\alpha_0}{2}\tilde{A}(z, \omega_c). \qquad (1.2.31)$$

The propagating power in a linear waveguide is given by Eq. (1.2.9),

$$P(z) = \left|\tilde{A}(z)\right|^2 = \left|\tilde{A}(0)\right|^2 e^{-\alpha_0 z}. \qquad (1.2.32)$$

To calculate the power transmission of practical waveguides, the coupling losses $a_{\text{cp}}^{(\text{in})}$ from the measurement system to the waveguide and $a_{\text{cp}}^{(\text{out})}$ from the waveguide to the measurement system need to be taken into account. The total transmission of a linear waveguide of length L is then given by

$$T(L) = \frac{P_{\text{out}}}{P_{\text{in}}} = a_{\text{cp}}^{(\text{in})} a_{\text{cp}}^{(\text{out})} e^{-\alpha_0 L}. \qquad (1.2.33)$$

1.2.3 Free Carrier Effects

Free carriers can have a strong influence on the optical properties of a material. This is especially true for semiconductor waveguides. Injection of carriers allows a large change in the carrier concentration, and as a consequence, the change of the optical parameters is large, too.

Free carriers can be easily exited, i.e. by photons, which gives rise to an additional absorption mechanism, the *free-carrier absorption* (FCA). Due to the Kramers-Kronig relations, the change of the imaginary part of the refractive index also causes the real part of the refractive index to change. Both this *free-carrier dispersion* (FCD) effect and the free-carrier absorption have the same physical origin, the excitation of a free-electron plasma. As a consequence, both are summarized by the name *plasma effect*.

In a mathematical treatment, both effects can be described as small perturbations to the real-valued refractive index n and to the propagation loss α. The Drude model predicts [22],

$$\Delta n = -\frac{e^2 \lambda^2}{8\pi c^2 \varepsilon_0 n} \left[\frac{\left(\Delta N_e\right)^{\xi_e}}{m_e^*} + \frac{\left(\Delta N_h\right)^{\xi_h}}{m_h^*} \right],$$

$$\Delta \alpha = \frac{e^3 \lambda^2}{4\pi^2 c^3 \varepsilon_0 n} \left[\frac{\left(\Delta N_e\right)^{\xi_e}}{\left(m_e^*\right)^2 \mu_e} + \frac{\left(\Delta N_h\right)^{\xi_h}}{\left(m_h^*\right)^2 \mu_h} \right],$$

(1.2.34)

where λ is the wavelength, $m_{e,h}^*$ are the effective masses of electrons and holes, $\mu_{e,h}$ are the respective mobilities and $\Delta N_{e,h}$ is the change in carrier concentration of electrons and holes, respectively. In a Drude model, a linear dependence on the carrier concentration change is predicted, thus $\xi_{e,h} = 1$.

For the special case of silicon waveguides, the free-carrier effects are well known. An early investigation by Soref and Bennett [22] found the predictions of Eqs. (1.2.34) to be accurate for effective masses of $m_e^* = 0.26 m_0$ and $m_h^* = 0.39 m_0$, where m_0 is the free-electron mass. In order to improve the accuracy even further, they introduced the phenomenological exponents

$$\xi_e = 1.05,$$
$$\xi_h = 0.85.$$

(1.2.35)

In practice however, the deviation of the exponents from the theoretical value of are often neglected $\xi_e = \xi_h = 1$, along with the dependence on the carrier type, so $\Delta N_e = \Delta N_h = \Delta N$. All parameters of Eqs. (1.2.34) can be combined to effective cross-sections, such that

$$\Delta n = \sigma_n \Delta N \left(\lambda / \lambda_0\right)^2,$$

$$\Delta \alpha = \sigma_\alpha \Delta N \left(\lambda / \lambda_0\right)^2,$$

(1.2.36)

where in silicon the free-carrier cross-sections for a wavelength $\lambda_0 = 1.55\,\mu\text{m}$ take values of $\sigma_n = -1.47 \times 10^{-27}\,\text{m}^3$ [23] and $\sigma_\alpha = 1.45 \times 10^{-21}\,\text{m}^2$ [24, 25].

The free-carrier dispersion is a strong effect in silicon. A change of the hole concentration of $\Delta N_h = 10^{18}\,\text{cm}^{-3}$ yields a refractive index change of $\Delta n = -2.1 \times 10^{-3}$ for a wavelength of $\lambda = 1.55\,\mu\text{m}$. However, FCD-based modulator designs suffer from the relatively long carrier lifetime, which requires technological measures like ion implantation treatment [26] or reverse-biased p-i-n junctions [25] in order to achieve a bandwidth around 40 GHz.

1.3 Third-Order Nonlinear Waveguides

The second-order nonlinear polarization can usually be neglected, as $\underline{\chi}^{(2)} = 0$ holds for inversion symmetric materials like silica-glass fibers and most semiconductor materials. The third nonlinear polarization in Eq. (1.1.10) describes nonlinear effects like third-harmonic generation (THG), third-order sum-frequency generation (TSFG), four-wave mixing (FWM), cross-phase modulation (XPM) and self-phase modulation (SPM). It is given by

$$\mathbf{P}_{\text{NL}}^{(3)}(\mathbf{r},t) = \varepsilon_0 \int\!\!\!\int\!\!\!\int_{-\infty}^{+\infty} \underline{\chi}^{(3)}(t-t',t-t'',t-t''') \vdots \mathbf{E}(\mathbf{r},t')\mathbf{E}(\mathbf{r},t'')\mathbf{E}(\mathbf{r},t''')\,\mathrm{d}t'\,\mathrm{d}t''\,\mathrm{d}t''', \quad (1.3.1)$$

We consider an optical signal with a limited bandwidth around a carrier frequency ω_c, which is sufficiently far away from all material resonances. Analogously to Eqs. (1.1.11)–(1.1.12), we can assume the third-order optical susceptibility $\underline{\tilde{\chi}}^{(3)}(\omega_1, \omega_2, \omega_3)$ as the Fourier transform of the influence function $\underline{\chi}^{(3)}(t',t'',t''')$ to be approximately constant in a small angular frequency interval,

$$\underline{\tilde{\chi}}^{(3)}(\omega_1, \omega_2, \omega_3) \approx \text{const.}$$
$$\underline{\chi}^{(3)}(t',t'',t''') = \underline{\tilde{\chi}}^{(3)}\delta(t-t')\delta(t-t'')\delta(t-t'''). \quad (1.3.2)$$

As a consequence of Eq. (1.3.2), $\underline{\chi}^{(3)}$ now describes an instantaneous response of the material, without any 'memory' of previous states. Assuming an immediate response of the polarization to the incident optical field, the convolution in Eq. (1.3.1) can be replaced by a simple multiplication with the susceptibility tensor $\underline{\chi}^{(3)}$ and the third-order polarization term for self-phase modulation becomes

$$\mathbf{P}_{\text{NL}}^{(3)}(\mathbf{r},t) = \frac{3}{4}\varepsilon_0 \underline{\chi}^{(3)} |\mathbf{E}(\mathbf{r},t)|^2 \mathbf{E}(\mathbf{r},t). \quad (1.3.3)$$

As the polarization is now dependent on the optical field intensity given in Eq. (1.1.17), the (real-valued) refractive index $n(\mathbf{r},t)$ and the absorption $\alpha(\mathbf{r},t)$ become dependent on the optical field intensity as well,

$$n(\mathbf{r},t) = n_0 + n_2 I(\mathbf{r},t) = n_0 + \frac{n_0}{2Z_0} n_2 \left| \mathbf{E}(\mathbf{r},t) \right|^2, \tag{1.3.4}$$

$$\alpha(\mathbf{r},t) = \alpha_0 + \alpha_2 I(\mathbf{r},t) = \alpha_0 + \frac{n_0}{2Z_0} \alpha_2 \left| \mathbf{E}(\mathbf{r},t) \right|^2. \tag{1.3.5}$$

To simplify the calculations, it is helpful to specify the complex refractive index

$$
\begin{aligned}
\underline{n}(\mathbf{r},t) &= n(\mathbf{r},t) - \mathrm{j}\frac{\alpha(\mathbf{r},t)}{2k_0} = n_0 - \mathrm{j}\frac{\alpha_0}{2k_0} + n_2 I(\mathbf{r},t) - \mathrm{j}\frac{\alpha_2}{2k_0} I(\mathbf{r},t) \\
&= n_0 - \mathrm{j}\frac{\alpha_0}{2k_0} + \underline{n}_2 I(\mathbf{r},t),
\end{aligned}
\tag{1.3.6}
$$

where the complex quantity

$$\underline{n}_2 = n_2 - \mathrm{j}\frac{\alpha_2}{2k_0} \tag{1.3.7}$$

comprises the nonlinear refractive index change as well as the nonlinear loss due to two-photon absorption (TPA). In optical waveguides, the nonlinear losses are usually small and the intensity dependent contributions can be treated as small perturbations to the refractive index n_0,

$$\underline{\Delta n}(x,y) = \underline{n}_2(x,y) I(x,y) - \mathrm{j}\frac{\alpha_0}{2k_0}, \tag{1.3.8}$$

To a first-order approximation, we can assume that the transverse mode distributions $\mathcal{E}(x,y,\omega_c)$ and $\mathcal{H}(x,y,\omega_c)$ are not affected by the refractive index change in Eq. (1.3.8). Again, the perturbation to the propagation constant is obtained from perturbation theory as

$$\Delta\beta(z,t) = \frac{k_0}{Z_0} \frac{\iint n(x,y)\underline{\Delta n}(x,y) \left| \mathcal{E}(x,y,\omega_c) \right|^2 \mathrm{d}x\,\mathrm{d}y}{\iint \mathrm{Re}\left[\mathcal{E}(x,y,\omega_c) \times \mathcal{H}^*(x,y,\omega_c) \right] \cdot \mathbf{e}_z \mathrm{d}x\,\mathrm{d}y}. \tag{1.3.9}$$

For low confinement waveguides the modal fields can be approximated by scalar fields $\mathcal{E}(x,y) \approx f(x,y)$ and $\mathcal{H}(x,y) \approx f(x,y)n_0/Z_0$ and the change of the propagation constant reduces to the well known expression [15, 27],

$$\Delta\beta = k_0 \frac{\iint \Delta n |f(x,y)|^2 \, dx \, dy}{\iint |f(x,y)|^2 \, dx \, dy}. \tag{1.3.10}$$

With these perturbations and an appropriate choice of the reference propagation constant in Eq. (1.2.4), we derive the *nonlinear Schrödinger equation* (NLSE) from Eq. (1.2.20). If we abbreviate $A(z,t,\omega_c) = A(\omega_c)$, we have

$$\frac{\partial A(\omega_c)}{\partial z} + \beta_1 \frac{\partial A(\omega_c)}{\partial t} - j\frac{\beta_2}{2}\frac{\partial^2 A(\omega_c)}{\partial t^2} + \frac{1}{2}\alpha_0 A(\omega_c) = -j\underline{\gamma}|A(\omega_c)|^2 A(\omega_c). \tag{1.3.11}$$

In this common formulation of the NLSE, $\underline{\gamma}$ is the complex nonlinearity parameter of the waveguide.

For a material i, the nonlinearity parameter is

$$\underline{\gamma}_i = \frac{\omega_c}{c}\frac{n_{2,i}}{A_{\text{eff},i}^{(3)}} = \frac{3}{4}\frac{\omega_c}{c}\frac{Z_0}{n_{0,i}^2}\frac{\chi_i^{(3)}}{A_{\text{eff},i}^{(3)}}, \tag{1.3.12}$$

where the integrals of Eq. (1.3.9) are included in the third-order effective area $A_{\text{eff}}^{(3)}$, which is discussed in the following section. A generalized expression for the nonlinearity parameter which takes into account the contributions of an arbitrary number of materials is given in Section 1.3.2.

1.3.1 Effective Area

The third-order interaction effective area $A_{\text{eff}}^{(3)}$ is determined by the ratio of an integral over the interaction area and an integral over the whole waveguide mode area,

$$A_{\text{eff},i}^{(3)} = \frac{Z_0^2}{n_{0,i}^2} \frac{\left| \iint\limits_{D_{\text{int},i}} \text{Re}\left[\mathcal{E}(x,y,\omega_c) \times \mathcal{H}^*(x,y,\omega_c) \right] \cdot \mathbf{e}_z \, dx \, dy \right|^2}{\iint\limits_{D_{\text{tot}}} |\mathcal{E}(x,y,\omega_c)|^4 \, dx \, dy} \tag{1.3.13}$$

In the special case of optical fibers, the low index contrast allows to simplify the equations, as all refractive indices are practically identical, $n_{0,i} \approx n_0$ and the nonlinearity is homogeneously distributed over the total waveguide area, $D_{\text{int}} = D_{\text{tot}}$. The transverse field distributions can be approximated by a scalar function $f(x,y)$ as $\mathcal{E}(x,y) = f(x,y)\mathbf{e}_x$ and $\mathcal{H}(x,y) \approx (n_0/Z_0) f(x,y)\mathbf{e}_y$.

As a result, Eq. (1.3.13) is simplified to

$$A_{\text{eff}}^{(3)} \approx \frac{\left(\iint_{D_{\text{tot}}} |f(x,y)|^2 \, dxdy \right)^2}{\iint_{D_{\text{tot}}} |f(x,y)|^4 \, dxdy}, \tag{1.3.14}$$

which is the commonly used definition of $A_{\text{eff}}^{(3)}$ in fiber optics [15] and monolithically integrated nonlinear optics [27].

As the intensity-dependent refractive index n_2 is a material parameter, the only other design parameter for optimizing the nonlinearity of a waveguide is the effective area. Depending on the refractive index contrast and the waveguide dimensions, the effective area can vary in the range between 100 μm^2 and 0.1 μm^2. To illustrate this fact, Fig. 1.1 compares the third order effective areas of a single mode fiber (SMF) [28], a holey fiber [28], a silicon rib waveguide [28, 29], a silicon strip nanowire [30], and a slot waveguide [30].

	SMF	Holey Fiber	Si Rib	Si Strip	Si Slot
Schematic Cross Section	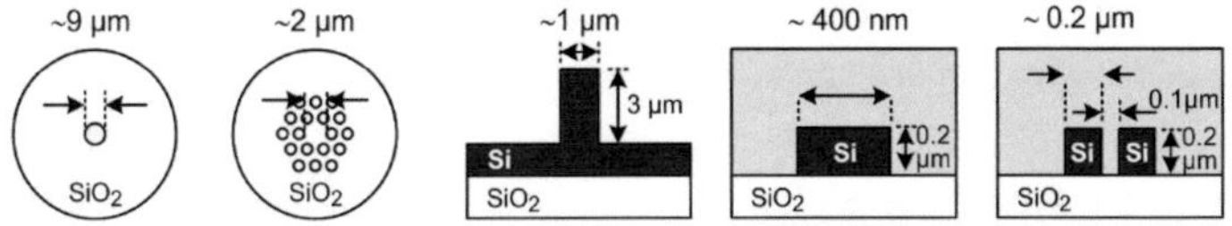				
$A_{\text{eff}}^{(3)}$	40...80 μm^2	2...5 μm^2	2...5 μm^2	~0.1 μm^2	~0.1 μm^2

Fig. 1.1 Comparison of third-order effective areas $A_{\text{eff}}^{(3)}$ of a single-mode fiber (SMF) [28], a holey fiber [28], a silicon rib waveguide [28, 29], a silicon strip nanowire [30] and a slot waveguide [30]. Refractive index illustrated by gray shading.

1.3.2 Waveguides with Hybrid Material Composition

Hybrid waveguide structures comprise different materials with largely different properties. Therefore, the nonlinearity cannot be described with a single γ_i as given by Eq. (1.3.12), which originally has been derived for silica fibers.

In heterogeneous waveguides, where several materials contribute to the complex susceptibility tensor, the nonlinear effects of Eqs. (1.3.1) and (1.3.3) need to be evaluated carefully over the whole modal cross-section D_{tot}. The nonlinear Schrödinger equation (1.3.11) then defines the total nonlinearity parameter of the hybrid waveguide as [31]

$$\underline{\gamma}_{\text{tot}} = \frac{3}{16}\frac{\omega_c \varepsilon_0}{\mathcal{P}^2} \iint_{D_{\text{tot}}} \left[\underline{\tilde{\chi}}^{(3)}(x,y,\omega_c)\mathcal{E}(x,y,\omega_c)\mathcal{E}(x,y,\omega_c)\mathcal{E}^*(x,y,\omega_c) \right] \mathcal{E}^*(x,y,\omega_c)\,dxdy$$

$$(1.3.15)$$

In the integral over the cross-section D_{tot}, the nonlinear interaction due to the local susceptibility $\underline{\chi}^{(3)} = \underline{\chi}^{(3)}(x,y,\omega_c)$ can be split into separate contributions by homogeneous cross-sectional domains D_i with susceptibilities $\underline{\chi}_i^{(3)}$, where the index varies with the domain, $i \in \{\text{Si}, \text{SiO}_2, \text{Cladding},...\}$. Using Eq. (1.2.8), the total nonlinearity parameter is given by

$$\underline{\gamma}_{\text{tot}} = \frac{3}{4}\omega_c \varepsilon_0 \sum_i \underline{\chi}_i^{(3)}(\omega_c) \frac{\displaystyle\iint_{D_i} |\mathcal{E}(x,y,\omega_c)|^4 \,dxdy}{\displaystyle\iint_{D_{\text{tot}}} \text{Re}\left[\mathcal{E}(x,y,\omega_c) \times \mathcal{H}^*(x,y,\omega_c) \right] \mathbf{e}_z \,dxdy}. \quad (1.3.16)$$

With the third-order effective area definition (1.3.13), the total nonlinearity parameter is given by

$$\underline{\gamma}_{tot}(\omega_c) = \frac{3}{4}\omega_c \varepsilon_0 \sum_i \frac{Z_0^2}{n_i^2} \frac{\underline{\chi}_i^{(3)}}{A_{\text{eff},i}^{(3)}} = \sum_i \underline{\gamma}_i(\omega_c). \quad (1.3.17)$$

As a result, the nonlinearity parameter $\underline{\gamma}_{\text{tot}}$ of a hybrid waveguide is the sum of the complex nonlinearity parameters of the constituent materials in Eq. (1.3.12), which need to be evaluated individually over the cross-sectional areas of the interaction [32].

1.3.3 Four-Wave Mixing

Two photons of a strong pump are transformed into one photon of the signal wave and a new photon at the idler (converted) frequency $f_i = 2f_p - f_s$. For sufficiently low power levels nonlinear losses due to two-photon absorption can be neglected. For a given launch power $P_p(z=0)$ of the pump and of the signal $P_s(z=0)$, the power P_i of the idler wave after a propagation length L is

$$P_i(L) = e^{-\alpha_0 L} \left(\eta \,\text{Re}\{\gamma\} P_p(0)L_{\text{eff}} \right)^2 P_s(0), \quad (1.3.18)$$

where η is the four-wave mixing efficiency and L_{eff} is the effective waveguide length

$$L_{\text{eff}} = \int_0^L \frac{P(z)}{P_0}\,dz = \frac{1-e^{-\alpha_0 L}}{\alpha_0}. \quad (1.3.19)$$

For a center wavelength λ_p in a waveguide with the dispersion factor D_2 from Eq. (1.2.25), the mismatch in propagation constants for a detuning $\Delta\lambda = \lambda_p - \lambda_s$ is

$$\Delta\beta = \frac{2\pi c D_2}{\lambda_p^2}(\Delta\lambda)^2 . \tag{1.3.20}$$

This creates a phase mismatch $L\Delta\beta$, which limits the four-wave mixing efficiency [33, 34]

$$\eta^2 = \frac{\alpha_0^2}{\alpha_0^2 + \Delta\beta^2}\left[1 + 4e^{-\alpha_0 L}\frac{\sin^2(L\Delta\beta/2)}{\left(1 - e^{-\alpha_0 L}\right)^2}\right] . \tag{1.3.21}$$

1.3.4 Cross-Phase Modulation

Cross-phase modulation is a third-order nonlinear effect, where an intensity modulated signal influences the phase of a second signal.

Analogue to the description of self-modulation in Eq. (1.3.11), we can derive the NLSE in the case of XPM as

$$\frac{\partial A_1(\omega_c)}{\partial z} + \beta_1\frac{\partial A_1(\omega_c)}{\partial t} - j\frac{1}{2}\beta_2\frac{\partial^2 A_1(\omega_c)}{\partial t^2} + \frac{1}{2}\alpha_0 A_1(\omega_c) = -j\gamma 2\left|A_2(\omega_c)\right|^2 A_1(\omega_c), \tag{1.3.22}$$

where $A_1(z,t)$ and $A_2(z,t)$ are the complex amplitudes of both waves. The right hand side of Eq. (1.3.22) describes the interaction between both waves: The field intensity of the second wave $I_2 \propto \left|A_2\right|^2$ influences the optical phase of the first wave.

It is convenient to express the achievable phase-shift not as a function of complex amplitudes, but as a function of optical signal power levels. In a phasor representation, we split the complex amplitude into a real amplitude and a phase,

$$A(t,\omega_c) = A_0 e^{j\omega_c t}e^{j\Delta\phi(t)} . \tag{1.3.23}$$

The phase of a continuos wave signal which experiences cross-phase modulation by a signal of power $P_s(t)$ is then given by

$$\Delta\phi(t) = -2\gamma L_{\text{eff}}P_s(t), \tag{1.3.24}$$

where the effective waveguide length is defined in Eq. (1.3.19).

The magnitude of the nonlinear phase shift is of great importance all applications like wavelength conversion, all-optical switching or regeneration. It is hard to determine experimentally, but it can be easily extracted from the optical spectrum by comparing measured spectra to simulation results. For a set of simplifying assumptions, also an approximative analytic solution can be found, where only a single free parameter is needed.

For an arbitrary bit sequence, the phase shift can be described as

$$\Delta\phi(t) = \Delta\phi_0 \sum_{n=0}^{\infty} B_s\left(nT_s\right) s\left(t - nT_s\right), \qquad (1.3.25)$$

where $\Delta\phi_0$ is the peak phase shift, $B_s(t) = \{0,1\}$ is a bit sequence with a symbol rate of T_s, and $s(t)$ describes the pulse shape used. Under the assumption, that the main contribution to XPM is due to the fundamental sinusoidal contained in the bit sequence, we can approximate

$$\Delta\phi(t) \approx b_1 \Delta\phi_0 \sin(\omega_s), \qquad (1.3.26)$$

where b_1 and $\omega_s = 2\pi/T_s$ are the Fourier series coefficient and the angular frequency of the fundamental wave. With this approximation, Eq. (1.3.23) becomes

$$A(t,\omega_c) = A_0 e^{j\omega_c t} e^{j b_1 \Delta\phi_0 \sin \omega_s}. \qquad (1.3.27)$$

We can expand the $e^{jy\sin x}$ function in Eq. (1.3.27) in terms of Bessel functions,

$$\exp\{jy\sin x\} = \sum_{n=-\infty}^{\infty} J_n(y)\exp\{jnx\}. \qquad (1.3.28)$$

Using just the fundamental Fourier component from Eq. (1.3.26), the complex field amplitude in Eq. (1.3.23) can be written as

$$A(t,\omega_c) = A_0 e^{j\omega_c t} \sum_{n=-\infty}^{\infty} J_n(b_1 \Delta\phi_0) e^{jn\omega_s t}, \qquad (1.3.29)$$

which is an infinite series of harmonic waves, which are weighted by Bessel function coefficients $J_n(x)$. In frequency domain, the spectrum consists of discrete lines around the carrier at frequency ω_c, separated by the angular frequency ω_s of the fundamental wave.

All discrete tones are dependent on the same argument, $b_1 \Delta\phi_0$. To determine the acquired phase-shift from the spectrum, the magnitudes of only two frequency components have to be known. Looking at the carrier ($\omega = \omega_c$, $n = 0$) and the first sideband ($\omega = \omega_c + \omega_s$, $n = 1$) we get the relation

$$\frac{|A(\omega_c)|^2}{|A(\omega_c + \omega_s)|^2} = \frac{|J_0(b_1 \Delta\phi_0)|^2}{|J_1(b_1 \Delta\phi_0)|^2}, \qquad (1.3.30)$$

in which the only free parameter is the Fourier coefficient b_1. We define the carrier-to-sideband ratio (CSR) as

$$\left. \text{CSR} \right|_{\text{dB}} = 10 \log_{10} \frac{P_{\text{carrier}}}{P_{\text{sideband}}} = 20 \log_{10} \frac{\left| J_0(b_1 \Delta \varphi_0) \right|}{\left| J_1(b_1 \Delta \varphi_0) \right|}. \tag{1.3.31}$$

The value of b_1 depends on the exact shape and duration of the pulses used. A simple way to determine the correct value of b_1 is to compare the predicted CSR of Eq. (1.3.31) to simulations, where the transmitter is modeled precisely and the nonlinear phase shift is described by Eq. (1.3.24).

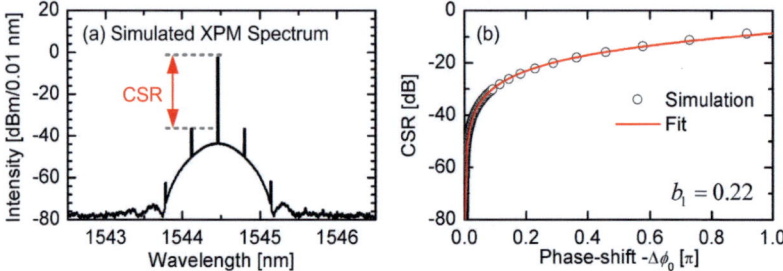

Fig. 1.2 (a) Simulated optical spectrum of a continuous wave that has experienced cross-phase modulation in a nonlinear waveguide. Depending on the acquired phase-shift $-\Delta\phi_0$, the modulation depth varies and can be characterized by the carrier-to-sidebande-ratio (CSR). (b) CSR as a function of the phase-shift. Simulation results (o) of XPM by a 33% RZ-OOK input signal are compared to a fit (–) of the analytic expression in Eq. (1.3.31), which yields a value of $b_1 = 0.22$.

The simulated optical spectrum of a continuous wave that experienced cross-phase modulation in a nonlinear waveguide is presented in Fig. 1.2(a). Depending on the acquired phase-shift $-\Delta\phi_0$, the modulation depth varies and can be characterized by the carrier-to-sidebande-ratio. Fig. 1.2(b) shows the CSR as a function of the phase shift. Simulation results (o) of XPM by a 33% RZ-OOK input pseudo-random bit sequence of length 2^9-1 are compared to a fit (–) of the analytic expression in Eq. (1.3.31), with $b_1 = 0.22$.

1.3.5 Two-Photon Absorption Figure of Merit

In a realistic Kerr-type waveguide, the nonlinear loss due to two-photon absorption is significant and the peak power that can be used for cross and self-phase modulation is reduced. This places a fundamental limit on the achievable nonlinear effect at high power levels. In this case, the nonlinearity parameter γ is complex-valued: The real part $\mathrm{Re}\{\underline{\gamma}\}$ corresponds to the nonlinear refractive index change, and the imaginary part $\mathrm{Im}\{\underline{\gamma}\}$ represents the nonlinear loss, see Section 1.3.5, Eqs. (1.3.7), (1.3.12), and (1.3.17), respectively.

The acquired phase change due to the Kerr nonlinearity of a nonlinear waveguide is

$$\Delta\phi = -L_{\mathrm{eff}} \,\mathrm{Re}\{\underline{\gamma}\} P_0, \tag{1.3.32}$$

where $P_0 = P(z=0)$ is the peak power inside the waveguide, and $L_{\mathrm{eff}} = \left(1 - e^{-\alpha_0 L}\right)/\alpha_0$ is the effective waveguide length. Depending on the switching scheme, the phase-shift required for complete all-optical switching varies [27, 35, 36] from $\left|\Delta\phi_{\mathrm{NLDC}}^{\min}\right| = 4\pi$ for nonlinear directional couplers, to $\left|\Delta\phi_{\mathrm{MZI}}^{\min}\right| = \pi$ for Mach-Zehnder interferometers.

Taking into account the nonlinear loss due to two-photon absorption, the evolution of the power is described by Eqs. (1.2.32) and (1.3.5) as ($\mathrm{Im}\{\underline{\gamma}\} < 0$)

$$\frac{d}{dz}P(z) = \left(-\alpha_0 - 2\left|\mathrm{Im}\{\underline{\gamma}\}\right| P(z)\right) P(z) \tag{1.3.33}$$

and the solution of this differential equation is given by

$$P(z) = \frac{e^{-\alpha_0 z}}{1 + 2L_{\mathrm{eff}} \left|\mathrm{Im}\{\underline{\gamma}\}\right| P_0} P_0, \tag{1.3.34}$$

From Eq. (1.3.34) a simple criterion for the characteristic length associated with two-photon absorption can be derived. Two-photon absorption reduces the power along propagation. Over a length where a nonlinear phase shift of $\left|\Delta\phi_{\mathrm{MZI}}^{\min}\right| = \pi$ is achieved, the nonlinearity should decrease the linearly reduced power by less than a factor of two,

$$-2L_{\mathrm{eff}} \,\mathrm{Im}\{\underline{\gamma}\} P_0 < 1. \tag{1.3.35}$$

By combining Eqs. (1.3.32) and (1.3.35) we introduce the characteristic *two-photon absorption figure of merit* $\mathrm{FOM_{TPA}}$,

$$\mathrm{FOM_{TPA}} = -\frac{1}{4\pi} \frac{\mathrm{Re}\{\underline{\gamma}\}}{\mathrm{Im}\{\underline{\gamma}\}}. \tag{1.3.36}$$

Please note that in this definition $\mathrm{FOM_{TPA}}$ is independent of power and waveguide length. It represents a property of the waveguide and is a fundamental limitation for the maximum achievable nonlinear effect [37]. Using Eq. (1.3.35) we can rewrite the criterion to achieve a minimum phase-shift of $\Delta\phi_{\mathrm{MZI}}^{\min} = \pi$ over a characteristic two-photon absorption length as,

$$\mathrm{FOM_{TPA}} > \frac{1}{2}. \qquad (1.3.37)$$

The power evolution in Eq. (1.3.34) is then given by

$$P(z) = \frac{e^{-\alpha_0 z}}{1 + \dfrac{1}{2\pi}\dfrac{-\Delta\phi}{\mathrm{FOM_{TPA}}}} P_0. \qquad (1.3.38)$$

Waveguides with a small figure of merit show strong two-photon absorption even for small phase-shifts. Waveguides with a large figure of merit show are not limited by two-photon absorption even for large phase-shifts. Increasing the device length or the power increases the nonlinear phase-shift and the two-photon absorption at the same time. Thus, the two-photon absorption figure of merit poses a limit to increase the nonlinear effects by scaling up the operating power.

For waveguide cross-sections with a constant nonlinearity, the figure of merit can also be defined to be a material property, relating the nonlinear index n_2 to the nonlinear two-photon absorption coefficient α_2. Following the same steps as above and using Eqs. (1.3.7) and (1.3.12), the nonlinear phase-shift is

$$\Delta\phi = -k_0 I_0 L n_2. \qquad (1.3.39)$$

The nonlinear interaction is limited by the characteristic two-photon absorption length

$$\alpha_2 I_0 L < 1, \qquad (1.3.40)$$

which for a required phase-shift of π leads to the common definition of the two-photon absorption figure of merit criterion [37, 38]

$$\mathrm{FOM_{TPA}} = \frac{n_2}{\lambda\alpha_2} > \frac{1}{2}. \qquad (1.3.41)$$

1.4 Media with Gain

Another important class of nonlinear effects can be found in media with gain. Transitions from an excited state to the ground state give rise to stimulated emission. These photons are quantum mechanically identical to incident photons. As the transitions involved are transitions between real states, this effect is orders of magnitude stronger than the Kerr effect, which is based on the purely virtual transitions. Semiconductors with interband transitions are particularly interesting, as they allow population inversion by electric pumping.

Also in media with gain, the wave propagation is governed by the Helmholtz equation (1.2.3)

$$\nabla^2 \tilde{\mathbf{E}}(\mathbf{r}, \omega_c) + \underline{n}^2(\omega_c) k_0^2 \tilde{\mathbf{E}}(\mathbf{r}, \omega_c) = 0,$$

where $\tilde{\mathbf{E}}(\mathbf{r}, \omega_c)$ is the electric field vector of the wave, ω_c is the center angular frequency of the light, $k_0 = \omega_c / c$ is the propagation constant, c is the speed of light in vacuum and $\underline{n}(\omega_c)$ is the complex refractive index.

Similarly to Eq. (1.2.29), we will treat the gain change Δg and the associated refractive index change $\Delta n'$ as perturbations to the refractive index of a passive waveguide

$$\underline{n} = n_0 + \Delta n' + \mathrm{j} \frac{\Delta g - \alpha_0}{2k_0}, \tag{1.4.1}$$

where $k_0 = 2\pi/\lambda$ is the propagation constant in vacuum and α_0 denotes the internal linear waveguide power loss.

Each interband transition changes the gain as well as the refractive index due to the plasma effect, see Section 1.2.3. Both effects are related by the Kramers-Kronig relations, which can be linearized in the operating point. As a result, the refractive index change $\Delta n'$ can be related to the gain change Δg by a constant *linewidth enhancement factor* (LEF), *Henry factor* or *alpha-factor* [39],

$$\alpha_{\mathrm{LE}} = -2k_0 \frac{\partial n'/\partial N}{\partial g/\partial N} \approx -2k_0 \frac{\Delta n'}{\Delta g}, \tag{1.4.2}$$

where the derivative with respect to the carrier concentration N is to be taken at a fixed operating point.

Practical waveguides with gain possess an active core region and a passive cladding. Therefore, the gain varies across the mode cross-section, $g = g(x, y)$. Only a fraction of the guided mode interacts with the active region and experiences gain.

The change of the propagation constant is given by Eq. (1.3.10). The refractive index change inside the active region is given by Eq. (1.4.1) and dominated by the gain. Outside the active region, the refractive index change is equal to Eq. (1.2.29), where only the waveguide loss enters.

As the strongest perturbations of the refractive index of the underlying passive waveguide are due to gain effects, it is convenient to rewrite Eq. (1.4.1) as

$$\underline{n} = n_0 - \frac{1}{2k_0}[\alpha_{\mathrm{LE}} - \mathrm{j}]\Gamma g - \mathrm{j}\frac{\alpha_0}{2k_0}, \qquad (1.4.3)$$

where Γ is the confinement factor and contains the integrals over the mode cross-section,

$$\Gamma = \frac{\displaystyle\iint_{D_{\mathrm{act}}} |f(x,y)|^2 \, \mathrm{d}x \, \mathrm{d}y}{\displaystyle\iint_{D_{\mathrm{tot}}} |f(x,y)|^2 \, \mathrm{d}x \, \mathrm{d}y}. \qquad (1.4.4)$$

These surface integrals extend over the active region D_{act} and the total mode cross-section D_{tot}. The confinement factor Γ is a simple measure of the confinement of the mode inside the active region. The effective refractive index in Eq. (1.4.3) allows to solve the Helmholtz equation (1.2.3) with the ansatz in Eq. (1.2.4). The transverse mode profiles $\mathcal{E}(x,y,\omega_{\mathrm{c}})$ and $\mathcal{H}(x,y,\omega_{\mathrm{c}})$ need to be determined numerically and are assumed to be unaffected by gain changes.

Identical to the treatment of losses in Section 1.2.2, Eqs. (1.2.28)–(1.2.30) describe the evaluation of the slowly-varying envelope,

$$\frac{\partial}{\partial z}\tilde{A}(z,\omega_{\mathrm{c}}) - \mathrm{j}\frac{1}{2}[\alpha_{\mathrm{LE}} - \mathrm{j}]\Gamma g \tilde{A}(z,\omega_{\mathrm{c}}) + \frac{1}{2}\alpha_0 \tilde{A}(z,\omega_{\mathrm{c}}) = 0. \qquad (1.4.5)$$

For waveguides without gain ($g = 0$), Eq. (1.4.5) is identical to the differential equation of a passive waveguide, Eq. (1.2.31).

1.4.1 Gain and Phase

The description of the gain effects on the optical signal in terms of the mode envelope $\tilde{A}(z,\omega_{\mathrm{c}})$ has its shortcomings, as optical fields are experimentally not easily accessible. Therefore, it is convenient to separate the amplitude and phase information and transform Eq. (1.4.5) to the time domain.

Amplitude and phase of the wave can be separated by using a phasor representation

$$A(z,t) = \sqrt{P(z,t)}e^{j\phi(z,t)} \tag{1.4.6}$$

where $P(z,t)$ and $\phi(z,t)$ are the power and the phase of the wave.

Usually the waveguide losses are negligible compared to the gain. Additionally, we assume the gain, confinement factor, and linewidth enhancement factor to be independent of the propagation distance z. We obtain separate differential equations for the amplitude

$$\frac{\partial P(z,t)}{\partial z} = (\Gamma g - \alpha_0) P(z,t) \approx \Gamma g P(z,t), \tag{1.4.7}$$

and find for the phase

$$\frac{\partial \phi(z,t)}{\partial z} = -\frac{1}{2}\alpha_{\text{LE}}\Gamma g. \tag{1.4.8}$$

Integration along the propagation in z direction yields the well known expressions for the power and phase evolution in a waveguide of length L, defining the gain G,

$$P(L) = P(0)e^{\Gamma g L} = GP(0),$$
$$\phi(L) = \phi(0) - \frac{1}{2}\alpha_{\text{LE}}\Gamma g L, \tag{1.4.9}$$

As a result, the power increases exponentially with the propagation length, while the phase increases linearly only.

1.4.2 Noise Figure

It is impossible to construct an completely noise free amplifier, as it would violate Heisenberg's uncertainty principle [40]. A measure for the characteristic noise added by an amplifier is the noise figure, which is discussed in the following paragraphs.

In a quantum mechanic description, any amplifier can be viewed as a photon number multiplier. Even in the case, where the amplification process is not accompanied by spontaneous emission, the amplification process itself increases the photon number variance, which is the quantum mechanic equivalent to classic amplitude noise [41, 42]. In the case of real amplifiers with spontaneous emission, the quantum mechanical description gives the same results with regard to the amplitude noise variance as the well known semiclassical description found in many textbooks [43]. In the following, a simple noise figure definition for a polarization sensitive amplifier is introduced [44, 45]. A more detailed discussion of the quantum mechanic description can be found in Refs. [42, 46, 47]. The modifications necessary for the case of polarization insensitive amplifiers are discussed afterwards.

1.4.2.1 Noise Figure Definition

The impact of the additional noise on the amplified signal is measured by the noise figure, which is defined as the signal-to-noise ratio (SNR) at the input of the amplifier divided by the SNR at the output of the amplifier,

$$F = \frac{\text{input SNR}}{\text{output SNR}}. \qquad (1.4.10)$$

It is common to use the square of the average photon number $\langle n_s \rangle^2$ to define the SNR. This corresponds to the square of the optical power and—after direct detection in an ideal detector—the square of the photocurrent.

For coherent light with a large average photon number, the photon statistics is Poissonian and the input SNR is given by

$$\text{input SNR} = \frac{\langle n_s \rangle^2}{\langle \Delta n_s^2 \rangle} = \langle n_s \rangle. \qquad (1.4.11)$$

After amplification by a factor of G, the square of the photon number of the signal is

$$\langle n_o \rangle^2 = G^2 \langle n_s \rangle^2 \qquad (1.4.12)$$

and the fluctuations at the output are given by [42]

$$\langle \Delta n_o^2 \rangle = G \langle n_s \rangle + 2 n_{sp} G (G-1) \langle n_s \rangle + n_{sp} (G-1)[1 + n_{sp}(G-1)], \qquad (1.4.13)$$

where n_{sp} is the *noise enhancement factor* or *inversion factor*. The different terms in Eq. (1.4.13) can be interpreted in a semiclassical picture. The first term describes the Poisson statistics of the amplified signal. The second term describes the beating between the signal and the amplified spontaneous emission. The last term describes the Bose-Einstein statistics of the spontaneous emission with an average photon number of $\langle n_{\text{ASE}} \rangle = n_{sp}(G-1)$, which corresponds to the available noise power at the output. The inversion factor n_{sp} is defined as

$$n_{sp} = \frac{N_2}{N_2 - N_1}, \qquad (1.4.14)$$

where N_2 and N_1 are the occupation numbers of the excited state and ground state of a two-level system. The SNR at the output is

$$\text{output SNR} = \frac{G^2 \langle n_s \rangle^2}{G \langle n_s \rangle + 2G \langle n_s \rangle n_{sp} (G-1) + n_{sp} (G-1)[1 + n_{sp} (G-1)]}. \quad (1.4.15)$$

With the input and output signal to noise ratios in Eqs. (1.4.11) and (1.4.15), the noise figure (1.4.10) is then given by

$$F = \frac{1}{G} + 2n_{sp} \left(1 - \frac{1}{G} \right) + \frac{1}{\langle n_s \rangle} n_{sp} \left(1 - \frac{1}{G} \right) \left[\frac{1}{G} + \left(1 - \frac{1}{G} \right) \right]. \quad (1.4.16)$$

While this noise figure is input-signal dependent and—strictly speaking—not a valid noise figure definition [44], it still bears practical value. Typically the signal photon number is relatively large and the last term in Eq. (1.4.16) can be safely neglected to yield the common noise figure definition

$$F \approx \frac{1}{G} + 2n_{sp} \left(1 - \frac{1}{G} \right), \quad (1.4.17)$$

which is approximately independent of the input signal, obeys the cascading rules for amplifiers [48], and may be also derived from purely quantum mechanical first principles [44, 45]. For an ideally inverted amplifier ($n_{sp} = 1$) and large gain ($G \gg 1$), Eq. (1.4.17) gives the well known minimum noise figure of an optical amplifier with direct detection as $F_{\min} = 2$.

In a semiclassical interpretation with $G \gg 1$, the photon energy $\hbar\omega$, and a signal bandwidth B, the noise figure takes the well known form [41]

$$F \approx \frac{1}{G} + \frac{2n_{sp}(G-1)}{G} = \frac{1}{G} + \frac{2P_{ASE}}{G\hbar\omega B}, \quad (1.4.18)$$

where P_{ASE} is the available noise power measured in the bandwidth B. It is customary to use logarithmic units,

$$\text{NF} = 10\log_{10}(F). \quad [\text{dB}] \quad (1.4.19)$$

1.4.2.2 Polarization-Dependent Correction

Historically, the most important application for this noise figure definition has been the systems design for erbium-doped fiber amplifier (EDFA) based long-haul networks. As EDFA are practically polarization insensitive, the amplified spontaneous is polarized in random state. In that case, only half of the total available noise power $P_{ASE,tot}$ is co-polarized with the signal and enters in Eq. (1.4.18) [49],

$$P_{ASE} = P_{ASE,\parallel} = \frac{1}{2} P_{ASE,tot}. \quad (1.4.20)$$

Standard noise-figure measurement programs of optical spectrum analyzers often tacitly use the assumption in Eq. (1.4.20), which is correct for polarization-independent amplifiers.

For polarization-dependent amplifiers, the gain for orthogonal polarizations can be different, $G_\parallel \neq G_\perp$. As $P_{\mathrm{ASE,pol}} \propto G_{\mathrm{pol}}$, the assumption in Eq. (1.4.20) leads to an underestimation of the real noise figure. For the same total measured noise power $P_{\mathrm{ASE,tot}}$, the real noise figure $F_\parallel$ relative to the noise figure of a polarization-independent amplifier with $\Delta G = G_\parallel - G_\perp = 0$ is [49]

$$F_\parallel = \frac{2}{1+\dfrac{G_\perp}{G_\parallel}} F_{\Delta G=0}. \tag{1.4.21}$$

For strongly polarization-dependent amplifiers like quantum dot semiconductor optical amplifiers, the gain orthogonal to the main polarization is negligible, $G_\perp \approx 0$. In this case, all of the measured amplified spontaneous emission is co-polarized with the input signal. With the (invalid) assumption in Eq.(1.4.20), the noise figure measured by a standard noise figure measurement program of an optical spectrum analyzer underestimates the real noise figure of a strongly polarization-dependent amplifier by 3 dB.

1.4.3 Cross-Gain Modulation

Saturation effects play a key role for the accuracy of the description of amplifiers. Each amplification process requires energy, and the amount of energy that can be delivered by an amplifier is limited. As a consequence, for high power signals the gain of the amplifier is reduced.

A multitude of microscopic processes can contribute to saturation effects in optical amplifiers, with a varying extend of the nature and magnitude of the respective effect. A comprehensive description of saturation effects in optical amplifiers is beyond the scope of this work and only a basic description is given here.

In the literature, more detailed description of microscopic saturation effects in erbium-doped fiber amplifiers [42, 50], bulk [50-52], and quantum-dot semiconductor optical amplifiers [53-55] can be found.

In a simple two-level system model, the gain constant is dependent on the frequency ω and power P of the input signal [50], Eq. (6.1.2),

$$g(\omega, P) = \frac{g_0}{1 + (\omega - \omega_0)^2 T_2^2 + P/P_s}, \tag{1.4.22}$$

where T_2 is the dipole relaxation time and P_s is the saturation power. Let us consider the center frequency ω_0 where the gain is maximized. If the input power level is increased up to the saturation power, the gain is reduced to $g(P_s) = g_0/2$, half the value of the small signal gain.

If more than one signal is launched into the amplifier, the available gain can be saturated by each of the input signals. If the gain experienced by one signal is modulated by another signal, this is called cross-gain modulation (XGM). In general, the available gain needs to be described as

$$\begin{aligned}
g_1(\omega_1, P_1) &\rightarrow g_1(\omega_1, P_1, \omega_2, P_1, \ldots, \omega_\mu, P_\mu), \\
g_2(\omega_2, P_2) &\rightarrow g_2(\omega_1, P_1, \omega_2, P_1, \ldots, \omega_\mu, P_\mu), \\
&\vdots \\
g_\mu(\omega_\mu, P_\mu) &\rightarrow g_\mu(\omega_1, P_1, \omega_2, P_1, \ldots, \omega_\mu, P_\mu),
\end{aligned} \tag{1.4.23}$$

where ω_i and P_i describe the frequencies and power levels of all input waves, $i = 1, 2, \ldots, \mu$. There are two important special cases to consider.

First, if the total power of all input waves does not exceed the saturation power $\sum P_i \ll P_s$, no saturation effects are observed,

$$\begin{aligned}
g_\mu &= \text{const.} \\
\Delta g_\mu &= 0.
\end{aligned} \tag{1.4.24}$$

Without saturation effects, the gain is constant and therefore no cross-gain modulation and no cross-phase modulation (XPM) is possible, see Eq. (1.4.9). This is the operating regime of linear amplifiers.

Second, if one of the waves ($P_1 \gg P_s$) now deeply saturates the amplifier, it directly modulates the gain of all other waves simultaneously. For digital optical signals, the change of the strong wave dominates,

$$\Delta P_1 \gg \Delta P_2, \ldots, \Delta P_\mu, \tag{1.4.25}$$

such that Eq. (1.4.23) can be considerably simplified,

$$\begin{aligned}
g_1(\omega_1, P_1, \omega_2, P_1, \ldots, \omega_\mu, P_\mu) &\approx g_1(\omega_1, P_1), \\
g_2(\omega_1, P_1, \omega_2, P_1, \ldots, \omega_\mu, P_\mu) &\approx g_2(\omega_2, P_1), \\
&\vdots \\
g_\mu(\omega_1, P_1, \omega_2, P_1, \ldots, \omega_\mu, P_\mu) &\approx g_\mu(\omega_\mu, P_1).
\end{aligned} \tag{1.4.26}$$

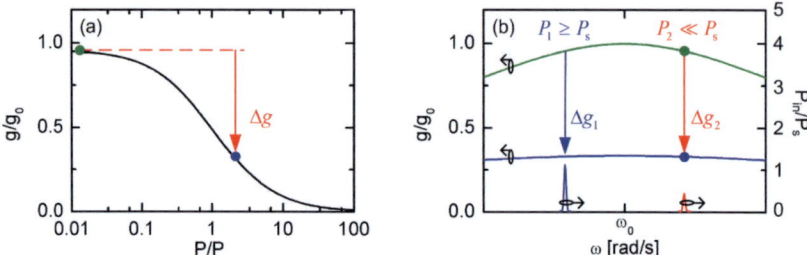

Fig. 1.3 (a) Saturation of the gain constant g as a function of the input power P. The gain is normalized to the maximum small-signal value g_0, the input power is normalized to the saturation power P_s. For high input power levels, the gain is reduced by Δg. (b) Gain spectrum with a maximum at ω_0. Two waves are launched into the device. A strong wave with $P_1 \geq P_s$ saturates the amplifier gain. A weak wave with $P_2 \ll P_s$ experiences a gain reduction by $\Delta g_2 = \Delta g_2(P_1)$.

Fig. 1.3(a) illustrates the saturation of the gain constant constant g as a function of the input power P. The gain is normalized to the maximum small-signal value g_0, the input power is normalized to the saturation power P_s. For high input power levels, the gain is reduced by Δg.

To illustrate the cross-gain effect, the gain spectrum with a maximum at ω_0 is shown in Fig. 1.3(b). Two waves are launched into the device. A strong wave with $P_1 \geq P_s$ saturates the amplifier gain. A weak wave with $P_2 \ll P_s$ experiences a gain reduction by $\Delta g_2 = \Delta g_2(P_1)$. Important applications of cross-gain and cross-phase modulation in semiconductor optical amplifiers are all-optical wavelength conversion [56, 57] and regeneration [58, 59].

1.5 Pump-Probe Spectroscopy

A possible use of ultra-fast processes in highly nonlinear waveguides for next generation all-optical signal processing requires intimate knowledge of the involved dynamics. Unfortunately, the bandwidth limitation present in electronic measurement equipment, severely limits the resolution of direct measurement techniques to a time scale of >15 ps. In order to experimentally determine dynamics on a sub-picosecond time scale, special effort needs to be expended.

Pump-probe spectroscopy is easily one of the most versatile measurement techniques with applications in biology [60], chemistry [61], and optics [62]. It uses short optical pulses to measure device dynamics with sub-picosecond resolution. The heterodyne pump-probe technique [63] offers an important advantage over classic pump-probe spectroscopy. In combination with an advanced heterodyne detection scheme, it allows the simultaneous measurement of the amplitude dynamics and the phase dynamics. Information on the phase dynamics is of utmost importance for optimum filtering schemes [64] and future communication systems, which are like to use phase-encoded signals [65]. Heterodyne pump-probe spectroscopy even allows using the same state of polarization for all pulses, which is a strong advantage for the characterization of polarization sensitive devices like quantum dots in Section 2.3.2 and silicon-photonic waveguides in Section 3.3.3.

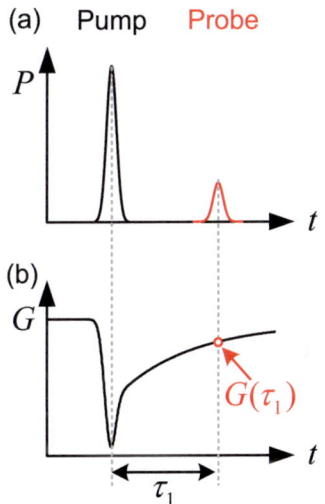

Fig. 1.4 Pump-probe principle. (a) Two pulses are needed for the measurement. The strong pump pulse drives the device under test into nonlinearity. The weak probe pulse cannot perturb the device, but is instead used to sample the propagation properties. (b) As an example, the gain G of an amplifier is investigated. The pump pulse at zero time delay depletes the gain. The delayed probe pulse experiences a reduced gain, depending on the time delay τ_1. By sweeping the time delay, the gain dynamics can be sampled with a time resolution determined by the probe pulse width.

Fig. 1.4 illustrates the basic pump-probe principle. Fig. 1.4(a) shows the two pulses which are needed for the measurement. The strong pump pulse drives the device under test into nonlinearity. The weak probe pulse cannot perturb the device, but is instead used to sample the propagation properties. As an example, Fig. 1.4(b) shows the gain G of an amplifier. The pump pulse at zero time delay depletes the gain. The delayed probe pulse experiences a reduced gain, depending on the time delay τ_1. By sweeping the time delay, the gain dynamics can be sampled with a time resolution determined by the probe pulse width.

As the aforementioned heterodyne pump-probe technique is significantly more complicated than the basic principle, Sections 1.5.1 and 1.5.2 discuss the experimental setup and the mathematical description needed. As a specialty, the heterodyne detection technique simultaneously measures the amplitude and phase dynamics. Section 1.5.3 shows that the characteristic two-photon absorption figure of merit can be directly measured with greatly reduced uncertainties.

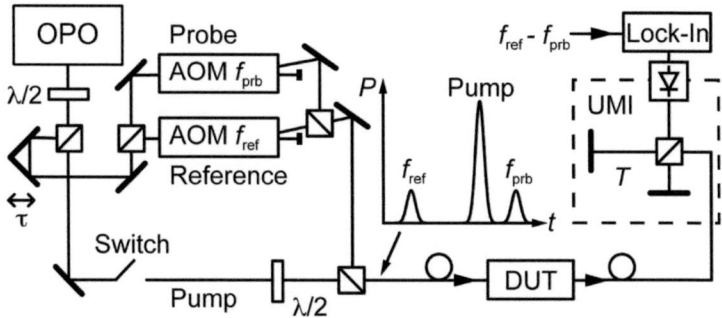

Fig. 1.5 Schematic of the heterodyne pump-probe setup. Short pulses are generated by an optical parametric oscillator (OPO) and split into pump, probe and reference pulses in a polarizing beam splitter (PBS). Probe and reference pulses are tagged by a frequency shift f_{prb} and f_{ref}, respectively, which is induced by acousto-optic modulators (AOM). A strong pump pulse drives the SOA into its nonlinear regime and can be attenuated by the combination of the half-wave plate and the second polarizing beam splitter. A weak pulse probes these nonlinearities in gain and phase. After the device under test (DUT), the pulse train is split and recombined in a Michelson interferometer with unbalanced arm lengths such that the resulting probe-reference beat signal with frequency $\Delta f = f_{\mathrm{prb}} - f_{\mathrm{ref}}$ can be detected in amplitude and phase by a lock-in amplifier.

1.5.1 Pump-Probe Setup

Fig. 1.5 shows the schematic of the setup. For a measurement of the amplitude and phase dynamics we implemented a heterodyne pump-probe technique with sub-picosecond resolution [63, 66-68].

Pulses with a FWHM of 130 fs are generated by an optical parametric oscillator (OPO) and split into pump, probe and reference pulses. Probe and reference pulses are tagged by a frequency shift f_{prb} and f_{ref}, respectively, which is induced by acousto-optic modulators (AOM). The pulse repetition rate is $f_{\text{rep}} = 80\,\text{MHz}$. The pulses are coupled into a polarization-maintaining fiber (PMF) from where they are launched into the device under test (DUT). First, the weak reference pulse is guided through the unperturbed SOA. Next, a strong pump pulse drives the SOA into its nonlinear regime. A weak pulse probes these nonlinearities in gain and phase. A polarizing beam splitter (PBS) acts as a variable attenuator for the pump and ensures the co-polarization of all pulses.

After the device, the pulse train is split in a Michelson interferometer with unbalanced arm lengths. Both copies of the pulse train are then superimposed in such a way that the reference pulse leaving the long arm coincides with the probe pulse leaving the short arm. Because of the respective frequency shifts, the lock-in amplifier detects amplitude and phase of the photodiode current at the difference frequency $\Delta f = f_{\text{prb}} - f_{\text{ref}}$.

For each data point, a reference measurement without pump pulses is used to correct for phase and amplitude drift. By varying the optical delay τ between -10 ps and 300 ps, the temporal evolution of gain and phase can be measured. To reduce the impact of the mean-zero noise, the data is over-sampled by using a step width much smaller than the pulse width.

Due to the periodicity of the measurement, the device always assumes a stationary state on the time scale of the repetition rate $\tau_{\text{rep}} = 1/f_{\text{rep}}$, which for our setup is 12.5 ns. This has two important consequences. First, it limits the temporal resolution to time constants $\tau < \tau_{\text{rep}}$, which might seem a minor problem. Transient behavior of devices like fiber amplifiers which happen on millisecond time scales, are inaccessible by this technique. As a second consequence, phase changes measured with this technique always are maximum values. At higher repetition rates (like in transmission experiments), a different stationary state will be reached, with a generally smaller phase shift for the same input power levels.

1.5.2 Heterodyne Detection Principle

The heterodyne pump-probe technique is an extension to the simple pump-probe technique shown in Fig. 1.4. The phase sensitivity of the measurement is achieved by comparing the weak probe pulse to a reference pulse. As this resembles the classic heterodyne detection scheme, where a local oscillator is mixed with the signal in order to detect the intermediate frequencies, the technique is called "heterodyne" pump-probe technique.

Small differences in the path length experienced by probe and reference pulses would lead to large phase errors. To minimize these phase fluctuations, both pulses should have nearly the same path. As a result, the reference pulse needs to propagate in the device the same way as the probe pulse. A beneficial side effect, this scheme also minimizes amplitude fluctuations due to fluctuating coupling conditions.

Fig. 1.6 shows the pulse sequence and the associated spectra for the heterodyne pump-probe measurement technique. Each pulse of a f_{rep}-periodic sequence is split into three individual pulses, which are shifted in time and frequency such that the contained information can be unambiguously retrieved. Fig. 1.6(a) shows a strong pump pulse, which is used to drive the device into nonlinearity. In its spectral representation in Fig. 1.6(d), the carrier at frequency f_c and the tones at $f_c \pm f_{rep}$. Fig. 1.6(b) shows the weak reference pulse, which acquires a negative time delay and gets frequency-shifted by Δf_{ref}, as shown in Fig. 1.6(e). Fig. 1.6(c) shows the weak probe pulse, which is delayed by τ_1 with respect to the pump pulse and propagates in the perturbed waveguide. The delay τ_2 with respect to the reference pulse is kept constant. The applied frequency-shift f_{prb} makes all three pulses discernible, see Fig. 1.6(f).

To extract the amplitude and phase information contained in the probe pulse, an unbalanced Michelson interferometer is used to superimpose the pulse train in the short interferometer arm with an identical but delayed copy of itself in the long interferometer arm, see Fig. 1.6(g) and Fig. 1.6(h). If the time delay $\Delta\tau$ is sufficiently low, reference and probe pulses coincide. Fig. 1.6(m) shows the optical spectrum for that moment. In a photodetector, a beating signal at the difference frequency $\Delta f = f_{prb} - f_{ref}$ can be detected in amplitude and phase.

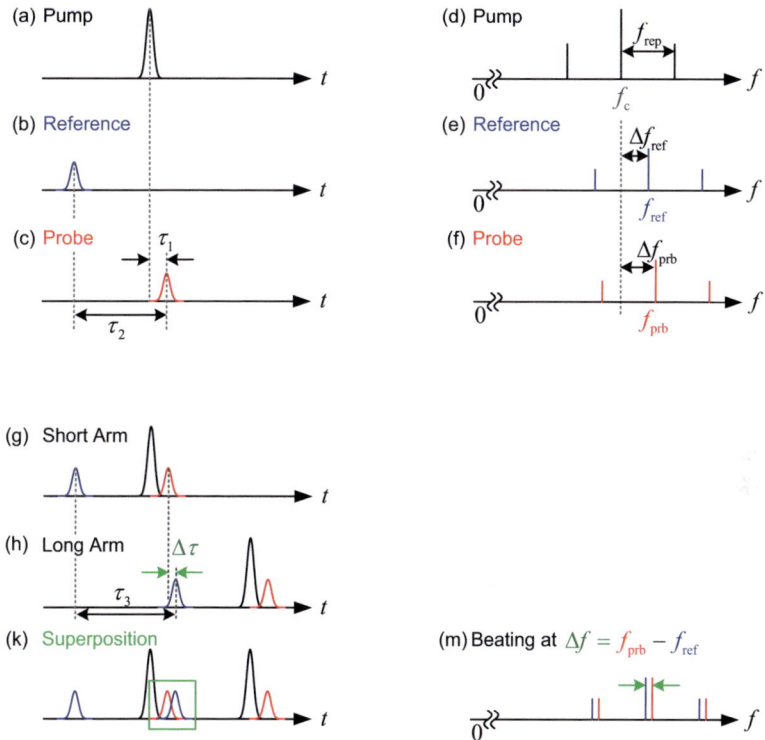

Fig. 1.6 Pulse sequence and associated spectra for the heterodyne pump-probe measurement technique. Each pulse of a f_{rep}-periodic sequence is split into three individual pulses, which are shifted in time and frequency such that the contained information can be unambiguously retrieved. (a) A strong pump pulse, is used to drives the device into nonlinearity. In its spectral representation (d), the carrier at frequency f_c and the tones at $f_c \pm f_{rep}$. (b) The weak reference pulse acquires a negative time delay and (e) gets frequency-shifted by Δf_{ref}. (c) The weak probe pulse is delayed by τ_1 with respect to the pump pulse and propagates in the perturbed waveguide. The delay τ_2 with respect to the reference pulse is kept constant. (f) The applied frequency-shift f_{prb} makes all three pulses discernible. To extract the amplitude and phase information contained in the probe pulse, an unbalanced Michelson interferometer is used to superimpose (g) the pulse train in the short interferometer arm with an identical but delayed copy of itself in (h) the long interferometer arm. If the time delay $\Delta \tau$ is sufficiently low, reference and probe pulses coincide. (m) That moment, in a photodetector a beating signal at the difference frequency $\Delta f = f_{prb} - f_{ref}$ can be detected in amplitude and phase.

Mathematically, reference, pump and probe pulse trains at the output of the short arm of the unbalanced Michelson interferometer are described by

$$a_{\text{pump}}(t) = \sum_{\nu=-\infty}^{\infty} A_{\text{pump}}(t - \nu\tau_{\text{rep}}) e^{j(\omega_c t + \varphi_{\text{pump}})},$$

$$a_{\text{ref}}(t) = \sum_{\nu=-\infty}^{\infty} A_{\text{ref}}(t - \tau_1 + \tau_2 - \nu\tau_{\text{rep}}) e^{j((\omega_c + \omega_{\text{ref}})(t - \tau_1 + \tau_2) + \varphi_{\text{ref}})}, \qquad (1.5.1)$$

$$a_{\text{prb}}(t) = \sum_{\nu=-\infty}^{\infty} A_{\text{prb}}(t - \tau_1 - \nu\tau_{\text{rep}}) e^{j((\omega_c + \omega_{\text{prb}})(t - \tau_1) + \varphi_{\text{prb}})},$$

where A_μ are the slowly-varying envelopes of the pulses. The summation is carried out over all pulses in the infinite pulse train. The pulse trains originating from the long arm are obtained by substituting t with $t - \tau_3$ in Eq. (1.5.1).

A photodetector at the output of the Michelson interferometer receives the pulse sequence

$$a_{\text{tot}}(t) = a_{\text{ref}}(t) + a_{\text{pump}}(t) + a_{\text{prb}}(t) + a_{\text{ref}}(t - \tau_3) + a_{\text{pump}}(t - \tau_3) + a_{\text{prb}}(t - \tau_3). \quad (1.5.2)$$

If the electrical bandwith B_e is smaller than the repetition frequency f_{rep}, the photodetector has as a low-pass filter characteristic and integrates over several signal periods. The photodetector with built-in transimpedance amplifier averages over one integration period and the electrical signal is given by

$$u(t) = \frac{G_{\text{TIA}} S}{\tau_{\text{int}}} \int_{t - \tau_{\text{int}}/2}^{t + \tau_{\text{int}}/2} |a_{\text{tot}}(t')|^2 \, dt', \qquad (1.5.3)$$

where G_{TIA} is the transimpedance gain, S is the responsivity of the photodiode, and $\tau_{\text{int}} = 1/B_e$ is the integration period associated with the limited bandwidth. In the square-law detector, spectral components at the difference frequency $\Delta\omega = \omega_{\text{prb}} - \omega_{\text{ref}}$ are generated, which carry the information of the beating of the frequency-shifted probe and reference pulses as shown in Fig. 1.6(m). The beating signal is

$$u(t, \Delta\omega) = \left[\frac{G_{\text{TIA}} S}{\tau_{\text{rep}}} \int_{-\infty}^{\infty} A_{\text{prb}}(t') A_{\text{ref}}^*(t' - \Delta\tau) \, dt' \right] e^{j\Delta\omega t} e^{j(\omega_c + \omega_{\text{ref}})\Delta\tau} e^{j\Delta\phi}, \quad (1.5.4)$$

where we have abbreviated the constant phase difference $\Delta\phi = \phi_{\text{prb}} - \phi_{\text{ref}} - \Delta\omega\tau_2$ and the time delay $\Delta\tau = \tau_3 - \tau_2$ between the probe and the reference pulses in Fig. 1.6(h).

A lock-in amplifier that is locked to the difference frequency $\Delta\omega$ extracts the complex amplitude of Eq. (1.5.4) and integrates over a large number of periods,

$$U = \left[\frac{G_{\text{TIA}} S}{\tau_{\text{rep}}} \int_{-\infty}^{\infty} A_{\text{prb}}(t') A_{\text{ref}}^*(t' - \Delta\tau) \, dt' \right] e^{j(\omega_c + \omega_{\text{ref}})\Delta\tau} e^{j\Delta\phi}. \tag{1.5.5}$$

Although the information on the nonlinearity of the device is only contained in the probe pulse, the measured complex amplitude also depends on the reference pulse, which is only influenced by the (linear) propagation in the device. In order to unambiguously determine the nonlinear amplitude and phase of the probe pulses, the linear influences need to be calibrated out. A possible calibration procedure is described in the following.

When a strong pump pulse is present, the complex amplitude of Eq. (1.5.5) shall be denoted

$$U^{(\text{on})} = \left[\frac{G_{\text{TIA}} S}{\tau_{\text{rep}}} \int_{-\infty}^{\infty} A_{\text{prb}}^{(\text{on})}(t') \left[A_{\text{ref}}^{(\text{on})}(t' - \Delta\tau) \right]^* dt' \right] e^{j(\omega_c + \omega_{\text{ref}})\Delta\tau} e^{j\Delta\phi}. \tag{1.5.6}$$

In the case where the beam of pump pulses is completely blocked and only the linear device is measured, the complex amplitude is

$$U^{(\text{off})} = \left[\frac{G_{\text{TIA}} S}{\tau_{\text{rep}}} \int_{-\infty}^{\infty} A_{\text{prb}}^{(\text{off})}(t') \left[A_{\text{ref}}^{(\text{off})}(t' - \Delta\tau) \right]^* dt' \right] e^{j(\omega_c + \omega_{\text{ref}})\Delta\tau} e^{j\Delta\phi}. \tag{1.5.7}$$

As $A_{\text{prb}}^{(\text{on})}(t)$ depends on the pump-probe time delay τ_1, so do $U^{(\text{on})}$ and the ratio $R = U^{(\text{on})} / U^{(\text{off})}$. If for each delay the complex amplitude with and without pump pulses are measured, the ratio R can fully describe the system.

The envelopes $A_{\text{prb}}^{(\text{off})}$ and $A_{\text{ref}}^{(\text{off})}$ already contain the information on the linear propagation of the pulses, like insertion loss and pulse broadening due to dispersion. In the presence of the strong pump pulses, probe and reference pulses get modified by a time-dependent transmission factor $T(t)$ and a time-dependent phase shift $\phi(t)$,

$$\begin{aligned} A_{\text{prb}}^{(\text{on})}(t) &= A_{\text{prb}}^{(\text{off})}(t) T(t + \tau_1) e^{j\phi(t+\tau_1)}, \\ A_{\text{ref}}^{(\text{on})}(t) &= A_{\text{ref}}^{(\text{off})}(t) T(t + \tau_1 - \tau_2) e^{j\phi(t+\tau_1-\tau_2)}. \end{aligned} \tag{1.5.8}$$

In this general case, the complex amplitude of Eq. (1.5.6) takes the form

$$U^{(\text{on})} = \frac{G_{\text{TIA}} S}{\tau_{\text{rep}}} e^{j(\omega_c + \omega_{\text{ref}})\Delta\tau + \Delta f}$$

$$\times \int_{-\infty}^{\infty} A_{\text{prb}}^{(\text{off})}(t') T(t'+\tau_1) e^{j\phi(t'+\tau_1)} \left[A_{\text{ref}}^{(\text{off})}(t'-\Delta\tau) T(t'-\Delta\tau+\tau_1-\tau_2) e^{j(t'-\Delta\tau+\tau_1-\tau_2)} \right]^* dt'. \tag{1.5.9}$$

In order for the reference pulse to provide a reference that is independent of the pump pulse, it has to enter the device ahead of the pump pulse. The transmission factor becomes independent of the time, and we can use the simplification

$$A_{\text{ref}}^{(\text{off})}(t'-\Delta\tau)T(t'-\Delta\tau+\tau_1-\tau_2)e^{j(t'-\Delta\tau+\tau_1-\tau_2)} \approx A_{\text{ref}}^{(\text{off})}(t'-\Delta\tau)T(\tau_1-\tau_2)e^{j(\tau_1-\tau_2)}. \quad (1.5.10)$$

With Eq. (1.5.10) we can bring Eq. (1.5.9) to the following form

$$U^{(\text{on})} = \frac{G_{\text{TIA}}S}{\tau_{\text{rep}}}e^{j(\omega_c+\omega_{\text{ref}})\Delta\tau+\Delta\phi}T(\tau_1-\tau_2)e^{j\phi(\tau_1-\tau_2)}$$
$$\times \int_{-\infty}^{\infty} w(t)T(t'+\tau_1)e^{j\phi(t'+\tau_1)}\,dt' \int_{-\infty}^{\infty} A_{\text{prb}}^{(\text{off})}(t')\left[A_{\text{ref}}^{(\text{off})}(t'-\Delta\tau)\right]^*\,dt', \quad (1.5.11)$$

where $w(t)$ is the a window function

$$w(t) = \frac{A_{\text{prb}}^{(\text{off})}(t)\left[A_{\text{ref}}^{(\text{off})}(t-\Delta t)\right]^*}{\int_{-\infty}^{\infty} A_{\text{prb}}^{(\text{off})}(t')\left[A_{\text{ref}}^{(\text{off})}(t'-\Delta t)\right]^*\,dt'}. \quad (1.5.12)$$

The window function ultimately determines the measurement resolution. It depends on the pulse-width of probe and reference pulses, and on the non-ideal overlap of both pulses due to the misalignment of both interferometer arms. In the case of ultra-short pulses, and slow device dynamics, the window function of an optimally tuned interferometer reduces to a delta-function $\delta(t)$.

The complex ratio R in terms of the time-dependent transmission factor $T(t)$ and the time-dependent phase shift $\phi(t)$ is given by

$$R(\tau_1) = \frac{U^{(\text{on})}}{U^{(\text{off})}} = T(\tau_1-\tau_2)e^{j\phi(\tau_1-\tau_2)} \int_{-\infty}^{\infty} w(t)T(t'+\tau_1)e^{j\phi(t'+\tau_1)}\,dt'. \quad (1.5.13)$$

For a negative time delay, $\tau_1 \ll 0$, also the probe pulse is unaffected by the pump pulse. Analogously to Eq. (1.5.10), the probe transmission factor and phase are given by T_0 and ϕ_0

$$R(\tau_1 \ll 0) = \frac{U^{(\text{on})}}{U^{(\text{off})}} = T(\tau_1-\tau_2)e^{j\phi(\tau_1-\tau_2)} \int_{-\infty}^{\infty} w(t)T_0 e^{j\phi_0}\,dt', \quad (1.5.14)$$

which can be used to normalize the complex transmission ratio $R(\tau_1)$ in Eq. (1.5.13) to the value of the undisturbed device of Eq. (1.5.14).

The complex transmission $T(\tau_1)$, which contains the complete amplitude and phase dynamics of the device is then defined as

$$T(\tau_1) = \frac{R(\tau_1 > 0)}{R(\tau_1 \ll 0)} = \int_{-\infty}^{\infty} w(t) \frac{T(t' + \tau_1)}{T_0} e^{j\phi(t' + \tau_1) - \phi_0} \, dt'. \qquad (1.5.15)$$

As only changes to the linear case are of interest, a convenient simplification is to define $T_0 = 1$ and $\phi_0 = 0$ as the base point for the analysis.

1.5.3 Measurement of Two Photon Absorption Figure of Merit

Simultaneous measurements of amplitude and phase dynamics allow to determine the two-photon absorption figure of merit (1.3.37) of passive waveguides with high precision and without any free parameters like the effective area $A_{\text{eff}}^{(3)}$. As in integrated optics the refractive index contrast is high and the waveguide cannot be assumed to be homogeneous over the complete mode cross-section, it is advantageous to use a formulation in terms of a complex nonlinearity parameter, γ. An identical derivation in terms of material parameters can be found in Appendix A.1 and leads to Eq. (1.3.41), which is identical to Eq. (1.3.37) for homogeneous waveguides.

Fig. 1.7 shows a schematic illustration of the effects found in the (a) amplitude and (b) phase dynamics of nonlinear silicon waveguides. At zero time delay, the Kerr effect causes an instantaneous phase change. For the time dependency of $\exp(j\omega t)$ used in electrical engineering, the change of the refractive index caused by the Kerr effect is positive and given by $\Delta n = -\phi_{\text{NL}} \lambda / (2\pi L_{\text{eff}})$. If free carriers are created by two-photon absorption, the plasma effect leads to an undesired phase change with the opposite sign and a long time constant. The amplitude transmission Fig. 1.7(a) shows the instantaneous loss caused by two-photon absorption, and a permanently reduced transmission due to free carrier absorption.

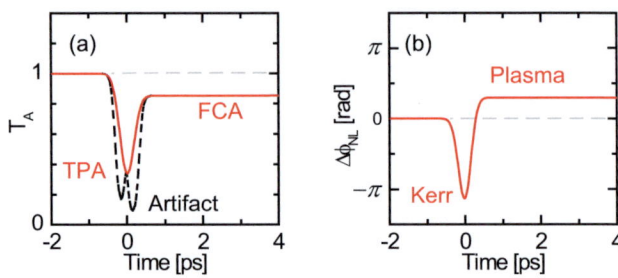

Fig. 1.7 Schematic illustration of (a) amplitude and (b) phase effects of nonlinear silicon waveguides. At zero time delay, the Kerr effect causes an instantaneous phase change. If free carriers are created by two-photon absorption of the pulse, the plasma effect leads to an undesired phase change with the opposite sign and a long time constant. The amplitude transmission (a) shows the instantaneous loss caused by two-photon absorption and a permanently reduced transmission due to free carrier absorption. The dashed line shows the spectral artifact of the measurement principle, which is expected for strong Kerr media [69].

The dashed line depicts an artifact of the measurement technique. In strong Kerr media the nearly instantaneous phase shift causes a very strong frequency shift $\Delta f = \mathrm{d}\phi_{\mathrm{NL}}/\mathrm{d}t$ of the probe pulse for non-zero time delay. This violates the assumption that the frequency difference between probe and reference pulses is fixed. A lock-in amplifier tuned to this difference frequency is unable to correctly detect the signal. Hence, the measured transmission seems to drop to nearly zero. As this drop is only caused by a violation of the measurement assumptions, it is treated as an artifact [69].

The strong pump signal with power P_P experiences linear losses α_0 and nonlinear losses α_2 due to two-photon absorption (TPA) and self-phase modulation (SPM) due to the Kerr effect. With the results of Section 1.3.5, the two-photon absorption figure of merit can be determined directly from pump-probe measurements.

The change of the power $P_P(z)$ and phase $\phi_{P,\mathrm{NL}}$ are given by Eqs. (1.3.32) and (1.3.33) [37],

$$\frac{\mathrm{d}P_P(z)}{\mathrm{d}z} = -\alpha_0 P_P(z) + 2\,\mathrm{Im}\left\{\underline{\gamma}\right\} P_P^2(z), \tag{1.5.16}$$

$$\frac{\mathrm{d}\phi_{P,\mathrm{NL}}(z)}{\mathrm{d}z} = -\mathrm{Re}\left\{\underline{\gamma}\right\} P_P(z), \tag{1.5.17}$$

where α_0 is the linear loss and λ is the center wavelength. Third-order nonlinearities are described by the nonlinear refractive index n_2 and the two-photon absorption coefficient α_2. The resulting pump power $P_P(z)$ for a launched pump power $P_{P,0}$ is given by Eq. (1.3.34),

$$P_P(z) = \frac{e^{-\alpha_0 z}}{1 - 2L_{\text{eff}} \, \text{Im}\{\underline{\gamma}\} \, P_{P,0}} P_{P,0}. \tag{1.5.18}$$

For zero time delay, pump and probe pulses occupy the same time slot. The weak probe pulse experiences negligible two-photon absorption, but considerable cross-two-photon absorption (XTPA) as well as cross-phase-modulation (XPM). The change of power $P_S(z)$ and phase $\phi_{\text{NL}}(z)$ are

$$\frac{dP_S(z)}{dz} = -\alpha_0 P_S(z) + 4 \, \text{Im}\{\underline{\gamma}\} \, P_P(z) P_S(z), \tag{1.5.19}$$

$$\frac{d\phi_{\text{NL}}(z)}{dz} = -2 \, \text{Re}\{\gamma\} \, P_P(z). \tag{1.5.20}$$

Because of the known pump power (1.5.18), equation (1.5.19) can be integrated to yield

$$P_S(z) = \frac{e^{-\alpha_0 z}}{\left(1 - 2L_{\text{eff}} \, \text{Im}\{\underline{\gamma}\} \, P_{P,0}\right)^2} P_{S,0}. \tag{1.5.21}$$

If for each time delay two measurements are taken, one with a pump of known power $P_{P,0}$ and one with a blocked beam $P_{P,0} = 0$, the power transmission T_P and the nonlinear phase change $\Delta\phi_{\text{NL}}$ become

$$T_P = \frac{P_S(P_P > 0)}{P_S(P_P = 0)} = \frac{1}{\left(1 - 2L_{\text{eff}} \, \text{Im}\{\underline{\gamma}\} \, P_{P,0}\right)^2}, \tag{1.5.22}$$

$$\Delta\phi_{\text{NL}} = \frac{\text{Re}\{\gamma\}}{\text{Im}\{\underline{\gamma}\}} \ln\left(1 - 2L_{\text{eff}} \, \text{Im}\{\gamma\} \, P_{P,0}\right). \tag{1.5.23}$$

If the linear loss can be neglected, the result is identical to Eqs. (1.5.22) and (1.5.23), except that the effective waveguide length is the total waveguide length, $L_{\text{eff}} = L$ [70].

Amplitude transmission $T_A = T_P^{0.5}$ and nonlinear phase change $\Delta\phi_{\text{NL}}$ are quantities that can be directly measured using the heterodyne pump-probe technique. Without the need to calculate an effective area $A_{\text{eff}}^{(3)}$, solving Eqs. (1.5.22) and (1.5.23) with respect to $\text{Re}\{\gamma\}/\text{Im}\{\underline{\gamma}\}$ yields an expression for the two-photon absorption figure of merit that only relies on these measured quantities, and is a characteristic property of the waveguide,

$$\mathrm{FOM}_{\mathrm{TPA}} = -\frac{1}{4\pi}\frac{\mathrm{Re}\{\underline{\gamma}\}}{\mathrm{Im}\{\underline{\gamma}\}} = \frac{\Delta\phi_{\mathrm{NL}}}{4\pi\ln T_A}. \tag{1.5.24}$$

If the effective area of a nonlinear waveguide is known, the pump-probe traces also allow to determine the two-photon absorption parameter α_2. For a simple silicon strip waveguide the intensity is known, as the effective area $A^{(3)}_{\mathrm{eff,Si}}$ can be easily derived numerically. For a peak pulse power P_{P0}, the inverse power transmission of the strong pump pulse depends linearly on the on-chip intensity $I_{P,0} = P_{P,0}\big/A^{(3)}_{\mathrm{eff,Si}}$,

$$\frac{1}{T_P} = \frac{1}{T_A^2} = 1 - 2\,\mathrm{Im}\{\underline{\gamma}\}\,P_{P,0}L_{\mathrm{eff}}. \tag{1.5.25}$$

2 Quantum Dot Semiconductor Optical Amplifiers

Self-assembled quantum dots (QD) have been studied intensively for more than a decade due to their δ-function-like density of states [71] and possible defect-free incorporation into semiconductor heterostructures [72]. Numerous device applications like QD laser diodes [73-75], mode-locked laser diodes [76-78], semiconductor optical amplifiers [79-81], and single photon emitters [82-84] have been realized and further applications, e. g. in spintronics [85, 86], are envisaged. The special reputation of quantum dots is due to a long list of predicted advantages over conventional bulk and quantum-well technologies.

Compared to conventional technologies, the stronger carrier confinement in quantum dots should enable temperature insensitive devices [87-90] with high gain [81, 91, 92] and noise figures below 5 dB [81].

The δ-like density of states increases the differential gain [93] and—due to the Kramers-Kronig relations—reduces the linewidth enhancement factor below 1 [92-98]. Additionally, the use of isolated dot groups could be used to enable multi-wavelength operation [99].

For high dot densities and strong pumping, contrary to the expected phonon bottleneck [100], fast processes on the order of 100 fs–1 ps have been found [97, 101], which enable high-speed operation [81, 102, 103].

The strong dependence of the quantum dot formation on the exact growth conditions can be used to tailor the properties, allowing a broad bandwidth of 120 nm [80, 104] and possibly polarization insensitive operation [73, 105].

Curiously, apart from the ultrafast nonlinearities, the low confinement factor inherent to quantum dots [53] improves linear properties like the input power dynamic range [106, 107], the burst mode tolerance [106]. Also, in the unsaturated regime the decoupling of dot states and wetting layer states causes the differential gain to be extremely low [53], which increases the saturation power considerably.

However, only few of these advantages have been reported at the same time for a single device. While some advantages are inherent only to quantum dots, it is unclear to what extend quantum dot devices can really outperform devices based on conventional technologies. Some advantages like the strong carrier confinement are compensated by disadvantages like an increase in homogeneous linewidth, which neutralizes the advantage of an increased differential gain [108]. Additional effects like the low intrinsic quantum efficiency [109] that have not been taken into account can further reduce the performance.

This chapter is structured as follows. In Section 2.1, the current state of the art in quantum dot semiconductor optical amplifiers is presented, ranging from basic epitaxy to linear and nonlinear applications. In Section 2.2, a detailed description of quantum dot device fabrication is given and the influence of the growth conditions and the InGaAs capping layer on the dot properties is investigated. In Section 2.3, quantum dot semiconductor optical amplifiers are characterized. From an analysis of the device dynamics and the homogeneous linewidth, possible applications are identified. In Section 2.4, the application of quantum dot semiconductor optical amplifiers as linear in-line amplifiers for amplitude-encoded and phase-encoded signals is investigated. Large input power dynamic ranges are found, which is attributed to fundamental quantum dot properties.

2.1 State of the Art in Quantum Dot Semiconductor Optical Ampflifiers

Material technology and corresponding device fabrication constitute the basis for the development and exploitation of new nanophotonic materials that offer new functionalities. Quantum dot (QD) materials promise advanced miniaturized devices for applications in the field of telecom systems at the core, metro, and access level. In the following, the state of the art in quantum dot devices with regard to fabrication and applications as broadband amplifiers as well as nonlinear devices is discussed.

2.1.1 Fabrication

The Stranski-Krastanow (SK) growth mode of universal self-organization on surfaces in lattice mismatched hetero-epitaxial growth can be used to realize active regions with high optical quality and homogeneous QD distributions [110]. Improved models of QD devices that take finite barrier heights and the broadening of the QD distribution due to strain into account allow the development of specialized photonic components with improved operation characteristics. Recently, a new growth technique based on droplets has been proposed. However, the required control of the growth conditions proves to be extremely challenging [111].

To achieve large gain, large differential gain and in turn a fast carrier capture, a high QD density is necessary. Unfortunately, the Stranski-Krastanow growth mode couples the size and density of the QD and might reach a limitation because of the existence of the wetting layer. By using the deposition of sub-monolayers (SML) for so-called localization layers these parameters are decoupled [112, 113]. Large dot densities of over 10^{11} cm^{-2} with a modal gain of more than 40 cm^{-1} [92] as well as ultra fast vertical cavity surface-emitting lasers (VCSEL) based on SML-QD were reported [114].

Optimized QD laser structures show in general a low transparency current density (<6 A/cm^2 per QD layer), low internal losses (~1.5 cm^{-1}), high internal quantum efficiency up to 98% and high output powers 18.2 MW/cm^2 [115]. The epitaxial growth of pseudomorphic layers on GaAs substrates facilitates to shift the emission wavelength of the devices to 1.3 μm and beyond, which exceeds the O-band of fiber-based communications [116-118]. InP-based technology is used for the 1.5 μm range [119], using low temperature molecular beam epitaxy (MBE) or gas source MBE (GSMBE) [120]. The resulting QD are usually elongated dashes (QDash) [121], limiting the performance of the device [122]. Presently, stable lasers reach transparency current densities with values slightly below 100 A/cm^2 per dot layer [123].

Devices of the current generation are strongly polarization sensitive due to the high aspect ratio of the QD and their inherent strain. Unfortunately, the polarization diversity technique cannot be used for nonlinear applications. Several new growth techniques have been proposed to overcome this severe limit of QD based optical amplifiers [124, 125]. However, constraints like the maximum strain without the introduction of dislocations render the realization a complex and challenging task. As a consequence, the maximum fiber-to-fiber gain of polarization insensitive quantum dot semiconductor amplifiers is well below 1 dB [105].

2.1.2 Broadband Amplification in Access Networks

Present deployments of optical access networks [126] are mostly based on gigabit passive optical network (GPON, G.984) [127-130] or Ethernet passive optical network (EPON, (IEEE 802.3av) standards or on active Ethernet in point-to-multipoint configuration (IEEE 802.3ah) [131]. Although none of these networks up to now include any kind of optical amplification, both standardization bodies now include optical amplifiers in their roadmaps. Particularly in access networks the available spectrum of the fiber must be exploited to a much larger extent than in other networks, e. g. the upstream wavelengths in PON are allocated within the O-band (1260–1360 nm) and the downstream in the S-band (1480–1500 nm). In terms of efficiency and maturity of the technology, especially QD SOA are very attractive components to fill this gap. They support a wide range of bit rates at modest bias power requirements and a small active volume. Although they provide less gain and higher noise figures compared to EDFA, the optical bandwidth of QD SOA is much larger and the gain dynamics are faster so they can more easily amplify the burst-mode traffic of the PON.

In the 1.5 µm range, the state of the art on single channel amplification with QD SOA is a QD SOA device that exhibits a gain bandwidth of 120 nm, 23 dBm output power and noise figure of less than 5 dB up to 40 Gbit/s [104]. Recently, a –3dB bandwidth of 120 nm in semi-cooled operation was demonstrated [80]. At 1.3 µm, the Fujitsu group has also successfully demonstrated pattern effect free amplification of QD SOA with 40 Gbit/s signals [132]. Undistorted amplification of mode-locked laser (MLL) pulse trains been shown at even higher rates of 80 GHz at 1.3 µm [133, 134] and the simultaneous amplification of 8 channels at 10 Gbit/s at 1.5 µm [119].

Very likely, future gigabit passive optical networks with extended reach of up to 60 km will support subscribers at fiber spans with strongly varying lengths. For the upstream path at 1.3 µm, this requires an amplifier technology with moderate gain but an input power dynamic range (IPDR) as large as possible. QD SOA are a very promising approach, as they combine burst mode tolerant operation [106], a sufficient signal fiber-to-fiber gain of >10 dB, and an IPDR of >26 dB for a single channel and >18 dB for two channels [64, 106], which is comparable to the values published for specifically designed linear optical amplifiers [135, 136]. For phase-shift keying signals, QD SOA at 1.5 µm show an IPDR improvement of 10 dB over comparable bulk SOA [137].

2.1.3 Nonlinear Devices and Applications

The nonlinear properties are the most unique features offered by the QD-based devices. The strong nonlinear optical properties of semiconductors are combined with ultra-fast carrier dynamics and an unprecedented bandwidth.

Ultra-fast gain and phase dynamics have been found in the 1.3 μm and the 1.55 μm wavelength region using the heterodyne pump-probe technique [68, 96, 97, 138-142]. For the first time, the magnitudes and the time constants for these gain and phase responses were extracted for various 1.3 μm InAs/GaAs QD SOA devices and the associated Henry factors were calculated. It was found, that the fast processes have a small Henry factor and become even faster for higher bias current densities, while the slow processes have Henry factors in the order of 5 and remain slow under all conditions. As the phase response is dominated by slow processes, QD SOA should be used only for regenerative schemes that are mostly based on cross-gain effects [97].

More system oriented experiments on the cross saturation dynamics of InAs/InP QDash optical amplifiers operating in 1.5 μm have been performed. The dependence of the cross saturation mechanism on the bit rate of the saturating signal, as well as on the spectral overlapping due to the finite homogeneously broadened width of every dash size population was examined. It was shown that for large detuning, slow rate signals experience large crosstalk, while at high bit rates the QDash SOA shows less cross-talk on the amplification of multi channel signals [141].

Four-wave mixing (FWM) is a very fast nonlinear process that is often used for wavelength conversion or dispersion compensation by optical phase conjugation. For QD SOA, experiments have shown high conversion efficiencies of 0 dB over the whole gain bandwidth, which was attributed to the low linewidth enhancement factor [143, 144]. However, for practical applications and high conversion efficiency, improved carrier confinement in the ground state of the dots is necessary [145].

For all-optical regeneration the single channel regenerative amplification at 40 Gbit/s has been reported [104, 146]. This scheme exploits the nonlinear behavior of the device at the saturation region for suppressing the "1"-level amplitude distortions of the input pulses, as well as its ultra-fast gain recovery which ensures pattern effect free performance. Wavelength conversion up to 40 Gbit/s has been experimentally demonstrated based on cross gain modulation, both in the small signal regime [147, 148] as well as the large signal regime [149]. However, no regenerative performance was achieved. From simulations, regenerative wavelength conversion is expected

[150], even for multiple input channels at high bit rates [58]. Despite the low Henry factor found in QD devices, new interferometric configurations at medium power levels promise excellent extinction ratios and novel all-optical regeneration schemes for advanced modulation formats [151-153].

2.2 Fabrication of Quantum Dot Active Regions

For the application of InAs/GaAs QD structures in information technology, emission at communication wavelengths of 1.3 µm (and 1.5 µm) is an indispensable prerequisite. This requires the epitaxial growth of large defect-free QD containing a high In concentration, which is technologically challenging. Several strategies were applied successfully in molecular-beam epitaxy (MBE) to maximize In incorporation and mobility of surface atoms, e. g. low InAs deposition rates [154-157], cycled sub-monolayer deposition [158], and utilization of InGaAs cap layers [156, 157, 159]. Some advances of the underlying growth technology that lead to emission in the 1.3 µm wavelength region are detailed in this section.

After a short introduction into the Stranski-Krastanov growth mode of molecular-beam epitaxy (MBE) grown self-assembled quantum dots in Section 2.2.1, the typical structure of quantum dot semiconductor optical amplifiers and edge emitting lasers is presented in Section 2.2.2. The formation of the InAs dots for the active region critically depends on multiple MBE growth parameters at the same time. In previous investigations, only the effect of one or two parameters was typically analyzed [154-157, 160-173].

In Section 2.2.3, we investigate the effects of multiple parameters like the deposited amount of InAs, growth temperature, As pressure, the growth rate during InAs deposition as well as the growth interruption time before cap layer growth. Photoluminescence (PL) spectroscopy, plan-view and cross-section transmission electron microscopy (TEM) of capped InAs QD structures are combined to analyze the optical and structural properties rather than solely interpreting PL data with respect to the structural properties or applying atomic force microscopy or scanning tunneling microscopy. The two latter methods require uncapped structures which might lead to an unintended annealing if sample cooling after growth is not performed properly [174]. Furthermore, overgrowth of the QD with GaAs modifies the structures due to In segregation during GaAs cap layer growth which can be assessed by TEM [175-177].

In Section 2.2.4, the use of InGaAs (instead of GaAs) cap layers with different In concentrations is investigated in order to increase the In content of the quantum dots. Different TEM techniques can be combined to determine the shape, size, and composition of the QD. By applying a post-processing procedure the composition of the layers can be reconstructed on an atomic scale. We find the In concentration in the QD to increase in growth direction up to a value of 90%. It is shown that redistribution of In during the InGaAs cap layer growth leads to a decrease of the In concentration in the cap layer with respect to the nominal In concentration.

2.2.1 Self-organized Growth in Molecular Beam Epitaxy

Most advanced optical nanostructures like photonic crystals require sophisticated fabrication technologies, as they require a control of device dimension and structure size on a nanometer scale. Quantum dot devices offer the advantage of a self-organized growth process, where the lateral dimensions of the quantum dots can be controlled simply by choosing the appropriate growth parameters. The *Stranski-Krastanov* (SK) growth regime in which self-assembled quantum dots are formed is based on the interplay between a 2D and 3D growth, due to a slight lattice mismatch between the substrate and the quantum dot material [111, 155, 156, 171, 178, 179]. In the case of InAs dots on GaAs substrate, this lattice mismatch is ~7%.

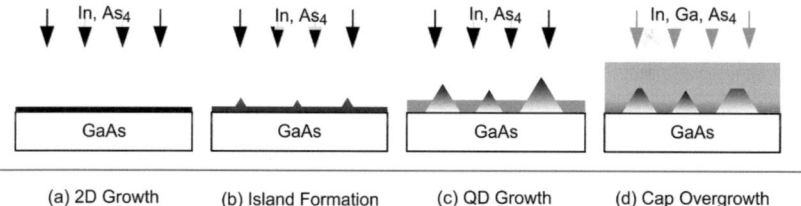

(a) 2D Growth   (b) Island Formation   (c) QD Growth   (d) Cap Overgrowth

Fig. 2.1   Stranski-Krastanov self-assembled quantum dot growth mode. (a) At the beginning, a fully lattice matched compressively strained 2D film (*wetting layer*) is formed. (b) At a critical coverage of 1.8 ML InAs, the accumulated strain is elastically relieved by randomly forming small 3D islands. (c) Additional InAs can freely migrate on the sample surface, adding to the 3D island growth. (d) The growth of a capping layer finishes the dot formation. If the capping layer material has a smaller bandwidth than the substrate, a quantum well structure around the dots is formed.

Fig. 2.1 illustrates the SK self-assembled quantum dot growth mode. At the beginning, a fully lattice matched compressively strained 2D film (*wetting layer*) is formed, see Fig. 2.1(a). At a critical coverage of 1.8 ML InAs, the accumulated strain is elastically relieved by forming small 3D islands [180], shown in Fig. 2.1(b). This nucleation process is random and does not depend on the growth rate [155]. Above the critical thickness, the additional InAs can freely migrate on the sample surface, adding to the 3D island growth, see Fig. 2.1(c). The growth of a capping layer in Fig. 2.1(d) finishes the dot formation. If the capping layer material has a smaller bandwidth than the substrate, a quantum well structure around the dots is formed. This technique is commonly used to extend the emission wavelength of the dots [156].

Depending on the temperature, the growth of the capping layer can cause an intermixing between the dot material and the capping layer material. As a result, both the composition and the shape of the quantum dots can change, and need to be investigated experimentally. As both parameters have a strong influence on key quantum dot parameters like the carrier confinement and the emission wavelength, the exact control of all growth parameters is essential for the fabrication of quantum dot based opto-electronic devices.

2.2.2 Device Structure

For the purpose of wave guiding and electrical pumping it is necessary to incorporate the quantum dot material into a device structure. Naturally, as the requirements are identical to conventional bulk and quantum well devices, the device structure surrounding the quantum dots is identical as well. Contrary to the assumptions found in many theoretical works on quantum dot devices [53, 58] that mainly concentrate on the dot properties, the influence of the surrounding structure cannot be safely neglected and might dominate the device performance.

In the following, the physical structure and the electronic structure are discussed and the concept of homogeneous and inhomogeneous broadening of quantum dot emission lines is quickly introduced.

2.2.2.1 Physical Structure

An accurate understanding of quantum dot devices cannot be solely based on some theory on quantum dots, it needs to adequately include the influence of the device structure. Thus, it is helpful to start the discussion of quantum dot devices with the description of the physical device structure.

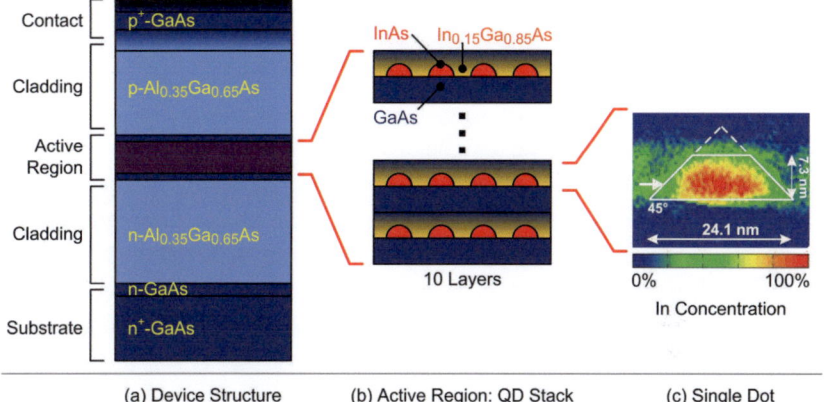

(a) Device Structure   (b) Active Region: QD Stack   (c) Single Dot

Fig. 2.2 (a) Structure of a quantum dot device grown on a GaAs substrate. For wave guiding and in order to avoid coupling of the optical mode to the substrate, the active region is surrounded by conductive $Al_{0.35}Ga_{0.65}As$ cladding layers of ~1.5 µm thickness. (b) The 0.4 µm thick active region consists of a stack of 10 layers of quantum dots. $In_{0.15}Ga_{0.85}As$ cap layers are used to increase the emission wavelength of the dots to the 1.3 µm wavelength region. (c) Composition analysis of a single quantum dot in cross-sectional view.

Fig. 2.2(a) shows the structure of a quantum dot device grown on a GaAs substrate. For wave guiding and in order to avoid coupling of the optical mode to the substrate, the active region is surrounded by conductive $Al_{0.35}Ga_{0.65}As$ cladding layers of ~1.5 µm thickness, in order to avoid coupling to substrate modes. The 0.4 µm thick active region shown in Fig. 2.2(b) consists of a stack of 10 layers of quantum dots. $In_{0.15}Ga_{0.85}As$ cap layers are used to increase the emission wavelength of the dots to the 1.3 µm wavelength region. As discussed in Section 2.2.1, the overgrowth changes the dot shape and composition. Fig. 2.2(c) shows the composition analysis of a single quantum dot in cross-sectional view.

2.2.2.2 Electronic Structure

The lifetime of an exited state of any oscillator is finite, when it is coupled to its environment. In time domain, the emission of such a state is given by an exponentially decaying oscillation. In frequency domain, its Fourier transform is given by a Lorentzian function,

$$l(x) = \frac{1}{\pi} \frac{\frac{\Gamma_{\text{hom}}}{2}}{\left(x - x_0\right)^2 + \left(\frac{\Gamma_{\text{hom}}}{2}\right)^2}, \qquad (2.2.1)$$

which is centered around x_0 and has a full-width at half maximum (FWHM) of Γ_{hom}.

As single quantum dots with their zero dimensional density of states (DOS) resemble artificial atoms, the emission of a single dot can be fully described by Eq. (2.2.1). Changes of the carrier lifetime affect all dots identically. As this homogeneously changes the emission spectrum, the broadening due to the finite lifetime of the excitation is called *homogeneous broadening*. A small homogeneous linewidth can be expected when the lifetime of the excited state is long. In general this is the case for low dot densities, where the coupling to other dots is effectively eliminated. Measurements at low temperatures with weak optical excitation are needed to validate this experimentally. Note that in practical devices these conditions are violated and the lifetimes are low due to coupling between two dots, coupling between a dot and a quantum well state, and most importantly due to Coulomb scattering [181]. At room temperature, a simple theory estimates the homogeneous linewidth of quantum dot interband transitions at 1.3 μm to be 15 meV [159].

Due to the random nature of the island formation for each independent quantum dot as discussed in Section 2.2.1 Fig. 2.1(c), the size distribution of the quantum dots is described by Gaussian function,

$$g(x) = \frac{1}{\sigma\sqrt{2\pi}} e^{\frac{-\left(x - x_0\right)^2}{2\sigma^2}}, \qquad (2.2.2)$$

which is centered around x_0 with a variance σ. Its FWHM is $\Gamma_{\text{inhom}} = 2\sigma\sqrt{2\ln 2} \approx 2.3548\sigma$. If each group of dots with identical properties can be regarded independent, a change of the distribution of the active dots can influence the spectrum asymmetrically. The broadening of the emission spectrum due to size variations of the dots is thus called *inhomogeneous broadening*. As the FWHM of the dot ensemble can be easily increased by varying the InAs coverage of consecutive quantum dot layers, typical values for Γ_{inhom} range between 30 nm and 120 nm. For quantum dot semiconductor optical amplifiers, the inhomogeneous broadening determines the optical bandwidth of the amplifier.

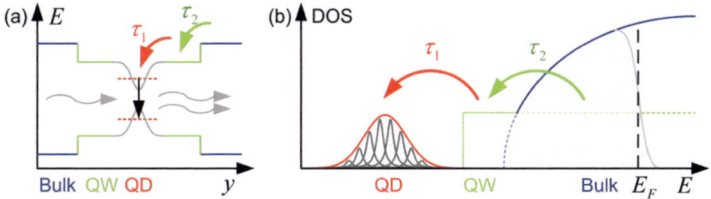

Fig. 2.3 (a) Band structure of a single layer of identical quantum dots (QD) embedded in a quantum well (QW) which is surrounded by a bulk structure (Bulk). Interband transitions in the QD cause stimulated (and spontaneous) emission (gray arrows). Under strong bias, two time constants are expected. One associated with the refilling of the dots τ_1, and one associated with the refilling of the QW states τ_2. (b) Schematic of the electron density of states (DOS) of the device shown in Fig. 2.2. Homogeneous quantum dot groups with a 0D density of states (grey) are inhomogeneously broadened (red). Quantum well and bulk states are described by the characteristic 2D (green) and 3D (blue) density of states. E_F denotes the Fermi energy.

Fig. 2.3(a) shows the band structure of a single layer of identical quantum dots (QD) embedded in a quantum well (QW) which is surrounded by a bulk structure (Bulk). Interband transitions in the QD cause stimulated (and spontaneous) emission (gray arrows). Under strong bias, two time constants are expected. One associated with the refilling of the dots τ_1, and one associated with the refilling of the QW states τ_2. Fig. 2.3(b) shows the schematic of the electron density of states (DOS) of a typical quantum dot device, see Fig. 2.2. Homogeneous quantum dot groups with a 0D density of states (grey) are inhomogeneously broadened (red). Quantum well and bulk states are described by the characteristic 2D (green) and 3D (blue) density of states. E_F denotes the Fermi energy. Obviously, in order to refill quantum dot states, carriers must traverse the cascade of bulk and quantum well states. Under strong saturation (or low bias conditions), the slowest time constant will dominate the device dynamics.

Although this description is extremely simplified, more elaborate models which involve a large number of quantum dot states and take into account the ground state as well as multiple possible excited states, still arrive at the same conclusions [53].

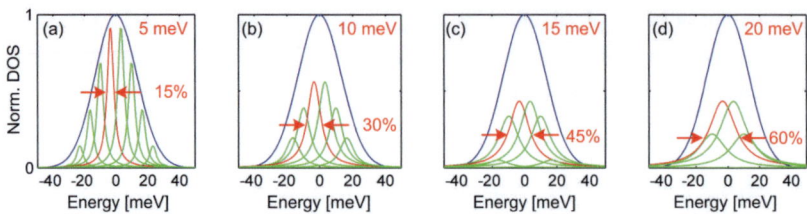

Fig. 2.4 Illustration of the inhomogeneous broadening of groups of quantum dots in the normalized density of states (DOS). The Gaussian distribution $g(\Delta E)$ (blue) is centered at 1300 nm with a full width at half maximum (FWHM) of $\Gamma_{\text{inhom}} = 33\,\text{meV}\,(\sim 45\,\text{nm})$. Each dot group is homogeneously broadened with a Lorentzian line shape (red). Ensembles of homogeneously broadened quantum dots (green) with linewidths Γ_{hom} of (a) 5 meV (~ 6.8 nm, 15%), (b) 10 meV (~ 13.6 nm, 30%), (c) 15 meV (~ 20.4 nm, 45%), and (d) 20 meV (~ 27.3 nm, 60%).

The influence of the homogeneous linewidth on the device performance is illustrated in Fig. 2.4. It shows the normalized density of states for a dot ensemble of at 1300 nm with a full width at half maximum (FWHM) of $\Gamma_{\text{inhom}} = 33\,\text{meV}\,(\sim 45\,\text{nm})$. Each dot group is homogeneously broadened with a Lorentzian line shape (red). Ensembles of homogeneously broadened quantum dots (green) with linewidths Γ_{hom} of (a) 5 meV (~ 6.8 nm, $\Gamma_{\text{hom}}/\Gamma_{\text{inhom}} = 15\%$), (b) 10 meV ($\sim 13.6$ nm, $\Gamma_{\text{hom}}/\Gamma_{\text{inhom}} = 30\%$), (c) 15 meV ($\sim 20.4$ nm, $\Gamma_{\text{hom}}/\Gamma_{\text{inhom}} = 45\%$), and (d) 20 meV ($\sim 27.3$ nm, $\Gamma_{\text{hom}}/\Gamma_{\text{inhom}} = 60\%$). In all four cases the emission spectrum is unchanged, the number of individual homogeneous lines contributing to the spectrum changes strongly.

The crosstalk between two homogeneous groups of dot is given by the overlap of their respective homogeneous lines. As a rule of thumb, a Lorentzian line reduces to 3% of its maximum value for a detuning of $3 \times \Gamma_{\text{hom}}$, $l(3\Gamma_{\text{hom}})/l(0) \approx 0.03$. The result is directly visible looking at Fig. 2.4(a) and Fig. 2.4(c). If only every third group of dots can carry a signal, multi-wavelength operation is only possible for a very low homogeneous linewidth, see Fig. 2.4(a). For homogeneous linewidths >15 meV and realistic gain bandwidths <60 nm ($\Gamma_{\text{hom}}/\Gamma_{\text{inhom}} > 30\%$), Fig. 2.4(c) and Fig. 2.4(d) show a significant overlap of all homogeneous lines. As a result, true multi-wavelength operation of quantum dots in a saturated regime is extremely unlikely.

2.2.3 Influence of Growth Conditions on Quantum Dot Properties [J10]

The influence of the conditions during growth of InAs/GaAs quantum-dot structures on GaAs(001) by molecular-beam epitaxy was investigated systematically with respect to achieving quantum-dot photoluminescence in the 1 eV range. The growth temperature, As flux, growth rate, InAs deposit, and growth interruption time before cap layer growth were varied. Photoluminescence (PL) spectroscopy and transmission electron microscopy (TEM) were used to study the optical and structural properties.

Large InAs quantum dots with photoluminescence in the 1 eV range are obtained at a low growth rate of 0.0056 ML/s. Focusing in particular on the low-growth-rate regime, it is found that an InAs deposition of at least 2.4 ML and a growth temperature of 500–510°C are crucial to obtain large quantum dots with a high size uniformity. Composition analyses by transmission electron microscopy reveal a significantly higher In concentration in the quantum dots grown at low growth rate compared to high-growth-rate samples.

2.2.3.1 Sample Fabrication and Experimental Details

The samples were grown on GaAs(001) substrates in a Riber Compact 21 molecular-beam epitaxy system equipped with effusion cells for Ga and In, as well as a valved cracker cell for As. A GaAs buffer layer was deposited at a substrate temperature of 580°C and an As:Ga beam equivalent pressure ratio (BEPR) of about 15:1. Afterwards growth was interrupted and the substrate temperature reduced to the value chosen for QD growth. The InAs QD were embedded into a 35–40 nm (below) and a 25–30 nm thick (above) GaAs layer, respectively, grown at the same substrate temperature as the QD. The As:Ga BEPR was set to about 10:1 for the GaAs layers. This preserved a (2×4) reconstruction during GaAs growth at the lower temperature. The QD formation was monitored by reflection high energy electron diffraction (RHEED). The intensities of the specular spot and one 3-dimensional (3D) diffraction spot were recorded. A 5 nm thick $In_{0.1}Ga_{0.9}As$ quantum well (QW) covered by a 35–40 nm thick GaAs layer was introduced below the QD for many samples to determine the In flux by measuring RHEED specular spot intensity oscillations.

Table 2.1 Overview of growth conditions used for the sample series used to investigate the influence of growth conditions on the InAs/GaAs quantum dot properties.

Series	Substrate temperature [°C]	Amount of InAs [ML]	Growth rate [ML/s]	Growth interruption time [s]	As precursor	As:In BEPR
As pressure series						
1	485	2.2	0.09	120	As_4	10, 21, 33
2	485	2.2	0.09	30	As_2	9, 15, 40
3	520	2.2	0.09	30	As_2	15, 130
Substrate temperature series						
4	485, 500, 520	2.2	0.09	60	As_4	20
5	485, 500	2.2	0.09	120	As_4	20
6	485, 500, 520, 535	2.2	0.09	30	As_2	15
Growth interruption series						
7	485	2.2	0.09	60, 120, 180	As_4	20
8	500	2.2	0.09	60, 120	As_4	20
9	485	2.2	0.09	2, 30, 60	As_2	15
Growth rate series						
10	500	2.4	0.0056, 0.01, 0.08	10	As_4	80
Layer thickness at low growth rate						
11	500	1.74-2.9	0.0056	10	As_4	80
Substrate temperature series at low growth rate						
12	485, 500, 510, 530	2.4	0.0056	10	As_4	80
13	500, 510	2.6	0.0056	10	As_4	80
Single samples at low growth rate						
14	500	1.74	0.0056	30	As_4	80
15	500	1.73	0.0056	30	As_4	80
16	500	2.2	0.01	30	As_4	80
17	500	2.2	0.01	10	As_4	55

Several sample series were investigated which are summarized in Table 2.1. The As:In BEPR during InAs deposition was varied from 9:1 to 130:1, the substrate temperature from 485–535°C, and the growth rate from 0.0056–0.09 monolayers/s (ML/s). Both As_2 as well as As_4 were used as As precursors. The deposited amount of InAs was about 2.2 ML unless stated otherwise. A growth interruption of 2–180 s was introduced before cap layer growth. The As pressure provided during InAs growth was retained during growth interruption until 10 s before the start of the GaAs deposition. The last 10 s were necessary to increase the As pressure again because of the higher GaAs growth rate.

Plan-view TEM samples were prepared by chemical etching from the substrate side using a 5:1 solution of NaOH (1 mol/l) and H_2O_2 (30%). Standard procedures [182] were used for cross-section sample preparation. A Philips CM 200 FEG/ST electron microscope with an electron energy of 200 keV was used for TEM investigations. High-resolution TEM lattice-fringe images were taken under two-beam conditions using the (002) reflection close to the [001]-zone axis. The QD morphology and local In concentration were determined on an atomic scale on the basis of lattice-fringe images utilizing composition evaluation by lattice fringe analysis (CELFA) [183].

At a temperature of about 6 K PL spectra were measured using a HeCd laser at $\lambda = 442\,nm$, a 0.275 m monochromator with 600 mm^{-1} grating, and an InGaAs photodiode. The signal was amplified by a standard lock-in technique.

2.2.3.2 Experimental Results

The transition from a two-dimensional to a 3D growth mode could be observed in-situ by RHEED after about 1.8 ML InAs deposition. This value was calibrated by CELFA measurements. It was in good agreement with the InAs growth rate calculated by extrapolating the In fluxes determined at higher In cell temperatures (and hence higher In fluxes) assuming an Arrhenius dependence of the In flux on In cell temperature. The intensity of the 3D diffraction spots in the RHEED pattern saturated at an InAs deposition of 2.2 ML for a growth rate of 0.09 ML/s. Hence, most samples contain 2.2 ML InAs.

In the following subsections we describe and discuss the influence of all relevant growth parameters on the PL and QD density as well as the In distribution of selected samples.

As flux

The inset of Fig. 2.5 shows a typical low-temperature PL spectrum for samples deposited with a growth rate of 0.09 ML/s. The intense and broad QD emission occurs at around 1.2 eV. The emission of the QW and GaAs substrate are visible at 1.472 eV and 1.492 eV, respectively. An emission of the wetting layer (WL), expected at about 1.42 eV [158, 184], is not visible. The assignment of the first peak to the QW emission was easily possible by changing the In concentration in the QW and observing the peak position.

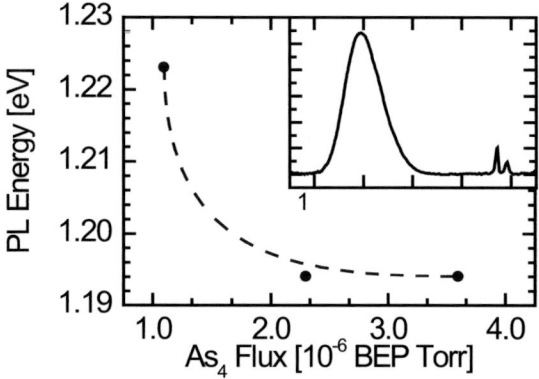

Fig. 2.5 Dependence of the low-temperature (6 K) PL emission energy on the As$_4$:In BEPR for a growth temperature of 485°C, a growth rate of 0.09 ML/s, a growth interruption of 120 s and 2.2 ML InAs deposition. The line is a guide to the eye. The inset shows the spectrum of the sample grown with a BEPR of 21:1.

Fig. 2.5 depicts the low-temperature PL emission energy dependence on the As$_4$ flux for samples grown at 485°C with a growth rate of 0.09 ML/s and a growth interruption of 120 s. The As$_4$ flux is given as As$_4$:In BEPR. Increasing the BEPR from 10:1 to 21:1 lowers the emission energy by about 30 meV. An increase of the As$_4$:In BEPR to about 33:1 does not introduce a further shift of the emission energy. The emission full width at half maximum (FWHM) rises from 65 meV to more than 80 meV with increasing As pressure (not shown). A similar shift of emission energy with increasing As pressure was found for samples grown with As$_2$ and a growth interruption of 30 s.

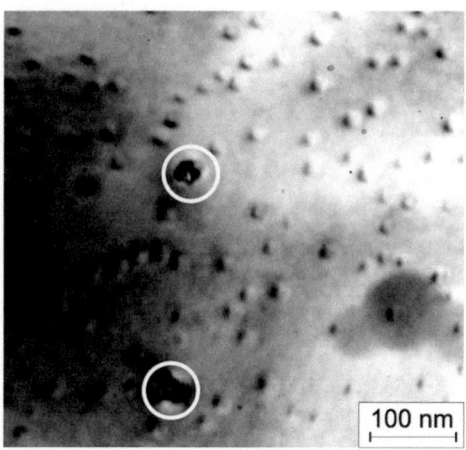

Fig. 2.6 Bright-field plan-view TEM micrograph along the [001]-zone axis of a sample containing 2.2 ML InAs grown with an As_2:In BEPR of 130:1 at a temperature of 520°C with a rate of 0.09 ML/s. The growth interruption was 30 s. The density of coherent quantum dots is $3.6\times10^{10}\,cm^{-2}$. Dislocated islands are marked by circles.

Plan-view TEM micrographs show a decrease of the density of coherent QD from 9.2 to $3.6\times10^{10}\,cm^{-2}$ for an increasing As_2:In BEPR from 15:1 to 130:1, a substrate temperature of 520°C, and a growth interruption of 30 s. Large relaxed islands occur for the highest As_2:In BEPR (see Fig. 2.6). The decreasing QD density with increasing As flux is consistent with the shift of the PL emission to lower energy because larger QD are expected for a reduced QD density and a constant deposited amount of InAs. The confinement energy is smaller for larger QD which leads to a lower PL energy. A higher In concentration in the QD which could explain the experimental results as well cannot be ruled out completely by our results. However, we assume that QD enlargement is more relevant due to the increasing surface energy with increasing As pressure leading to a smaller number of larger QD for a higher As flux [185].

Reports in literature about the influence of the As flux differ significantly [154, 158, 163-165, 185]. This may be related to the fact that the beam equivalent pressure values given in different reports are basically not comparable because they are machine dependent. Only a qualitative discussion of the observed phenomena is possible. The As flux was discussed in connection with the mobility of atomic species on the surface [158, 164, 165], surface energy [185], In desorption [154, 166], and In segregation efficiency [186].

The most striking observation was made by Ledentsov *et al.* [185] who found the formation of stable QD with equilibrium (pyramidal) shape within a narrow window of optimum As pressures and relatively high deposition rates (0.3 ML/s). Plan-view TEM images of the present samples do not show square-shaped strain contrast associated with pyramidal structures within the range of studied BEPR. We will see later (Fig. 2.10) that low growth rates are the essential ingredient for achieving large pyramidal QD. We speculate that the present As pressures are comparatively low because we observe a reduction of QD density and an increase of QD size with rising BEPR. This is consistent with the observation of Ledentsov *et al.* [185] who found a growing QD size with increasing As pressure in the range of low arsenic pressures while they found a size reduction of (coherent) QD with increasing As pressure in the range of high arsenic pressures. The change of the island size distribution and corresponding reduction of the PL energy indicates that the mobility of surface atoms is not limited by the impinging atomic fluxes in the present range of As:In BEPR. We presume that Chu *et al.* [158] worked in the high-flux regime because they observed the opposite effect: a reduced PL energy occurred for lower As pressure which was associated with an enhanced surface length and the formation of larger QD. Compositional changes and corresponding effects on the PL energy cannot be completely excluded because the In-segregation efficiency was shown to depend on the BEPR value by Muraki *et al.* [186] for InGaAs QW with a lower In concentration. A higher BEPR led to the enhancement of In incorporation during GaAs cap layer deposition which might be favorable if higher average In concentrations are desired. Enhanced In desorption at lower As fluxes with its corresponding influence on the QD size and PL energy are supposed not to be relevant for the substrate temperature used for the samples discussed in this section [166]. However, it can explain differing experimental results for higher substrate temperatures.

Substrate Temperature

The dependence of the PL emission energy and FWHM on substrate temperature is shown in Fig. 2.7 for samples grown with a rate of 0.09 ML/s an As_4:In BEPR of 20:1, and a growth interruption of 60 s or 120 s, respectively.

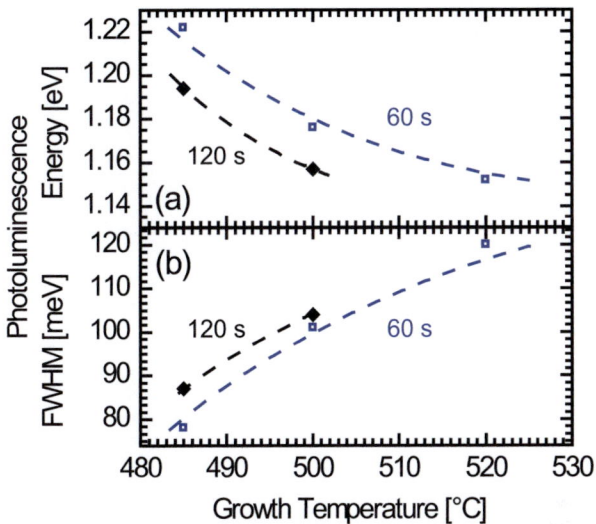

Fig. 2.7 Dependence of the low-temperature (6 K) PL emission energy (a) and FWHM(b) on substrate temperature for 2.2 ML InAs deposition, a growth rate of 0.09 ML/s, and an As$_4$:In BEPR of 21:1. The growth interruption duration is given in the key. The lines are guides to the eye.

The PL energy decreases and the FWHM increases with increasing substrate temperature for both growth interruptions. Only a generally lower emission energy is found for a longer growth interruptions. A comparable behavior was observed for sample grown with As$_2$ instead of As$_4$, where the As$_2$:In BEPR was 15:1 and the growth interruption was 30 s. Fig. 2.8 presents plan-view TEM micrographs of three of the latter samples. The diameter of the QD is less than 20 nm. The QD density is in the order of 10^{11} cm^{-2} and decreases with increasing growth temperature from 1.6 (485°C) to 0.9×10^{11} cm^{-2} (520°C). Lower emission energies at higher substrate temperatures indicate a smaller confinement energy due to larger QD or a higher In concentration.

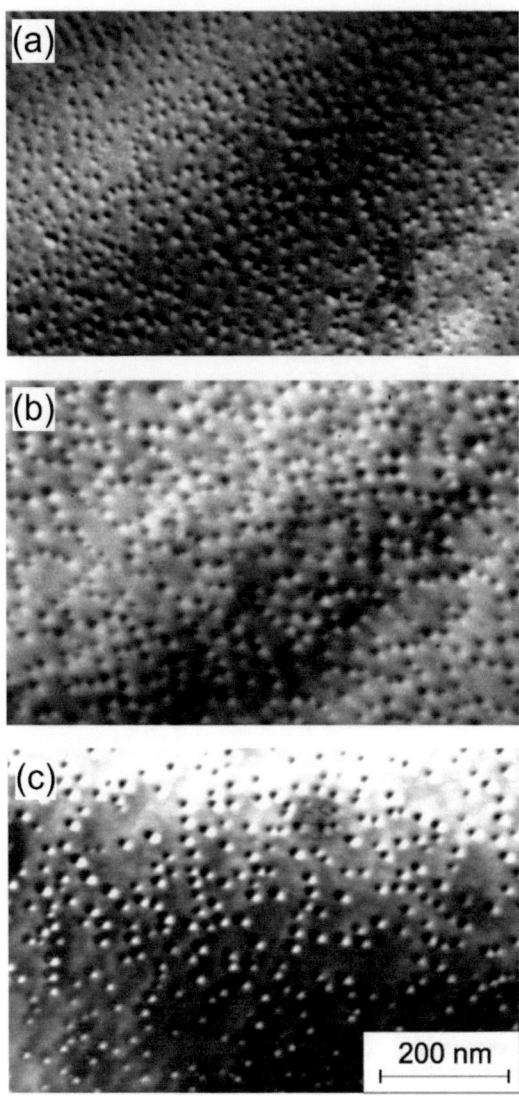

Fig. 2.8 Bright-field plan-view TEM micrographs along the [001]-zone axis of samples grown with a rate of 0.09 ML/s, an As2:In BEPR of 15:1, and a growth interruption of 30 s with an InAs deposit of 2.2 ML. The substrate temperatures (QD densities) are (a) 485°C $(1.6 \times 10^{11}\,\mathrm{cm}^{-2})$, (b) 500°C $(1.2 \times 10^{11}\,\mathrm{cm}^{-2})$, and (c) 520°C $(0.9 \times 10^{11}\,\mathrm{cm}^{-2})$.

The latter is in contradiction with enhanced In segregation at elevated temperature [187]. Hence, larger QD are the most likely origin for the lower emission energy. A corresponding reduced QD density was indeed detected by TEM. These trends are in agreement with several previous studies [158, 163, 167-170]. The formation of fewer but larger QD at a higher substrate temperature can be explained by an increase of the surface diffusion length of adatoms with increasing substrate temperature. An exception from the generally observed behavior was reported by Ledentsov *et al.* [171]. They found a lower density of *smaller* QD emitting at higher energy for higher growth temperatures. This was explained by assuming equilibrium conditions for QD formation. Hence, kinetically limited QD formation is likely for the present growth conditions.

Growth Interruptions

The influence of a GI introduced before cap layer growth on the PL is shown in Fig. 2.9 for a growth rate of 0.09 ML/s, an As$_4$:In BEPR of 20:1, and two different substrate temperatures.

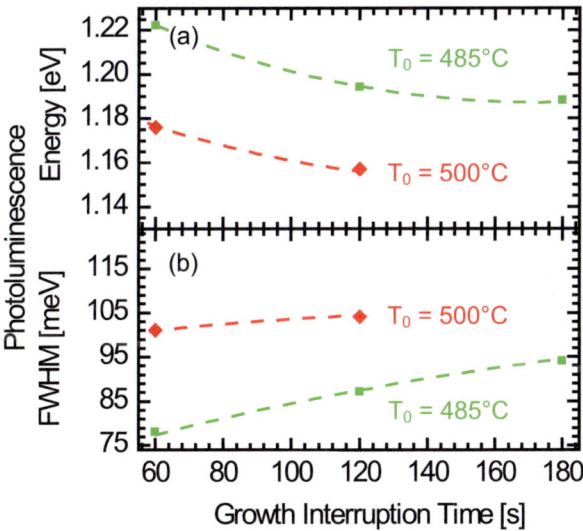

Fig. 2.9 Dependence of the low-temperature (6 K) PL emission energy (a) and FWHM (b) on the growth interruption time for 2.2 ML InAs, a growth rate of 0.09 ML/s, and an As$_4$:In BEPR of 21:1. The substrate temperature is given in the key. The lines are guides to the eye.

Fig. 2.9 shows that the PL energy decreases and the FWHM increases with increasing growth interruption duration for both temperatures. As expected, the emission energy is lower and the FWHM is larger for higher temperature. A comparable dependence was observed for an As_2:In BEPR of 15:1 and a growth temperature of 485°C. Plan-view TEM of selected samples of the latter series reveals a decreasing QD density for extended growth interruptions with densities of $2.15 \times 10^{11} \, cm^{-2}$ (2 s), $1.6 \times 10^{11} \, cm^{-2}$ (30 s), and $1.0 \times 10^{11} \, cm^{-2}$ (60 s), respectively. Some dislocated islands were observed in plan-view TEM images (not shown here) for a growth interruption of 60 s. These results show the ongoing development of the QD morphology during the GI leading to a lower density of larger QD or QD with a higher In concentration.

A reduction of the QD density accompanied by a size increase of the QD can be interpreted in terms of a reorganization of the InAs to an energetically more advantageous state. It is important to note that the FWHM increases with increasing growth interruption time for the samples under study, i. e., the size uniformity decreases. This indicates that the islands will not reach a stable size distribution which is in contradiction to a picture of highly uniform quantum dots in thermodynamic equilibrium [188, 189]. The continuing development of the QD ensemble is corroborated by the appearance of dislocated islands for a long growth interruption.

A possible explanation is the dependency of the surface energy on the As flux [185]. A high surface energy favors ripening of the QD which yields finally few but large InAs islands.

The reports in literature are quite diverse. Kiravittaya *et al.* [172] found similar results for samples grown with a high rate of 0.2 ML/s but an optimum growth interruption time with respect of a small PL FWHM for a growth rate of 0.01 ML/s. Ledentsov *et al.* [171] observed stable QD ensembles for short growth interruptions and the development of large relaxed clusters at the cost of the small islands for very long growth interruptions. Krzyzewski *et al.* [174] reported a deterioration of QD size uniformity for shorter growth interruptions but an improvement for longer ones. We suggest that these discrepancies are related to differing As fluxes or the amount of deposited InAs which might also influence the evolution of the QD morphology during a growth interruption.

Growth Rate

Fig. 2.10 presents the spectra of three samples containing 2.4 ML InAs, deposited with different growth rates. The other parameters (substrate temperature 500 C, As_4:In BEPR about 80:1, growth interruption 10 s) were kept constant. The As_4:In BEPR was the lowest value which could be set reproducibly for a growth rate of 0.0056 ML/s. Reducing the growth rate from 0.08 ML/s to 0.0056 ML/s leads to a shift of the emission energy as large as 180 meV reaching 1.046 eV for 0.0056 ML/s.

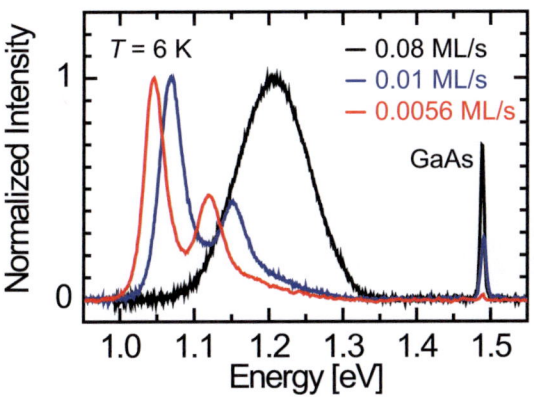

Fig. 2.10 Low-temperature PL spectra for 2.4 ML InAs deposition at 500°C and different growth rates of 0.08 ML/s (–, black), 0.01 ML/s (–, blue), and 0.0056 ML/s (–, red). The As_4:In BEPR was 80:1, and the growth interruption 10 s.

The shape of the spectra in Fig. 2.10 changes drastically in the growth-rate regime from 0.08 ML/s to 0.01 ML/s and remains similar for a further decrease to 0.0056 ML/s. The emission of the high-growth-rate sample consists of one broad peak (118 meV FWHM). In contrast, the emission of the low-growth-rate samples consists of two peaks where the (more intense) low-energy peak has a FWHM of only 39 meV (0.01 ML/s) or even 33 meV (0.0056 ML/s), respectively. Excitation intensity-dependent measurements indicate that the low-energy peak corresponds to the ground and the high-energy peak to the first excited QD state. Hence, a growth rate reduction to very low values leads to larger QD with improved size uniformity in agreement with earlier reports [155-157, 170, 172]. This behavior can be explained by the extended time during growth to reach conditions close to thermodynamic equilibrium. However, we want to point out that low growth rates cannot be compensated by long growth interruptions although the system has more time to approach thermodynamic equilibrium in both cases.

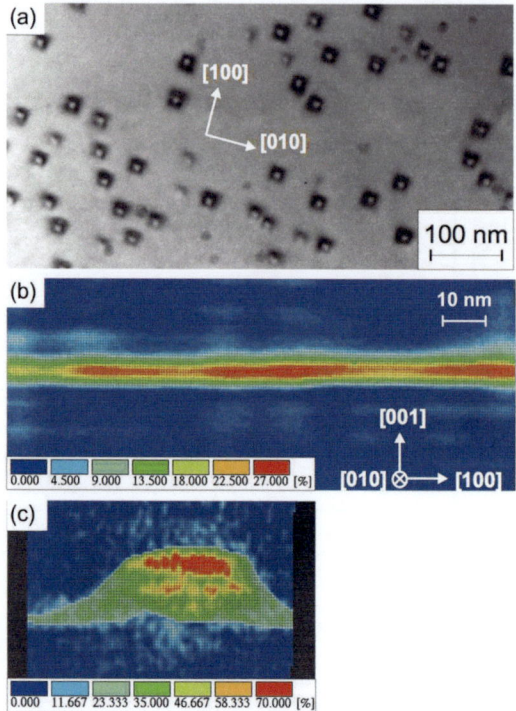

Fig. 2.11 Bright-field plan-view TEM micrograph along [001]-zone axis for an InAs growth rate of 0.0056 ML/s. (b) and (c) Color-coded cross-section images of the In distribution for QD obtained with a deposition rate of (b) 0.08 ML/s and (c) 0.0056 ML/s under otherwise identical conditions (InAs deposit 2.4 ML, substrate temperature 500°C, As$_4$:In BEPR 80:1, and growth interruption 10 s).

In the following we present plan-view and cross-section TEM images to compare the structural properties and In distribution of low-growth-rate and high-growth-rate samples. The plan-view TEM micrograph of the sample grown with a rate of 0.0056 ML/s is shown in Fig. 2.11(a). The QD density is 2.0×10^{10} cm^{-2} which is reduced compared to higher growth rates. The contrast is square shaped and very strong. It is considerably different from the high-growth-rate sample which shows a contrast similar to all other samples deposited with a rate of about 0.09 ML/s (see,

e. g., Fig. 2.6). The change of contrast is indicative for a shape transition of the QD and larger strain fields. The pronounced strain contrast is likely to be induced by higher In concentrations for which we expect stronger distortions. Fig. 2.11(b) and Fig. 2.11(c) depict cross-section views of the color-coded In concentration obtained by CELFA evaluations of a high (0.08 ML/s) and a low-growth-rate (0.0056 ML/s) sample, respectively.

We emphasize that the WL and QD consist of ternary InGaAs although binary InAs was deposited which results from the incorporation of segregated In during the GaAs cap-layer growth [155, 177]. A layer with fluctuating In concentration up to 27% and a slightly varying thickness around 6 nm is visible for the high-growth-rate sample. The regions with high In concentration are assigned to the QD although the interpretation of Fig. 2.11(b) is not straight forward. We have to consider the high density of small QD (1.1×10^{11} cm^{-2} according to plan-view TEM micrographs) with respect to the finite TEM sample thickness between approximately 10 and 25 nm. Thus, QD may overlap in the projection along the electron-beam. Furthermore, the evaluated In concentration is in general lower than the real one because the QD are embedded in GaAs or in the wetting layer with a lower In concentration. In fact, quantitative results cannot be obtained for the In concentration inside the QD and the diameter of the QD. However, it is clear that the height of the QD is rather small. The QD are embedded almost completely in the WL due to In segregation during GaAs cap layer growth. According to Fig. 2.11(c), the QD deposited with a low rate have the shape of a truncated pyramid with a base width of about 45 nm and a top width of about 20 nm. The height of the QD is approximately 12 nm. The CELFA results confirm the shape change deduced from the QD contrast of plan-view images, see Fig. 2.11(a). Thus, the low-growth-rate QD are indeed much larger (both in diameter and height) than the high-growth-rate QD in accordance with other reports [170]. Joyce *et al.* [155] speculated that the In concentration could be increased at reduced growth rates based on volume measurements using scanning tunneling microscopy. Although care must be exercised with respect to the interpretation of the evaluated composition in Fig. 2.11(b) and Fig. 2.11(c) we find extremely high In concentrations in QD of the low-growth-rate sample which are not observed in all other samples. The efficient In incorporation could be aided by the high BEPR which was found to reduce In segregation during GaAs cap layer growth [186].

The In concentration increases from the bottom to the top of the QD with the maximum close to the top. This kind of In concentration profile was observed earlier by us and other groups using TEM evaluated by CELFA [177, 187], grazing incidence x-ray diffraction [190], cross-sectional scanning tunneling microscopy [191], and medium-energy ion scattering [192], and can be understood by In segregation during growth. Some groups reported more complicated inverse (truncated) cone or trumpet-shaped In concentration profiles by cross-sectional scanning tunneling microscopy [193-196] which are not corroborated by the present results.

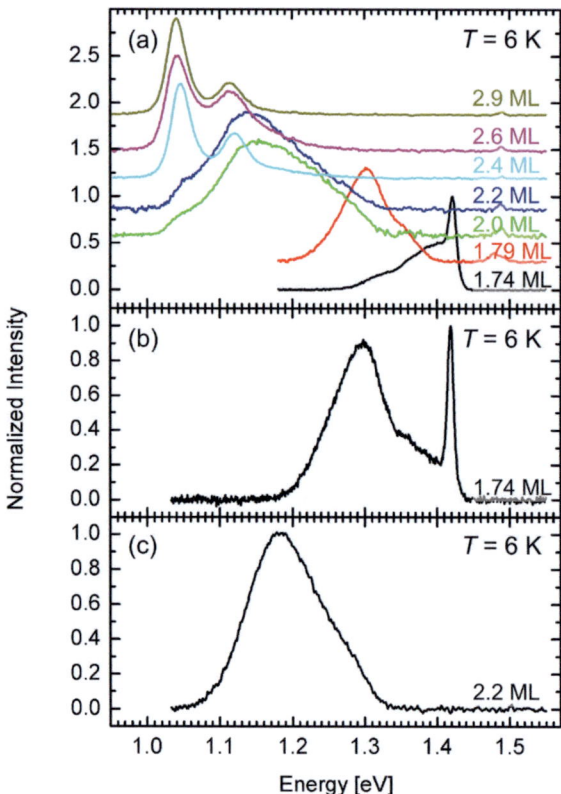

Fig. 2.12   (a) Low-temperature (6 K) PL spectra for a growth rate of 0.0056 ML/s, a growth interruption of 10 s, an As$_4$:In BEPR of about 80:1, a substrate temperature of 500°C, and an InAs deposit of (1) 1.74, (2) 1.79, (3) 2.0, (4) 2.2, (5) 2.4, (6) 2.6, and (7) 2.9 ML. The spectra are shifted for clarity. (b) Same as (1) but with a growth interruption of 30 s. (c) Low-temperature (6 K) PL spectrum for 2.2 ML InAs deposition but with a growth interruption of 30 s. The growth rate was 0.01 ML/s, the substrate temperature 500°C, and the As$_4$:In BEPR about 80:1.

Quantum Dot Formation at Low Growth Rate

After optimizing the growth conditions with respect to obtaining large QD with a high size uniformity, the deposited amount of InAs was varied between 1.74 and 2.9 ML leaving all other parameters (growth rate 0.0056 ML/s, growth interruption 10 s, As_4:In BEPR about 80:1, substrate temperature 500°C) unchanged.

Fig. 2.12(a) depicts the corresponding PL spectra. A sharp peak at 1.421 eV combined with a broad shoulder on the low-energy side down to about 1.275 eV is visible for 1.74 ML InAs. The emission of the sample with 1.79 ML InAs has its maximum at 1.302 eV and a FWHM of 72 meV. A further increase of the amount of InAs (2.0 and 2.2 ML) leads to an extremely broad emission from 1.01 to 1.34 eV which seems to consist of several overlapping peaks. The maxima are at about 1.15 (2.0 ML) and 1.14 eV (2.2 ML), respectively. Samples containing 2.4 ML InAs or more show a long wavelength emission of two peaks as already demonstrated in Fig. 2.10. There is a slight shift of the PL emission of 5 meV (low-energy peak) and 7 meV (high-energy peak) to lower energies by increasing the InAs deposit from 2.4 to 2.9 ML.

We first discuss the samples with small InAs deposits with respect to early stages of QD formation. The peak at 1.421 eV for 1.74 ML InAs is attributed to WL emission. The broad emission on the low-energy side points to a beginning formation of QD which are small at first. A growth-mode transition is not yet detected by RHEED suggesting that the QD density was too low to observe QD formation by this technique. Only WL emission appeared for samples with less than 1.73 ML InAs indicating a critical thickness of 1.73 ML in case of these growth conditions. Another sample was grown with 1.74 ML InAs deposition and an extended growth interruption of 30 s under otherwise unchanged parameters to provide more time for QD formation. However, a growth-mode transition could not be observed by RHEED even during a 30 s growth interruption. Fig. 2.12(b) presents the PL spectrum of this sample. The WL emission is still visible. However, a second peak appears, almost separated from the WL peak and similar to the PL emission of the 1.79 ML sample in Fig. 2.12(a). The growth-mode transition was just detected by RHEED when the In shutter was closed for the latter sample. PL indicates that similar QD are formed in the samples with 1.79 ML and 1.74 ML with 30 s GI, but the strong WL emission and lack of a growth-mode transition suggests a lower QD density in the 1.74 ML sample. Hence, the growth interruption leads to an increase of QD size which is nevertheless much smaller than in the sample containing 2.4 ML InAs. The QD emission for a sample containing a further reduced amount of InAs of only 1.73 ML (instead of 1.74 ML) and a growth interruption of 30 s occurs at the same spectral position but with lower intensity compared to the spectrum presented in Fig. 2.12(b), which is a sign of a further reduced QD density. Preliminary spatially resolved luminescence experiments indicate a two orders of magnitude lower QD density below 5×10^8 cm^{-2} for the latter compared to the 1.79 ML sample.

In the following paragraphs we consider the role of the deposited amount of In and growth interruptions with respect to achieving large QD with a uniform size distribution. The PL emission broadens extremely for 2.0 and 2.2 ML InAs and narrows strongly for higher InAs coverage. The spectra of the latter samples consist of two relatively narrow peaks at low energy where the low-energy peak originates from the ground and the high-energy peak from the first excited state of large QD with a high size uniformity. The small shift of the emission peaks with highest InAs deposit indicates that the size of the QD increases only slightly. (A higher In concentration can be ruled out due to the reduced distance of both emission peaks which is explained in more detail below.) This is in agreement with Ref. [173] where large InAs clusters appear in atomic force microscopy images for higher InAs deposits. Joyce *et al.* [173] supposed that these clusters are dislocated and do not contribute to the almost unchanged PL emission energy and size of coherent QD with increasing amount of InAs.

The broad emission for 2.0 and 2.2 ML InAs seems to consist of (at least) two overlapping peaks pointing to a bimodal size distribution. The shoulder at the low-energy side is located nearly at the same position as the low-energy peak of samples containing more than 2.2 ML InAs. This can be interpreted as a general change in the QD properties from samples with less than 2.0 ML to samples with more than 2.2 ML InAs deposition. A similar change in QD properties between 2.2 and 2.4 ML InAs was observed for a growth rate of 0.01 ML/s. The present results are in agreement with Joyce *et al.* [173] who found a significantly narrowed size distribution above an InAs deposit of 2.2 ML for similar growth rates. However, is the amount of InAs really the important parameter? One should take into account that for a growth rate of about 0.09 ML/s the change in QD properties cannot be observed (see Fig. 2.10) and that the QD evolution can take place also during a growth interruption after InAs deposition as demonstrated for an InAs coverage close to the critical thickness, see Fig. 2.12(b). Fig. 2.12(c) shows the spectrum of a sample with a slightly reduced InAs coverage (2.2 ML) deposited with a rate of 0.01 ML/s and an extended growth interruption of

30 s, i. e., the sum of growth time and the duration of the growth interruption was the same for this sample and the 2.4 ML sample (grown with a rate of 0.01 ML/s, too) shown in Fig. 2.10. The spectra of both samples differ significantly. The emission of the 2.2 ML sample with a longer growth interruption in Fig. 2.12(c) is characterized by a higher energy and a much larger FWHM than the emission of the 2.4 ML sample in Fig. 2.10. Thus, during the growth interruption an evolution towards larger QD with improved size uniformity does not take place. Effects of the varying As pressures are excluded because the flux ratio was similar for all samples. Therefore, both the amount of InAs and a low growth rate are crucial to obtain large QD with good size uniformity.

The ineffectiveness of a growth interruption to obtain similar QD as for a longer deposition time in case of deposition of 2.2 ML InAs is a specific property of the low-growth-rate regime at these optimum InAs deposits in contrast to a lower InAs coverage of 1.74 ML, see Fig. 2.12(a) and Fig. 2.12(b). The result also differs from the result obtained for a higher growth-rate, where growth interruptions lead to a shift of the PL emission to lower energy, see Fig. 2.9(a). Kiravittaya *et al.* [172] found a shift of the PL to lower energy and a smaller PL FWHM for a growth interruption of 30 s in case of a growth rate of 0.01 ML/s. This seems to contradict the present results. However, they deposited only 1.8 ML InAs which is close to the critical thickness. In addition, the emission shifts to higher energy and becomes broader again for a longer growth interruption. Hence, the results of Ref. [172] are in accordance with the present results.

The dependence of the PL energy on the substrate temperature is presented in Fig. 2.13(a) for a growth rate of 0.0056 ML/s, an As_4:In BEPR of about 80:1, a growth interruption of 10 s, and nominal InAs deposits of 2.4 ML and 2.6 ML. The energy decreases to 1.030 eV (2.4 ML) and 1.020 eV (2.6 ML), respectively, with increasing temperature up to 510°C. A drastic change of the emission energy to 1.448 eV occurs at 530°C (2.4 ML). The PL peak is narrow (11 meV) as expected for a quantum well. The emission consists of one broad peak for 485°C and two relatively narrow peaks for 500°C and 510°C, see Fig. 2.12(a). Thus, the formation of large QD with uniform size occurs only at intermediate substrate temperatures.

The distance between the ground and the first excited QD state shown in Fig. 2.13(b) decreases from 500°C to 510°C as a result of a reduced confinement energy. This indicates that the shift towards lower PL energies is correlated with a QD enlargement rather than an In enrichment. Hence, the QD grow to larger sizes for rising substrate temperatures up to 510°C in agreement with the results for a growth rate of 0.09°ML/s.

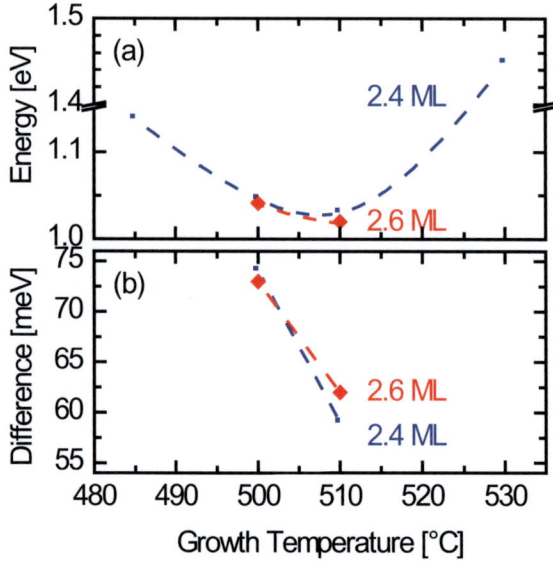

Fig. 2.13   (a) Dependence of the low-temperature (6 K) PL emission energy on the substrate temperature.   (b) Difference between the low-temperature (6 K) PL emission energy of the ground and the first excited QD state as a function of substrate temperature. Growth rate 0.0056 ML/s, growth interruption 10 s, and the As_4:In BEPR of 80:1. The amount of deposited InAs is given in the key. Lines are guides to the eye.

Chu *et al.* [158] observed a blue-shift of the QD emission at high growth temperatures due to a stronger GaAs/InAs intermixing. In contrast, the PL emission of the present sample grown at 530°C indicates a drastic temperature dependence of the InAs growth rate. RHEED did not show a growth-mode transition despite a nominal InAs deposit of 2.4 ML whereas growth-mode transitions were detected at 1.8 ML up to 510°C and at nominally 2.0 ML for 520°C. The same apparently increased critical thickness (2.0 ML) at 520°C was determined for a growth rate of 0.09 ML/s, an As_2:In BEPR of 15:1, and a growth interruption of 30 s. The QD PL was very weak for a substrate temperature of 535°C and a nominal deposition of 2.2 ML InAs under the otherwise identical growth conditions. Plan-view TEM did not reveal any QD in this sample. The temperature dependence of the growth-mode transition can be attributed to a reduced In sticking coefficient at higher temperatures [166, 167]. The deviating observation of Chu *et al.* [158] may be related to higher As fluxes because Ohtake *et al.* [166] found a strong dependence of the In sticking coefficient on the As flux.

Heyn *et al.* [197] reported a temperature dependence of the growth-mode transition which cannot be explained by a reduced In sticking coefficient. Recently, they explained their findings by GaAs/InAs intermixing but also presented a growth-rate dependent reduced In sticking coefficient at further increased temperatures [198]. No hints to a temperature dependence of the critical thickness up to 510°C were found in the present study in contradiction to Heyn *et al.* [197, 198] However, this might be related to the smaller temperature window of 485°C up to 535°C compared to 400°C up to 600°C in Refs. [197, 198]. The PL emission energy of the low-growth-rate sample grown at 530°C is higher than the PL energy of the WL in other samples. However, a lower energy would be expected if the critical thickness was really higher due to a thicker WL. Hence, the PL emission energy provides a strong indication that a reduced In sticking coefficient is the reason for the temperature dependent time of the growth-mode transition in the present work.

The present results provide no clear evidence for an influence of the growth rate on the In sticking coefficient which seems to contradict Ref. [198]. However, the As pressure influences the In sticking coefficient as well [166]. Thus, discrepancies are possibly caused by different As:In BEPR in the present study and Ref. [198], respectively. Unfortunately, the lacking comparability of the As-pressure values in the literature does not allow a detailed comparison.

2.2.3.3 Summary

To summarize, we have performed PL and TEM investigations on InAs QD structures grown by molecular-beam epitaxy using a broad range of conditions in the high and low growth-rate regimes. As general trends, we find that the QD size increases while the PL emission energy and QD density decrease with increasing substrate temperature, As:In BEPR, and growth interruption time or decreasing growth rate. The QD do not reach a stable size distribution during a growth interruption in the studied range of growth conditions. Large dislocated InAs clusters are formed for longer growth interruptions. Increasing growth temperature, increasing As:In BEPR, and increasing growth interruptions decrease the size uniformity of the QD ensemble for high growth rates.

Spectrally narrow PL around 1 eV is achieved for a low growth rate (0.006 ML/s) and substrate temperatures between 500°C and 510°C. The amount of deposited InAs must exceed 2.4 ML. TEM demonstrates that large QD with a high degree of size uniformity and high In concentration are formed under these conditions. QD grown at higher rates are typically smaller and tend to be embedded in a wetting layer which is broadened by In segregation during GaAs cap layer growth. An extended growth interruption at low growth rate does not compensate a reduced InAs coverage with respect to the formation of large QD with a uniform size distribution. However, a growth interruption can be used to obtain a low density of small QD for InAs deposits close to the critical thickness. The In sticking coefficient is significantly reduced at temperatures above 510°C for the conditions chosen in this study. The broad range of analyzed growth conditions yields a unique and consistent data set leading to a comprehensive understanding of InAs QD formation which allows tuning of the QD PL at low temperatures within the range from about 1.35 eV to 1.02 eV.

2.2.4 Influence of InGaAs Cap-Layers on Quantum Dot Properties [J8]

To achieve the highest possible In concentration in the QD, the use of InGaAs (instead of GaAs) cap layers with different In concentrations is a promising approach. Different TEM techniques can be combined to determine the shape, size, and composition of the QD. The In concentration in the QD is measured too low in TEM due to the embedding of the QD in material with lower In concentration and averaging along the finite TEM sample thickness. By applying a post-processing procedure, we are able to reconstruct the composition of the layers on an atomic scale.

We find that the In concentration in the QD increases in growth direction and reaches values up to 90%. Redistribution of indium during the InGaAs cap layer growth leads to a decrease of the In concentration in the cap layer with respect to the nominal In concentration. The observed red-shift of the PL peak with increasing In concentration in the cap layer can be attributed to the enlargement of island size and the change of the strain in the QD layers.

2.2.4.1 Sample Fabrication and Experimental Details

A series of samples was produced by MBE on GaAs(001) substrates. The growth direction will be denoted in the following by [001] in contrast to the in-plane [100] and [010] directions. After the growth of a GaAs buffer layer at 570°C, the substrate temperature was reduced to 500°C. Then, an InAs QD layer with a nominal thickness of 2.6 ML was deposited at a low growth rate of 0.006 ML/s. After a 10 s interruption, an $In_xGa_{1-x}As$ cap layer with a nominal thickness of 6 nm and In concentrations of $x = 0$, 0.05, 0.1, 0.15, 0.2, and 0.25 was subsequently grown. Finally, an additional 30 nm thick GaAs layer was deposited. The growth of all layers and transitions between the two and three-dimensional growth modes was controlled *in situ* by reflection high-energy electron diffraction (RHEED).

The structural properties of the InAs/GaAs layers were studied by TEM of cross-section samples prepared by standard procedures including ion milling [182] and viewed along the [010] and <110>-zone axes. Plan-view samples were prepared by chemical etching from the substrate side using a solution of NaOH (1 mol/l) and H_2O_2 (30%) with a ratio of 5:1. This route was chosen to prevent the formation of additional defects during preparation. For conventional and high-resolution tunneling electron microscope (HRTEM) investigations, a Philips CM 200 FEG/ST electron microscope was used at an accelerating voltage of 200 kV. The microstructure of the plan-view and cross-section samples was characterized by conventional TEM. The In concentration within the InGaAs layers was determined on the atomic scale using composition evaluation by lattice-fringe analysis (CELFA) [199]. For this purpose, HRTEM lattice-fringe images are taken using (002) two-beam conditions near the [010]-zone axis with a center of Laue circle (COLC) corresponding to (0,20,1.5). In addition, lattice-fringe images were also taken with a strongly excited (200) reflection and a COLC (1.5,20,0). The (200) planes—being oriented perpendicular to the buffer/QD-layer interface—are less affected by lattice-plane bending and errors in the composition evaluation. The following image conditions are used for the application of CELFA: The chemically selected sensitive {200} reflection [(200) or (002)] is centered on the optical axis of the transmission electron microscope. Only the (000) and (200) reflections are selected for the formation of the lattice-fringe images. The local In concentration is determined by measuring the local amplitude of the {200} Fourier component of the image intensity which is normalized with respect to the corresponding {200} Fourier component in the adjacent GaAs. The local normalized

{200} amplitudes are then compared to the values calculated by the Bloch-wave method using structure factors [200].

The relative position of the QD within the TEM cross-section sample and the local sample thickness are determined by recording a tilt series of two-beam dark-field TEM images using also the chemically sensitive (200) reflection. The sample is tilted around an axis parallel to the [100] direction in steps of 5° starting from an [010]-zone axis orientation. With increasing tilt angle, the projection of the thin wetting-layer (WL) region broadens. From the tilted (200) dark-field images, the relative position of the QD within the specimen can then be derived from its position relative to the projection of the WL. The local sample thickness is estimated by measuring the width of the projected WL at a given tilt angle by applying simple trigonometry.

Low-temperature (5 K) PL spectra were acquired using an InGaAs detector and a spectrometer equipped with a 600 mm^{-1} grating. The excitation was carried out by the 442 nm and 325 nm lines of a HeCd laser.

2.2.4.2 Experimental Results

By using capping layers with increasing In content, a strong red-shift is observed. At best, the red-shift of the ground state energy between the samples capped with GaAs and $In_{0.2}Ga_{0.8}As$ is 47 meV.

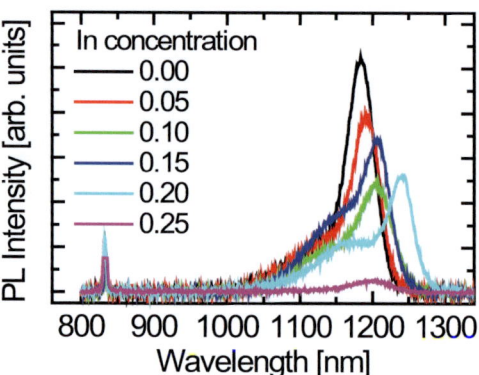

Fig. 2.14 Low-temperature (5 K) PL spectra of quantum dots covered with an InGaAs layer. With increasing In content, the emission wavelength is red-shifted. For a $In_{0.25}Ga_{0.75}As$ cap layer the PL emission is greatly reduced.

Fig. 2.14 shows PL spectra of all samples recorded at a low temperature of 5 K. The PL peak positions shift to lower energies with increasing In concentration in the cap layer. The maximum PL intensities decrease with increasing In concentration in the cap layer. The only exception is the sample with $x = 0.1$ with a PL peak energy that almost coincides with the PL peak energy of the sample with $x = 0.15$ but with a lower intensity.

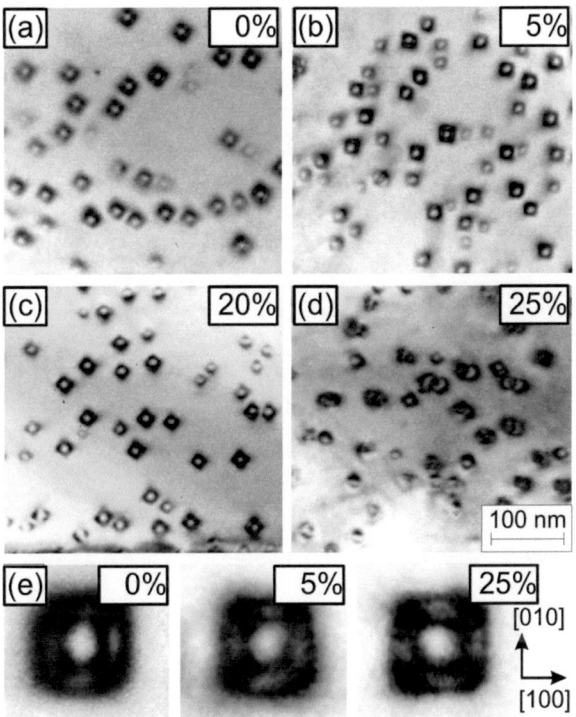

Fig. 2.15 Bright-field TEM images along the [001]-zone axis of plan-view samples with (a) 0%, (b) 5%, (c) 20%, and (d) 25% of indium in the InGaAs cap layer. (e) Enlarged view of the QD from (a)–(c).

Furthermore, for all samples a second PL peak appears which corresponds to the first excited state [201]. The energy separation between the PL peaks associated with the ground and first excited state is about 60 meV for all samples according to fits of the spectra using Gaussians.

Fig. 2.15 shows bright-field [001]-zone axis TEM images of plan-view samples with different $In_xGa_{1-x}As$ cap layers with indium concentrations of (a) 0%, (b) 5%, (c) 20%, and (d) 25%, as well as enlarged views of the QD (e). A square-shaped base is observed for all QD independent of the In concentration. The irregular QD contrast in the sample capped with $In_{0.25}Ga_{0.75}As$ shown in Fig. 2.15(d) results from defect formation.

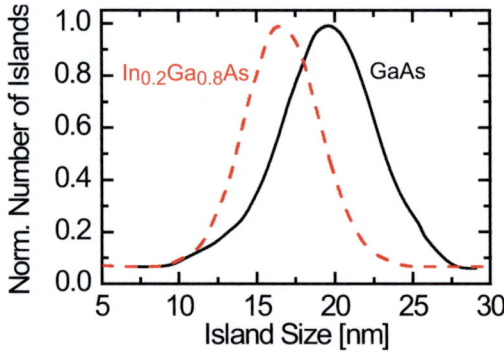

Fig. 2.16 Size distribution of the quantum dots, taken from plan-view images of samples without In and with 20% indium in the InGaAs cap layer.

Fig. 2.16 shows the size distribution of the QD bases in the samples without In and with an $In_{0.2}Ga_{0.8}As$ cap layer. The QD area was measured using the *IMAGEJ* software from plan-view images for approximately 200 islands. Taking into account the square-shaped base of the islands, the length of the base line was extracted from the measured QD area. For the area measurement, contrast clipping was performed which may induce a systematic error to the determination of the area but does not affect the measured size distribution. The quantum dots in the sample with $x = 0$ are larger than those in the sample with $x = 0.2$. The full width at half maximum (FWHM) of the size distributions decreases from 7.1 nm for the sample with $x = 0$ to 6.3 nm for the sample with $x = 0.2$ which demonstrates the improvement of the size distribution with increasing In concentration in the cap layer.

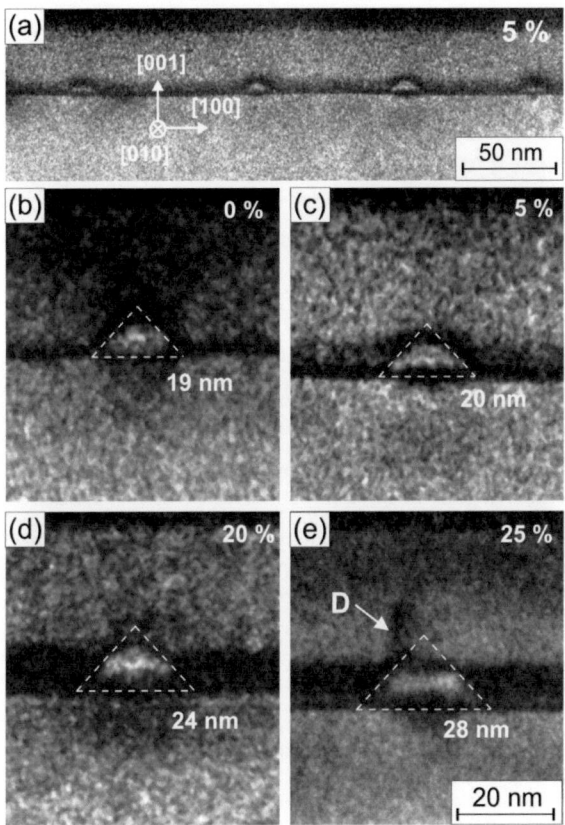

Fig. 2.17 (002) dark-field TEM images close to the [010]-zone axis. (a) Overview of the sample with a In$_{0.05}$Ga$_{0.95}$As cap layer. Enlarged views of the layers with different In$_x$Ga$_{1-x}$As cap layers with (b) $x = 0$, (c) $x = 0.05$, (d) $x = 0.2$, and (e) $x = 0.25$.

Fig. 2.17 shows dark-field TEM images of cross-section samples close to the [010]-zone axis taken with the (002) reflection which is chemically sensitive in InGaAs. Fig. 2.17(a) presents an overview image of the sample with an In$_{0.05}$Ga$_{0.95}$As cap layer with four embedded QD. Fig. 2.17(b)–Fig. 2.17(e) are enlarged sections of the samples with different In$_x$Ga$_{1-x}$As cap layers with (b) $x = 0$, (c) $x = 0.05$, (d) $x = 0.2$, and (e) $x = 0.25$. Calculated intensities of the (002) beam with the Bloch-wave method based on structure factors [200] show that InGaAs displays a decreasing brightness with respect to the embedding GaAs with a minimum intensity at an In concentration of

17% for thin sample regions. For higher In concentrations, the intensity rises and exceeds the GaAs intensity above $x = 0.34$. According to Fig. 2.17(b)–(d), the brightness of the WL regions decreases which can be understood by an increasing In concentration in the chosen range whereas the bright QD contrast is indicative for a high In concentration. The projected shape of the QD can be roughly approximated by a triangle with a base size increasing with x from 19 nm to 24 nm. In the sample with $x = 0.25$, a dark line above the QD appears in the cap layer [marked by 'D' in Fig. 2.17(e)] which is induced by a defect.

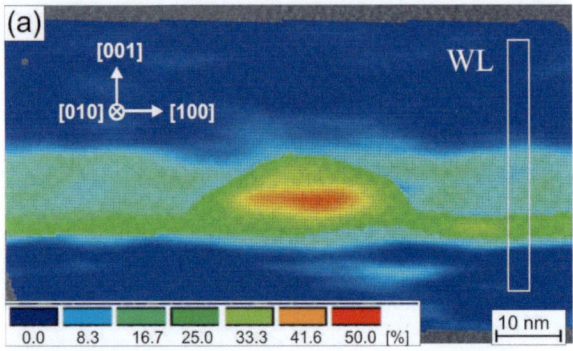

Fig. 2.18   Color-coded maps of the In concentration obtained with CELFA in the sample capped by $In_{0.2}Ga_{0.8}As$. A region where only the wetting layer exists is marked by WL. The wetting layer extends over the whole height of the quantum dot and causes the CELFA to underestimate the In concentration in the quantum dot.

For the sample capped with $In_{0.2}Ga_{0.8}As$, a color-coded map of the local In concentration obtained by CELFA is presented in Fig. 2.18. A region where only the wetting layer exists is marked by WL. The wetting layer extends over the whole height of the quantum dot. The In concentrations in the QD measured with CELFA do not correspond to the real composition due to the three-dimensional shape of the QD which are embedded in a matrix with lower In concentration and the averaging effect due to a TEM sample with finite thickness. For the determination of the real In distribution within the QD, a suitable post-processing procedure of the CELFA data is required [202]. For the CELFA evaluation, only QD were chosen which are fully embedded in the InGaAs layer, without any sectioning due to the TEM specimen preparation.

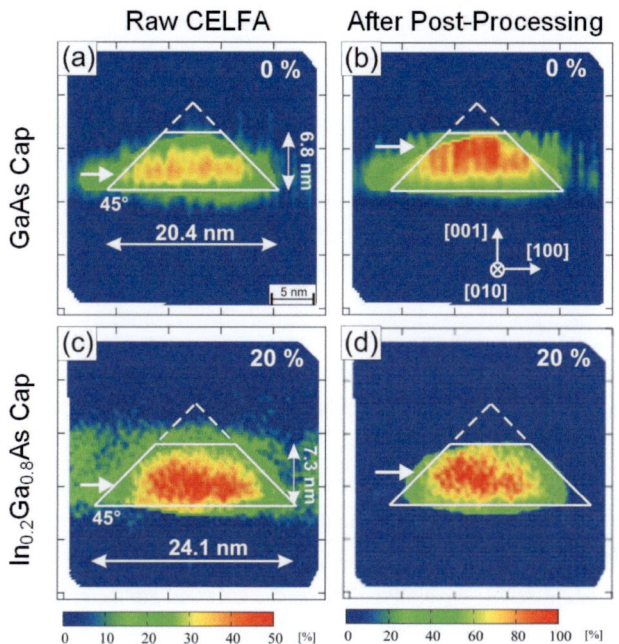

Fig. 2.19 Color-coded In-concentration maps obtained with CELFA using the (200) reflection in samples capped by (a/b) GaAs and (c/d) $In_{0.2}Ga_{0.8}As$ before (left-hand side) and after post-processing of the CELFA data (right-hand side). The white triangles delineate the QD shape.

Comparing the presented TEM images of plan-view and cross-section samples Fig. 2.15, Fig. 2.17, and Fig. 2.18, according to simulations of TEM images [200] and results from cross-section scanning-tunneling microscopy investigations [191], a truncated pyramid with a base along the [010] and [100] directions and {101} facets is the most probable QD shape. Applying the above-described procedure to the originally obtained CELFA data in a restricted field of view containing only the QD, a thickness-corrected In-concentration map can be reconstructed. Fig. 2.19(a) and Fig. 2.19(c) are color-coded maps of the In concentration obtained for the samples capped by GaAs and $In_{0.2}Ga_{0.8}As$. For comparison, Fig. 2.19(b) and Fig. 2.19(d) display the corresponding maps after the post-processing. The thicknesses of the TEM specimens are 33 nm for the GaAs-capped QD and 38 nm for the $In_{0.2}Ga_{0.8}As$-capped QD. Since the correction was only applied to the QD region, the WL is not visible in the corrected maps. In the corrected data, high In concentrations up to 90% are reached. We emphasize that imaging was carried out with the (200) lattice fringes (perpendicular to the substrate/ layer interface), which are only weakly affected by strain in contrast to the (002) lattice planes. The latter are oriented parallel to the interface and their lattice distance and orientation changes within a QD, where the strain field gives rise to lattice-plane bending [203]. The white triangles indicate the approximate QD shape and size. Obviously, the lateral size of the QD increases with the In concentration in the cap layer from about 20 nm for the sample with $x = 0$ to 24 nm for the island with $x = 0.2$, while the dot height increases only slightly from 6.8 nm to 7.3 nm. The white arrows mark the maximum of the In concentration within the dots which shifts upward after the correction. The maximum In concentration reaches almost 90% in both QD with steep concentration gradients at the lower and upper interfaces.

The main motivation for this study was the analysis of the effect of $In_xGa_{1-x}As$ cap layers with x up to 0.25 on the structural and chemical properties of InAs QD and, based on the obtained comprehensive data, the evaluation of the corresponding red-shift of the PL. Before discussing this issue in more details, we have to explain contradictory results regarding the measured QD sizes. We observe an increase of the QD size with increasing In concentration in the cap layer on the basis of images taken with the chemically sensitive (002) beam, see Fig. 2.17 and Fig. 2.19. In contrast, a reduction of the lateral extension is observed according to plan-view bright- field imaging along the [001]-zone axis, see Fig. 2.15 and Fig. 2.16. This apparent contradiction can be resolved by taking into account that (i) bright-field images are mainly sensitive to distortions and lattice-plane bending induced by strain and (ii) the general difficulty of size measurements based on strain contrast. Images taken under these conditions are therefore not well suited to evaluate the real QD size. For example, the strain field of the QD does not only depend on the real QD size and QD composition but also on the lattice-parameter mismatch between QD and the surrounding cap layer. With respect to understanding the behavior of the PL, size measurements on the basis of images taken under chemically sensitive conditions are more relevant because the size of the region with high In content determines the PL energy rather the extension of the strain field. From this point of view, it is more reasonable to use the results of Fig. 2.17 and Fig. 2.19 which indicate an increase of the In-rich QD regions with increasing In concentration in the cap layer.

Most likely, the enlargement of the In-rich QD regions is strain driven [204, 205]. During the InGaAs cap-layer growth, In atoms tend to migrate to the partially relaxed side faces of the QD because the lattice parameter there is larger compared to the strained InGaAs cap layer. This effect is expected to be enhanced for cap layers enriched with indium which results in enlarged QD. The accumulation of indium in the QD also explains the reduction of measured In concentration in the cap-layer regions compared to the nominal values.

Although the measured QD sizes on the basis of bright-field TEM images do not yield the real QD size, the FWHM of the size distribution can be assumed to reflect the homogeneity of the QD sizes. The reduction of the FWHM for the $In_{0.2}Ga_{0.8}As$ cap layer in Fig. 2.16 is consistent with the PL data in Fig. 2.14, which also show a narrowing of the ground state PL peak from a FWHM of 59 meV for the GaAs cap layer to 47 meV for the $In_{0.2}Ga_{0.8}As$ cap layer. Thus, both techniques demonstrate the improvement of the size distribution for an increasing In concentration in the cap layer. The sample with an $In_{0.25}Ga_{0.75}As$ cap layer will not be further considered because it displays a strong reduction of the PL intensity. Fig. 2.15(e) and Fig. 2.17(e) show that this effect is clearly associated with defect formation, causing non-radiative recombination.

The experimental results can be summarized in the following way:
- A red-shift of the ground state PL peak energy of 47 meV is observed if the nominal In concentration in the InGaAs cap layer increases from 0% to 20%. The energy separation between ground state and first excited state of 60 meV is virtually independent of the cap layer composition.

- The density and QD shape (truncated pyramids) are essentially independent of the cap-layer composition, see Fig. 2.15-Fig. 2.17.

- The QD base width increases from approximately 20 nm to 24 nm (Fig. 2.17) with increasing In concentration in the cap layer. The QD heights increase slightly, e. g., 6.8 nm for a GaAs-capped QD, and 7.2 nm for an $In_{0.2}Ga_{0.8}As$-capped QD according to Fig. 2.19. Almost identical aspect ratios of 0.33 (GaAs cap layer) and 0.30 ($In_{0.2}Ga_{0.8}As$ cap layer) are obtained.

- The In concentration and In distribution in the QD depend only marginally on the cap-layer composition with a maximum of ~90% of indium in the upper part of the QD, see Fig. 2.19(b) and (d). The QD are only laterally embedded in InGaAs.

In general, the PL energy of InAs QD depends on the QD composition, shape, size, and strain as well as barrier height as demonstrated by the calculated PL energies in Refs. [206-208]. The QD composition and shape do not depend on the In concentration in the cap layer as presented above. Thus changes of these attributes cannot explain the observed red-shift. Stier *et al.* [207] and Pryor [208] calculated the electron and hole confinement energy levels for (truncated) pyramidal InAs QD in GaAs with base widths up to 20 nm and find a strong dependence of the confinement energies on the base width. Taking these results as a trend suggests that the increase of the QD size could well account for the PL red-shift of our samples. In addition, the reduced lateral barrier height would support the shift to lower energies. However, the negligible change of the energy separation between ground state and first excited state excludes a pure effect of size and lateral barrier height. The change of strain due to the decrease of the misfit between QD and capping layers is expected to play a role as well [209, 210]. For example, Shin *et al.* [210] estimated a red-shift of about 40 meV for InAs QD capped with $In_{0.2}Ga_{0.8}As$ in comparison to a GaAs cap. Although the calculations are based on a lower QD height, their value is in good agreement with our experimental results. Finally, we note that the calculation of electronic states still does not fully account for the real chemical morphology of InGaAs/GaAs QD systems despite the high level of sophistication achieved by theory.

2.2.4.3 Summary

In this study, size, morphology, composition, and PL of MBE-grown InAs QD layers capped by GaAs and InGaAs with different In concentrations up to 25% were investigated. Different TEM techniques were applied which are appropriate for obtaining quantitative data on the QD size and composition despite complex contrast generation in TEM. Composition-sensitive imaging with the (002) and (020) reflections contains reliable information about the size of the In-rich regions as opposed to conditions where merely the extension of the strain field is measured. The determination of the local TEM sample thickness and QD shape nallows for the correction of the primary data on the In concentration in the QD.

After correction we find a maximum In concentration of 90% in the QD core independent of the cap layer composition. The observed enlargement of the QD with increasing In concentration in the cap layer is caused most likely by In redistribution during the cap layer growth which is consistent with the observed In depletion in the cap layers compared to the nominal cap-layer composition. The size distribution of the islands is improved when the In concentration in the cap layer increased from 0% to 20%. A red-shift of 47 meV for the PL peak associated with the ground state energies is observed with increasing In concentration in the cap layer. The red-shift is related to the enlargement of the QD and strain change due to the decrease of the mismatch between the QD and cap layer.

2.2.5 Summary

We have performed PL and TEM investigations on InAs QD structures grown by molecular-beam epitaxy using a broad range of conditions in the high and low growth-rate regimes. As general trends, we find that the QD size increases while the PL emission energy and QD density decrease with increasing substrate temperature, As:In BEPR, and growth interruption time or decreasing growth rate. The QD do not reach a stable size distribution during a growth interruption in the studied range of growth conditions. Large dislocated InAs clusters are formed for longer growth interruptions. Increasing growth temperature, increasing As:In BEPR, and increasing growth interruptions decrease the size uniformity of the QD ensemble for high growth rates.

The dependence of size, morphology, composition, and PL of MBE-grown InAs QD layers on the capping material was investigated. A maximum In concentration of 90% in the QD core is found, independent of the cap layer composition. The observed enlargement of the QD with increasing In concentration in the cap layer is caused most likely by In redistribution during the cap layer growth which is consistent with the observed In depletion in the cap layers compared to the nominal cap-layer composition. A red-shift of 47 meV for the PL peak associated with the ground state energies is observed with increasing In concentration in the cap layer. The red-shift is attributed to the enlargement of the QD and strain change due to the decrease of the mismatch between the QD and cap layer.

The broad range of analyzed growth conditions yields a unique and consistent data set. The comprehensive understanding of InAs QD formation allows tuning of the QD PL at low temperatures within the range from about 1.35 eV to 1.02 eV.

2.3 Characterization of Quantum Dot Semiconductor Optical Amplifiers

For applications based on quantum dot semiconductor optical amplifiers to show optimum performance, characteristic advantages and disadvantages of quantum dot devices have to be known precisely.

In addition to basic amplifier characteristics like gain and noise figure which are investigated in Section 2.3.1, the device dynamics are of great importance. In Section 2.3.2, the carrier dynamics of quantum dot SOA are investigated for the first time from an engineering perspective and with sub-picosecond resolution. Finally in Section 2.3.3, possible multi-wavelength operation of typical quantum dot SOA is investigated by evaluating the homogeneous linewidth at the normal operating point.

2.3.1 Gain and Noise Figure

The two most prominent device parameters are gain and noise figure, which are discussed in Sections 1.4.1 and 1.4.2. Using an automated setup, the dependence of both parameters on wavelength and input power can be investigated.

The gain and noise figure measurement setup is shown in Fig. 2.20. A high power (~ 8 dBm) tunable laser source (TLS) and a variable optical attenuator (VOA1) are used to vary the cw input signal in wavelength and power. A polarization controller allows optimizing the polarization for the device under test (DUT). Two power meters (PM1, PM2) are used to continuously monitor the coupling efficiency of the lensed fibers. A second variable optical attenuator (VOA2) is used to keep the photodetector in the optical spectrum analyzer (OSA) in its linear detection region. Signal and noise power levels are measured with a resolution bandwidth of 0.1 nm at the signal wavelength and with 1 nm detuning from the peak, respectively. For an accurate measurement of the noise figure, a low-noise TLS is needed.

To calibrate the setup and the power levels detected by the OSA, the device under test (including the lensed fibers) is replaced by a strand of single mode fiber. First, the output ports of the second 90/10 coupler are exchanged, so that PM2 measures the total signal power. In a second step, the original configuration is restored with VOA2 set to 0 dB attenuation. This is used to calibrate the OSA readings to actual power levels as would be measured by a photo diode with appropriate filters. This procedure allows eliminating most systematic errors caused by the measurement equipment. For the actual measurements, VOA2 is set to 15 dB, which allows even measuring gain and noise figure of high power amplifiers with more than 25 dBm saturation output power.

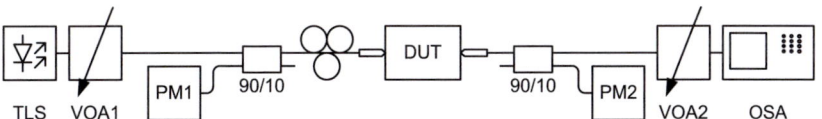

Fig. 2.20 Gain and noise figure measurement setup. A high power (~ 8dBm) tunable laser source (TLS) and a variable optical attenuator (VOA1) are used to vary the cw input signal in wavelength and power. A polarization controller allows optimizing the polarization for the device under test (DUT). Two power meters (PM1, PM2) are used to continuously monitor the coupling efficiency of the lensed fibers. A second attenuator (VOA2) is used to keep the optical spectrum analyzer (OSA) in its linear detection region.

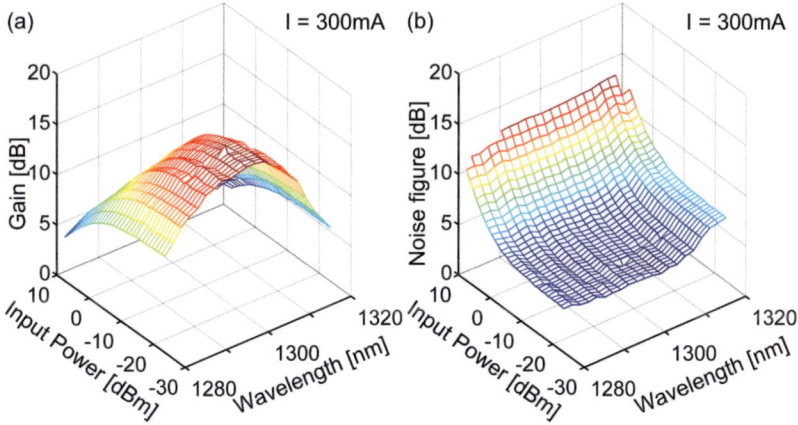

Fig. 2.21 (a) Fiber-to-fiber gain and (b) fiber-to-fiber noise figure of a quantum dot SOA as a function of the wavelength and the input power for a fixed bias current of 300 mA. The maximum gain is 17 dB for small input power levels at a wavelength of 1296 nm. The corresponding noise figure is 6 dB.

Fig. 2.21 shows the fiber-to-fiber gain (a) and the fiber-to-fiber noise figure (b) of a quantum dot SOA as a function of the wavelength and the input power for a fixed bias current of 300 mA, which corresponds to a bias current density per QD layer of $i_0 = 0.375\,\text{kA}/\text{cm}^2$. The device contains a stack of 10 layers of InGaAs/GaAs quantum dots having a dot in a well structure. The device length is 4 mm and the waveguide width is 2 μm. The maximum gain is 17 dB for small input power levels at a wavelength of 1296 nm. The 3 dB gain bandwidth is 35 nm and the polarization dependence reaches 10 dB. The noise figure is 6 dB.

2.3.2 Device Dynamics [J7]

Of paramount importance is the dynamic response of an SOA when it becomes saturated. This will ultimately determine the performance of QD SOA for use as broadband amplifiers or as fast nonlinear signal processing elements. Therefore, pump-probe measurements of gain parameters have been published for QD SOA both in the 1.55 μm and in the 1.3 μm wavelength region [96, 98, 139, 140, 211]. Fast gain recovery has been observed, but fast gain dynamics does not necessarily come along with fast phase dynamics. Particularly, long-reach telecommunications require un-chirped signals with a fast response both for gain and phase. However, so far the strength and relevance of the slow and fast phase dynamics under various operating conditions have never been clarified.

In this Section, gain and phase dynamics of 1.3 μm InAs/GaAs QD SOA extracted from heterodyne pump-probe measurements are presented. Fast and slow processes of both gain and phase are quantified. Also the relative strength of the various processes with respect to the current bias and input power operating conditions is shown. It is found that gain recovery is predominantly fast, while phase recovery is predominantly slow under almost any operation conditions of a QD SOA. These findings have strong implications for potential applications: QD SOA are efficient nonlinear amplitude modulators and thus well suited for cross-gain signal processing applications. If phase effects should be avoided then QD SOA are best operated under high bias current densities with very small or very high input power levels.

2.3.2.1 Experimental Setup and Device Structure

For a measurement of the amplitude and phase dynamics we implemented a heterodyne pump-probe technique with sub-picosecond resolution as discussed in Section 1.5.

The investigated samples are QD SOA grown with MBE on a GaAs substrate. The active region consists of a stack of 10 layers of self-assembled InAs quantum dots with an areal density of approximately $1.3 \times 10^{11}\,cm^{-2}$, each layer covered with InGaAs and a spacer of 33 nm thickness. The active region is surrounded by 1.5 µm thick p and n-doped $Al_{0.35}Ga_{0.65}As$ cladding layers. The deeply etched ridge waveguide is $W = 4$ µm wide and $L = 2$ mm long. The facets are anti-reflection coated and tilted by 7° to avoid lasing. The SOA chip gain is 18 dB and the coupling losses of the structure are about 3 dB per facet.

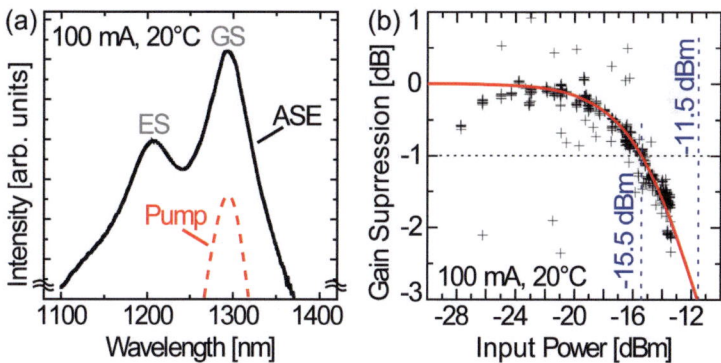

Fig. 2.22 Pump spectrum and ASE without optical pump (different intensity scales.) Ground state and excited state are marked by GS and ES, respectively. (b) Gain suppression measured under pump probe conditions. In the fiber before the SOA, we measured an input power of -11.5 dBm (-15.5 dBm) for a 3 dB (1 dB) gain compression. This corresponds to a pulse energy of 0.89 pJ (0.35 pJ).

Fig. 2.22(a) shows the amplified spontaneous emission (ASE) of the SOA and the spectrum of the pulsed laser source that was tuned to $\lambda = 1295\,nm$. Fig. 2.22(b) shows the suppression of the measured gain relative to the small-signal gain under pump probe conditions, where the pump beam is blocked and the power of probe and reference pulses are varied. The obvious outliers are insignificant, as they are outnumbered by more than a factor of 20 by the total number of measurement points (620). For a gain compression of 3 dB, an input saturation power of -11.5 dBm is found, which equals to a pump pulse energy of 0.89 pJ. Pump, probe and reference pulses are co-polarized and coupled into the same quasi-TE mode of the waveguide, where the dominant component of the electric field is parallel to the substrate plane.

2.3.2.2 Device Model and Fitting Procedure

We fitted the measured data by a simple empirical model that reproduces all observed features. Starting with a physical model and taking into account the finite temporal width of the laser pulses, the complex amplitude transmission function is calculated and finally used to fit the measured data.

Detailed models predict complex carrier dynamics taking into account several different relaxation processes [96], each associated with a characteristic time constant. However, in pump-probe experiments the number of measurable time constants is limited by temporal resolution and by noise. Therefore, it is only possible to draw conclusions regarding the dominant relaxation processes, each of which is commonly approximated by an exponential time dependence [139].

In this thesis, we consider a fast process associated with the quantum dot carrier capture time τ_1 and a slow process associated with the wetting layer capture time τ_2. Both processes influence the material gain $\Delta g(t)$ and the phase dependence $\Delta n(t)$ simultaneously, but with different magnitudes Δg_1, Δg_2 and Δn_1, Δn_2. To confirm this assumption, we have fitted the measured data allowing for individual time constants for the gain and phase recovery. These time constants turned out to be equal within the experimental margin of error. In addition, the probe also experiences instantaneous cross two-photon absorption (XTPA) under the influence of a strong pump.

The change of the net gain $\Delta g(t)$ and the refractive index $\Delta n(t)$ in response to an ideal impulse $\delta(t)$ then becomes

$$\begin{aligned}\Delta g(t) &= u(t)\left[\Delta g_1 \exp\{-t/\tau_1\} + \Delta g_2 \exp\{-t/\tau_2\}\right] + \Delta g_{\text{TPA}}\delta(t) \\ \Delta n(t) &= u(t)\left[\Delta n_1 \exp\{-t/\tau_1\} + \Delta n_2 \exp\{-t/\tau_2\}\right],\end{aligned} \tag{2.3.1}$$

where $u(t)$ is the unit step function and Δg_{TPA}, Δg_1, Δg_2, Δn_1, and Δn_2 are gain and phase parameters, respectively. To keep the number of free parameters small, the instantaneous influence on the phase due to Kerr-nonlinearities was neglected in this empirical model.

The measurement setup has a limited temporal resolution, caused by the finite width of pump and reference pulses. Therefore, before fitting the experimental data, we need to convolve the ideal impulse response in Eq. (2.3.1) with the pump pump-probe cross-correlation $F^{(2)}$ [212].

Fitting of the measured data is then performed to Eq. (1.5.15) the normalized complex amplitude transmission factor $T(\tau) = |T| e^{j\varphi}$ of the probe pulse

$$T(\tau) = \int_{-\infty}^{\infty} F^{(2)}(\tau - t) \exp\left\{ \Gamma L \left(\Delta g(t) / 2 - j k_0 \Delta n(t) \right) \right\} dt, \qquad (2.3.2)$$

where the delay τ is the pump-probe-delay, Γ denotes the field confinement factor, L is the length of the SOA, and $k_0 = 2\pi / \lambda$ is the vacuum wave vector at the center wavelength λ. In relation to the single pass gain G_0, the gain suppression G / G_0 is then related to the normalized amplitude transmission by $G / G_0 = |T|^2$.

Fig. 2.23 shows the results of the fitting procedure (blue solid line) and the separate contributions by fast (black dashed line), slow (red long-dashed line) and XTPA processes (green dash-dotted line).

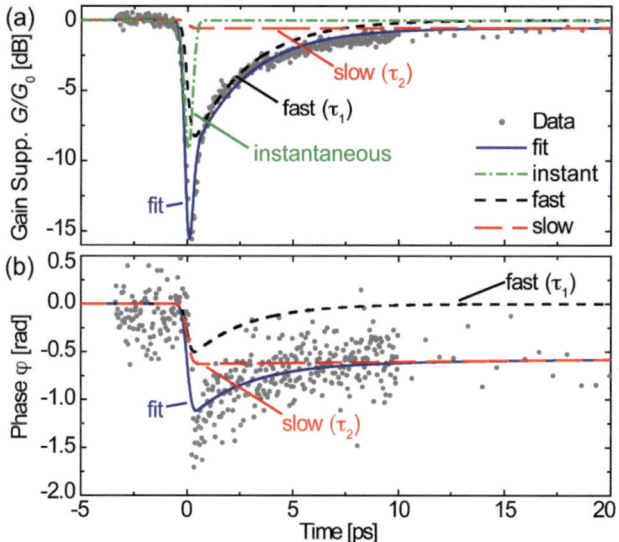

Fig. 2.23   Time evolution of (a) gain suppression G/G_0 and (b) phase dynamics of a typical QD SOA device for a bias current density of $J = 1.25\,\text{kA}/\text{cm}^2$. The fit (blue solid line) well reproduces the measured data (gray dots). The model assumes a fast process (black dashed line), a slow process (red long-dashed line) and instantaneous two-photon absorption (XTPA, green dash-dotted line).

2.3.2.3 Dependence of Fast and Slow Processes on Pump Power and Bias Current Density

The dependence of the process time constants on pump power and bias current density for both the fast and the slow process are plotted in Fig. 2.24. The time constants depend only weakly on the input pump power.

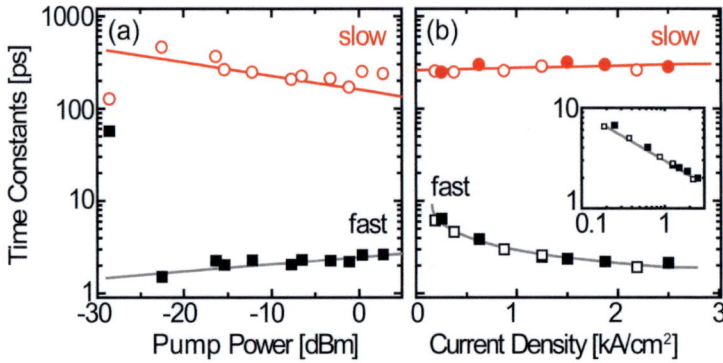

Fig. 2.24 Dependence of time constants on (a) pump power and (b) bias current density for fast and slow processes. Both processes show only a weak dependence on input power. The time constant of the fast process is $\tau_1 < 10\,\text{ps}$ and of the slow process $100\,\text{ps} < \tau_2 < 500\,\text{ps}$. The pump power dependence was measured at a bias current density of $J = 1.25\,\text{kA}/\text{cm}^2$ and the bias current dependence with pump powers of -6 dBm (open symbols) and -11 dBm (filled symbols). The inset shows the power law of the bias current density dependence of the time constant of the fast process on doubly logarithmic scales.

For all measurements a fast process with a typical time constant of $\tau_1 < 10$ ps and a slow process with a typical time constant of $\tau_2 > 100$ ps up to 500 ps are found. The two outliers in Fig. 2.24(a) are due to the small changes introduced by low input powers, which marks the noise limit.

We attribute the smaller time constant to carrier capture from the wetting layer into the QD states, and the larger one to the recovery of the carrier numbers in the wetting layer. When changing the pump power by more than two orders of magnitude, the time constants change by less than a factor of two. The dependence on the bias current density shown in Fig. 2.24(b) is much stronger.

For the fast process a power-law behaviour is found (see inset),

$$\tau_1 \propto i^{\beta}, \quad \beta = -0.5 \pm 0.1 \tag{2.3.3}$$

the exponent of which slightly differs from the value of $\beta = 0.69$ expected for an Auger assisted capturing process [211]. We estimate the bias current density where the fast process becomes nearly instantaneous on the scale of the pump pulse width by extrapolating the fit to a value of $J = 10\,\mathrm{kA/cm^2}$, in agreement with theoretical predictions [54].

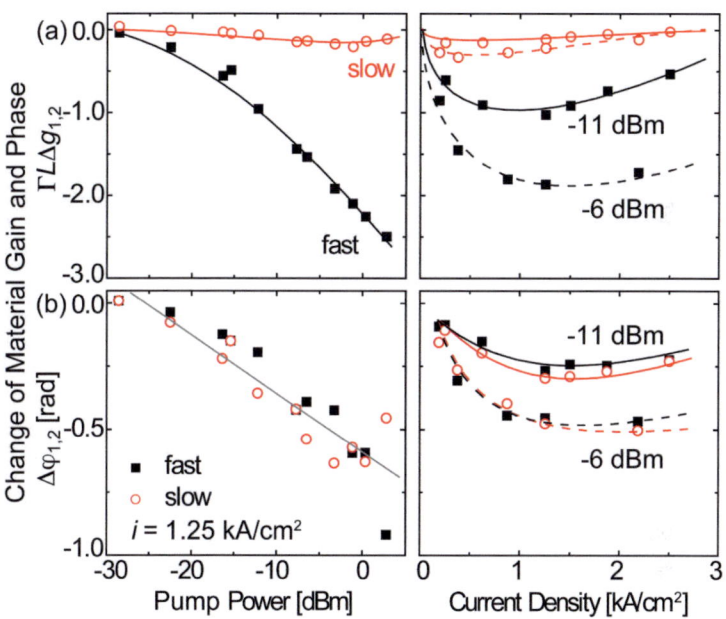

Fig. 2.25 Change of (a) net gain $\Gamma L \Delta g_{1,2}$ and (b) phase $\Delta \varphi_{1,2} = -k_0 \Gamma L \Delta n_{1,2}$ as a function of pump power and bias current density. The strength of the response increases with input power. The slow process has a weak effect on the gain, but influences the phase as strongly as the fast process.

For all practical applications it is not only important to know the time constants but rather the strengths of the respective processes. Fig. 2.25 shows to what extent the various slow and fast nonlinear processes contribute to the overall nonlinearity, depicted as a function of input pump power and bias current density. Fig. 2.25(a) shows that the gain dynamics is mostly dominated by the fast process while the slow process hardly contributes. This finding has often led to the conclusion that QD dynamics are fast in general.

However, our measurements of the phase changes depicted in Fig. 2.25(b) confirm theoretical predictions, that phase recovery is to a large extent dominated by slow processes [213].

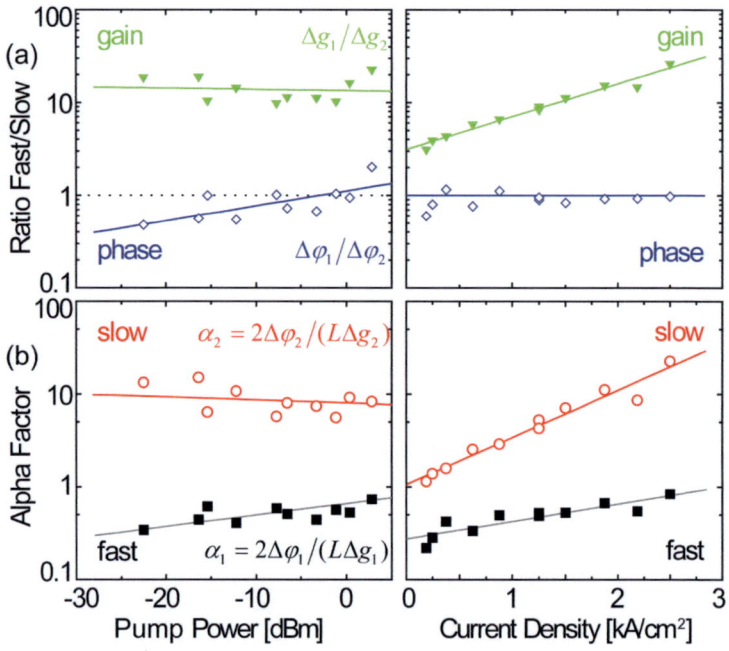

Fig. 2.26 (a) Ratio of strengths of fast and slow processes for phase ($\Delta\varphi_1/\Delta\varphi_2$) and gain ($\Delta g_1/\Delta g_2$. and of (b) alpha-factors for the fast ($2\Delta\varphi_1/(L\Delta g_1)$) and the slow processes ($2\Delta\varphi_2/(L\Delta g_2)$) as a function of input power and bias current density. The material gain response is dominated by the fast process. The phase response is only weakly influenced by the input power but both processes are of equal strength. In (b) it is seen that the fast process has a very low alpha-factor $\alpha_1 < 1$ that changes for large parameter variations by a factor of 2 only. The slow process has an alpha-factor of $1 < \alpha_2 < 22$ that strongly increases with the bias current density.

The relevance of the contributions of fast and slow processes are probably best visualized in Fig. 2.26(a), where the ratios of the parameters $\Delta g_1/\Delta g_2$ and $\Delta\varphi_1/\Delta\varphi_2$

are plotted. The figure shows that the gain is dominated by the fast process (the ratio is larger than 1). For the phase change both fast and slow processes contribute alike (a ratio around 1).

It is interesting to note, that the bias current density has no measurable influence on the ratio $\Delta\varphi_1/\Delta\varphi_2$, while the relative strength of the fast process for the gain rapidly increases, Fig. 2.26(a). Identical changes of the number of free carriers in the wetting layer and inside the QD lead to virtually identical phase changes, even if the current density increases. For the gain, which is determined by the QD states, the situation is different. The QD carriers deplete strongly and rapidly, and the refilling of the QD states is mostly determined by the capture time of carriers into the quantum dots but also limited by carrier number in the wetting layer. This is the reason why $\Delta g_1/\Delta g_2$ increases with the bias current density.

By comparing the relative amplitudes of the net gain changes and phase changes we use Eq. (1.4.2) to calculate the alpha-factors α_1 and α_2 from Eq. (2.3.1) for the slow and fast processes independently

$$\alpha_{1,2} = -\frac{4\pi}{\lambda}\frac{\partial\left(\Delta n_{1,2}\exp(-t/\tau_{1,2})\right)/\partial t}{\partial\left(\Delta g_{1,2}\exp(-t/\tau_{1,2})\right)/\partial t} = -\frac{4\pi}{\lambda}\frac{\Delta n_{1,2}}{\Delta g_{1,2}} = \frac{2}{L}\frac{\Delta\varphi_{1,2}}{\Delta g_{1,2}}. \tag{2.3.4}$$

Alpha-factors calculated from these coefficients are shown in Fig. 2.26(b). The fast process has a very low alpha-factor $\alpha_1 < 1$ that is close to zero for small current densities and low input pump powers, which is expected for quantum dot devices [96]. The slow process has an alpha-factor of $1 < \alpha_2 < 22$ that strongly increases with the bias current density.

To visualize the temporal evolution of the phase response of Eq. (2.3.1), it is convenient to introduce an effective time dependent alpha-factor [214],

$$\alpha_{\text{eff}}(t) = -\frac{4\pi}{\lambda}\frac{\partial(\Delta n(t))/\partial t}{\partial(\Delta g(t))/\partial t} = \frac{2}{L}\frac{\partial(\Delta\varphi(t))/\partial t}{\partial(\Delta g(t))/\partial t}. \tag{2.3.5}$$

In the literature, the absolute phase change $\Delta\varphi(t)$ is often related to the absolute gain change $\Delta g(t)$ by using an alpha-factor definition that integrates over the infinitesimal changes used in our definition of $\alpha_{\text{eff}}(t)$ in Eq. (2.3.5) [98]. This integrated alpha-factor then takes the form

$$\alpha_{\text{int}}(t) = -\frac{4\pi}{\lambda}\frac{\Delta n(t)}{\Delta g(t)} = \frac{2}{L}\frac{\Delta\varphi(t)}{\Delta g(t)}. \tag{2.3.6}$$

This definition is useful to calculate the absolute phase change at a given time $\Delta\varphi(t)$ in comparison to the reference phase for an un-depleted device. The differential definition of $\alpha_{\text{eff}}(t)$ in Eq. (2.3.5) gives insight to the temporal evolution of the alpha-factor experienced by the pulse.

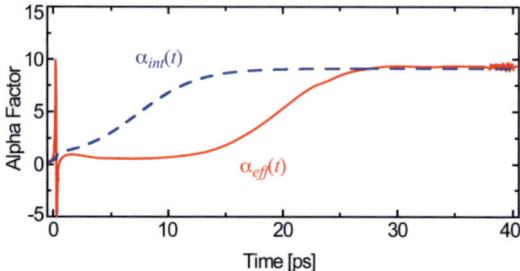

Fig. 2.27 Effective time dependent alpha-factors $\alpha_{\text{eff}}(t)$ (red solid line) and $\alpha_{\text{int}}(t)$ (blue dashed line) for the traces shown in Fig. 2.23. The dynamic response of the first 10 ps is governed by the fast process with an alpha-factor close to zero. Later, the slow process with a large alpha-factor dominates.

Fig. 2.27 shows a characteristic plot of the time dependent effective alpha-factors $\alpha_{\text{eff}}(t)$ and $\alpha_{\text{int}}(t)$ based on data from Fig. 2.23. The plot shows an almost negligible effective alpha-factor during the first 10 ps. The quantum dot processes therefore can be regarded as almost chirp free in this time window.

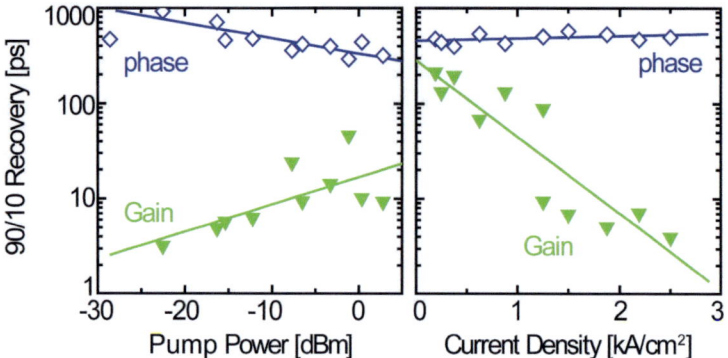

Fig. 2.28 Dependence of effective 90/10 recovery time of chip gain and phase on input power and bias current density. The phase recovery is dominated by the slow process. The gain recovery is fastest for low input power and high current densities and might be sped up by very strong input powers.

The situation dramatically changes when the slow regime becomes dominant. The alpha-factor becomes large and might contribute significantly to the overall chirp. As predicted, the integrated alpha-factor also shows strong dynamics during the first 20 ps [96]. After this time, both dynamic alpha-factors give the same value, which is identical to the alpha-factor α_2 of the slow recovery process.

For practical applications effective 90% to 10% recovery times of gain G and phase φ might be more useful. Fig. 2.28 shows the dependence on pump power and bias current density of the effective 90/10 recovery times calculated from the fitted device response. The phase recovery is clearly dominated by the slow process. It shows an effective recovery time of hundreds of picoseconds and cannot be improved considerably by changing the input power or the bias current density. The gain recovery is considerably faster. The associated effective time constant increases with input power, because the gain depletion is much stronger, but rapidly decreases for higher bias current densities, as the capturing process into the QD states becomes more efficient.

2.3.2.4 Results

Pump-probe measurements of QD SOA reveal two characteristic timescales, firstly a small time constant attributed to quantum dot carrier capture times. This fast process that dominates the quantum dot dynamics during the first 10 picoseconds determines mainly the material gain response and shows a very small alpha-factor, i.e. a small chirp. Secondly a large time constant associated with the slow refilling of the wetting layers governs the quantum-dot dynamics in the time frame after 15 ps. It contributes only little to the gain dynamics but since the associated alpha-factor is large (between 1 and 22, depending on the operating conditions) it dominates the phase response of the device and may significantly contribute to chirp.

Because of their fast gain dynamics, QD SOA are well suited as ultra-fast nonlinear elements for switching applications and regeneration schemes based on cross-gain modulation [59]. Distortions from chirp can be avoided either by using high input powers thereby improving the effective phase recovery time, or by using very low input powers where the total phase distortion becomes negligible. For both operating points, the effective gain recovery can be additionally improved by using high bias current densities.

2.3.3 Homogeneous Linewidth and Cross-Gain Modulation

Probably the single most interesting advantage of quantum-dot based devices is the predicted multi-channel capability. A simple model assumes homogeneous dot groups which show an inhomogeneously broadened gain spectrum due to the size variations of the dots. This let to predictions of high-speed nonlinear devices [215] with the promise of multiple-wavelength operation for high bit rate pulse trains over 40 Gbit/s under gain saturation [216]. However, up to date only amplification of multiple channels with large spacing has been demonstrated [99, 106, 217].

A numerical investigation of multi-channel cross-gain modulation (XGM) in QD SOA [58] finds strict requirements for the homogeneous linewidth in order to avoid strong signal degradation. At 40 Gbit/s and 160 Gbit/s, regenerative properties are found for a linewidth of 6.2 nm and a channel spacing of >10 nm and >15 nm, respectively. However, devices with a larger linewidth of 18.6 nm introduce strong signal degradations in both cases, even for a large channel spacing of 20 nm.

The homogeneous linewidth obviously is a key parameter for all quantum dot models. In the case that the assumed value does not correspond to the physical reality, it remains unclear to what extend the theoretical results can predict the real device performance. While an extremly small homogeneous linewidth of a single quantum dot is measured for low dot densities at low temperatures and weak excitation levels [218], the homogeneous linewidth of real devices with high dot densities, operated at room temperature and with electrical bias can be significantly larger [219]. This is also discussed in more detail in Section 2.2.2.2.

A simple technique to measure the homogeneous linewidth is a stationary gain measurement in the presence of a strong cw signal. In the absence of the strong signal, the small-signal gain is measured. In the presence of the strong cw signal, a spectral hole is burned and the small signal gain is reduced by XGM as a function of the wavelength.

Fig. 2.29(a) shows the wavelength dependence of cross-gain modulation for a QD SOA with a fiber-to-fiber gain of 10 dB at a wavelength of 1296 nm. The 3 dB gain bandwidth is 36 nm at a current of $I = 200 \, \text{mA}$. The gain of the undepleted device (black) is compared to the gain in the presence of a +5 dBm cw input signal at 1305 nm (blue). The gain is reduced by 3 dB over the whole bandwidth and completely depleted at the signal wavelength.

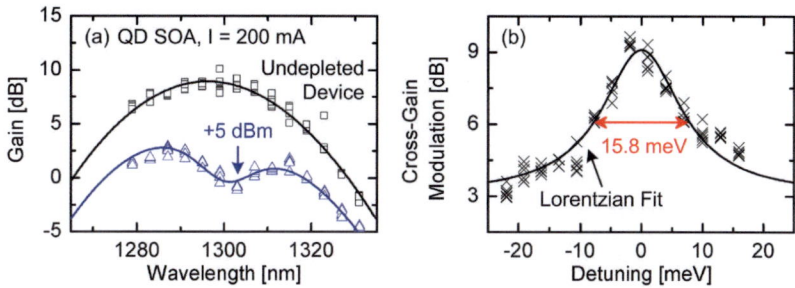

Fig. 2.29　Wavelength dependence of cross-gain modulation for a QD SOA with a 3 dB gain bandwidth is 36 nm. (a) Gain of an undepleted device (black) compared to the gain in the presence of a +5 dBm cw input signal at 1305 nm (blue). The gain is reduced by 3 dB over the whole bandwidth and completely depleted at the signal wavelength. (b) Cross-gain modulation as a function of the detuning from the photon energy of the +5 dBm cw signal, data points (×) and Lorentzian fit (–). The FWHM is 15.8 meV (~ 21.6 nm), which is about 60% of the total gain bandwidth and in good agreement with the theoretical lower limit of 15 meV for interband transitions [159].

Fig. 2.29(b) shows the cross-gain modulation as a function of the detuning from the photon energy of the +5 dBm cw signal, data points (×) and Lorentzian fit (–) to Eq. (2.2.1). The full-width at half maximum (FWHM) is 15.8 meV (~ 21.6 nm), which is about 60% of the total gain bandwidth. This value is in very good agreement with the theoretical lower limit of 15 meV predicted for interband transitions at 1.3 μm at room temperature [159].

To put the experimentally determined homogeneous linewidth into perspective, Table 2.2 compares published values of the homogeneous linewidth of quantum dots under optical (Opt.) and electrical (El.) excitation. It includes values for various dot densities and emission energy levels measured between cryogenic temperatures and room temperature. For comparison, parameters commonly used for detailed quantum dot models are given. Note that for the comparision the relevant physical quantity is the energy broadening ΔE, as it is independent of the emission wavelength and directly corresponds to the lifetime of emitting state.

As a result, at room temperature the value of 15.8 meV measured for a quantum dot ensemble with high dot density is in very good agreement both with the theoretical lower limit of 15 meV [159] as well as the average value of 16.8 meV of the published results listed in Table 2.2. If a channel spacing of more than three times the homogeneous linewidth is required, multi-wavelength operation is still theoretically possible in ultra-large bandwidth devices [80]. In practice, this is contradicted by the strong cross-gain modulation over the complete gain bandwidth. Due to the depletion of the refilling states, this allows broadband wavelength conversion [220] but it also prevents useful multi-wavelength operation under gain saturation conditions.

2.3.4 Summary

To achieve high gain, in practical devices the dot density is maximized. The close proximity of the dots and the refilling by shared quantum wells leads to a strong coupling between dots. While this hybridization has a beneficial side-effect of reducing the dot recovery time it also increases the homogeneous linewidth at the same time. Worse yet, as the quantum dot layers are surrounded by quantum wells and bulk cladding layers, the carrier transport into the active region is limited by the slowest process. In the limit of very strong carrier depletion, the performance of a quantum dot device thus is expected to be identical to conventional bulk devices.

Pump-probe measurements of QD SOA confirm the presence of two characteristic timescales, firstly a small time constant attributed to quantum dot carrier capture times. This fast process that dominates the quantum dot dynamics during the first 10 picoseconds determines mainly the material gain response and shows a very small alpha-factor, i.e. a small chirp. Secondly a large time constant associated with the slow refilling of the wetting layers governs the quantum-dot dynamics in the time frame after 15 ps. It contributes only little to the gain dynamics but since the associated alpha-factor is large (between 1 and 22, depending on the operating conditions) it dominates the phase response of the device and may significantly contribute to chirp.

Distortions from chirp can be avoided by using very low input powers where the total phase distortion becomes negligible. Far from saturation, quantum dot SOA combine ultra-fast carrier dynamics with low distortions due to phase effects. Because of this behaviour quantum dot SOA are promising devices for applications as linear amplifiers in metro and access networks.

Table 2.2 Homogeneous linewidth of quantum dots under optical (Opt.) and electrical (El.) excitation. Published values include measurements of quantum dots of various densities and emission energy levels, measured between cryogenic temperatures and room temperature (RT). For comparison, parameters commonly used for detailed quantum dot models are given.

Material	Density $[10^{10}\,cm^{-2}]$	Energy E [eV]	Δ [meV]	Wavelength λ [nm]	Δ [nm]	Temp. [K]	Exc.	Ref.
Spectroscopic Methods								
InAs/GaAs		1.29	<0.1	961	<0.07	10	Opt.	[71][†]
InGaAs/GaAs	30	1.31	5	946	3.61	150	Opt.	[185][‡]
InAs/GaAs	1	0.92	21	1350	30.87	RT	Opt.	[159]
InAs/GaAs	<10	0.93	<25	1300	<34	RT	Opt.	[155]
InAs/GaAs	3.5	1.04	18.6	1192	21.32	14	Opt.	[164]
InAs/GaAs	2	0.82	22	1520	41.00	RT	Opt.	[221]
InGaAs/GaAs	<0.1	1.22	7...15	1014	5.80...12.43	RT	Opt.	[222][†]
GaAs/AlGaAs	>1	1.64	16	756	7.38	4.2	Opt.	[223]
InAs/GaAs	2	0.92	14	1348	20.52	10	Opt.	[224]
InGaAs/GaAs	0.5	1.30	0.0002	954	0.0015	4.2	Opt.	[218][†]
InAs/GaAs	1.7	0.94	18	1320	25.30	RT	Opt.	[219]
InAs/GaAs	<1	0.93	0.036	1300	0.05	13	Opt.	[157][†]
InAs/GaAs	<1	0.93	0.160	1300	0.22	70	Opt.	[157][†]
InAs/GaAs	<10	1.18	6	1055	5.39	RT	Opt.	[225]
InAs/GaAs	1	0.89	17.5	1400	27.66	300	Opt.	[226]
InGaAs/GaAs	0.5	1.42	6.5	873	4.00	10	Opt.	[227]
InAs/GaAs	5	1.10	<0.15	1127	0.15	RT	El.[*]	[185][†]
InAs/GaAs		0.96	<24	1290	<32.21	RT	El.	[228]
InGaAs/GaAs		1.13	16	1100	15.61	80	El.	[229]
InGaAs/GaAs		1.13	19	1100	18.54	298	El.	[229]
InAs/InGaAs		1.18	5.00	1050	4.50	RT	El.	[230]
InAs/InGaAs		1.13	10...20	1100	9.76...19.52	RT	El.	[138]
InAs/GaAs		1.17	13.24	1060	12.00	RT	El.	[89, 143]
InAs/InGaAs	5	0.93	5.87	1300	8.00	RT	El.	[117]
InGaAs/GaAs		1.08	5...25	1150	5.3...26.7	4...300	El.	[181]
InAs/GaAs	3	0.99	5...20	1260	6.40...25.61	295	El.	[231]

Material	Density $[10^{10}\,cm^{-2}]$	Energy E [eV]	Δ [meV]	Wavelength λ [nm]	Δ [nm]	Temp. [K]	Exc.	Ref.
InAs/GaAs	4	0.93	10...20	1300	13.6...27.3		El.	[232]
InAs/InP		0.80	3.6...6.2	1550	7...12	RT	El.	[233]
Cross-Gain Modulation								
InAs/GaAs		1.07	11	1160	12.00	RT	El.	[215]
InAs/GaAs		0.93	22	1300	30.00	RT	El.	[234]
InAs/GaAs		0.93	22	1300	30.00	RT	El.	[148, 220]
InAs/GaAs	13	0.93	15.8	1300	21.56	RT	El.	this work
Theoretical Works								
			5..20					[235]
		1.00	16...19	1240	19.8..23.6	289		[236, 237]
	5	0.90	12	1377	18.30		El.	[54, 55]
		0.84	5...10	1485	8.89...17.79			[238]
		0.83	10	1439	16.70		El.	[108]

*) Cathodoluminescence from electron beam excitation.

†) Measurement on single quantum dots.

‡) Measurement on group of identical quantum dots.

2.4 Applications of Quantum Dot Semiconductor Optical Amplifiers

Of all predicted advantages of quantum dot semiconductor optical amplifiers (QD SOA), only few are found in real-world devices. The characterization results presented in Section 2.3 allow drawing several conclusions with respect to possible applications.

For nonlinear applications like wavelength conversion or regeneration, QD SOA are not well suited, as they exhibit slow amplitude and phase dynamics for high input power levels. The inherently large homogeneous linewidth prohibits multi-wavelength operation and offers no advantage over conventional bulk and quantum-well SOA.

For linear applications QD SOA combine ultra-fast carrier dynamics with low distortions due to phase effects. In combination with the high gain, the moderate noise figure, and the relative temperature insensitivity, QD SOA fulfill all requirements for in-line amplifiers.

In Section 2.4.1, the performance of QD SOA as in-line amplifiers of amplitude encoded signals in access networks is investigated and a large input-power dynamic range is found. In Section 2.4.2, in-line amplification of advanced modulation formats and phase-encoded signals is investigated. For this application, QD SOA are found to be particularly well suited due to their low alpha factor.

2.4.1 In-line Amplification of Amplitude-Shift Keying Signals [C29]

All-optical networks, like extended reach coarse wavelength-division multiplexing (CWDM) based gigabit passive optical networks (GPON), have a need for optical amplifiers. Bulk and quantum well semiconductor optical amplifers (SOA) offer polarization insensitive gain, high saturation output power and reasonably low noise figure. This makes such devices promising for in-line amplification to increase the number of customers served by the same central office [239-241]. On the other hand, the slow gain dynamics even under moderate gain saturation limit their input power dynamic range (IPDR) and their multi-wavelength capability.

Quantum dot SOA promise an ultra-fast gain response, greatly expanded bandwidth, low noise figure, the enhanced multi-wavelength capability and the possibility of uncooled operation. While extended studies of the nonlinear capabilities of QD SOA have been performed [81], an in-depth characterization of the linear performance of QD SOA is still missing.

In this section QD SOA are investigated for applications as linear amplifiers. A large input power dynamic range with error-free single and multi-wavelength amplification at bit rates from 2.5 Gbit/s to 43 Gbit/s is found.

2.4.1.1 Experimental Setup

The investigated device is a quantum dot SOA containing a stack of 10 layers of InAs quantum dots in a dot in an InGaAs quantum well structure. The device length is 4 mm and the waveguide width is 2 μm. It is operated with a bias current of 500 mA, corresponding to a bias current density per QD layer of $i_0 = 0.625\,\text{kA}/\text{cm}^2$. The maximum gain is 20 dB for small input power levels at a wavelength of 1296 nm. The 3 dB gain bandwidth is 35 nm and the polarization dependence reaches 10 dB. The noise figure is 6 dB.

The experimental setup is shown in Fig. 2.30. Signals from two transmitters (Tx) at 1310 nm and 1290 nm are combined, amplified and launched into the device under test (DUT) with varying power levels. At bitrates of 2.5 Gbit/s (NRZ-OOK), 10 Gbit/s (NRZ-OOK), and 40 Gbit/s (RZ-OOK) the Q^2-factor (see Appendix A.2) is measured in a pre-amplified receiver (Rx).

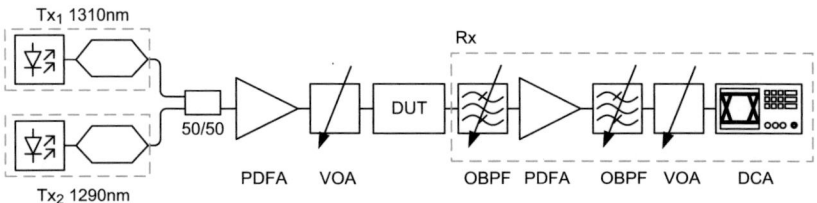

Fig. 2.30 Experimental setup to measure Q^2-factor of data signals after amplification in a QD SOA. Signals from two transmitters (Tx) at 1310 nm and 1290 nm are combined, amplified and launched into the device under test (DUT) with varying power levels. At bitrates of 2.5 Gbit/s (NRZ-OOK), 10 Gbit/s (NRZ-OOK), and 40 Gbit/s (RZ-OOK) the Q^2-factor is measured in a pre-amplified receiver (Rx). For the single channel case only a single transmitter is used. For the two channel case, both channels are launched into the DUT with identical input power levels. PDFA: Praseodymium-doped fiber amplifier; VOA: Variable optical attenuator; OBPF: Optical band-pass filter; DCA: Digital communications analyzer.

For the single channel case only a single transmitter is used. For the two channel case, both channels are launched into the DUT with identical input power levels. The IPDR for amplification of single and multiple data signals with a 1.3 μm QD SOA is studied by evaluating the Q^2-factor. Error-free amplification is achieved for quality factors exceeding $Q^2 > 15.6\,\mathrm{dB}$ [42].

2.4.1.2 Input Power Dynamic Range in QD SOA for ASK Signals

The sensitivity of the Q^2-factor to variations in the power launched into the QD SOA is investigated for bit rates and modulation formats of 2.5 Gbit/s NRZ-OOK, 10 Gbit/s NRZ-OOK and 43 Gbit/s RZ-OOK in the presence of one and two data signals. In general, the signal quality is limited by two effects. For low input power levels, it is limited by noise. For high input power levels it is limited by bit-patterning effects.

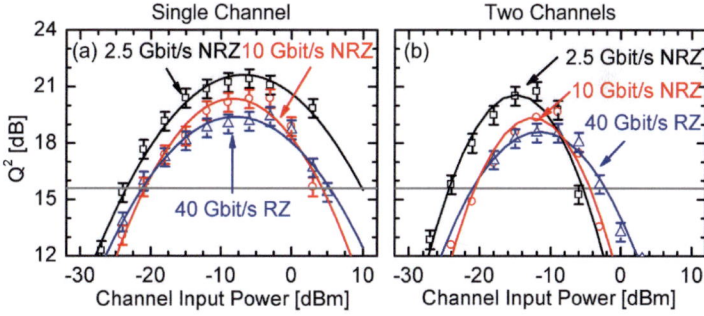

Fig. 2.31 Dependency of Q^2-factor of one and two channels amplified with a QD SOA on input-power per channel. (a) A large IPDR between 25 dB and 34 dB is found for bitrates of 2.5 Gbit/s (black), 10 Gbit/s (red), and 40 Gbit/s (blue) for the single channel case at 1310 nm. (b) Q^2-factor for two de-correlated data signals at 1290 nm and 1310 nm entering the DUT with equal power levels. IPDR values of 19 to 16 dB for bitrates of 2.5, 10 and 40 Gbit/s are found.

Fig. 2.31 shows the dependency of the Q^2-factor on input-power per channe lof (a) one and (b) two channels amplified with a QD SOA . In general, for low input power levels, error free operation is limited by noise. For high input power levels, it is limited by saturation effects. The lower limit is designated P_1, the upper limit is designated P_2.

A large IPDR between 25 dB and 34 dB is found for bitrates of 2.5 Gbit/s (black), 10 Gbit/s (red), and 40 Gbit/s (blue) for the single channel case at 1310 nm. The Q^2-

factor for two de-correlated data signals at 1290 nm and 1310 nm is measured for both channels having equal power levels. IPDR values of 19 dB to 16 dB for bitrates of 2.5, 10 and 40 Gbit/s are found. All results are summarized in Table 2.3.

Table 2.3 IPDR of a 1.3 μm QD SOA for bit rates of 2.5 Gbit/s, 10 Gbit/s, and 40 Gbit/s in single channel and two channel operation. The IPDR is defined by error free operation with a quality factor of $Q^2 > 15.6\,\mathrm{dB}$.

Bitrate [Gbit/s] Mod. Format	IPDR [dB] 1 channel	IPDR [dB] 2 channel
2.5 Gbit/s - NRZ-OOK	34.5±0.5	19.0±0.5
10 Gbit/s - NRZ-OOK	24.9±0.5	16.0±0.5
40 Gbit/s - RZ-OOK	26.7±0.5	18.8±0.5

2.4.1.3 Input Power Dynamic Range Dependence on Bias Current

As the gain strongly depends on the bias current, a strong effect on the input power range is expected. In a worst-case scenario of 40 Gbit/s RZ-OOK operation, the IPDR is investigated for various bias current densities.

Fig. 2.32(a) shows the amplified spontaneous emission (ASE) spectrum for bias currents between 150 mA and 400 mA. The ASE spectra are virtually identical to the gain spectra. The emission from the quantum dot ground state around 1300 nm is already saturated even for small bias currents. For higher currents, the emission from the excited state around 1220 nm increases. Additionally, the temperature of the active region increases which causes the spectra to shift to longer wavelengths. Fig. 2.32(b) shows the fiber to fiber gain at 1300 nm as a function of the device input power and bias current density. The gain shows a variation of 5 dB for various bias currents and reaches the maximum value of 16.8 dB for a bias current of 350 mA. Circles (○) mark the saturation input power levels. The Q^2 after amplification of 40 Gbit/s data as a function of the input power and bias current is shown in Fig. 2.32(c).

Despite the gain variations, for all bias current densities the device allows error-free operation for the same range of input power levels. All measured IPDR values are summarized in Table 2.4.

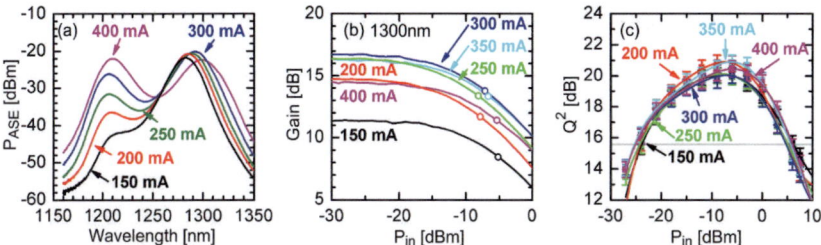

Fig. 2.32 Bias current dependence of 1.3 μm QD SOA parameters. (a) Amplified spontaneous emission (ASE) spectrum for bias currents between 150 mA and 400 mA. The ASE spectra are virtually identical to the gain spectra. The emission from the quantum dot ground state around 1300 nm is already saturated even for small bias currents. For higher currents, the emission from the excited state around 1220 nm increases. Additionally, the temperature of the active region increases which causes the spectra to shift to longer wavelengths. (b) Fiber to fiber gain at 1300 nm as a function of the device input power and bias current density. The gain shows a variation of 5 dB for various bias currents and reaches the maximum value of 16.8 dB for a bias current of 350 mA. Open circles (○) mark the saturation input power levels. (c) Q^2 after amplification of 40 Gbit/s RZ-OOK data as a function of the device input power and bias current. Despite the gain variations, for all bias current densities the device allows error-free operation for the same range of input power levels. The measured IPDR values are summarized in Table 2.4.

Table 2.4 IPDR of a 1.3 μm QD SOA with 40 Gbit/s RZ-OOK data in single channel operation. The IPDR is defined by error-free operation with a quality factor of $Q^2 > 15.6\,\text{dB}$. P_1: lowest input power level, limited by noise. P_2: maximum input power level, limited by saturation effects.

I	P_1	P_2	IPDR
[mA]	[dBm]	[dBm]	[dB]
150	-23.8	6.1	29.9
200	-24.1	4.9	29.0
250	-24.2	5.0	29.2
300	-25.1	4.6	29.7
350	-25.3	5.6	30.9
400	-25.0	6.0	31.0

2.4.2 In-line Amplification of Phase-Shift Keying Signals [J1]

SOA have attracted new interest in the last few years due to their ability to amplify signals across the whole spectral range from 1250 nm up to 1600 nm at reasonable costs [242]. A new and interesting question has thereby been the ability of SOA to amplify phase-encoded signals. As a result, it has been shown that the constant envelope of differential phase encoded signals provides higher tolerance towards SOA nonlinear impairments such as cross-gain (XGM) and cross-phase modulation (XPM) compared to on-off keying (OOK) formats [243]. This higher tolerance has its limit once the SOA is operated in saturation where nonlinear impairments reduce the input power dynamics even for phase encoded signals [244, 245]. While quantum dots (QD) as an active medium in SOA have been shown to extend the input power dynamic range (IPDR) for OOK formats, their suitability for differential-phase encoded signals has not been studied up to now. QD SOA offer low alpha-factor [97], ultra-fast QD gain response (~1 ps) [97], greatly expanded gain bandwidth (~120 nm) [80], high gain (>25 dB) [81], large IPDR for OOK signals, and high burst mode tolerance [106].

In this section, for the first time an input power dynamic range improvement for a 28 GBd non-return to zero differential quadrature phase-shift keying (NRZ-DQPSK) signal amplified in a 1.5 μm QD SOA is reported. The IPDR is improved up to 10 dB compared to a low confinement bulk SOA especially designed for amplification. This enhancement found for QD SOA is attributed to the reduced phase error on the differential encoded phase signal, due to the lower alpha-factor. The IPDR of the QD SOA is 20 dB at a bit-error ratio (BER) of $BER = 10^{-9}$ and exceeds 32 dB for $BER = 10^{-3}$.

2.4.2.1 QD and bulk SOA characteristics

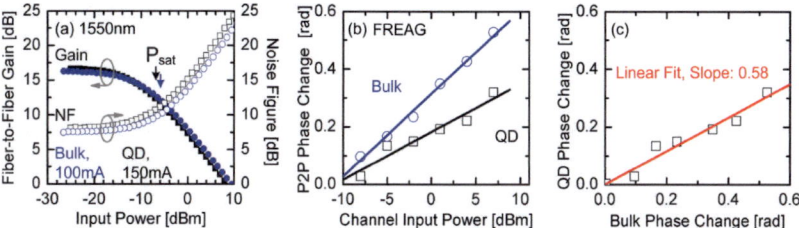

Fig. 2.33 Comparison of QD and bulk SOA characteristics. (a) Fiber-to-fiber gain, noise figure (NF) and saturation power levels for a 1.5 μm QD SOA (black) and a bulk SOA (blue) with a low optical confinement of 20%. For equal current densities all characteristics are comparable. (b) Peak-to-peak (P2P) phase changes of the bulk SOA compared to the QD SOA as a function of the channel input power. The phase changes are measured as XPM of a 33 % RZ-OOK 40 Gbit/s "1010" data sequence at a wavelength of 1557.4 nm on a cw signal at a wavelength of 1554.1 nm. The average input power of the cw (ch. 1) and data (ch. 2) channels is always adjusted to be equal, thereby defining the channel input power. (c) Measured phase changes of bulk SOA versus QD SOA from (b). For all input power levels the phase effect of the QD SOA is less than the phase effect of the bulk SOA by a factor of 0.58.

A comparison for phase encoded signals of two SOA with different active media requires similar device performance. Fig. 2.33(a) shows comparable fiber-to-fiber gain, noise figure (1.4.21) and saturation powers of the 1.5 μm QD SOA device (6 layers of InAs/InP quantum dashes) and the bulk SOA operated with the same current density [90]. The low optical confinement (20%) bulk SOA is especially designed for linear applications. For both devices, the gain peak is around 1530 nm and the 3 dB bandwidth is 60 nm.

Fig. 2.33(b) shows the peak-to-peak (P2P) phase changes of the QD and bulk SOA as a function of channel input power. The phase changes are measured as XPM of a 33% RZ-OOK 40 Gbit/s "1010" data sequence at a wavelength of 1557.4 nm on a cw signal at a wavelength of 1554.1 nm. The average input power of the cw (ch. 1) and data (ch. 2) channels is always adjusted to be equal, thereby defining the channel input power. The phase change is measured using the frequency resolved electro-absorption gating technique (FREAG) based on linear spectrograms [246]. In Fig. 2.33(c) the measured phase changes of the bulk SOA are plotted versus the phase changes of the QD SOA using the results from Fig. 2.33(b). For all input power levels the phase effect of the QD SOA is less than the phase effect of the bulk SOA. The ratio of the alpha-factors (1.4.2) is obtained by linear fit of the data to $\alpha_{QD}/\alpha_{Bulk} = 0.58$.

2.4.2.2 Experimental Setup

The power penalty caused by SOA for NRZ-DQPSK data is investigated using the experimental setup shown in Fig. 2.34. It comprises two data signals at 1554.1 nm (ch. 1) and 1557.4 nm (ch. 2), which are de-correlated by 69 bit. The power levels of both channels are adjusted to be equal before launching them into the device under test (DUT). After amplifying both data signals in the DUT, the 1557.4 nm channel is blocked by a band-pass filter while the BER of the remaining data channel is analyzed. The DQPSK receiver (Rx) consists of a delay interferometer (DI) based demodulator followed by a balanced detector and a bit-error ratio tester (BERT). In the experiment, no data encoder circuit was employed. To allow bit-error ratio measurements, the error detector is programmed with the expected data sequence, which allows a pseudo-random bit sequence (PRBS) length of up to 2^9-1.

The IPDR for amplification of one and two 28 GBd NRZ-DQPSK channels is studied by evaluating the power penalty for two selected bit-error ratios of BER = 10^{-9} and BER = 10^{-3}. This guarantees error-free transmission when forward error correction (FEC) is used [247, 248].

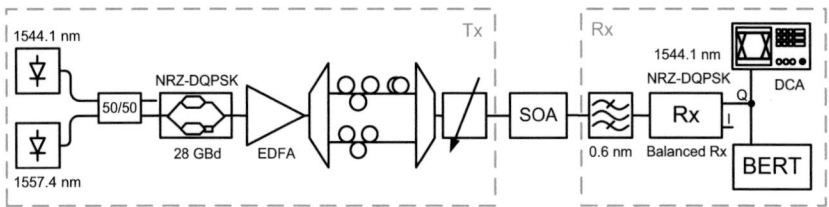

Fig. 2.34 Experimental Setup. Two 28 GBd NRZ-DQPSK channels are equalized and de-correlated using 0.5 m of fiber. The average power of both channels is varied and launched into a bulk or QD SOA. A single channel is selected, amplified and demodulated in a DQPSK receiver (Rx), consisting of a delay interferometer (DI) followed by a balanced detector. The electrical signal is then analyzed using a digital communications analyzer (DCA) and a bit-error ratio tester (BERT).

2.4.2.3 Dynamic Range Improvement in QD SOA for PSK Signals

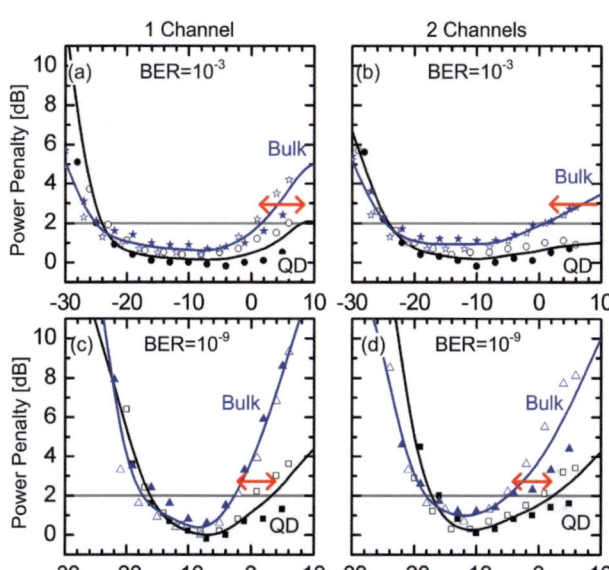

Fig. 2.35 Power penalty vs. channel input power levels. The input power dynamic range (IPDR) is defined as the range of input power levels with less than 2 dB power penalty compared to the back-to-back case. Red arrows indicate the IPDR enhancement of the QD SOA (black) over the bulk SOA (blue). (a), (b) QD SOA improve the IPDR at a BER of 10^{-3} by 5 dB and >10 dB compared to bulk SOA for one and two 28 GBd NRZ-DQPSK channels, respectively. (c), (d) For a BER of 10^{-9}, the QD SOA IPDR is enhanced by 5 dB. The filled symbols correspond to the I-channel, whereas the open symbols represent the Q-channel.

We define the IPDR as the range of input power levels with less than 2 dB power penalty compared to the back-to-back case. Fig. 2.35 shows the power penalty as a function of the SOA channel input power for one and two channels at specific BER. Fig. 2.35(a) and (b) show an IPDR improvement of 5 dB for the single channel and >10 dB for the two channel case at a BER of 10^{-3}, respectively. Fig. 2.35(c) and (d) show around 5 dB IPDR improvement for the QD SOA compared to the bulk SOA for one and two NRZ-DQPSK channels at a BER of 10^{-9}. The filled symbols correspond to the I-channel, whereas the open symbols represent the Q-channel. The QD SOA exhibits a large IPDR of around 20 dB for BER = 10^{-9} and exceeds 30 dB for

BER = 10^{-3}. We attribute the increased IPDR in the two-channel case to the effect of cross-gain modulation (XGM), which reduces the gain for each channel. This leads to larger saturation power levels, less patterning effects and thus smaller power penalties. The results are summarized in Table 2.5.

To illustrate this advantage of QD SOA over bulk SOA, Fig. 2.36 shows the observed eye diagrams of the demodulated 28 GBd NRZ-DQPSK Q-channel for high SOA input power levels of 6 dBm. The comparison of the back-to-back eye diagram in Fig. 2.36(a) for high input power to the QD SOA eye diagrams in Fig. 2.36(b) shows no signal degradation at optimum receiver sensitivity. In contrast, for high input power to the bulk SOA, the eye opening in Fig. 2.36(c) is reduced, and the signal quality is significantly degraded.

Table 2.5 Input power dynamic range (IPDR) at 2 dB power penalty for bulk and QD SOA. In all cases, the QD SOA shows a significant IPDR enhancement compared to a conventional bulk SOA.

		1 Channel		2 Channels	
	BER	10^{-3}	10^{-9}	10^{-3}	10^{-9}
IPDR [dB]	QD	> 32	19.5	> 36	19.4
	Bulk	26.9	15.0	25.7	13.4
	Enhancement	> 5.1	4.5	> 10	6.0

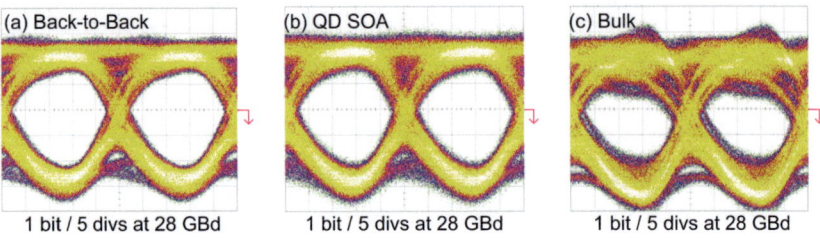

(a) Back-to-Back	(b) QD SOA	(c) Bulk
1 bit / 5 divs at 28 GBd	1 bit / 5 divs at 28 GBd	1 bit / 5 divs at 28 GBd

Fig. 2.36 Demodulated NRZ-DQPSK eye diagrams for high SOA input power levels of 6 dBm. (a) Back-to-back eye diagram of 28 GBd Q-channel at optimum receiver sensitivity. (b) No signal degradation for QD SOA high input powers. (c) Reduced eye opening and signal quality degradation for SOA.

2.4.2.4 Dominant Sources for Impairments of PSK Signals in SOA

The unexpected IPDR enhancement found in QD SOA needs explanation. As it is well known from ASK formats, SOA can introduce strong amplitude distortions like overshoots [249] and patterning effects [250] when operated in saturation. For ideal phase encoded signals, these effects should be strongly suppressed [243].

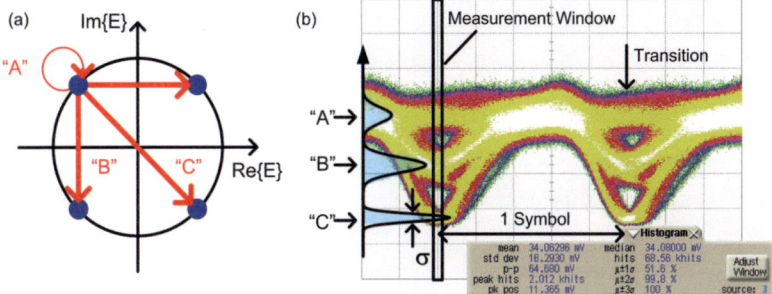

Fig. 2.37 Amplitude distortions of the NRZ-DQPSK envelope in QD and bulk SOA. (a) Possible transitions in the constellation diagram. To increase transmitter long time stability, instead of pure phase modulation (all states on the circle) some transitions ("B", "C") are generated using amplitude modulation. (b) Example eye diagram of the power envelope of the 28 GBd NRZ-DQPSK signal, showing all possible transitions. A histogram is taken at the transition in a 1.6 ps time window. Assuming a Gaussian distribution, the mean value and standard deviation are investigated as a function of the device input power for both device types.

Fig. 2.37(a) shows all possible transitions in the constellation diagram of DQPSK signals. Instead of pure phase modulation (all states on the circle), most practical implementations generate some transitions ("B", "C") using amplitude modulation in order to increase transmitter long time stability. Fig. 2.37(b) shows an example eye diagram of the power envelope of the 28 GBd NRZ-DQPSK signal with constant power at the decision point in the middle of the bit slot. All expected transitions are observed. A histogram is taken at the transition in a 1.6 ps time window. To investigate the influence of the amplitude effects for both SOA types, the power envelope of the 28 GBd NRZ-DQPSK signal is analyzed as a function of the channel input power. Assuming a Gaussian distribution, the mean value and standard deviation are calculated.

In DQPSK systems with direct detection, the signals are received using a delay interferometer (DI) followed by a balanced receiver. Fluctuations of the received power as well as deviations from ideal phase transitions can strongly degrade the signal.

As a comparison of the amplitude and phase characteristics of bulk and QD SOA will show, both SOA types are practically identical with respect to *amplitude* effects. However, QD SOA cause less *phase* errors due to their inherently lower alpha-factors, which can significantly improve the input power dynamic range.

Amplitude fluctuations

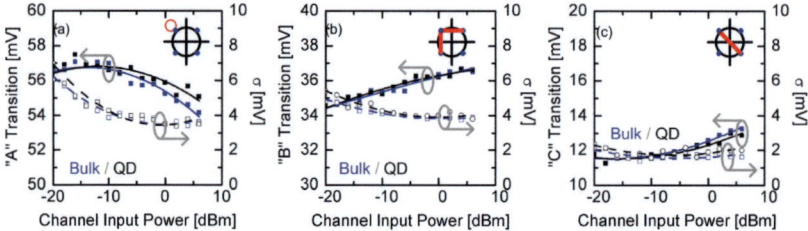

Fig. 2.38 Amplitude transitions in bulk (blue) and QD SOA (black): Dependence of mean values (■, filled symbols) and standard deviations (□, open symbols) as a function of the channel input power. For all three possible transitions, bulk and QD SOA show an identical behavior. Measured at optimum receiver input power, the standard deviations are unaffected by input power levels above -10 dBm. No difference between bulk and QD SOA is observed with respect to the signal amplitude.

Fig. 2.38 shows the dependence of mean values (■, filled symbols) and standard deviations (□, open symbols) of bulk (blue) and QD SOA (black) as a function of the channel input power. In all cases, bulk and QD SOAbehave identically. Measured at optimum receiver input power, the standard deviations are unaffected by input power levels above -10 dBm. No difference between bulk and QD SOA is observed with respect to the signal amplitude, so the observed dynamic range difference must be caused by phase effects.

Phase fluctuations

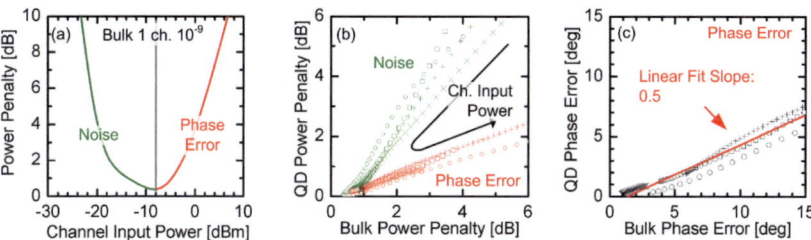

Fig. 2.39 Comparison of QD and bulk power penalty for all channels and BER. (a) Bulk SOA 1 ch. power penalty for BER = 10^{-9} as an example. The power penalty curves are marked according to the corresponding limits of the IPDR. For low input power levels, the DQPSK signal is degraded by noise (green). For high input powers, saturation of the SOA induces phase errors (red). (b) Power penalty for QD SOA vs. power penalty for bulk SOA when increasing the channel input power for BER = 10^{-9} (○: 1 ch., +: 2 ch) and BER = 10^{-3} (□: 1 ch., ×: 2 ch.). The penalty is attributed to either noise or phase errors. All measurements shown in Fig. 2.35 displayed a similar ratio of the penalties. The largest difference between the samples arises for high input powers. (c) The power penalty for high input powers can be related to an effective phase error of the delay interferometer by the relation presented in [251]. The slope of a linear fit is 0.5, which actually corresponds to the ratio of the respective alpha-factors. The very good agreement between the calculated and measured ratio of the alpha-factors provides the explanation of the advantage of QD SOA in terms of IPDR: The smaller alpha-factor of QD SOA reduces the phase impairments.

Direct detection receivers for differential phase encoded signals are particularly susceptible to errors caused by deviations from the ideal phase transitions. For a power penalty less than 2 dB the phase error at the DI must be less than 10° [251, 252]. Due to the fact that typical NRZ-DQPSK transmitters show a fast amplitude transition if a phase change occurs [253], SOA can induce errors by amplitude and phase fluctuations [254]. Since the gain saturation of both devices is similar the observed IPDR difference must be attributed to phase induced errors. Typically, in SOA the phase recovery is slower than the amplitude recovery [97, 214]. As a consequence amplitude transitions between bit slots influence the signal phase also at the decision point in the middle of the bit slot which introduces bit-errors.

As an example, the bulk SOA 1 ch. power penalty for BER = 10^{-9} is depicted in Fig. 2.39(a).The power penalty curves are marked according to the corresponding limits of the IPDR. For input power levels below -10 dBm, the DQPSK signal is limited by noise. For input power levels above -10 dBm, saturation of the SOA induces phase errors. The main difference between the samples arises for high input powers. Therefore, the phase limitations on the DQPSK signal performance is studied.

Fig. 2.39(b) shows the penalty for the QD SOA vs. the power penalty for the bulk SOA when increasing the channel input power levels for BER $= 10^{-9}$ ($\circ$: 1 ch., $+$: 2 ch.) and BER $= 10^{-3}$ ($\square$: 1 ch., $\times$: 2 ch.). The penalty is attributed to either noise or phase errors. All measured data which have been displayed in Fig. 2.35(a)–(d) resulted in a similar penalty ratio.

The influence of small phase errors is equivalent to the effect of deviations from the optimum operating point of the delay interferometer. For demonstrating this influence on the power penalty, we calculate the equivalent phase misalignment of a DI that would lead to the actually measured power penalty [251]. The absolute value of this phase error contains large uncertainties due to the fact that the phase error probability density is unknown. However, bulk and QD SOA are operated under identical conditions, and the calculated phase errors of the bulk SOA can be therefore compared to the phase errors of the QD SOA. As the biggest phase error will determine the bit-error ratio, the calculated values give an estimate of the worst-case phase error.

Fig. 2.39(c) compares the calculated equivalent phase errors for the bulk SOA to the equivalent phase errors for the QD SOA. A linear fit of the data shows a slope of 0.5. Assuming that the observed power penalty can be completely attributed to phase errors, this slope gives the ratio of the alpha-factors of both devices. It is in good agreement with the results extracted from the independently measured P2P phase changes using the FREAG technique, shown in Fig. 2.33(c).

The fast amplitude transients in NRZ-DQPSK signals induce amplitude fluctuations in the SOA. These fluctuations induce carrier density fluctuations, which in turn cause refractive index variations and such create phase errors. Due to the fact that the alpha-factor in QD SOA is low, the amplitude to phase conversion is reduced compared to bulk SOA, so less phase errors are introduced. This general advantage of QD SOA also applies for other differential phase encoded formats like NRZ/RZ-DPSK or RZ-DQPSK.

2.4.3 Summary

The performance of QD SOA was studied for applications as linear amplifiers. For amplitude-shift keying signals, error-free amplification is found for a large input power dynamic range exceeding 25 dB in the single channel experiment at bit rates of 2.5, 10 and 43 Gbit/s. In the multi-channel case the IPDR is still large showing 19 dB at 43 Gbit/s. The large IPDR cannot be explained by evaluating the device gain, but must be attributed to a complex interplay of various device parameters. QD SOA at 1.3 μm with gain of 10–20 dB and large IPDR are promising candidates for in-line amplification in future access networks with simple amplitude based modulation formats.

For phase-shift keying signals, an input power dynamic range improvement for a 28 GBd NRZ-DQPSK signal amplified in a 1.5 μm QD SOA was demonstrated. The IPDR is improved more than 10 dB compared to a low confinement bulk SOA especially designed for amplification. This enhancement found in QD SOA is attributed to the lower alpha-factor which reduces impairments to the differentially encoded phase signal by phase errors. The IPDR of the QD SOA is about 20 dB at a bit-error ratio of BER $= 10^{-9}$ and exceeds 32 dB for a bit-error ratio of BER $= 10^{-3}$.

3 Beyond Silicon Photonics: Silicon-Organic Hybrid Waveguides

Silicon photonics is expected to be one of the key technologies of the future. Boosted by billions of dollars of annual investments, complementary metal oxide-semiconductor (CMOS) technology has reached a maturity level that allows the production of integrated electronic devices with nanometer precision on an industrial scale. In a world with exponentially growing bandwidth needs [1], the promise of silicon photonics is tempting: to combine the availability and low price offered by CMOS technology with the large bandwidth and high speed offered by optics.

Silicon is transparent at infrared wavelengths, and so the material lends itself to dense on-chip integration of photonic devices. Over the last years, particularly intense research in the field of silicon photonics has proven the viability of high index-contrast silicon-on-insulator (SOI) integrated optical devices such as strip waveguides and resonators [255-257], filters [258-260] and photonic crystal waveguides [261].

However, there are still functionalities that cannot be realized when relying solely on the intrinsic properties of silicon. A prominent example is on-chip integration of active devices, which is hindered by the indirect band gap of silicon. Therefore, all-silicon light emitting devices realized so far rely on optically pumped Raman emission [262].

Another problem is the lack of desirable intrinsic nonlinear optical properties: Due to crystal symmetry, silicon does not feature a second-order nonlinear optical effect. Therefore, electro-optic modulators have been realized only based on free-carrier injection, whereby the electro-optical bandwidth is currently limited to 30 GHz by carrier dynamics [263]. Third-order nonlinearities in silicon nanophotonic waveguides can be strong, but are always impeded by two-photon absorption (TPA) and by TPA-induced free carrier absorption (FCA). All-optical signal regeneration has been demonstrated at 10 Gbit/s [264], but for higher data rates, free carriers generated by TPA have to be removed by appropriate technological measures to prevent free-carrier absorption [265].

Reports on combining conventional silicon strip waveguides with polymer claddings suggest that ultrafast all-optical signal processing beyond 10 Gbit/s is possible in hybrid systems [266]. In fact, the dominant electronic nonlinearity of organic molecules with strongly polarizable delocalized electron systems would allow to reach Tbit/s in off-resonant interactions.

By embedding properly designed SOI waveguide templates into organic cladding materials, it is possible to combine silicon's outstanding technological maturity with specifically engineered optical properties of organic materials such as high optical nonlinearities. The unique combination of optimized core structures and organic nonlinear cladding materials allows building waveguides, which show record nonlinearity parameters of $\gamma > 100\,000\,(\text{Wkm})^{-1}$ yet are fully integrated with CMOS-compatible silicon photonic devices. The resulting silicon-organic hybrid (SOH) waveguides fulfill the ultra-high speed requirements of the future already today.

This chapter introduces novel device concepts based on silicon-organic hybrid integration. It is organized as follows. Section 3.1 gives an overview over the rapid progress of the state of the art in silicon photonics. In Section 3.2, basic waveguide designs that maximize the third-order nonlinearity are discussed. Section 3.3 presents characterization results, which show the unique advantages offered by hybrid silicon-organic integration. Finally, applications like all-optical high-speed wavelength conversion and switching are demonstrated in Section 3.4.

3.1 State of the Art in Silicon Photonics

The main advantages offered by silicon as a base for integrated optics have been outlined in the seminal paper *"Single-crystal silicon: a new material for 1.3 and 1.6 µm integrated-optical components"* of Soref and Lorenzo [267], which appeared in *Electronics Letters* in October 1985. Silicon material properties are well suited for near-infrared operation in the 1.3 µm and 1.5 µm communication windows, the high index contrast in the silicon/glass/air material system enables small structures, and, most importantly, highly developed complementary metal-oxide-semiconductor (CMOS) fabrication technology can be leveraged, which enables integration of optics and electronics on the same chip.

Today, all silicon photonic devices are fabricated using the silicon-on-insulator (SOI) technology, where a thin layer of crystalline silicon is separated from silicon bulk wafer by a thin layer of buried silicon oxide (BOX). As in state of the art microprocessor technology, standard deep-ultraviolet (UV) lithography, etching steps, and regrowth processes are used to fabricate nanophotonic devices. Although chemical wet etching might be used to define low loss structures [268], silicon photonic devices up to now are based on dry etching processes.

Apart from closed-access fabrication facilities of universities and companies like Intel, IBM, and Luxtera, there are several freely accessible facilities which operate with a foundry concept. In Europe, the efforts are bundled through the European project Epixfab [269], comprising the CMOS fabrication lines of CEA LETI [270] and IMEC [271]. In the US, silicon photonic circuits are offered by a number of commercial CMOS fabs of Freescale [272], BAE systems [273], Texas Instruments [274]. In all cases, the fabrication of photonic devices is limited to CMOS-compatible processing conforming to the design guidelines established by electronics. Depending on the layer in which the photonic functionalities are needed, this includes devices fabricated of amorphous silicon (a-Si) [275], polycrystalline silicon (p-Si) [276], and strained silicon [277].

Silicon is transparent at communication wavelengths, which makes the fabrication of sources, modulators and detectors difficult. To overcome this limitation, on-chip integration of germanium, III-V semiconductors, and nonlinear organic materials is used.

Technologically very close to silicon, epitaxy of silicon-germanium (SiGe) on a silicon chip promises easy integration into the standard CMOS process. Very recently, all key functionalities have been reported, like lasers [278], modulators [279, 280], and photodetectors with bandwidths of up to 40 GHz [270, 281, 282].

Hybrid integration of III-V materials promises orders of magnitude more efficient devices, but is hardly CMOS compatible. Complete devices like GaInAsP/InP lasers [283, 284] and ring resonators [285], but also membranes of active materials have been wafer-bonded to silicon waveguides. Evanescent coupling between the modes in the silicon waveguides and modes in the active membrane material is used to implement efficient lasers [286-290], modulators [291], amplifiers [292], and photodetectors [293].

Ultra high-speed devices become possible through hybrid integration of organic electro-optic [294] and Kerr [295] materials. Using slot waveguides to incorporate the organic cladding material, electro-optic modulation at 40 Gbit/s [296] and high speed demultiplexing of 170 Gbit/s signals have been demonstrated [297].

In the last decade, passive silicon photonic components have reached a level of maturity which enables the integration of multiple devices on the same chip. To achieve complex functionalities, high quality components are needed. The silicon photonic toolbox meanwhile consists of passive and active devices: Section 3.1.1 describes the state of the art on low loss waveguides, splitters, filters, and resonators. Then Section 3.1.2 discusses the state of the art on integrated optical sources, amplifiers, and modulators. Finally, Section 3.1.3 discusses the state of the art on slot waveguides as optimized nonlinear elements for future all-optical signal processing applications.

3.1.1 Passive Components

One of the main reasons for choosing a high index-contrast material system is the possibility of shrinking the device dimensions, as this allows the integration of much functionality in a small area on chip. On the other hand, losses due to sidewall scattering and absorption at Si/SiO_2 defects at interfaces increase with increasing confinement of the light, the realization of integrated components like low loss couplers, waveguides, and filters is technologically challenging.

Direct coupling from a standard single-mode fiber to an as-cleaved strip waveguide suffers from high losses of about 30 dB/facet, due to the large mode mismatch. While the use of lensed-fibers partly mitigates the issue, typical losses still exceed 8 dB/facet [298]. Several approaches have been used to overcome this problem. Inverse tapers have been used as spot converters, which in combination with Si_3N_4 or polymer supercladdings have led to coupling losses of less than 1 dB/facet [299]. Graded-index (GRIN) waveguide tapers have been shown to reduce losses to 0.5 dB/facet [300]. However, to form the index graded cladding structure additional plasma-enhanced vapor deposition steps are required, which are not yet available in the CMOS process.

Reduced sensitivity to fiber alignment is achieved by grating couplers where a periodic structure is used to deflect and focus the light into a waveguide [301]. Typical losses of about 5 dB/coupler [302] have been improved by optimizing the grating parameters and incorporating backside mirrors. Low grating coupler losses of 1.5 dB/coupler have been reported for metallic backside mirrors [303], as well as for dielectric Si/SiO_2 backside mirror [304]. Two-dimensional (2D) grating couplers can be used to split orthogonal polarization states [305, 306], enabling the implementation of polarization diversity schemes [307].

For the actual functionally of photonic integrated circuits, low-loss passive waveguides are the basic building block and have attracted the most interest. For large area single-mode waveguides with a width of 14 μm, ultralow losses of 0.1 dB/cm have already been achieved early on [308]. For rib waveguides with a height of 200 nm, losses of only 0.5 dB/cm have been reported [309]. For narrow strip waveguides, the scattering losses are increased to a value of about 2.4 dB/cm [257, 271, 310] to 2.0 dB/cm [311]. Further optimization of the dry-etch mask has led to improved losses of about 1 dB/cm for 500 nm wide strip waveguides [312].

Losses have been reduced even further by applying post processing steps—which smooth the surface by dry or wet oxidation [313]—down to a value of 0.8 dB/cm [314]. Very low loss waveguides have been fabricated without precise etching process. Just using thermal oxidation [315] resulted in losses of only 0.3 dB/cm [316]. Unfortunately, these waveguides are buried and thus hard to access, which creates issues for the integration with other devices.

Another key building block of photonic integrated circuits are waveguide bends. Improvements in the fabrication process have led to practically lossless bends [271, 317], which is in good agreement with 3D finite-difference in time-domain simulations [318]. In a different approach, overmoded waveguides have been used to increase the fabrication tolerances while maintaining low propagation and bending losses [319].

Using straight waveguides and bends, optical buffers have been realized. Delay lines based on cascaded ring resonators achieved a delay of 510 ps in a narrow wavelength region [320]. Recently, delays of up to 2 ns over the complete C-band have been realized in multi-mode waveguides with 45° mirror bends [321].

To take advantage of the possible parallelization offered by integrated optics, wavelength channels need to be separated in a compact way. For dense wavelength-division multiplexing (DWDM), demultiplexers are typically realized as arrayed waveguide gratings (AWG) [322]. Demultiplexing of 30 channels with less than -25 dB crosstalk and only 1.9dB insertion loss has been reported [323].

Due to their small footprint, most filter designs employ ring resonators, e.g. to create narrow-band notch filters [273] or tunable filters and switches. Telecom-grade channel add-drop filters that provide truly hitless reconfigurability have been reported with extinction ratios exceeding 30 dB [258]. A similar approach has been realized to implement 4×4 crossbar switches [324], which are needed for on-chip interconnects in multi-core microprocessor architectures [325]. The state of the art fabrication already allows constructing more complex structures. For example, monolithically integrated multi-channel receivers at 10 Gbit/s have been reported [272].

Historically even more limited by the underlying fabrication technology, photonic crystals (PhC) have attracted a lot of interest in the last years. The creation of a photonic band gap is used to reduce the speed of light close to the band edge, which significantly enhances the interaction of the light with the surrounding medium [326]. First demonstrations based on the plasma effect have confirmed the operation principle [327, 328]. In combination with electro-optic polymers, photonic crystal structures are promising candidates to realize ultra compact modulators for 100 Gbit/s with a drive voltage amplitude of only 1 V [329]. Although the fabrication still is challenging, a first low-speed proof of principle has been reported at 5 kHz [330]. Higher-order nonlinear effects benefit from the reduced speed of light even more. Recently, the predicted enhancement of third-order nonlinearities [331] was used to demonstrate enhanced self-phase modulation in an only 80 μm short photonic crystal defect waveguide [332].

3.1.2 Active Components

The integration of active components allows significant enhancements in functionality of photonic integrated circuits. As silicon is an indirect-bandgap semiconductor, sophisticated growth techniques or hybrid integration with III-V materials is needed to implement active devices like lasers, modulators, detectors, and even photonic integrated circuits on silicon.

The 'silicon laser' still is the biggest challenge. While optically pumped silicon Raman lasers [262] and epitaxially grown germanium lasers [278] have been reported, electrically pumped cw operation has so far only been demonstrated by die-to-wafer bonding of AlGaInAs/InP lasers [286, 333], GaInAsP/InP lasers [283], and InAsP/InP lasers [284]. In a distributed Bragg-reflector structure, direct modulation of an evanescent InP laser was shown up to a bit rate of 4 Gbit/s [288].

A multitude of modulators has been demonstrated based on the free-carrier plasma effect discussed in Section 1.2.3. In a Mach-Zehnder Interferometer (MZI) geometry, the field effect in a metal-oxide-semiconductor (MOS) was used to modulate the free-carrier concentration capacitively [334], up to a bit rate of 10 Gbit/s at an extinction ratio of 3.8 dB [335]. In p-n and p-i-n diode structures operated under reverse bias, modulation of the width of the depletion zone is used to modulate the free-carrier concentration [336, 337]. As an accumulation of carriers is avoided, the effect is fast and 3 dB bandwidths of 20 GHz are possible [338]. However, for high-speed operation at 40 Gbit/s, only a very limited extinction ratio of 1.1 dB was found [263]. Forward-biased diode structures usually show good extinction ratios of more than 9 dB, but due to the accumulation of charges the modulation speed is limited. Modulation in ring resonators [276] has been reported up to speeds of 12.5 Gbit/s [339]. In addition to the strictly CMOS-compatible silicon modulator schemes, advanced designs which integrate other materials are possible. The quantum-confined Stark effect in germanium quantum wells [340] or electro-optic polymers promise ultrafast modulation. A photonic crystal waveguide with an infiltrated electro-optic polymer would theoretically enable modulation up to 100 Gbit/s [329].

For the detection of light, multiple solutions seem practicable. Ion implantation of silicon increases the absorption at communication wavelengths and has been demonstrated up to 20 GHz [341]. Epitaxially integrated germanium diodes allow detection of 10 Gbit/s signals [272, 342] and are commercially used by Luxtera.

Hybrid integration of III-V materials is possible, although the evanescent coupling requires large devices which are RC limited to <1 GHz [293].

In the last years, the focus has begun to shift to the realization of complex photonic integrated circuits. First milestones were the integration of preamplifiers and photodetectors [343], the integration of lasers and photodetectors [344], and the integration of lasers and modulators [290]. Also, integrated 2×2 [325] and 4×4 [324] switches have been shown. Just recently, an integrated polarization and phase diversity coherent receiver has been reported [307].

3.1.3 Nonlinear Slot Waveguides

Despite the excellent optical properties of silicon discussed in the previous paragraphs, its nonlinear properties are severely limited. Its second-order electro-optic effect is too weak to be useful for modulators [22], and the third-order Kerr nonlinearity is impaired by two-photon absorption and free-carrier effects [345].

By embedding properly designed SOI waveguide templates into organic cladding materials [294, 295], it is possible to combine silicon waveguide structures with specifically engineered optical properties of organic materials and their high optical nonlinearities.

Waveguides consisting of two narrow silicon strips which form a slot are of particular interest, as the fundamental mode is strongly confined to the slot, which improves the interaction with the nonlinear cladding material. Additionally, if the refractive index of the cladding material is smaller than the refractive index of silicon, the continuity of the displacement field $\mathbf{D}(\mathbf{r},t)$ at each interface causes a strong enhancement of the electric field $\mathbf{E}(\mathbf{r},t)$ in the slot [346, 347]. This field enhancement is used to increase the sensitivity of bio-sensors, the efficiency of electro-optic modulators, and enables highest speed all-optical signal processing due to the Kerr effect.

A number of theoretical works on slot waveguides in general has been published in the last years [346, 348-351]. By optimizing the geometrical parameters, compact bends [352] and right-angle bends [353] are possible. With the slot width as an additional degree of freedom over conventional strip waveguides, also the waveguide dispersion can be engineered from near-zero dispersion [354], up to very strong dispersion of $-180\,000\,\mathrm{ps}/(\mathrm{km\,nm})$ [355].

For applications in bio-sensing, a strong sensitivity enhancement is predicted [350], up to a 5-fold to 100-fold increase [356]. High-Q silicon slot waveguide ring resonators have been fabricated [357] and and increased sensitivity to biomelecules in Si_3N_4-on-glass ring resonators has been experimentally demonstrated [358].

A novel approach to create fast electro-optic modulators on silicon is the combination of silicon slot waveguides and $\chi^{(2)}$-nonlinear organic cladding materials with ultrafast polarization response [359]. Due to the field enhancement in the slot and the small device dimensions, low-voltage operation is possible [360]. If the slot waveguides are surrounded by photonic crystals in order to reduce the optical group velocity, the interaction is increased even more, leading to very short devices [330] with a theoretical bandwidth of 78 GHz [329]. For conventional straight slot waveguides with an electro-optic polymer cladding, modulation up to a bandwidth of 192 GHz is predicted [361] and first experiments have demonstrated operation at 40 Gbit/s [296].

For nonlinear applications based on the Kerr effect, slot waveguides have been intensively studied. Small slot widths minimize the nonlinear effective area and maximize the nonlinear effect [349]. Different cladding materials like Al_2O_3 and TiO_2 [362], SiO_2 [363], and silicon nanocrystals [364] have been investigated. For slot waveguides cladded with an erbium-doped glass, even gain is predicted [365, 366]. By choosing an appropriate organic cladding material like P-toluene sulphonate (PTS) [367], extremely high nonlinearity parameters of up to $\gamma = 7 \times 10^6 (\text{Wkm})^{-1}$ [351] are possible. In combination with the organic cladding material 2-[4-(dimethylamino)phenyl]-3-{[4-(dimethylamino)phenyl]ethynyl}buta-1,3-diene-1,1,4,4-tetracarbonitrile) DDMEBT [295], slot waveguides have been demonstrated that show large nonlinearity parameters of $\gamma = 100000 (\text{Wkm})^{-1}$ [368, 369] without any slow patterning effects [298, 370]. Using these waveguides, all-optical signal processing experiments have been reported [371, 372], including the successful demultiplexing of a 170 Gbit/s stream to 42.7 Gbit/s [297].

3.2 Silicon-Organic Hybrid Waveguide Design

Nonlinear waveguides should feature a large nonlinearity parameter γ and a large two-photon absorption figure of merit $\mathrm{FOM_{TPA}}$ at the same time. By combining the excellent waveguiding properties of silicon with specially engineered nonlinear cladding materials, the fundamental limitations of the silicon two-photon absorption can be overcome.

In the following, the linear and nonlinear waveguide properties of silicon-organic hybrid waveguides are discussed in more detail. In Section 3.2.1, the basic material parameters of silicon are reviewed. Section 3.2.2 then introduces the silicon-organic hybrid waveguide geometries, where the waveguides are characterized according to the dominant source of the nonlinear interaction. In Section 3.2.3, dispersion, nonlinearity, and figure of merit are discussed by numerical modeling of the basic geometries.

3.2.1 Nonlinear Material Parameters of Silicon

It is possible to design highly nonlinear CMOS-compatible waveguides by exploiting the strong mode confinement, which is possible in the high index-contrast silicon-on-insulator technology. However, the device performance is limited by silicon material parameters like the nonlinear refractive index n_2 and the two-photon absorption coefficient α_2, see Section 1.3. Unfortunately, the two-photon absorption figure of merit, as defined in Eq. (1.3.41), for silicon has a value of $\mathrm{FOM_{TPA,Si}} = 0.39$, which is insufficient to achieve all-optical switching. An extensive list of published values for the nonlinear material parameters of crystalline silicon is compiled in Table 3.1 and Fig. 3.1.

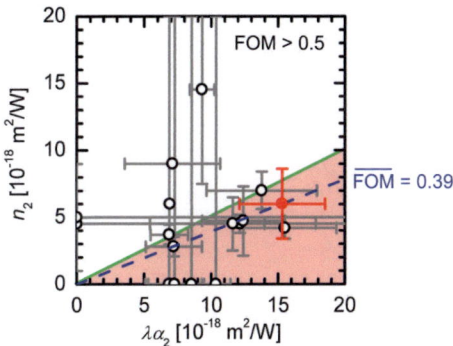

Fig. 3.1 Experimental values for silicon material parameters in a graphical representation. Nonlinear refractive index n_2 is plotted versus the product $\lambda\alpha_2$ of wavelength and two-photon absorption coefficient. The TPA figure of merit of Eq. (1.3.41) is the slope of the linear fit (– –). Open circles (○) with gray error bars are literature values, see Table 3.1. The red data point (●) is the value measured in Section 3.3.3. All-optical switching is possible in the white area and impossible in the red area. The linear fit has been obtained by a least-squares fit to all data points. With a value of $FOM_{TPA,Si} = 0.39$, silicon does not fulfill the criterion needed for all-optical switching.

Fig. 3.1 shows the nonlinear silicon material parameters in a graphical representation. The nonlinear refractive index n_2 is plotted versus the product $\lambda\alpha_2$ of wavelength and two-photon absorption coefficient. The TPA figure of merit (1.3.41) is the slope of the linear fit (– –). Open circles (○) with gray error bars are literature values, see Table 3.1. The red data point (●) is the value measured in Section 3.3.3. All-optical switching is possible in the white area and impossible in the red area. The dashed blue line is the least squares fit to all points.

Table 3.1 summarizes the published values of nonlinear material parameters of crystalline silicon. Reliable values at $\lambda = 1550\,\text{nm}$ are $\alpha_2 = 0.8\,\text{cm}/\text{GW}$ and $n_2 = 6.0 \times 10^{-18}\,\text{m}^2/\text{W}$, in good agreement with theory [373]. With a value of $FOM_{TPA,Si} = 0.39$, pure silicon waveguides not fulfill the criterion needed for all-optical switching. This limitation can be overcome using hybrid integration of nonlinear materials which do not suffer from two-photon absorption.

Table 3.1 Published values of nonlinear material parameters of crystalline silicon. Reliable values at $\lambda = 1550$ nm are $\alpha_2 = 0.8 \, \text{cm/GW}$ and $n_2 = 6.0 \times 10^{-18} \, \text{m}^2/\text{W}$. Methods: 1/T and T: pulse transmission; z-scan: far-field transmittance [374]; SPM: self-phase modulation, FWM: four-wave mixing.

λ [nm]	α_2 [cm/GW]	$\lambda\alpha_2$ [10^{-18} m^2/W]	n_2 [10^{-18} m^2/W]	FOM$_{TPA}$	Method	Refs.
1536	0.45	6.9	6	0.89	1/T	[375]
1560	0.44±0.10	6.9±1.6	–	–	1/T	[376]
1540	0.79±0.12	12.2±1.8	4.5±0.7	0.37	z-scan	[377]
1530	0.90±0.27	13.8±4.1	7.0±1.4	0.51	1/T	[378]
1455	0.50±0.15	7.3±2.2	–	–	T	[379]
1547	0.67±0.07	10.4±1.1	–	–	1/T	[380]
1550	0.60±0.06	9.3±0.9	14.5±7.0	1.56	T,SPM	[28]
1559	0.44±0.09	6.9±1.4	3.7±0.7	0.54	SPM	[381]
1547	0.46±0.23	7.1±3.6	9.0	1.26	FWM	[382]
1550	–	–	4.5	–	FWM	[383]
1500	–	–	5.0±4.0	–	SPM	[384]
1550	0.75±0.40	11.6±6.2	4.5±2.0	0.39	z-scan	[385]
1500	0.48±0.14	7.2±2.1	2.8±0.7	0.39	z-scan	[386]
1550	0.55	8.5	–	–	z-scan	[387]
1550	0.80±0.20	12.4±3.1	4.7±2.6	0.38	1/T	[369]
1550	1.00±0.25	15.5±3.9	4.2±0.8	0.27	T	[388]

3.2.2 Basic Waveguide Geometries

We consider here three generic nonlinear waveguide structures that exploit the nonlinearities of the core and the cladding material to a different extent. Fig. 3.2 shows the three proposed basic designs [351] along with the mode fields calculated for a cladding with $n = 1.8$.

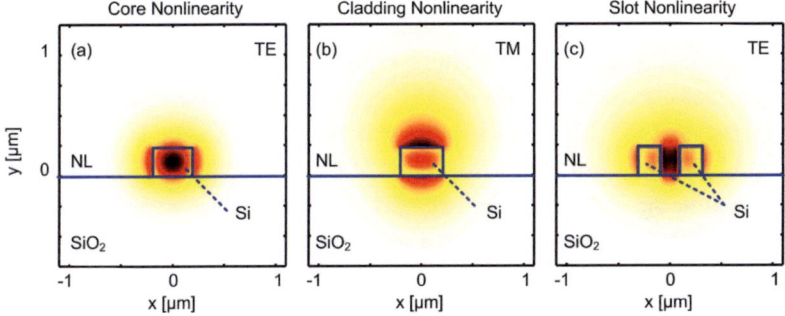

Fig. 3.2 Geometry and electric field distribution of three highly nonlinear CMOS-compatible waveguides. All SOI structures are covered with an organic nonlinear cladding material (NL). (a) *"Core nonlinearity"*: A strip waveguide operated in TE mode (dominant electric field component along the *x*-direction), where the light is concentrated in the waveguide core. The third-order nonlinearity is dominated by the complex-valued $\chi^{(3)}$ of silicon, while the effect of the cladding material is negligible. (b) *"Cladding nonlinearity"*: A strip waveguide operated in TM mode (dominant electric field component along the *y*-direction). The optical signal is squeezed into the cladding, allowing exploiting the real valued nonlinearity of the cladding. (c) *"Slot nonlinearity"*: In the slot geometry, the light is almost completely confined to the slot filled with nonlinear material. For a cladding material with a real susceptibility, the TPA figure of merit is high for (b) and (c). For better comparison, all waveguides have been fabricated on the same chip with the same cladding material.

All structures feature strong optical nonlinearities but show characteristic differences in nonlinear dynamics, dispersion, and the TPA figure of merit, Eq. (1.3.37). They can be classified according to their real and imaginary part of the dominant nonlinearity.

Core nonlinearity

The strip waveguide operated in TE mode (dominant electric field component along the x-direction) is shown in Fig. 3.2(a). It consists of a single silicon strip waveguide. The field is concentrated in the waveguide core ("*core nonlinearity*") and the nonlinear effect is maximized by the strong field confinement and dominated by the complex-valued $\chi^{(3)}$ of silicon. Hence, the figure of merit has a low value of $\text{FOM}_{\text{TPA}} \approx 0.35$ [377, 386]. This structure is simple to fabricate, although care needs to be taken to reduce the sidewall roughness.

Cladding nonlinearity

The strip waveguide operated in TM mode (dominant electric field component along the y-direction) is shown in Fig. 3.2(b). It consists of a single silicon strip waveguide with a nonlinear cladding material. The mode is mostly guided in the cladding ("*cladding nonlinearity*"). The discontinuity of the refractive index at the waveguide top gives rise to a strong field enhancement in the cladding [266]. If the two-photon absorption in the organic cladding material is negligible, the waveguide figure of merit will be greatly improved. The top surface of the silicon strip is protected in all fabrication steps, so it remains flat and the propagation loss is low.

Slot nonlinearity

A different approach uses two narrow silicon strips separated by a small slot. Again, the whole structure is covered by a nonlinear organic cladding material. The mode distribution of a slot waveguide operated in TE mode is shown in Fig. 3.2(c). The light is strongly confined to the slot ("*slot nonlinearity*") due to the field enhancement at the silicon-organic interface. Because the intensity in the silicon strips is low, two-photon absorption will be lowest in the slot geometry, which leads to a greatly improved figure of merit. The propagation loss is higher than for the strip waveguides as the structure has four sidewalls that suffer from surface roughness. Further technological improvements might solve this problem.

3.2.3 Numerical Modelling

The nonlinearity coefficient can be maximized for each basic design by the proper selection of the nonlinear material and by optimizing the geometry of the structure.

Taking into account the waveguide dimensions as well as the limits imposed by the fabrication technology, parameters like the complex nonlinearity and the dispersion can be predicted by numerical models.

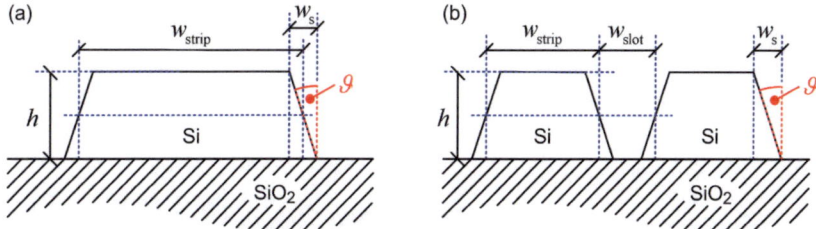

Fig. 3.3 Parameterization of (a) silicon strip waveguides and (b) silicon slot waveguides. Both waveguides are characterized by the waveguide height h and the silicon strip width w_{strip}. Slot waveguides consist of two silicon strips, separated by a slot of width w_{slot}. Due to shortcomings of the fabrication technology, usually the cross-section of the silicon strips deviates from the perfect rectangle and can be described by a trapezoid. The waveguide dimensions are defined at height $h/2$, in order to keep the silicon cross-section independent of the sidewall angle ϑ.

To investigate the influence of the geometrical parameters numerically, the waveguide dimensions are parameterized as depicted in Fig. 3.3. Strip and slot waveguides are characterized by the waveguide height h and the silicon strip width w_{strip}. Slot waveguides consist of two silicon strips, separated by a slot of width w_{slot}. Due to shortcomings of the fabrication technology, usually the cross-section of the silicon strips deviates from the perfect rectangle and can be described by a trapezoid. The waveguide dimensions are defined at height $h/2$, in order to keep the silicon cross-section independent of the sidewall angle ϑ. The angled sidewalls extend over a width $w_s = h \tan \vartheta$, which reduced the length of the top edge accordingly.

Commercially available mode solvers are used to calculate the field distribution. For the investigated high index contrast structures, two different simulation techniques are used to cross-check results and use the particular strength of each method.

The transient solver of CST Microwave Studio [19] is based on the finite-integration technique (FIT). The computation is fast and produces reliable results. But due to the limited control over the mesh generation, it can only simulate rectangular shapes and slot widths of approximately $w_{strip}/3 \approx 60$ nm.

RSoft FemSIM [20] is based on the finite-element method (FEM). It offers finer control over the mesh generation and higher resolution. Thus it is better suited to simulate small structures like narrow slots and non-rectangular shapes, like the angled-sidewall structures. However, it is computationally more expensive in terms of memory and time.

For all structures and parameter variations, the $\mathcal{E}$ and $\mathcal{H}$ field distributions of the fundamental transverse electric and transverse magnetic modes are calculated, the effective area (1.3.13) and the group velocity [329] are extracted, and dispersion and nonlinearity parameters are calculated.

3.2.3.1 Waveguide Dispersion

Nanophotonic devices have reached a miniaturization level, where the device dimensions are on the scale of the wavelength. Even small changes of the operating wavelength can cause significant changes of the actual field distribution. As a consequence, the group velocity becomes strongly dependent on the wavelength. A theoretical description of these dispersion effects is given in Section 1.2.1.

The main effect of dispersion in nonlinear signal processing is a broadening of pulses, which reduces the available peak power. For nonlinear interactions like four-wave mixing (FWM), the maximum nonlinear effect can additionally be limited by phase mismatch. While this limitation is detrimental e.g. for broadband wavelength conversion, it might be highly desired for multi-wavelength operation.

To evaluate the dependence of the dispersion parameters on the waveguide geometry, the $\mathcal{E}$ and $\mathcal{H}$ field distributions of the fundamental transverse electric and transverse magnetic modes are calculated for all basic SOH waveguide geometries, which allows to extract the group velocity [329]. In our case the total dispersion is dominated by waveguide dispersion and only waveguide dispersion will be considered in the following.

To narrow down the parameter space for the simulations, several parameters have been fixed at relevant values. The waveguide height and sidewall angle has been fixed at $h = 220\,\text{nm}$ and $\vartheta = 0°$, respectively. The refractive index of the cladding material has been fixed at $n_{0,\text{NL}} = 1.8$. Variations of the waveguide height and the cladding refractive index can be found in [351].

Core nonlinearity

To evaluate the dispersion parameters of silion strip waveguides with *core nonlinearity*, the width of the strip was varied between 300 nm and 500 nm, with a step width of 20 nm. The field distributions are grouped according to the dominant electric field contribution and the quasi-TE modes are evaluated.

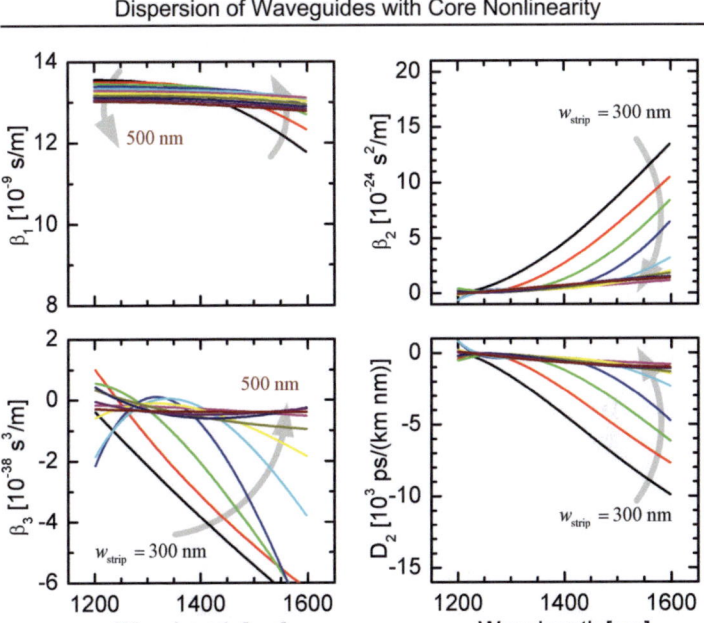

Fig. 3.4 Dispersion parameters for a waveguide with *core nonlinearity*. The strip width is varied from 300 nm to 500 nm in steps of 20 nm. The waveguide height is 220 nm and the sidewall angle is 0°. Up to a strip width of 380 nm, the group propagation constant $\beta_1 = v_g^{-1}$ changes significantly with increasing wavelength. As a result, the dispersion D_2 is nearly constant for strip widths above 380 nm, but strongly changes for narrow strips.

Fig. 3.4 shows the calculated dispersion parameters for a waveguide with *core nonlinearity*. Up to a strip width of 380 nm, the group propagation constant $\beta_1 = v_g^{-1}$ changes significantly with increasing wavelength. As a result, the dispersion D_2 is nearly constant for strip widths above 380 nm, but strongly changes for narrow strips.

Silicon strip waveguides with core nonlinearity can achieve constant and low dispersion values, which avoids phase mismatch in nonlinear applications.

Cladding nonlinearity

To evaluate the dispersion parameters of silion strip waveguides with *cladding nonlinearity*, the width of the strip was varied between 300 nm and 500 nm, with a step width of 20 nm. The field distributions are grouped according to the dominant electric field contribution and the quasi-TM modes are evaluated.

Dispersion of Waveguides with Cladding Nonlinearity

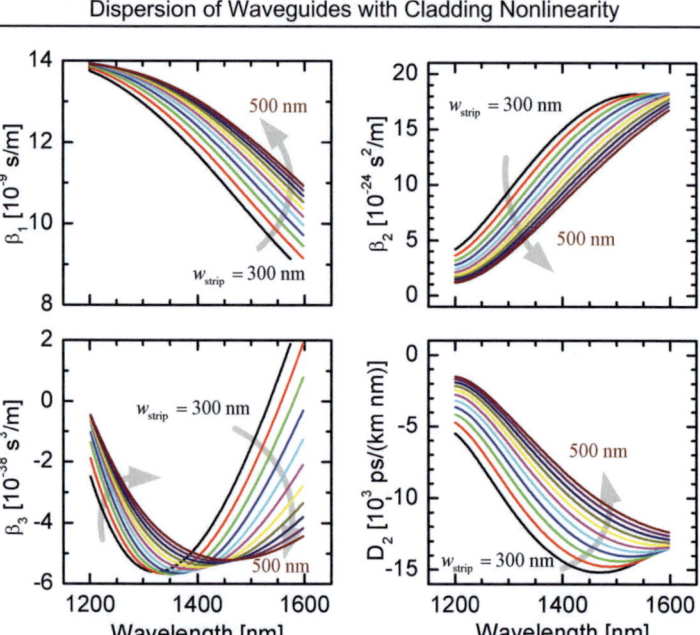

Fig. 3.5   Dispersion parameters for a waveguide with *cladding nonlinearity*. The strip width is varied from 300 nm to 500 nm in steps of 20 nm. The waveguide height is 220 nm and the sidewall angle is 0°. As the strip hight is always much smaller than the wavelength, the group propagation constant $\beta_1 = v_g^{-1}$ changes significantly with increasing wavelength and strip width. As a result, the dispersion D_2 takes very large values of the order of $-10\,000\,\text{ps}/(\text{km nm})$ and varies strongly with wavelength and strip width.

Fig. 3.5 shows the calculated dispersion parameters for a waveguide with cladding nonlinearity. As the strip hight is always much smaller than the wavelength, the group propagation constant $\beta_1 = v_g^{-1}$ changes significantly with increasing wavelength and strip width. As a result, the dispersion D_2 takes very large values of the order of $-10\,000\,\text{ps}/(\text{km nm})$ and varies strongly with wavelength and strip width.

Waveguides with cladding nonlinearity show an inherently large dispersion. In nonlinear applications, this could be used to enable multi-wavelength operation with only few nanometers of detuning.

Slot nonlinearity

To evaluate the dispersion parameters of silion strip waveguides with *slot nonlinearity*, the width of both silicon strips is fixed to 212 nm, and the slot width is varied from 0 nm to 200 nm with a step width of 20 nm. The field distributions are grouped according to the dominant electric field contribution and the quasi-TE modes are evaluated.

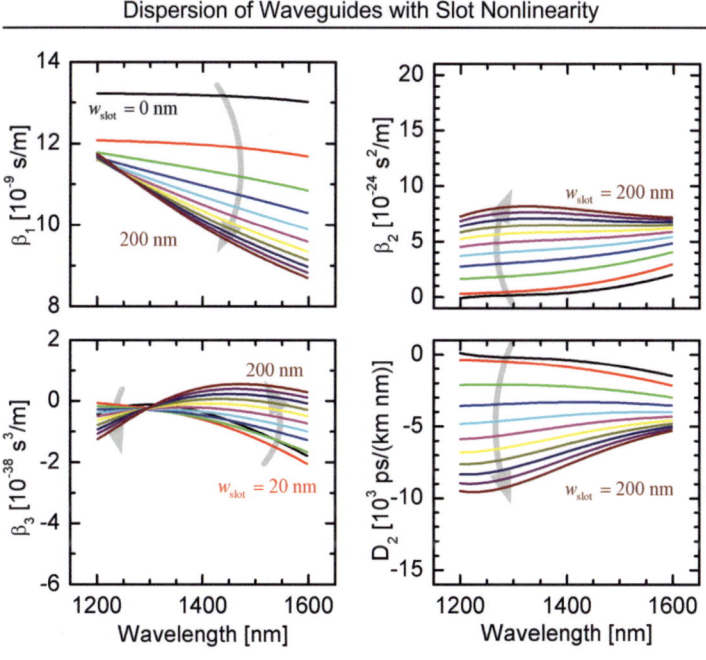

Fig. 3.6 Dispersion parameters of waveguides with slot nonlinearity as a function of slot width $w_{\text{slot}} = 0...200\,\text{nm}$, in steps of 20 nm, sidewall angle $\vartheta = 0°$. For a slot width of 0 nm, identical results to the waveguide with core nonlinearity and a width of 420 nm are found. For an increasing slot width, the mode is less confined to the core and the group propagation constant $\beta_1 = v_g^{-1}$ decreases. As a result, the dispersion D_2 takes large values of the order of $-5000\,\text{ps/(km\,nm)}$ and varies mainly with the slot width.

Fig. 3.6 shows the calculated dispersion parameters of waveguides with slot nonlinearity as a function of slot width. For a slot width of 0 nm, identical results to the waveguide with core nonlinearity and a width of 420 nm are found. For an increasing slot width, the mode is less confined to the core and the group propagation constant $\beta_1 = v_g^{-1}$ decreases. As a result, the dispersion D_2 takes large values of the order of $-5\,000\,\text{ps}/(\text{km}\,\text{nm})$ and varies mainly with the slot width.

Waveguides with slot nonlinearity show large group velocity dispersion coefficients D_2, but low third-order dispersion β_3. For short waveguide lengths, these dispersion values are sufficiently low to avoid phase-mismatch. In addition, for short optical pulses which are large in spectrum, the low third-order dispersion limits the experienced distortion of the pulse envelope. As a result, compact waveguides with slot nonlinearity are ideally suited for signal processing at highest bit rates.

3.2.3.2 Influence of Sidewall Angle

If the sidewalls are not perfectly vertical, i.e. $\vartheta > 0°$, the effective area increases because the guided mode is less confined in the slot region and the increase of the effective area restricts the enhancement of the nonlinear effect [349].

However, the extent of this effect strongly depends on the parameterization of the problem. If the sidewall angle is varied, while keeping the base width of the trapezoid constant, the total cross-section of the waveguide material is reduced. As a result, a sidewall angle of $\vartheta = 8°$ would reduce the cross-sectional area of a 300 nm wide strip already by 20%, which will result in an even larger increase in the effective area of up to 35%.

The parameterization illustrated in Fig. 3.3 avoids this main influence of the sidewall angle by keeping the cross-sectional areas of core and cladding materials constant. The main effect of angled sidewalls is a slight deviation from the ideal field distribution, and only in the nonlinear effective areas some differences can be expected. For linear quantities like e.g. the group velocity, the influence of the sidewall angle is negligible.

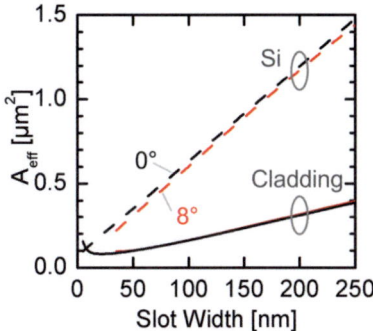

Fig. 3.7   Influence of sidewall angle on effective areas of a waveguide with slot nonlinearity. For a sidewall angle of 0° (black) and 8° (red), the effective area of silicon (– –, dashed line) and the nonlinear cladding material (—, solid line) are compared. The influence of the sidewall angle is largest for the effective area of silicon at small slot widths, close to the minimum value for the slot width of 30 nm. In general, the influence of the sidewall angle is negligible.

Fig. 3.7 illustrates the influence of the sidewall angle on effective areas of a waveguide with slot nonlinearity. For a sidewall angle of 0° (black) and 8° (red), the effective area of silicon (– –, dashed line) and the nonlinear cladding material (—, solid line) are compared. The influence of the sidewall angle is largest for the effective area of silicon at small slot widths, close to the minimum value for the slot width of 30 nm. In general, the influence of the sidewall angle is negligible.

3.2.3.3 Waveguide Nonlinearity Parameter

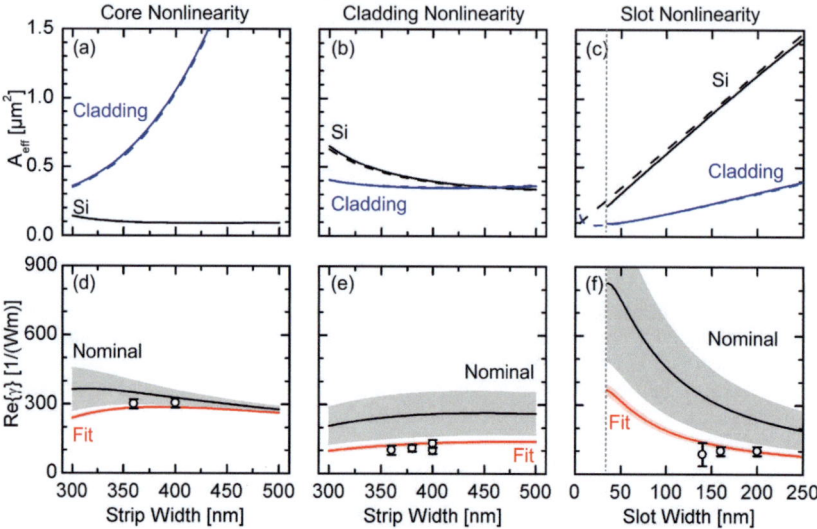

Fig. 3.8   Finite-element simulation results for (a)–(c) third order effective area $A_{\text{eff}}^{(3)}$ in silicon (-, Si) and in the nonlinear cladding material (-, Cladding) and (d)–(f) nonlinearity parameter $\text{Re}\{\gamma\}$ of the basic geometries, calculated for a sidewall angles of $\vartheta = 8°$ (solid lines) and $\vartheta = 0°$ (dashed lines). For the nonlinearity parameter, the contribution of the nonlinear cladding material is calculated for a nominal value of $n_{2,\text{Nom}} = (17 \pm 8) \times 10^{-18}\,\text{m}^2/\text{W}$ (black line) and for a value of $n_{2,\text{Fit}} = (6.0 \pm 0.5) \times 10^{-18}\,\text{m}^2/\text{W}$ (red line) obtained by a fit to measured values [ ]. Following Eqs. (1.3.12) and (1.3.17), the nonlinearity parameter is large for small effective areas. The dotted line (...) in (c) and (f) marks the minimum possible slot width for the case of a non-zero sidewall angle.

(a) In the waveguide with the core nonlinearity the dominant nonlinear contribution comes from the silicon, as the silicon effective area can be strongly minimized. (b) In waveguides with *cladding nonlinearity* both silicon and the nonlinear cladding material contribute alike. (c) The nonlinear effect of waveguides with *slot nonlinearity* depends on the slot width and the nonlinear cladding material. The total nonlinearity parameter for strip waveguides in (d) and (e) does not significantly depend on the strip width. (f) Decreasing the slot width decreases the effective area and thereby increases the nonlinearity parameter. For highly nonlinear cladding materials, a very strong nonlinearity parameter can be obtained.

The nonlinearity coefficient can be maximized by minimizing the effective areas of the mode fields in the respective nonlinear material, see Fig. 3.2. Apart from parameters which are fixed to technologically viable values, the main parameters that influence the waveguide properties are the strip and slot widths. For all waveguides, the height is fixed to $h = 220$ nm. For strip waveguides, the strip width is varied between 300 nm and 500 nm. For slot waveguides, the silicon strip width is fixed to $w_{strip} = 212$ nm, and the slot width is varied between 0 nm and 250 nm. For angled sidewalls, the minimum slot width is given by $w_{slot} > h \tan \vartheta$. Due to imperfections in the fabrication process, in reality all waveguides exhibit a sidewall angle of $\vartheta = 8°$.

In Fig. 3.8(a)–(c), effective areas for the third order interaction in silicon (-, Si) and the nonlinear cladding material (-, Cladding) are calculated using a finite-element method (FEM) for a sidewall angles of $\vartheta = 8°$ (solid lines) and $\vartheta = 0°$ (dashed lines). For a fixed waveguide height of 220 nm the width of the strip or slot is varied.

Fig. 3.8(a) shows that the nonlinearity of waveguides with *core nonlinearity* is dominated by the silicon effective area. For waveguides with *cladding nonlinearity* in Fig. 3.8(b) both silicon and the nonlinear cladding material contribute alike. The nonlinear effect of waveguides with *slot nonlinearity* in Fig. 3.8(c) depends on the slot width and the nonlinear cladding material. Decreasing the slot width decreases the effective area and thereby increases the nonlinearity parameter. For a waveguide with a slot with of 80 nm, a two-fold increase of the nonlinearity parameter over the values measured here is possible.

Fig. 3.8(d)–(f) shows the nonlinearity parameter $\mathrm{Re}\{\gamma\}$ of the basic geometries, calculated for a sidewall angles of $\vartheta = 8°$. Following Eqs. (1.3.12) and (1.3.17), the nonlinearity parameter is large for small effective areas. The contribution of the nonlinear cladding material is calculated for a nominal value of $n_{2,\mathrm{Nom}} = (17 \pm 8) \times 10^{-18}$ m^2/W (black line) and for a value of $n_{2,\mathrm{Fit}} = (6.0 \pm 0.5) \times 10^{-18}$ m^2/W (red line) obtained by a fit to measured values c). Shaded areas illustrate the uncertainties in the values. For the nonlinear refractive index of silicon a value of $n_{2,\mathrm{Si}} = 6.0 \times 10^{-18}$ m^2/W is used. Fig. 3.8(f) illustrates how a very strong nonlinearity parameter can be obtained for highly nonlinear cladding materials.

3.2.3.4 Two-Photon Absorption Figure of Merit

In a realistic Kerr-type waveguide, the nonlinear loss due to two-photon absorption is significant and the peak power that can be used for cross and self-phase modulation is limited.

As discussed in Section 1.3.5, to achieve a minimum phase-shift of $\Delta\phi_{MZI}^{min} = \pi$ over a characteristic two-photon absorption length, the two-photon absorption figure of merit has to exceed a value of $1/2$,

$$\text{FOM}_{TPA} = -\frac{1}{4\pi}\frac{\text{Re}\{\underline{\gamma}\}}{\text{Im}\{\underline{\gamma}\}} > \frac{1}{2}. \tag{1.3.37}$$

The nonlinearity parameter $\underline{\gamma}_{tot}$ of a hybrid waveguide is the sum of the complex nonlinearity parameters of the constituent materials in Eq. (1.3.12), which need to be evaluated individually over the cross-sectional areas of the interaction, see Eq. (1.3.17). As discussed in the previous section, for all basic geometries the constituent materials contribute to different extends. As a result, the maximum achievable figure of merit is strongly dependent on the waveguide geometry.

Based on the results shown in Fig. 3.8, the total nonlinearity parameter and the figure of merit are calculated for specific values of $n_{0,Si} = 3.48$, $n_{2,Si} = 6.0 \times 10^{-18}\,\text{m}^2/\text{W}$, and $\alpha_{2,Si} = 0.8\,\text{cm}/\text{GW}$ for silicon, see Table 3.1 and Fig. 3.1. The nonlinear cladding material is assumed to have a refractive index of $n_{0,Clad} = 1.8$. The nonlinear refractive index of $n_{2,Clad} = (6.0 \pm 0.5) \times 10^{-18}\,\text{m}^2/\text{W}$ is obtained from fits to the experimental values presented in Section 3.3, the two-photon absorption is set to zero, $\alpha_{2,Clad} = 0\,\text{cm}/\text{GW}$. Implicitly, this comparison to waveguides covered with DDMEBT assumes a rather large deviation from the published value of the nonlinear refractive index, $n_{2,DDMEBT} = (17 \pm 8) \times 10^{-18}\,\text{m}^2/\text{W}$.

Fig. 3.9 shows the dependence of nonlinearity parameter $\text{Re}\{\underline{\gamma}\}$ and two-photon absorption figure of merit FOM_{TPA} on the width of the silicon strip and the slot width. Fig. 3.9(a)–(c) show the contributions of silicon (black) and the nonlinear cladding material (blue) to the total nonlinearity parameter (red), as previously defined in Eq. (1.3.17). Shaded areas indicate the uncertainty of values. In waveguides with core nonlinearity shown in Fig. 3.9(d), the figure of merit is determined by the silicon core. In waveguides with cladding nonlinearity shown in Fig. 3.9(e), core and cladding material contribute alike. This significantly improves the figure of merit. In waveguides with slot nonlinearity shown in Fig. 3.9(f), the total nonlinearity is dominated by the nonlinearity of the cladding material. As a result, the figure of merit can be significantly improved.

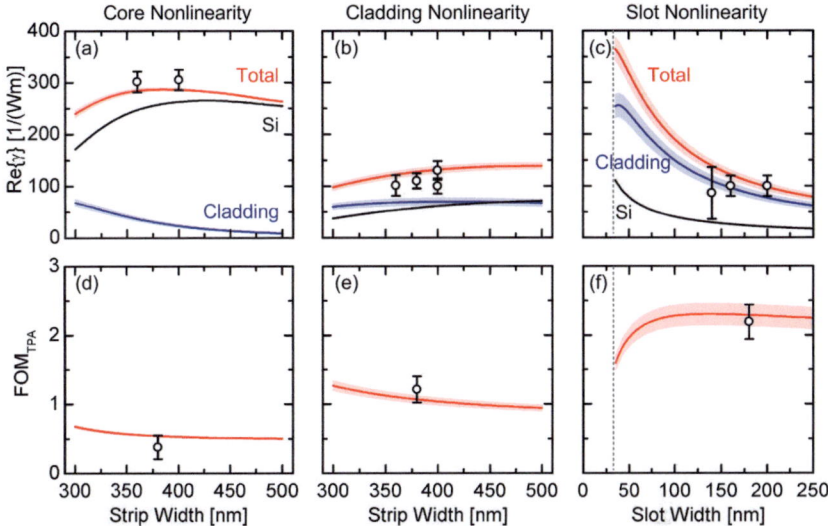

Fig. 3.9 Dependence of nonlinearity parameter $\mathrm{Re}\{\underline{\gamma}\}$ and two-photon absorption figure of merit $\mathrm{FOM_{TPA}}$ on the width of the silicon strip and the slot width. The waveguide height is fixed at 220 nm, the sidewall angle is fixed at $\vartheta = 8°$. Experimental results ($\circ$) are taken from Section 3.3. (a)–(c) Contributions of silicon (black) and the nonlinear cladding material (blue) to the total nonlinearity parameter (red). Shaded areas indicate the uncertainty of values. (d) In waveguides with core nonlinearity, the figure of merit is determined by the silicon core. (e) In waveguides with cladding nonlinearity, core and cladding material contribute alike. This significantly improves the figure of merit. (f) In waveguides with slot nonlinearity, the total nonlinearity is dominated by the nonlinearity of the cladding material. As a result, the figure of merit can be significantly improved.

While the uncertainty of the material parameters of the cladding material do not have an impact on the nonlinearit parameter and the figure of merit of waveguides with core nonlinearity, in waveguides with slot nonlinearity even small deviations from the assumed values can result in large deviations for the nonlinearity parameter and the figure of merit.

3.2.4 Summary

Simulations of the basic silicon-organic hybrid waveguide geometries reveal large differences regarding dispersion, nonlinearity parameter, and figure of merit. By using an appropriate parameterization, the influence of the sidewall angle becomes negligible.

Waveguides with core nonlinearity in general combine low dispersion with large nonlinearity parameters. As the nonlinearity is dominated by the core material, the figure of merit is limited and the nonlinear effect can only be exploited in long devices.

Waveguides with cladding nonlinearity in general show large dispersion values. In combination with the high nonlinearity parameters and sufficient values of the figure of merit, applications as a nonlinear element capable of multi-wavelength operation become possible.

Finally, waveguides with slot nonlinearity show tolerable dispersion, combined with high nonlinearity parameters and the best two-photon absorption figure of merit. The low third-order dispersion limits the experienced distortion of the pulse envelope. As a result, compact waveguides with slot nonlinearity are ideally suited for signal processing at highest bit rates.

3.3 Characterization [J4]

In order to experimentally evaluate the properties of silicon-organic hybrid waveguide designs, we have fabricated waveguides of all basic types on the same chip. Four-wave mixing is used to measure the nonlinearity parameter, propagation losses and the dispersion of the waveguides. Heterodyne pump-probe measurements are used to measure the amplitude and phase dynamics and to calculate the two-photon absorption figure of merit. To reduce measurement errors, we average the data of multiple waveguides having slight variations in waveguide dimensions.

The highly nonlinear silicon-organic hybrid slot waveguides [297] are based on silicon-on-insulator technology using the 193 nm deep-UV lithography [257] offered by ePIXfab [269]. Silicon strip waveguides with widths between 320 nm and 400 nm are fabricated from a 220 nm thick crystalline silicon layer on a 2 μm buried oxide buffer. Slot waveguides with slot widths between 160 nm and 200 nm are formed by two 220 nm wide silicon ribs.

The waveguides are filled and covered with molecular beam deposited DDMEBT. The nonlinear organic cladding obtained in such a way is highly homogeneous and has a refractive index of $n = 1.8$ with a nonlinear refractive index of $n_2 = (1.7 \pm 0.8) \times 10^{-17} \, \text{m}^2/\text{W}$ [295, 389]. Waveguide facets are cleaved and no anti-reflection coating is applied, leading to a coupling loss to the strip and slot waveguides of $(7...9)$ dB/facet and $(4...6)$ dB/facet, respectively. The devices are 6.9 mm long and are operated without any temperature control.

3.3.1 Linear Transmission

Low-loss passive waveguides are the basic building block for linear as well as for nonlinear applications. The main contributions to the propagation loss are absorption at Si/SiO_2 interface defects and scattering loss at rough top and sidewall interfaces. Without further postprocessing, the expected losses of strip waveguides fabricated in the 193 nm deep-UV process should take values of about 2.4 dB/cm [271].

The total transmission discussed in Section 1.2.2 in practical units of dB is given by

$$T\big|_{dB} = -\left(\alpha_0 \big|_{dB} \, L - 2 \, a_{cp} \big|_{dB} \right), \qquad (3.3.1)$$

where α_0 is the linear propagation loss per unit length and a_{cp} is the coupling loss per facet. As the total transmission is determined by two independent variables, cut-back measurement of the transmission of one waveguide at decreasing length L can reveal both main contributions at the same time [390].

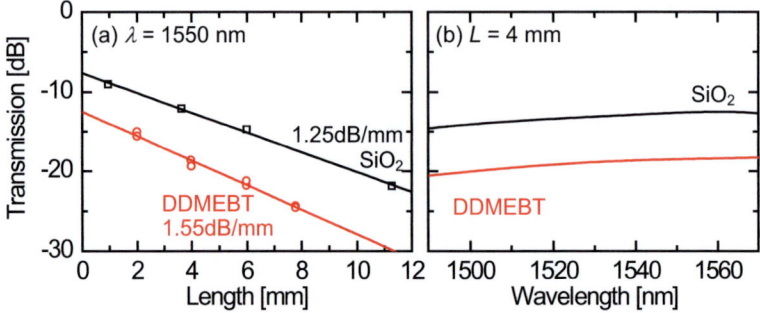

Fig. 3.10 Cut-back measurement of silicon-organic hybrid slot waveguides with 160 nm slot width and 220 nm ridge width. (a) The total transmission as a function of the waveguide length for waveguides covered with SiO$_2$ (black open squares) and DDMEBT (red open circles). The slope of the fit to Eq. (3.3.1) gives the linear propagation loss, α_0. The loss at $L = 0$ mm is due to two times the coupling loss per facet, a_{cp}. Waveguides covered with DDMEBT show a strongly increased coupling loss, but the propagation loss is only slightly increased. (b) Transmission spectrum for waveguides covered with SiO$_2$ (–) and DDMEBT (–). The flat transmission spectrum is characteristic for waveguides without periodic variations of the refractive index or coupling to adjacent structures.

Fig. 3.10(a) shows cut-back measurement of silicon-organic hybrid slot waveguides with 160 nm slot width and 220 nm ridge width as an example. The total transmission as a function of the waveguide length for waveguides covered with SiO$_2$ (black open squares, □) is compared to waveguides covered with DDMEBT (red open circles, ○). The slope of the fit to Eq. (3.3.1) gives the linear propagation loss, α_0. Even though the losses are much stronger than typically expected for fabrication process that has been used [310], slot waveguides push the fabrication technology to its limit and also include twice the number of rough sidewalls compared to simple strip waveguides. Moreover, the light is guided in the slot with the peak intensity close to the rough inner sidewalls.

The loss at $L = 0\,\text{mm}$ is due to two times the coupling loss per facet, a_{cp}. Waveguides covered with DDMEBT show a strongly increased coupling loss, but the propagation loss is only slightly increased. Cut-back measurement results on all investigated waveguides are summarized in Table 3.2.

Fig. 3.10(b) shows the transmission spectrum for waveguides covered with SiO$_2$ (black) and DDMEBT (red). The flat transmission spectrum is characteristic for waveguides without periodic variations of the refractive index or coupling to adjacent structures. Showing no features in the transmission spectrum, both waveguides are ideally suited for broadband signal processing.

3.3.2 Nonlinear Effects

The nonlinearity parameter, the dispersion and the propagation loss of the respective structures can be derived from four-wave mixing experiments, as discussed in Section 1.3.3.

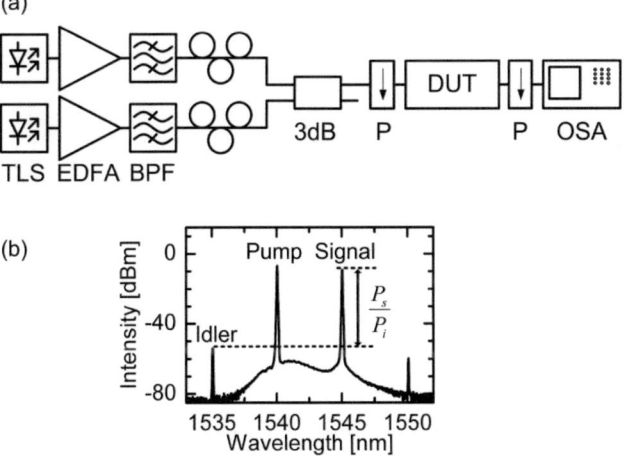

Fig. 3.11 (a) Four-wave mixing setup and (b) example spectrum measured in a bandwidth of 0.1 nm. Co-polarized light from two amplified laser sources is launched into the device under test (DUT) and the four-wave mixing spectrum is recorded in an optical spectrum analyzer (OSA). From the ratio of the idler to the signal the nonlinearity parameter γ can be extracted. (TLS: tunable laser source, EDFA: erbium-doped fiber amplifier, BPF: optical band pass filter, P: polarizer)

The four-wave mixing setup is shown in Fig. 3.11(a). Co-polarized light from two amplified laser sources is launched into the device under test (DUT) using polarization-maintaining lensed fibers. The four-wave mixing spectrum is recorded in an optical spectrum analyzer (OSA). Polarization controllers and polarizers (P) are used to strictly separate between TE and TM polarization. The example spectrum in Fig. 3.11(b) shows the pump and signal waves, as well as the up and down-converted four-wave mixing products.

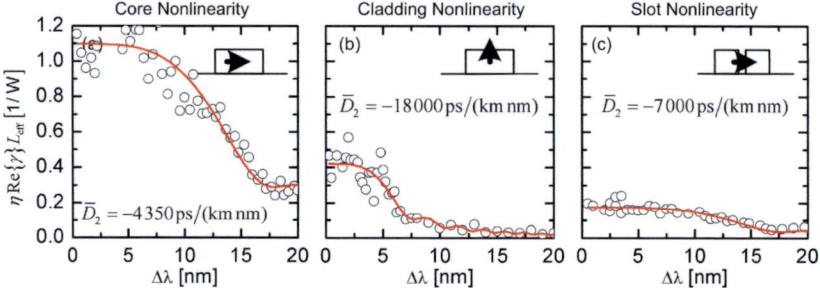

Fig. 3.12   Dependence of FWM conversion efficiency on the wavelength detuning $\Delta\lambda$; measurement (°) and fit (-). The given parameters are averaged over multiple waveguides and measurements. The given parameters are averaged over multiple waveguides and measurements. All waveguides show high nonlinearities. (a) The strip waveguides with pure silicon core nonlinearity show the largest effect. (b) Waveguides with cladding nonlinearity have low linear losses but significant waveguide dispersion, which causes a large phase mismatch for a detuning larger than 5 nm. (c) The slot waveguides show a strong nonlinear effect as well but provide larger phase-matching. The total nonlinear effect is limited by a low effective waveguide length, due to high linear losses of 1.5 dB/mm. All experimental results are summarized in Table 3.2.

Fig. 3.12 shows the dependence of the four-wave mixing conversion efficiency $\eta \operatorname{Re}\{\gamma\}L_{\text{eff}}$ on the wavelength detuning $\Delta\lambda$ for a 400 nm wide strip waveguide operated in TE and TM, and for a slot waveguide with a 160 nm slot. The quantity η describes the normalized degradation of the four-wave mixing efficiency with increasing phase mismatch; without mismatch $\eta = 1$ holds. The parameters extracted from the measurements are averaged over independent measurements of six waveguides for each design. Using a least squares fit procedure, the measurement of the idler power as a function of the frequency detuning between pump and signal allows to determine the nonlinearity parameter $\operatorname{Re}\{\underline{\gamma}\}$, the linear propagation loss α_0 and the dispersion factor D_2.

In our measurements, waveguides with pure silicon *core nonlinearity* and dimensions close to the theoretical optimum [351] show the largest nonlinear effect. For waveguide widths of $(360...400)$ nm an averaged nonlinearity parameter of $\bar{\gamma} = (307\,000 \pm 17\,000)/(\mathrm{W\,km})$ is found, close to the theoretical maximum of $\gamma_{\mathrm{max}} \approx 350\,000/(\mathrm{W\,km})$. Dispersion and propagation loss are measured to be $\bar{D}_2 = (-4350 \pm 150)\,\mathrm{ps}/(\mathrm{km\,nm})$ and $\bar{\alpha}_0 = (1.1 \pm 0.1)\,\mathrm{dB/mm}$, respectively.

Strip waveguides with *cladding nonlinearity* show a large averaged nonlinearity parameter of $\bar{\gamma} = (108\,000 \pm 17\,000)/(\mathrm{W\,km})$ for $(360...400)$ nm wide strips. A propagation loss of $\bar{\alpha}_0 = (1.0 \pm 0.1)\,\mathrm{dB/mm}$ is found. This value is higher than expected for a device with very low interface roughness. But because the mode extends deeply into the cladding, scattering at the sample surface gives rise to additional propagation loss. The significant waveguide dispersion of $\bar{D}_2 = (-18\,000 \pm 2300)\,\mathrm{ps}/(\mathrm{km\,nm})$ causes a large phase mismatch for a detuning larger than 5 nm, see Fig. 3.12(b).

Waveguides with slot nonlinearity also show a strong nonlinearity parameter of $\bar{\gamma} = (100\,000 \pm 13\,000)/(\mathrm{W\,km})$, although the waveguide height of 220 nm and the slot width of $(160...200)$ nm are far from the optimum that is reached for much smaller slot widths, see Fig. 3.8(c). An optimized waveguide could allow nonlinearity parameters beyond $10^6/(\mathrm{W\,km})$ [351]. The total nonlinear effect is limited by a low effective waveguide length of $L_{\mathrm{eff}} = 2.6\,\mathrm{mm}$, due to an increased linear loss of $\bar{\alpha}_0 = (1.5 \pm 0.1)\,\mathrm{dB/mm}$. The dispersion of $\bar{D}_2 = (-7\,000 \pm 400)\,\mathrm{ps}/(\mathrm{km\,nm})$ although large, is still sufficiently low to enable all-optical wavelength conversion at 42.7 Gbit/s [370] and demultiplexing at 170.8 Gbit/s [297] in a 4 mm long slot waveguide. All experimental results are summarized in Table 3.2.

3.3.3 Device Dynamics

To characterize the nonlinear dynamics, pump-probe measurements were performed. Simultaneous measurements of amplitude and phase dynamics allow to determine the two-photon absorption figure of merit (1.3.37) with high precision and without any free parameters like the effective area $A_{\mathrm{eff}}^{(3)}$. In order to resolve amplitude and phase dynamics of the proposed waveguide designs, we have used a heterodyne pump-probe technique [97].

In the pump-probe setup a strong pump pulse induces nonlinearities in the waveguide, at a center wavelength of 1550 nm. A weak probe pulse launched after the pump pulse then experiences changes in the amplitude transmission and the refractive index of the waveguide. By superimposing the probe pulse with a local reference pulse in an unbalanced Michelson interferometer, a beating signal is created in a photodiode. A lock-in amplifier is then used to resolve the amplitude and phase information. By changing the time delay between pump and probe pulses, we are able to sample the device dynamics with sub-picosecond resolution.

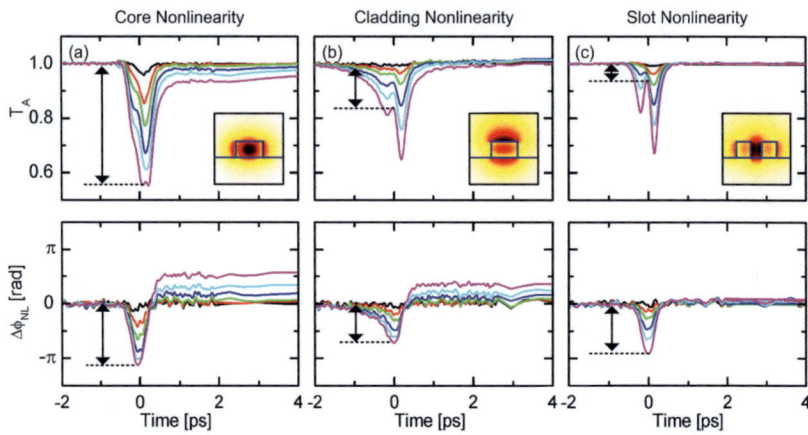

Fig. 3.13   Amplitude transmission T_A and phase $\Delta\phi_{NL}$ dynamics of the highly nonlinear waveguides for different pump power levels. All waveguides show strong Kerr nonlinearities. (a) However, the silicon *core nonlinearity* waveguide shows strong two-photon absorption accompanied by simultaneous strong free-carrier absorption. The experiment leads to a figure of merit $\text{FOM}_{\text{TPA}} = 0.38 \pm 0.17$. (b) The waveguide with *cladding nonlinearity* shows a significantly lower detrimental TPA effect. It has a $\text{FOM}_{\text{TPA}} = 1.21 \pm 0.19$. (c) Waveguide with *slot nonlinearity* showing a Kerr nonlinearity with nearly no two-photon absorption, negligible free carrier absorption, and a $\text{FOM}_{\text{TPA}} = 2.19 \pm 0.25$.

Fig. 3.13 shows amplitude transmission T_A and phase $\Delta\phi_{NL}$ dynamics of the three highly nonlinear waveguides. All waveguides show strong Kerr nonlinearities, the main difference is in the strength of the two-photon absorption and the amount of long lasting changes due to generated free carriers.

Pump-probe measurements of the silicon *core nonlinearity* in Fig. 3.13(a) show strong two-photon absorption and strong free-carrier absorption at the same time. This leads to a figure of merit of $\text{FOM}_{\text{TPA}} = 0.38 \pm 0.17$, in good agreement with values found for unclad silicon waveguides [345, 377]. As a side effect of the strong two-photon absorption, free carriers with a life time of 1.2 ns are generated, leading to free-carrier absorption and slow phase change due to the plasma effect. For high speed applications, free carriers will accumulate, thereby reducing the nonlinear effect and leading to patterning effects.

The waveguide with *cladding nonlinearity* is shown in Fig. 3.13(b). As only a minor fraction of the intensity is still guided in the silicon, the detrimental effects are already reduced and the figure of merit is improved to $\text{FOM}_{\text{TPA}} = 1.21 \pm 0.19$. At high peak power, smaller numbers of free carriers are generated, leading to a reduced plasma effect. The two lobes visible in the transmission dynamics are the spectral artifact due to the rapid phase change, as explained in Fig. 1.7 in Section 1.5.3.

Waveguides with *slot nonlinearity* in Fig. 3.13(c) show a strong Kerr nonlinearity with nearly no two-photon absorption and negligible free carrier absorption. The two-photon absorption figure of merit is $\text{FOM}_{\text{TPA}} = 2.19 \pm 0.25$, which enables all-optical signal processing at highest bit rates [297]. Though, while the nonlinearity parameter of the silicon strip waveguide with core nonlinearity is higher, the nonlinearity of the slot geometry shows much smaller nonlinear losses and thus a much better scalability with peak power.

Fig. 3.14 shows the inverse power transmission for a 390 nm wide silicon strip waveguide. By using the measured dispersion of $D_2 = -4400\,\text{ps}/(\text{km\,nm})$ (see Table 3.2) to calculate the average peak power, an effective area of $0.092\mu\text{m}^2$, and an effective length of $L_{\text{eff}} = 2.5\,\text{mm}$, the imaginary part of γ due to two-photon absorption is calculated from the slope of a linear fit to a value of $\text{Im}\{\underline{\gamma}\} = -41.6/(\text{W\,m})$. Since all the TPA originates form the silicon core, and since the effective area within the core is known, we can derive the TPA-coefficient of silicon, $\alpha_2 = 0.8\,\text{cm/GW}$. This is in good agreement with previous work [6, 19]. As the pulse width in the waveguide can only be estimated with an uncertainty of 20%, the total error for α_2 is $\pm 0.2\,\text{cm/GW}$. However, for the calculation of the figure of merit in Eq. (1.5.24), these and other inaccuracies (e. g., for $A_{\text{eff}}^{(3)}$) cancel.

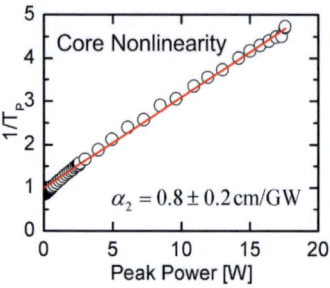

Fig. 3.14 Measured inverse power transmission $1/T_P$ of a silicon strip waveguide with core nonlinearity as a function of the on-chip peak power. For an effective waveguide length of $L_{\text{eff}} = 2.5\,\text{mm}$, the two-photon absorption coefficient is calculated from the slope of a linear fit to a value of $\alpha_2 = (0.8 \pm 0.2)\,\text{cm/GW}$.

3.3.4 Summary

Highly nonlinear silicon waveguides with core, cladding and slot nonlinearity have been fabricated. Key parameters have been analyzed and are summarized in Table 3.2. As each design shows characteristic advantages, the optimum design strongly depends on the intended application.

For applications at repetition rates below 1 GHz or if signal distortion due to free carrier effects can be tolerated, pure silicon strip waveguides with *core nonlinearity* are the easiest solution. By confining the light to small waveguide cross-sections, very high nonlinearity parameters can be reached, up to a record value measured in silicon of $\gamma = (307\,000 \pm 17\,000)/(\text{W km})$. However, this high value of the nonlinearity parameter is resonantly enhanced, and the fundamental two-photon absorption limitation for switching applications cannot be overcome. The waveguides are easy to fabricate and show low dispersion. By engineering the waveguide dimensions to optimize the zero dispersion wavelength, highly efficient wavelength conversion is possible [391].

For applications that simultaneously require good conversion efficiency, a high figure of merit and multi-wavelength operation, waveguides with *cladding nonlinearity* are the optimum design. Strip waveguides are easy to fabricate and easy to cover with nonlinear cladding materials. The figure of merit with a value of $\text{FOM}_{\text{TPA}} = 1.21 \pm 0.19$ is sufficient for all-optical switching. Because the electric field in TM mode is oriented perpendicularly to the wafer surface, even cladding materials which have very high nonlinear refractive indices but are difficult to deposit could be used, possibly increasing the nonlinearity parameter by a factor of 10 [367]. The significant waveguide dispersion can be even used to limit the nonlinear interaction to a detuning of 5 nm, enabling multi-wavelength operation.

For high speed applications, waveguides with *slot nonlinearity* will provide the best signal quality. The light is strongly confined to the slot, so two-photon absorption and associated free carrier effects in silicon can be avoided. Silicon-organic hybrid slot waveguides are highly nonlinear showing potential for nonlinearity parameters beyond $10^6/(\text{W km})$. In addition, they exhibit the best figure of merit of $\text{FOM}_{\text{TPA}} = 2.19 \pm 0.25$ reported for CMOS-compatible waveguides. As this allows the use of high peak powers, the waveguide length can be kept small, and phase mismatch due to dispersion is negligible, thus enabling all-optical signal processing at highest bit rates [297]. Future improvements in the fabrication process will reduce the limiting propagation loss and allow the move to even smaller slot widths, significantly increasing the confinement to the slot. In combination with improved nonlinear cladding materials, this will enable all-optical switching in millimeter-long devices.

Table 3.2 Dimensions and optical properties of basic silicon-organic hybrid waveguide designs determined from four-wave mixing and heterodyne pump-probe experiments at a center wavelength of $\lambda = 1.55\mu\text{m}$. For the definition of the dimensions see Fig. 3.3. *: Effective areas of silicon and nonlinear cladding material are obtained from a finite-element simulation.

Design	Core	Cladding	Slot
$\text{Re}\{\underline{\gamma}\}$ [1/(W km)]	307 000±17 000	108 000±17 000	100 000±13 000
FOM_{TPA}	0.38±0.17	1.21±0.19	2.19±0.25
D_2 [ps/(km nm)]	-4350±150	-18000±2300	-7000±400
α_0 [dB/mm]	1.1±0.1	1.0±0.1	1.5±0.1
a_{cp} [dB/facet]	8.8±0.2	7.5±0.2	5.0±1.0
h [nm]	220	220	220
w_{strip} [nm]	360...400	360...400	220
w_{slot} [nm]	0	0	160...200
$A^{(3)}_{\text{eff,Si}}$ [μm^2]	0.09*	0.39*	0.89*
$A^{(3)}_{\text{eff,NL}}$ [μm^2]	1.25*	0.39*	0.29*

3.4 Applications

Wavelength conversion is one of the corner stones of all-optical signal processing. While devices like semiconductor optical amplifiers or highly nonlinear fibers have been successfully used for some time [392], the research effort for silicon compatible wavelength converters that offer on-chip integration has been considerably increased [382, 383, 393]. However, all pure silicon implementations to date suffer from two-photon absorption (TPA) and free-carrier absorption (FCA) effects. Additional technological measures like a p-i-n structure are needed to mitigate these effects and scale to bit rates of 40 Gbit/s [265]. Combining the waveguiding properties of silicon with third order nonlinearities from organic cladding materials offers a technologically feasibly alternative that avoids free-carrier effects completely [298].

Of the third-order nonlinear effects, cross-phase modulation (XPM) and four-wave mixing (FWM) are of particular importance. All experiments demonstrated in this section represent the current state of the art in all-optical wavelength conversion in silicon waveguides.

XPM enables wavelength transparent switching and does not suffer from phase-mismatch. The wavelength conversion experiment demonstrated in Section 3.4.1 is the first proof-of-principle of XPM at communication wavelengths and speeds.

FWM is a versatile effect which creates signals at new wavelengths. As amplitude and phase information of the input signal are preserved, wavelength conversion of amplitude-shift keying (ASK) and phase-shift keying (PSK) signals is possible. In Section 3.4.2, wavelength conversion at 42.7 Gbit/s using FWM is demonstrated. As no patterning effects are found in slot waveguides, signal processing at highest bitrates becomes possible. Results on demultiplexing of 170 Gbit/s down to 42.7 Gbit/s are presented in Section 3.4.3. Finally, wavelength conversion of advanced modulation formats is demonstrated. The results on the conversion of 56 Gbit/s non-return-to-zero differential quadrature phase-shift keying (NRZ-DQPSK) data presented in Section 3.4.4 is the fastest wavelength conversion ever reported for silicon waveguides.

The highly nonlinear silicon-organic hybrid slot waveguides used for all wavelength conversion experiments are based on silicon-on-insulator (SOI) technology in the 193 nm deep-UV process offered by ePIXfab [271]. On a buried oxide buffer silicon strip waveguides and slot waveguides are formed with a height of 220 nm. The waveguides are covered with molecular beam deposited DDMEBT (2-[4-(dimethylamino)phenyl]-3-{[4-(dimethylamino)phenyl]ethynyl}buta-1,3-diene-1,1,4,4-tetracarbonitrile), an offresonant Kerr-type nonlinear organic cladding with a refractive index of $n = 1.8$ [295]. Waveguide facets are as cleaved and no anti-reflection coating is applied, leading to a coupling loss of 6...8 dB per facet. The linear propagation loss for strip and slot waveguides is 1.0 dB/mm and 1.55 dB/mm, respectively. For a typical device length of 4 mm this amounts to a total fiber-to-fiber loss of 18...20 dB.

3.4.1 Wavelength Conversion using Cross-Phase Modulation [C16]

Highly nonlinear waveguides are key components for on-chip integration of all-optical signal processing. Among the nonlinear effects, cross-phase modulation (XPM) is of great importance. It enables switching operation with virtually unlimited speed across a large spectral range, because there is no phase-matching restriction for XPM such as with four-wave mixing (FWM). So far, XPM in silicon has only been studied at low repetition rates, using pump-probe measurements that clearly show speed limitations imposed by two-photon absorption and free carrier effects [29, 394, 395]. Very recently NRZ-OOK to RZ-OOK conversion using XPM has been demonstrated in a pure silicon waveguide, limited to 10 Gbit/s [396]. Silicon waveguides with hybridly integrated nonlinear organic cladding materials offer a way to overcome these speed limitations [396].

The wavelength conversion experiment reported here is the first time error-free all-optical wavelength conversion at 42.7 Gbit/s based on XPM, using a 4 mm long highly $\chi^{(3)}$-nonlinear silicon-organic hybrid (SOH) slot waveguide for cross-phase modulation, and a tuneable one-bit delay interferometer (DI) for phase-to-amplitude conversion. The measured bit-error ratio (BER) of $\text{BER} = 2 \times 10^{-10}$ demonstrates error-free operation and underlines the potential of silicon-organic hybrid waveguides for all-optical switching applications.

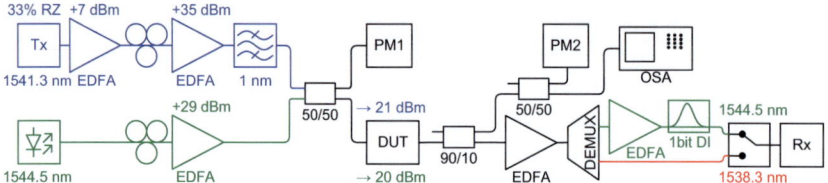

Fig. 3.15   Experimental setup for wavelength conversion of 42.7 Gbit/s data using either cross-phase modulation or four-wave mixing. A pseudo-random bit sequence (PRBS) of 33% RZ-OOK pulses is highly amplified, combined with a strong cw wave, and the composite signal is launched into the device under test (DUT) using lensed fibers. The $\chi^{(3)}$-nonlinearity of the waveguide causes a cross phase modulation (XPM) of the cw wave via the intensity of the data stream. At the same time new signals are created by four-wave mixing (FWM). Either one FWM signal or the XPM signal can be selected by the switch. A one-bit delay interferometer (DI) is used for phase-to-amplitude conversion of the XPM signal. A receiver with a pre-amplifier and a bit-error ratio tester are used to evaluate the signal quality. EDFA: Er-doped fiber amplifier, PMx: power meter, OSA: optical spectrum analyzer.

The experimental setup is shown in Fig. 3.15. A pseudo-random bit sequence (PRBS) of 42.7 Gbit/s 33% RZ-OOK pulses are highly amplified and band-pass filtered to suppress the out-of-band amplifier noise. Using a 3 dB coupler and short lensed fibers, the data stream is combined with a strong cw laser, and then launched into the nonlinear SOH waveguide. The 160 nm wide slot is formed by two silicon ribs of height 220 nm and width 220 nm, covered by DDMEBT [295]. On-chip power levels for data and cw are 21 dBm and 20 dBm, respectively. The phase of the cw is modulated via the intensity of the data stream by means of the $\chi^{(3)}$-nonlinearity of the waveguide. After amplification, the cross-phase modulated cw wave is band-pass filtered, amplified and launched into a tuneable one-bit delay interferometer for phase-to-amplitude conversion. Although the delay interferometer performs a differentiation of the data, in the experiment no data encoder circuit was employed. To allow bit-error ratio measurements, the error detector is programmed with the expected data sequence, which allows a pseudo-random bit sequence (PRBS) length of up to 2^9-1. A pre-amplified receiver is used to detect the signal in an optical bandwidth of 50 GHz or 70 GHz using a digital communications analyzer or a bit-error ratio tester, respectively.

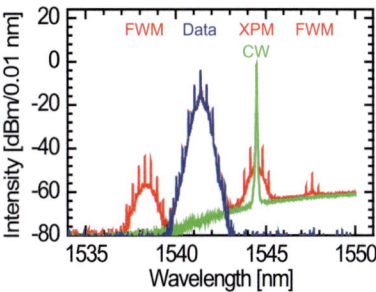

Fig. 3.16 Signal spectrum at the output of the nonlinear SOH waveguide. When data (blue) and cw (green) are launched together, the total spectrum (red) clearly shows the XPM signal as well as up and down-converted FWM signals.

Fig. 3.16 shows the spectrum of the data, the cw, and the total signal at the output of the nonlinear waveguide. Both the XPM spectrum and the up and down-converted FWM spectra (plotted in red) are clearly visible and can be detected after appropriate filtering. For further analysis, the achieved nonlinear phase shift can be determined by comparing the XPM spectrum to simulation results, as discussed in Section 1.3.4.

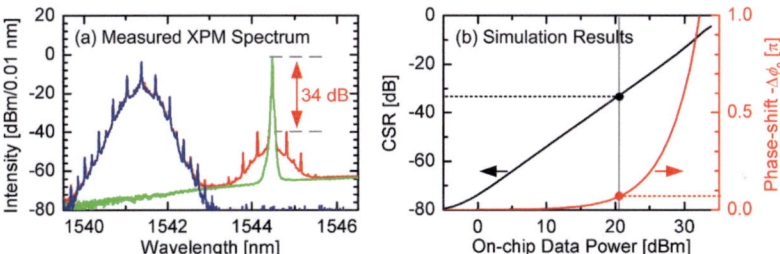

Fig. 3.17 Analysis of XPM phase shift. (a) The measured spectrum shows a carrier-to-sideband ratio (CSR) of 34 dB for an average on-chip data power of 21 dBm.   (b) Simulation results for XPM of a 33% RZ-OOK signal in a slot waveguide with parameters of $\mathrm{Re}\{\gamma\} = 100000\,(\mathrm{Wkm})^{-1}$, $L = 4\,\mathrm{mm}$, $\alpha_0 = 1.5\,\mathrm{dB/mm}$. For an on-chip power of 21 dBm, simulations predict the same CSR of 34 dB, which corresponds to a nonlinear phase shift of $\Delta\varphi_0 = -0.06\pi$.

Fig. 3.17(a) shows the optical spectrum measured at the output of the nonlinear waveguide. For an average on-chip data power of 21 dBm, a carrier-to-sideband ratio of 34 dB is measured, see Eq. (1.3.31). Fig. 3.17(b) compares the measured data to simulation results for XPM of a 33% RZ-OOK signal in a slot waveguide with parameters of $\mathrm{Re}\{\gamma\} = 100\,000\,(\mathrm{Wkm})^{-1}$, $L = 4\,\mathrm{mm}$, $\alpha_0 = 1.5\,\mathrm{dB/mm}$.

For an on-chip power of 21 dBm, simulations predict the same CSR of 34 dB, which corresponds to a nonlinear phase-shift of $\Delta\varphi_0 = -0.06\pi$. Although this phase-shift is small, it is ultrafast in nature and can be considerably improved by reducing the coupling loss and by using optimized slot waveguide geometries with smaller slot width.

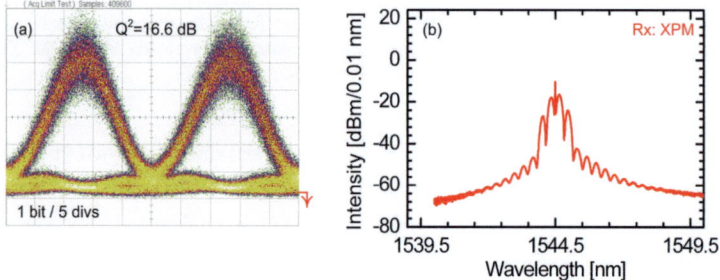

Fig. 3.18 (a) Received cross-phase modulated signal with a quality factor of $Q^2 = 16.6\,\mathrm{dB}$ and a simultaneously measured bit-error ratio of $\mathrm{BER} = 2\times10^{-10}$. (b) Received spectrum of the wavelength converted signal, showing a strongly suppressed carrier and characteristic AMI side lobes. No crosstalk from the original data signal at 1541 nm or the four-wave mixing products is found.

To detect the XPM data, the phase-encoded signal needs to be converted into an amplitude-encoded signal in the receiver. Fig. 3.18(a) shows the eye diagram in the pre-amplified receiver connected to the destructive port of the delay interferometer which was used for phase-to-amplitude conversion. The eye has a good quality factor of $Q^2 = 16.6\,\mathrm{dB}$ (see Appendix A.2) and a bit-error ratio of $\mathrm{BER} = 2\times10^{-10}$. No dependence on the PRBS length between 2^7-1 bits and 2^{31}-1 bits has been observed. Fig. 3.18(b) shows the received optical spectrum after narrow-band filtering in the receiver. It shows a strongly suppressed carrier and the expected shape of an alternate mark inversion (AMI) signal.

Error-free operation and a wide eye opening demonstrate the absence of strong patterning effects. This proves the suitability of silicon-organic hybrid waveguides for XPM-based all-optical switching applications.

3.4.2 Wavelength Conversion of Amplitude-Shift Keying Signals

The wavelength conversion of ASK signals reported here is the first wavelength conversion devoid of any patterning effects. All-optical wavelength conversion of 42.7 Gbit/s return-to-zero data is achieved using four-wave mixing in a 4 mm long silicon-organic hybrid waveguide. No patterning effects are observed and the signal quality is only limited by OSNR.

3.4.2.1 Wavelength Conversion of 33% RZ-OOK Signals

Compared to wavelength conversion by cross-phase modulation (XPM), the use of four-wave mixing (FWM) has distinct advantages. FWM products of amplitude-shift keying (ASK) signals also have an ASK format, which allows for straightforward direct detection. As these FWM products are generated at new wavelengths, appropriate filtering of the input wavelengths can improve the optical signal-to-noise ratio considerably. While phase matching usually is a big concern for FWM in highly nonlinear fibers (HNLF), the phase-matching length of SOH waveguides exceeds the effective length even for high dispersion values.

The experimental setup is identical to the one which is shown in Fig. 3.15 and discussed in Section 3.4.1. The device under test consists of a 160 nm wide slot, formed by two silicon ribs of height 220 nm and width 220 nm and covered by DDMEBT [295]. On-chip power levels for data and cw are 21 dBm and 20 dBm, respectively. As no format conversion is involved, the 1538.3 nm channel is selected in the DWDM demultiplexer and received in the preamplified receiver using direct detection.

Fig. 3.19(a) shows the received eye diagram of the four-wave mixing signal with a quality factor of $Q^2 = 18.0$ dB. Error-free operation is confirmed by bit-error ratio measurements, BER $= 8 \cdot 10^{-10}$. Fig. 3.19(b) shows the optical spectrum of the wavelength converted signal in the pre-amplified receiver. No crosstalk from the original data signal at 1541 nm is found. However, due to an imperfect transmitter, a weak 20 GHz component is visible in the spectrum and in the eye diagram.

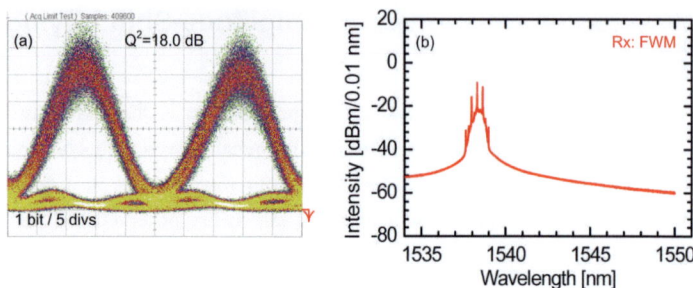

Fig. 3.19 (a) Received eye diagram of the four-wave mixing signal with a quality factor of $Q^2 = 18.0$ dB. Error-free operation is confirmed by bit-error ratio measurements, BER $= 8 \cdot 10^{-10}$. (b) Received spectrum of the wavelength converted signal. No crosstalk from the original data signal at 1541 nm is found.

The eye quality factor and the bit-error ratio are limited by amplifier noise and could be improved by a photodiode with a bandwidth smaller than 70 GHz. Decreasing the propagation loss of the nonlinear waveguide would increase the nonlinear effect and increase the output power at the same time, which would also improve the OSNR considerably.

3.4.2.2 Wavelength Conversion of 2.2 ps Mode-Locked Laser Signals [C17]

The real need for all-optical signal processing arises for communication at bitrates of 100 Gbit/s and above. Many technologies have been shown to work up to 40 Gbit/s, which corresponds to a typical time scale of 25 ps, but only few are able to work with mode-locked laser (MLL) pulses of a few picoseconds duration. In order to be able to achieve demultiplexing of high-bitrate optical time-division multiplexing (OTDM) streams, wavelength conversion, or even 3R (reamplification, reshaping, retiming) regeneration, a nonlinear medium is needed that does not exhibit patterning effects, even when operated with high-power MLL pulse streams.

The all-optical wavelength conversion experiment presented here shows that silicon-organic hybrid (SOH) slot waveguides are suitable for all-optical wavelength conversion. The absence of any patterning effects confirms the ultrafast device dynamics discussed in Section 3.3.3.

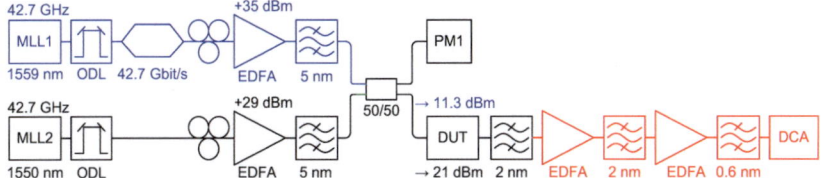

Fig. 3.20 Experimental setup of the wavelength conversion experiment. Mode-locked laser (MLL1) pulses are modulated at 42.7 Gbit/s. A second mode-locked laser (MLL2) provides a clock signal. Optical delay lines (ODL) are used to synchronize the pulse streams. Both signals are amplified, band-pass filtered and launched into the device under test (DUT) using polarization-maintaining lensed fibers. The four-wave mixing signal is amplified, band-pass filtered and detected with a digital communications analyzer (DCA).

Fig. 3.20 shows the setup of the wavelength conversion experiment. Mode-locked laser (MLL1) pulses at 1559 nm are modulated with a pseudorandom (2^{31}-1 bit) RZ signal at 42.7 Gbit/s ($Q^2 > 21$ dB). A second mode-locked laser (MLL2) at 1550 nm provides the clock pulses at a repetition rate of 42.7 GHz. The pulse width of both sources is approximately 2.2 ps. Optical delay lines (ODL) are used to synchronize the pulse streams. Both signals are amplified and band-pass filtered to suppress the strong amplified spontaneous emission (ASE) from both booster amplifiers. Using polarization-maintaining lensed fibers the TE polarized pulses are launched into the device under test (DUT), reaching maximum on-chip power levels of 21.0 dBm for the clock and 11.3 dBm for the data signal. The 157 nm wide and 4 mm long slot waveguide is formed by two silicon ribs of height 220 nm and width 216 nm. All waveguides are filled and covered with molecular beam deposited DDMEBT [295].

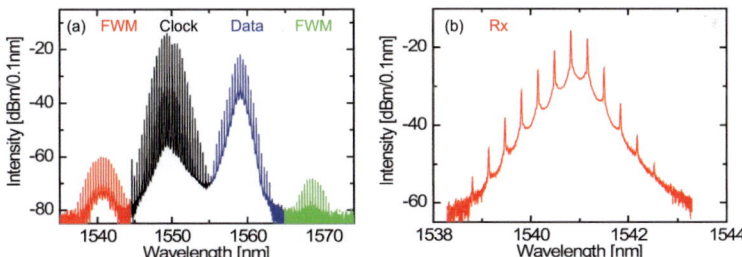

Fig. 3.21 Optical four-wave mixing spectra of 42.7 Gbit/s mode-locked laser pulse stream with a 42.7 GHz clock signal, measured (a) at the output of the nonlinear waveguide and (b) in the receiver after all band-pass filters. The FWM signal at 1541 nm was chosen to avoid cross-talk from the strong data pulses.

Fig. 3.21(a) shows the optical spectrum at the output of the nonlinear waveguide. Both four-wave mixing signals can be clearly observed. In order to avoid cross-talk from the strong data signal, the converted signal at 1541 nm is then amplified and filtered with a 0.6 nm narrow band-pass to avoid ringing in the photodiode., The resulting spectrum is shown in Fig. 3.21(b). A digital communications analyzer (DCA) with a bandwidth of 53 GHz is used to detect the signal. Compared to the 33% RZ-OOK wavelength conversion experiment, for data modulated onto short MLL pulses the use of a bandwidth-limited receiver carries a certain penalty.

For transform-limited Gaussian pulses of $T = 2.2\,\mathrm{ps}$ duration, a bandwidth of $B = 0.44/T = 200\,\mathrm{GHz}$ is needed. As short pulses increase the peak power, all nonlinear effects–including two-photon absorption–are increased. But as the input pulse spectrum is considerably larger compared to the spectrum of 33% RZ pulses, the power of the wavelength-converted signal is distributed over a larger part of the spectrum as well. In the bandwidth limited receiver, only part of the wavelength-converted signal can be used for detection, but all distortions due to patterning effects can degrade the quality of the received signal. If no patterning effects are found for very short optical pulse sequences, no inherently slow processes can be present, even for other communication signals.

The measurement results for the wavelength-converted signal are shown in Fig. 3.22. The eye diagram in Fig. 3.22(a) shows an open eye with a quality factor of $Q^2 = 11.3$ dB. Distortions of the 0-rail are due to the limited bandwidth of the DCA and weak cross-talk from the clock. For the bit sequences (PRBS of 2^{15}-1 bit) shown in Fig. 3.22(b)–(d) no pattern dependence is observed, which can be fully explained by the absence of free-carrier effects. The signal quality is only limited by OSNR degradations due to amplifier noise. This limitation could be easily overcome by increasing the input power to the nonlinear waveguide.

All-optical wavelength conversion at 42.7 Gbit/s over 18 nm in a passive 4 mm long CMOS-compatible device has been demonstrated. The quality of the received signal was only limited by amplifier noise. No pattern effects have been found. Increasing the input power will enable error free operation and allow nonlinear silicon-organic hybrid slot waveguides to scale to highest bit rates.

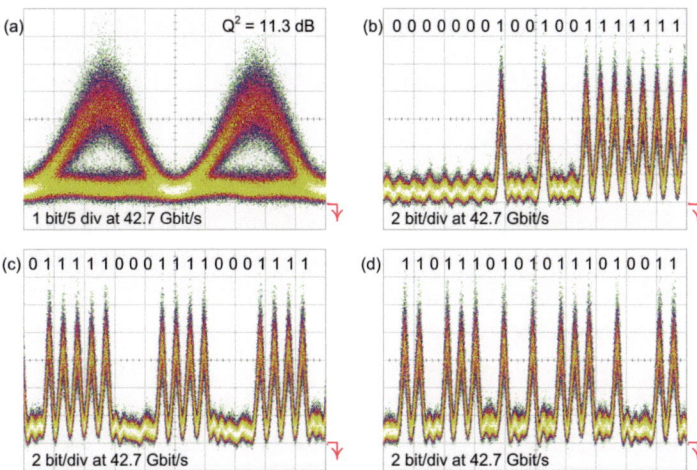

Fig. 3.22 (a) Eye diagram of the four-wave mixing signal at 1541 nm with a quality factor of $Q^2 = 11.3$ dB. Distortions of the 0-rail are due to the limited bandwidth of the DCA and weak cross-talk from the clock. (b)-(c) Bit sequences with different characteristics. No pattern dependence is observed. The eye quality is only limited by the OSNR due to amplifier noise.

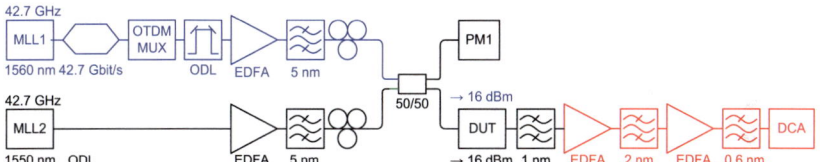

Fig. 3.23 Experimental setup of the demultiplexing experiment; MLL1, MLL2: mode-locked lasers; OTDM-Mux: optical time-division multiplexer; ODL: tuneable optical delay line, EDFA: erbium-doped fiber amplifier; DUT: device under test; DCA: digital communications analyzer.

3.4.3 Demultiplexing 170 Gbit/s to 42.7 Gbit/s [J5]

To demonstrate the viability of silicon-organic hybrid (SOH) slot waveguides for ultrafast all-optical processing of broadband telecommunication signals, we performed demultiplexing of a 120.0 Gbit/s (170.8 Gbit/s) return-to-zero (RZ-OOK) data stream to 10 Gbit/s (42.7 Gbit/s) using partially degenerate four-wave mixing (FWM). As demultiplexing in the electronic domain would take considerable effort and power, our all-optical approach is a proof-of-principle experiment that highlights the potential for energy efficient all-optical signal processing offered by the silicon-organic hybrid technology.

The experimental setup is depicted in Fig. 3.23. For the data and pump we used two synchronized mode-locked fiber lasers operating at repetition rates of 40.0 GHz (42.7 GHz) and emitting pulses of approximately 3 ps FWHM. The temporal overlap of signal and pump was adjusted by a tuneable optical delay. The 120.0 Gbit/s (170.8 Gbit/s) data stream was generated by modulating the basic 40.0 GHz (42.7 GHz) pulse train with a pseudo-random bit sequence (2^{31}-1 bit) and by subsequent optical time-division multiplexing. Data and pump were both amplified and coupled into a SOH slot waveguide of height $h = 220$ nm, strip width $w = 212$ nm, slot width $w_{slot} = 205$ nm, and geometrical waveguide length $L = 6.0$ mm ($L = 4.0$ mm). The propagation loss was $\alpha_0 = 1.5$ dB/mm and the fiber-chip coupling loss was $a_{cp} = 4.1$ dB/facet at 1550 nm.

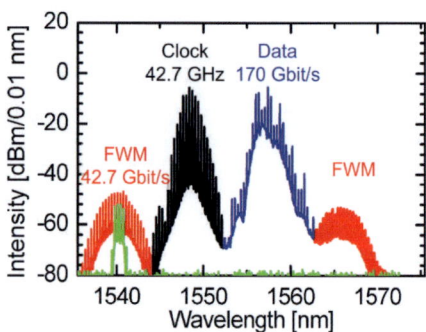

Fig. 3.24 Signal spectrum at the output of the nonlinear SOH waveguide. When 170 Gbit/s data (blue) and the 42.7 GHz clock are launched together, four-wave mixing creates new spectral components (red). The demultiplexed 42.7 Gbit/s signal is then filtered (green) and detected in the receiver.

The signal at the output of the SOH waveguide was bandpass-filtered at the converted wavelength and detected in a pre-amplified receiver. Fig. 3.24 shows the signal spectrum at the output of the nonlinear SOH waveguide. When 170 Gbit/s data (blue) and the 42.7 GHz clock are launched together, four-wave mixing creates new spectral components (red). The demultiplexed 42.7 Gbit/s signal is then filtered (green) and detected in the receiver.

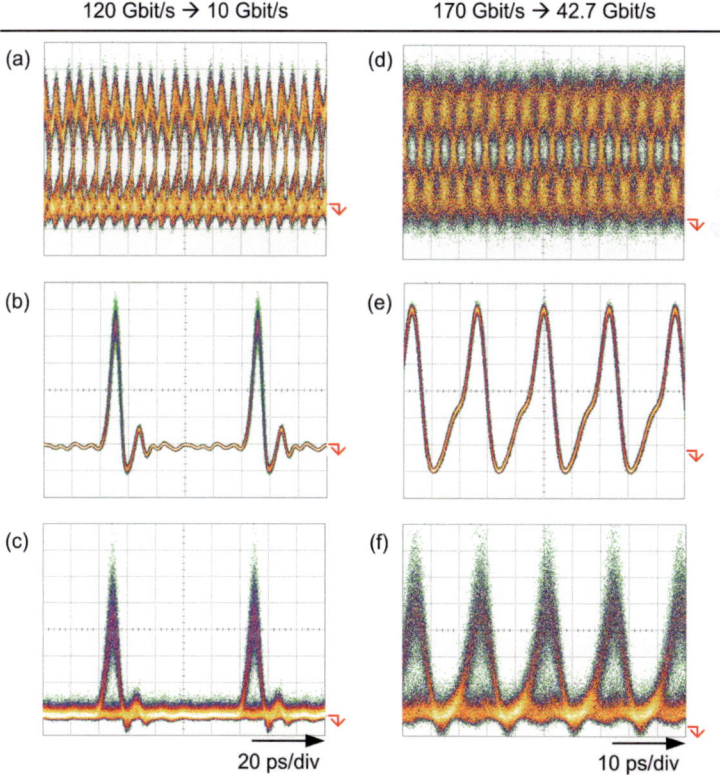

Fig. 3.25 Eye diagrams of demultiplexing experiments: (a) 120 Gbit/s signal, (b) 10 GHz pump, (c) demultiplexed 10 Gbit/s signal. (d) 170.8 Gbit/s signal, (e) 42.7 GHz pump, (f) demultiplexed 42.7 Gbit/s signal.

For both the 120 Gbit/s and the 172.8 Gbit/s experiments the optical signals were detected with a 120 GHz photodiode, and the eye diagrams were recorded using a digital communication analyzer (DCA). The eye diagrams of the respective data signals are depicted in Fig. 3.25, (a) 120 Gbit/s signal, (b) 10 GHz pump, (c) demultiplexed 10 Gbit/s signal. (d) 170.8 Gbit/s signal, (e) 42.7 GHz pump, (f) demultiplexed 42.7 Gbit/s signal. The average on-chip pump-power was $P_{1,pump} = 15.2\,dBm$ ($P_{1,pump} = 16.6\,dBm$). By varying the delay between the pump and the signal, different tributaries could be demultiplexed. Similar performances were found for the different tributaries. For the 120 Gbit/s experiment, a quality factor of $Q^2 = 11.1$ dB was measured.

Due to the limited electronic bandwidth of the photodiode and the DCA, the eye diagrams are noticeably distorted. The noise in the converted eye diagram is predominantly caused by amplified spontaneous emission (ASE) originating from the amplifiers (EDFA) after the DUT. The signal-to-noise ratio is lower for the 172.8 Gbit/s-to-42.7 Gbit/s demultiplexing experiment since the received energy per bit is less than for demultiplexing 120.0 Gbit/s to 10.0 Gbit/s.

This is the fastest all-optical signal processing experiment in a silicon waveguide to day. Signal quality and conversion efficiency still have a lot of potential for optimization, e.g. by improving the fiber-chip coupling, by reducing the waveguide loss, and by optimizing the waveguide geometry for maximum nonlinearity. The dispersion of the SOH slot waveguide is dominated by waveguide dispersion and can therefore be mitigated by appropriate waveguide design. It can further be expected that the converted signal experiences retiming due to the strictly periodic pump pulse train. The demonstrated demultiplexing scheme preserves both phase and amplitude information and is therefore transparent with respect to the modulation format.

3.4.4 Wavelength Conversion of Phase-Shift Keying Signals [C9]

Highly nonlinear waveguides are key components for on-chip integration of all-optical signal processing. Waveguides with ultrafast Kerr nonlinearity enable switching operation and wavelength conversion with virtually unlimited speed. Among the nonlinear effects found in waveguides, four-wave mixing (FWM) is special as it preserves the phase information and allows format-transparent operation [382, 391, 397]. Especially for advanced modulation formats, which are needed to increase the spectral efficiency [253], phase-preserving wavelength converters are needed.

For the silicon-organic hybrid (SOH) waveguide technology no fundamental speed limitation has been found, possibly scaling to bitrates up to 170 Gbit/s and beyond [297]. Of the basic silicon-organic waveguide geometries discussed in Section 3.2.2 [369], strip waveguides operated in TM mode are of particular interest, as they effectively exploit the cladding nonlinearity with nonlinearity parameters of $\mathrm{Re}\{\gamma\} = 110\,000\,(\mathrm{Wkm})^{-1}$, and are easy to fabricate [271]. Here, for the first time all-optical high-speed wavelength conversion of a phase-encoded signal is demonstrated, based on four-wave mixing in a 4 mm long silicon-organic hybrid strip waveguide operated in TM mode. The bitrate of 56 Gbit/s this is the fastest wavelength conversion reported for silicon waveguides, limited only by the available measurement equipment. Compared to previous results reported for waveguides with slot nonlinearity, strip waveguides operated in TM mode exploit the nonlinearity of the cladding material and have the advantage of a greatly reduced complexity in fabrication. Silicon-organic hybrid waveguides provide CMOS compatible nonlinearities for all-optical signal processing at highest bit rates.

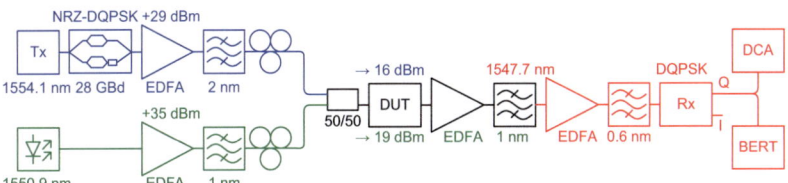

Fig. 3.26   Experimental setup of the NRZ-DQPSK all-optical wavelength conversion experiment. Data encoded at 28 GBd NRZ-DQPSK are amplified, bandpass filtered, combined with a strong cw pump, and launched into the device under test (DUT) using polarization-maintaining lensed fibers. The four-wave mixing signal is amplified, bandpass filtered and demodulated in a balanced receiver. The eye opening is monitored with a digital communications analyzer (DCA). The received signal is analyzed using a bit-error ratio tester (BERT).

Degenerate four-wave mixing is a parametric process frequently exploited for format-transparent wavelength conversion. Fig. 3.22 shows the setup of the wavelength conversion experiment. A pseudorandom data stream is encoded at 1554.1 nm using the 28 GBd NRZ-DQPSK format, amplified and band-pass filtered in order to suppress the out-of-band spontaneous emission noise. The signal is combined with a strong cw pump, and launched into the device under test (DUT) in quasi-TM (dominant electric field component parallel to the growth direction) using polarization-maintaining lensed fibers. The nonlinear waveguide has a length of 4 mm and consists of a silicon strip of 220 nm height and 400 nm width, covered by DDMEBT [295]. The on-chip power levels are +19 dBm for the pump and +16 dBm for the signal, respectively. The temperature of the device is controlled to 25°C in order to stabilize the fiber-to-chip coupling. The four-wave mixing signal is amplified, band-pass filtered and demodulated in a DQPSK receiver, consisting of delay interferometers and balanced detectors. The eye opening is monitored with a digital communications analyzer (DCA). Although the delay interferometer performs a differentiation of the data, in the experiment no data encoder circuit was employed. To allow bit-error ratio measurements, the error detector is programmed with the expected data sequence, which allows a pseudo-random bit sequence (PRBS) length of up to 2^9-1. The received signal is analyzed using a bit-error ratio tester (BERT).

In NRZ-DQPSK the information is differentially encoded, using phase shifts of $\{0, \pi/2, \pi, -\pi/2\}$ [253]. While NRZ-DQPSK ideally is a constant-envelope signal, for most practical implementations some state transitions in the constellation diagram cause residual amplitude modulation. Compared to 33% RZ-OOK signals of the same average power, the peak power of NRZ-DQPSK is reduced by 8 dB. However, patterning effects are significantly suppressed, as no long sequences of marks and spaces are possible. In the absence of patterning effects, TPA and FCA only act as additional loss mechanisms and limit the achievable conversion efficiency.

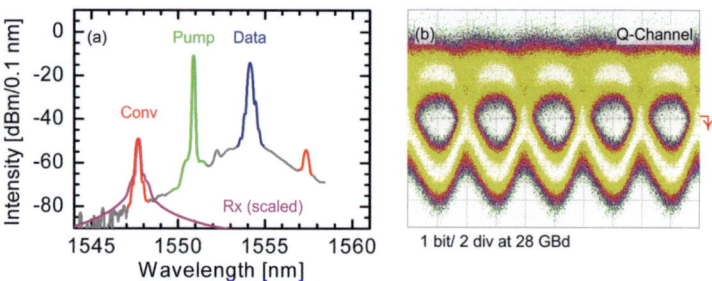

Fig. 3.27 (a) Optical spectra of the four-wave mixing (FWM) experiment, measured at the output of the nonlinear waveguide and in the receiver (Rx, scaled) after both band-pass filters. No crosstalk is observed. (b) Eye diagram of the Q-component of the four-wave mixing signal at 1547.7 nm, corresponding to a bit-error ratio of BER = 10^{-5}. The signal quality is limited only by the OSNR degradations due to amplifier noise.

The measurement results for the wavelength-converted signal are shown in Fig. 3. The optical spectrum at the output of the nonlinear waveguide in Fig. 3.27(a) shows the up-converted and down-converted FWM products. The FWM product at 1547.7 nm is selected for detection in the receiver. No crosstalk is observed. Fig. 3.27(b) shows the demodulated data of the Q-channel corresponding to a bit-error ratio of 10^{-5} measured for a pattern length of 2^7-1, showing no distortions from patterning effects. No influence of the pattern length on the performance is found up to 2^{31}-1. Compared to back-to-back measurements, the signal quality is only limited by OSNR degradations due to amplifier noise. This limitation could be easily overcome by reducing the coupling loss or by increasing the input power to the nonlinear waveguide.

All-optical wavelength conversion of a 56 Gbit/s NRZ-DQPSK signal based on four-wave mixing in a 4 mm long silicon-organic hybrid strip waveguide is demonstrated. The device is operated in TM mode and exploits the nonlinearity of the organic cladding material. Compared to previous results reported for waveguides with slot nonlinearity, strip waveguides operated in TM mode provide high nonlinearity at a greatly reduced complexity in fabrication. By reducing the coupling loss, error free operation will become possible. This allows scaling nonlinear applications to highest bit rates.

3.4.5 Summary

All-optical signal processing at highest bitrates has been demonstrated using silicon-organic hybrid (SOH) waveguides.

Due to their large two-photon absorption figure of merit, slot waveguides have enabled the first proof-of-principle demonstration of cross-phase modulation at communication speeds and wavelengths on a silicon chip.

In slot waveguides, no slow patterning effects have been found. This enables error-free wavelength conversion of 42.7 Gbit/s 33% RZ-OOK signals and demultiplexing of data streams up to 170 Gbit/s using four-wave mixing.

Silicon-organic hybrid strip waveguides with cladding nonlinearity also show a large nonlinearity, yet are easy to fabricate. This has enabled the fastest wavelength conversion experiment at 56 Gbit/s, using four-wave mixing in a SOH waveguide operated in transverse magnetic (TM) mode.

Although there is still a lot room for optimization in terms of linear losses and nonlinear organic cladding materials, current state of the art silicon-organic hybrid waveguides already demonstrate a huge potential for all-optical on-chip signal processing at highest bitrates.

4 Summary and Future Work

Quantum dot semiconductor optical amplifiers and silicon-organic hybrid waveguides are promising approaches to enabling all-optical signal processing at highest bitrates in compact and energy efficient devices.

In this thesis, state of the art quantum dot devices and nonlinear silicon-organic hybrid waveguides have been investigated. By detailed characterization of steady-state and dynamic device properties, advantageous applications have been identified and proof-of-principle experiments have been demonstrated. In this chapter, the key results are summarized and suggestions for future research are given.

Quantum Dot Fabrication

Careful control of the growth parameters allows shifting the quantum dot ground state emission to the 1.3 μm wavelength region. An extensive study of the influence of the growth parameters on quantum dot formation shows that this shift can be attributed to an increase in quantum dot size as well as to strain effects.

Especially the growth of a capping layer strongly influences the composition of the quantum dot. Contrary to previous assumptions, if the composition analysis is corrected for wetting layer effects, a high indium concentration of up to 90% is found at the top of the quantum dot.

In the future, quantum dot growth on pre-patterned substrates could allow for independent control of emission wavelength and inhomogeneous broadening. This additional degree of freedom is highly desirable for engineering the properties of the quantum dot ensemble.

Quantum Dot Semiconductor Optical Amplifier Device Characteristics

Quantum dot semiconductor optical amplifiers had been envisaged as multi-wavelength nonlinear elements at highest bit rates. An evaluation of the suitability for this particular application requires detailed knowledge of the device dynamics and the wavelength dependence of quantum dot devices.

Heterodyne pump-probe spectroscopy is used to investigate the device dynamics. Two characteristic time scales are found, which are attributed to different physical effects. Firstly, a small time constant which is attributed to carrier capture into quantum dots. This fast process that dominates the quantum dot dynamics during the first 10 picoseconds determines mainly the material gain response and shows a very small alpha-factor, i.e. a small chirp. Secondly a large time constant associated with the slow refilling of the wetting layers governs the quantum-dot dynamics in the time frame after 15 ps. It contributes only little to the gain dynamics but since the associated alpha-factor is large it dominates the phase response of the device and may significantly contribute to chirp.

The multi-wavelength operation capability is predicted on the basis of an investigation of the homogeneous linewidth. At room temperature, a value of 16 meV is measured for a quantum dot ensemble with high dot density, which is in very good agreement with theoretical predictions. However, this corresponds to a linewidth of 22 nm or 60% of the total gain bandwidth, which effectively prevents multi-wavelength operation under gain saturation conditions.

As a result, fast processes in quantum dot semiconductor optical amplifiers introduce a chirp, which is too small to efficiently exploit in nonlinear interferometric schemes. On the other hand, quantum dot semiconductor optical amplifiers introduce only small signal distortions, strongly suggesting a use as linear amplifiers.

Applications for Quantum Dot Semiconductor Optical Amplifiers

For nonlinear applications like wavelength conversion or regeneration, quantum dot semiconductor optical amplifiers are not well suited, as they exhibit slow amplitude and phase dynamics for high input power levels. The inherently large homogeneous linewidth prohibits multi-wavelength operation and offers no advantage over conventional bulk and quantum-well semiconductor optical amplifiers.

For linear applications quantum dot semiconductor optical amplifiers combine ultra-fast carrier dynamics with low distortions due to phase effects. In combination with the high gain, the moderate noise figure, and the relative temperature insensitivity, quantum dot semiconductor optical amplifiers fulfill all requirements for in-line amplifiers.

The application as an in-line amplifier of amplitude-shift keying signals is investigated for single and multi-channel cases. A large input power dynamic range with error-free single and multi-wavelength amplification at bit rates from 2.5 Gbit/s to 43 Gbit/s is found. For this wide range of bitrates, quantum dot semiconductor optical amplifiers exceed the performance of specially engineered linear optical amplifiers. For access networks, passive optical networks with quantum dot based range extenders might be a viable solution for providing cost efficient broadband internet access.

As inline amplifiers for phase-shift keying signals, clear advantages of quantum dot semiconductor optical amplifiers over bulk or quantum well semiconductor optical amplifiers are found. The fast amplitude transients in phase-shift keying signals without perfectly constant envelope induce amplitude fluctuations in the semiconductor optical amplifier. These fluctuations induce carrier density fluctuations, which in turn cause refractive index variations and such create phase errors. Due to the fact that the alpha-factor in quantum dot semiconductor optical amplifiers is low, the amplitude to phase conversion is reduced compared to bulk semiconductor optical amplifiers, so less phase errors are introduced.

In the future, engineering and optimization of semiconductor optical amplifier device parameters could allow increasing the input power dynamic range even more, which would allow further extending the reach of an access network. An investigation of the performance with advanced modulation formats could identify modulation formats and network scenarios, for which quantum dot semiconductor optical amplifiers can match the performance of Erbium-doped fiber amplifiers, with significantly reduced cost, device size, and power consumption.

Silicon-Organic Hybrid Waveguide Design

Hybrid integration of silicon waveguides and organic nonlinear cladding materials is a promising approach to create compact and highly nonlinear waveguides in a complementary metal-oxide-semiconductor compatible technology. By confining light to the nonlinear cladding material, silicon-organic hybrid waveguides achieve high nonlinearity parameters and avoid nonlinear impairments by two-photon absorption in silicon. Simulations of the basic silicon-organic hybrid waveguide geometries reveal large differences regarding dispersion, nonlinearity parameter, and figure of merit.

Waveguides with core nonlinearity in general combine low dispersion with large nonlinearity parameters. As the nonlinearity is dominated by the core material, the figure of merit is limited and the nonlinear effect can only be exploited in long devices.

Waveguides with cladding nonlinearity in general show large dispersion values. In combination with the high nonlinearity parameters and sufficient values of the figure of merit, applications as a nonlinear element capable of multi-wavelength operation become possible.

Silicon-organic waveguides with slot nonlinearity avoid two-photon absorption and free-carrier effects nearly completely. The excellent two-photon absorption figure of merit enables all-optical switching at highest bitrates.

Silicon-Organic Hybrid Waveguide Characterization

Highly nonlinear silicon waveguides with core, cladding and slot nonlinearity have been fabricated and key parameters have been analyzed using cut-back measurements, heterodyne pump-probe measurements, and four-wave mixing. In all devices, the theoretically predicted properties are confirmed.

For applications at repetition rates below 1 GHz or if signal distortion due to free carrier effects can be tolerated, pure silicon strip waveguides with *core nonlinearity* are the easiest solution. However, as the nonlinearity is resonantly enhanced, the fundamental two-photon absorption limitation for switching applications cannot be overcome. The waveguides are easy to fabricate and show low dispersion.

For applications that simultaneously require good conversion efficiency, a high figure of merit and multi-wavelength operation, waveguides with *cladding nonlinearity* are the optimum design. Strip waveguides are easy to fabricate and easy to cover with nonlinear cladding materials. The figure of merit is sufficient for all-optical switching. For the cladding, even materials which have very high nonlinear refractive indices but are difficult to deposit could be used, possibly increasing the nonlinearity parameter by a factor of 10.

For high speed applications, waveguides with *slot nonlinearity* will provide the best signal quality as two-photon absorption and associated free carrier effects in silicon can be avoided. Silicon-organic hybrid slot waveguides are highly nonlinear and exhibit the best figure of merit reported for complementary metal-oxide-semiconductor-compatible waveguides. As this allows the use of high peak powers, the waveguide length can be kept small. Phase mismatch due to dispersion is negligible, thus enabling all-optical signal processing at highest bit rates.

In the future, improvements in the fabrication process of the waveguides should have priority. A reduction of the limiting propagation loss will allow the move to even smaller slot widths and significantly increase the confinement to the slot. In combination with improved nonlinear cladding materials, this will enable all-optical switching in millimeter-long devices. On-chip integration with filters and Mach-Zehnder structures will enable further miniaturization of multiple all-optical switches on a single chip.

Applications for Silicon-Organic Hybrid Waveguides

All-optical signal processing at highest bitrates has been demonstrated using silicon-organic hybrid waveguides in proof-of-principle experiments.

Due to their large two-photon absorption figure of merit, slot waveguides have enabled the first proof-of-principle demonstration of cross-phase modulation at communication speeds and wavelengths on a silicon chip.

In slot waveguides, no slow patterning effects are found. This has enables error-free wavelength conversion of 42.7 Gbit/s 33% RZ-OOK signals and demultiplexing of data streams up to 170 Gbit/s using four-wave mixing.

Silicon-organic hybrid strip waveguides with cladding nonlinearity also show a large nonlinearity, yet are easy to fabricate. At 56 Gbit/s, this has enabled the fastest wavelength conversion experiment in silicon photonics, using four-wave mixing in a silicon-organic hybrid waveguide operated in transverse magnetic mode.

In the future, the research should be focused on three main areas. Firstly, the nonlinear effects need to be increased by reducing propagation loss and by improved cladding materials. This will significantly enhance the performance and at the same time reduce device size and energy consumption. Secondly, the ultrafast speed of the Kerr nonlinearity should be emphasized by increasing the speed. To that end, both the use of optical time-division multiplexed data of up to 640 Gbit/s as well as the use of advanced modulation formats, like multi-level quadrature amplitude modulation or orthogonal frequency-division multiplexing, is very promising. Lastly, the multi-wavelength operation of high dispersion waveguides should be investigated in single-pump and multi-pump configurations.

Appendix A.

A.1. Two-Photon Absorption Figure of Merit as Material Parameter

As homogeneous waveguides precede hybrid waveguides by a long time, it is often more common to express the equations for the nonlinear two-photon absorption figure of merit in terms of the material constants n_2 and α_2 (also often designated β_2). This derivation is identical to the derivation in Section 1.5.3, except for the use of n_2 and α_2 in place of the complex nonlinearity parameter γ.

The strong pump signal I_P experiences linear losses α_0 and nonlinear losses α_2 due to two-photon absorption (TPA) and self-phase modulation (SPM) due to the Kerr effect. The change of the intensity $I_P(z)$ and phase $\phi_{P,NL}$ are given by [37]

$$\frac{\mathrm{d}I_P(z)}{\mathrm{d}z} = -\alpha_0 I_P(z) - \alpha_2 I_P^2(z), \qquad (A.1)$$

$$\frac{\mathrm{d}\phi_{P,NL}(z)}{\mathrm{d}z} = -\frac{2\pi}{\lambda} n_2 I_P(z), \qquad (A.2)$$

where α_0 is the linear power loss and λ is the center wavelength. Third order nonlinearities are described by the nonlinear refractive index n_2 and the two-photon absorption coefficient α_2. The intensity of a pump with launch power $I_{P,0}$ then is

$$I_P(z) = \frac{1}{e^{\alpha_0 z}\left(L_{\mathrm{eff}}\alpha_2 I_{P,0} + 1\right)}. \qquad (A.3)$$

For zero time delay, pump and probe pulses co-propagate. The weak probe pulse experiences negligible two-photon absorption, but considerable cross-two-photon absorption (XTPA) as well as cross-phase-modulation (XPM). The change of intensity $I_S(z)$ and phase $\phi_{NL}(z)$ are

$$\frac{\mathrm{d}I_S(z)}{\mathrm{d}z} = -\alpha_0 I_S(z) - 2\alpha_2 I_P(z) I_S(z), \qquad (A.4)$$

$$\frac{\mathrm{d}\phi_{NL}(z)}{\mathrm{d}z} = -\frac{2\pi}{\lambda} 2n_2 I_P(z). \qquad (A.5)$$

Because of the known pump intensity (1.5.18), equation (1.5.19) can be integrated to yield

$$I_S(z) = \frac{e^{-\alpha_0 z}}{\left(L_{\text{eff}} \alpha_2 I_{P,0} + 1\right)^2} I_{S,0}. \tag{A.6}$$

If for each time delay two measurements are taken, one with a pump of known intensity $I_{P,0}$ and one with a blocked beam $I_{P,0} = 0$, the power transmission T_P and the nonlinear phase change $\Delta\phi_{NL}$ become

$$T_P = \frac{I_S(I_P \neq 0)}{I_S(I_P = 0)} = \frac{1}{\left(L_{\text{eff}} \alpha_2 I_{P,0} + 1\right)^2},$$

$$\Delta\phi_{NL} = -4\pi \frac{n_2}{\lambda \alpha_2} \ln\left(L_{\text{eff}} \alpha_2 I_{P,0} + 1\right). \tag{A.7}$$

Amplitude transmission $T_A = T_P^{0.5}$ and nonlinear phase change $\Delta\phi_{NL}$ are quantities that can be directly measured using the heterodyne pump-probe technique. Without the need to calculate an effective area $A_{\text{eff}}^{(3)}$, solving Eqs. (A.7) with respect to $n_2/(\lambda \alpha_2)$ yields an expression for the two-photon absorption figure of merit that only relies on these measured quantities and is a characteristic property of the waveguide,

$$\text{FOM}_{\text{TPA}} = \frac{n_2}{\lambda \alpha_2} = \frac{-\Delta\phi_{NL}}{2\pi \ln(1/T_P)} = \frac{\Delta\phi_{NL}}{2\pi \ln T_P} = \frac{\Delta\phi_{NL}}{4\pi \ln T_A} \tag{A.8}$$

If the effective area of a nonlinear waveguide is known, the pump probe traces also allow to determine the two-photon absorption parameter α_2. For a simple silicon strip waveguide the intensity is known, as the effective area $A_{\text{eff,Si}}^{(3)}$ can be easily derived numerically. For a peak pulse power P_0, the inverse power transmission depends linearly on the on-chip intensity $I_{P,0} = P_P(0)\big/A_{\text{eff,Si}}^{(3)}$,

$$\frac{1}{T_P} = \frac{1}{T_A^2} = 1 + \alpha_2 I_{P,0} L_{\text{eff}}. \tag{A.9}$$

A.2. Eye Quality-Factor and Bit-Error Ratio

The main figure of merit for a digital communication link is the bit-error ratio (BER). In the past, a $BER = 10^{-9}$ was considered the limit for error-free transmission. With the recent introduction of third generation forward error correction codes [398], a limit of $BER = 2 \times 10^{-3}$ has been widely accepted.

If the BER cannot be directly measured or in the case of low line speed where a statistically relevant measurement of BER values below 10^{-9} is impractical due to time constraints, the BER can be estimated by evaluating the received eye quality. Under the assumptions of i.) a Gaussian probability distribution, ii.) equiprobable transmission of marks and spaces and iii.) an optimum decision threshold, the BER of a binary on-off-keying transmission link can be calculated [42, 50].

The bit-error ratio is defined as

$$BER = P(1 \mid 0)P(0) + P(0 \mid 1)P(1), \qquad (A.10)$$

$$P(0) + P(1) = 1, \qquad (A.11)$$

where $P(0)$ and $P(1)$ represent the probabilities that a space or mark symbol is transmitted. $P(1 \mid 0)$ denotes the conditional probability for the electronics decision circuit of falsely detecting a mark symbol when a space symbol was transmitted and $P(0 \mid 1)$ represents the contrary event. To calculate these conditional probabilities for real world systems with various present noise sources like amplifiers, the probability distribution of the detected photocurrent needs to be known.

As the exact photon statistics is virtually impossible to determine, a common approach is the Gaussian approximation. For mark and space symbols denoted by $x = \{0,1\}$, the probability of measuring a voltage u at the decision instant t_D is

$$P_x(u) = \frac{1}{\sqrt{2\pi\sigma_x^2}} \exp\left(\frac{(u - u_x)^2}{2\sigma_x^2}\right), \qquad (A.12)$$

where u_x and σ_x for are the mean value and standard deviation of mark and space symbols. Fig. A 1(a) illustrates the probability distributions in a digital on-off-keying receiver.

For any given decision threshold u_D, the conditional probabilities of Eq. (A.10) are

$$P(1|0) = \int_{u_D}^{\infty} P_0(u')\,du' = \frac{1}{\sqrt{2\pi}} \int_{Q_0}^{\infty} \exp\left(-\frac{u'^2}{2}\right) du',$$

$$P(0|1) = \int_{0}^{u_D} P_1(u')\,du' = \frac{1}{\sqrt{2\pi}} \int_{Q_1}^{\infty} \exp\left(-\frac{u'^2}{2}\right) du',$$

(A.13)

where Q_1, Q_0 are defined as

$$Q_0 = \frac{u_D - u_0}{\sigma_0} \quad \text{and} \quad Q_1 = \frac{u_1 - u_D}{\sigma_1}.$$

(A.14)

The BER (A.10) now depends on the chosen decision threshold level and the probabilities $P(0)$ and $P(1)$. For long bit sequences and especially pseudo-random bit sequences, marks and spaces are uniformly distributed

$$P(0) = P(1) = \frac{1}{2}$$

(A.15)

and the optimum decision threshold can be obtained by minimizing the BER, $\partial \text{BER}/\partial u_D = 0$. As a result, the optimum threshold is

$$u_D = \frac{\sigma_1 u_0 + \sigma_0 u_1}{\sigma_0 + \sigma_1}$$

(A.16)

and the probabilities in Eq. (A.13) are set equal $P(1|0) = P(0|1)$. The BER is then given by Eqs. (A.10)–(A.16) as

$$\text{BER} = \frac{1}{2} \text{erfc}\left(\frac{Q}{\sqrt{2}}\right),$$

(A.17)

where Q is Personick's Q factor,

$$Q = \frac{u_1 - u_0}{\sigma_1 + \sigma_2}.$$

(A.18)

Typically, the Q-factor is specified either in linear units, or as Q^2 in logarithmic units,

$$Q^2\big|_{\text{dB}} = 10\log_{10} Q^2 = 20\log_{10} Q.$$

(A.19)

Using the first term of a series definition of $\text{erfc}(x)$, Eq. (A.17) can be approximated by

$$\text{BER} \approx \frac{1}{Q\sqrt{2\pi}} \exp\left(\frac{-Q^2}{2}\right).$$

(A.20)

Fig. A 1(b) shows the dependence of the BER on the Q^2-factor. A comparison shows that the exact expression in Eq. (A.17) can be approximated very well by Eq. (A.20) for Q^2-factor values over 10 dB. Error-free operation at $\text{BER} = 10^{-9}$ is achieved for a Q^2-factor value of 15.6 dB. Although this is a powerful and quick method of evaluating the BER, one needs to be aware of its limitations.

In the range of $10\,\text{dB} < Q^2 < 18\,\text{dB}$, the calculated BER of Eq. (A.17) usually corresponds nicely to directly measured BER. However, for values <10 dB, the Q^2-factor is very hard to measure reliably, leading to large errors in the BER. For values >18 dB, even small variations in the Q^2-factor cause large variations in the BER.

Although the Gaussian approximation in Eq. (A.12) typically holds, inter-symbol interference and nonlinear distortion effects can significantly alter the probability distributions. For example, transient overshoots typically lead to an underestimated quality factor and thus an overestimated BER.

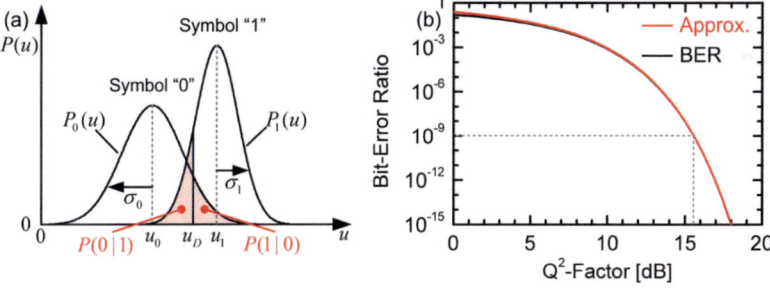

Fig. A 1 (a) Probability distributions corresponding to the photodetection of mark (1) and space (0) symbols of a digital transmission system. Gaussian distributions with mean value u_x and standard deviations σ_x are assumed. The shaded areas indicate the probabilities of false symbol detection. The chosen decision threshold is u_D. (b) Bit-error ratio as a function of the measured Q^2-factor. The exact expression (black) can be approximated very well for Q^2-factor values over 10 dB. Error-free operation at $\text{BER} = 10^{-9}$ is achieved for a Q^2-factor value of 15.6 dB.

A.3. Useful Formulae and Constants

Fourier Transformation

The Fourier transform is given by

$$\tilde{\mathbf{E}}(\mathbf{r},\omega) = \mathcal{F}\{\mathbf{E}(\mathbf{r},t)\} = \int\limits_{-\infty}^{+\infty} \mathbf{E}(\mathbf{r},t)e^{-j\omega t}\, dt,$$

$$\mathbf{E}(\mathbf{r},t) = \mathcal{F}^{-1}\{\tilde{\mathbf{E}}(\mathbf{r},\omega)\} = \frac{1}{2\pi}\int\limits_{-\infty}^{+\infty} \tilde{\mathbf{E}}(\mathbf{r},\omega)e^{j\omega t}\, d\omega.$$

(A.21)

For Fourier transformed quantities, the following equations hold [16]

$$\mathcal{F}\{\mathbf{E}^*(\mathbf{r},t)\} = \tilde{\mathbf{E}}^*(\mathbf{r},-\omega),$$

(A.22)

$$\mathcal{F}\{\mathbf{E}(\mathbf{r},t-t_0)\} = e^{-j\omega t_0}\, \tilde{\mathbf{E}}(\mathbf{r},\omega),$$

(A.23)

$$\mathcal{F}^{-1}\{\tilde{\mathbf{E}}(\mathbf{r},\omega-\omega_0)\} = e^{j\omega_0 t}\, \mathbf{E}(r,t),$$

(A.24)

$$\mathcal{F}\{\mathbf{A}(\mathbf{r},t)*\mathbf{B}(\mathbf{r},t)\} = \mathcal{F}\left\{\int_{-\infty}^{\infty} \mathbf{A}(\mathbf{r},t-t')\mathbf{B}(\mathbf{r},t')\, dt'\right\}$$
$$= \mathcal{F}\{\mathbf{A}(\mathbf{r},t)\}\,\mathcal{F}\{\mathbf{B}(\mathbf{r},t)\}$$
$$= \tilde{\mathbf{A}}(\mathbf{r},\omega)\tilde{\mathbf{B}}(\mathbf{r},\omega),$$

(A.25)

$$\mathcal{F}^{-1}\{\tilde{\mathbf{A}}(\mathbf{r},\omega)*\tilde{\mathbf{B}}(\mathbf{r},\omega)\} = \mathcal{F}^{-1}\left\{\int_{-\infty}^{\infty} \tilde{\mathbf{A}}(\mathbf{r},\omega-\omega')\tilde{\mathbf{B}}(\mathbf{r},\omega')\, d\omega'\right\}$$
$$= 2\pi\,\mathcal{F}^{-1}\{\mathbf{A}(\mathbf{r},t)\}\,\mathcal{F}^{-1}\{\mathbf{B}(\mathbf{r},t)\}$$
$$= 2\pi\,\mathbf{A}(\mathbf{r},t)\mathbf{B}(\mathbf{r},t),$$

(A.26)

$$\mathcal{F}\{\mathcal{F}\{\mathbf{E}(\mathbf{r},t)\}\} = 2\pi\,\mathbf{E}(\mathbf{r},-t),$$

(A.27)

$$\mathcal{F}\left\{|\mathbf{E}(\mathbf{r},t)|^2\right\} = \frac{1}{2\pi}\int_{-\infty}^{\infty} \tilde{\mathbf{A}}(\mathbf{r},\omega')\tilde{\mathbf{A}}^*(\mathbf{r},\omega'-\omega)d\omega',$$

(A.28)

$$\frac{d^n \mathbf{E}(\mathbf{r},t)}{dt^n} = F^{-1}\{(jn)^n\,\tilde{\mathbf{E}}(\mathbf{r},\omega)\},$$

(A.29)

$$\mathcal{F}\{\delta(t)\} = 1,$$

(A.30)

$$\mathcal{F}\{1\} = 2\pi\delta(\omega),$$

(A.31)

$$\mathcal{F}\{H(t)\} = \pi\delta(\omega) + \mathcal{P}\frac{1}{j\omega} \quad \text{for} \quad H(t) = \begin{cases} 0 & t<0, \\ 1 & t>0. \end{cases}$$

(A.32)

Analytic Signals

Physically meaningful quantities $\mathbf{F}(\mathbf{r},t)$ have to be real-valued, so the spectrum $\tilde{\mathbf{F}}(\mathbf{r},\omega)$ fulfills the relation [31]

$$\tilde{\mathbf{F}}(\mathbf{r},-\omega) = \tilde{\mathbf{F}}^{*}(\mathbf{r},\omega), \tag{A.33}$$

where the lower part of the spectrum $\omega < 0$ can be derived from the upper part of the spectrum $\omega \geq 0$. This redundancy is removed by using analytic signals $\underline{\mathbf{F}}(\mathbf{r},t)$ in the time domain. The real part of the analytic signal represents the physically meaningful quantity,

$$\mathbf{F}(\mathbf{r},t) = \mathrm{Re}\left[\underline{\mathbf{F}}(\mathbf{r},t)\right], \tag{A.34}$$

and the imaginary part is chosen such that the Fourier-transform is single sided, $\tilde{\underline{\mathbf{F}}}(\mathbf{r},\omega < 0) = 0$. In this case, the real and the imaginary part form a Hilbert pair and are connected by the Hilbert transformation.

If the spectrum consists of lines at discrete angular frequencies ω_i, $i = 1,2,\ldots,N$, instead of using the Fourier transform, complex amplitudes $\hat{\underline{\mathbf{F}}}(\mathbf{r},\omega_i)$ of harmonic contributions $e^{j\omega_i t}$ can be used to construct the time-domain signal,

$$\underline{\mathbf{F}}(\mathbf{r},t) = \sum_{i=0}^{N} \hat{\underline{\mathbf{F}}}(\mathbf{r},\omega_i)e^{j\omega_i t}, \tag{A.35}$$

with the real valued physical quantity

$$\mathbf{F}(\mathbf{r},t) = \frac{1}{2}\sum_{i=-N}^{N} (1+\delta_{i,0})\hat{\underline{\mathbf{F}}}(\mathbf{r},\omega_i)e^{j\omega_i t}, \tag{A.36}$$

where $\delta_{i,0}$ is the Kronecker delta. The spectrum of the signals in Eqs. (A.35) and (A.36) can be expressed in terms of complex amplitudes as

$$\tilde{\underline{\mathbf{F}}}(\mathbf{r},\omega) = 2\pi\sum_{i=0}^{N} \hat{\underline{\mathbf{F}}}(\mathbf{r},\omega_i)\delta(\omega-\omega_i), \tag{A.37}$$

$$\tilde{\mathbf{F}}(\mathbf{r},t) = \pi\sum_{i=-N}^{N} (1+\delta_{i,0})\hat{\underline{\mathbf{F}}}(\mathbf{r},\omega_i)\delta(\omega-\omega_i). \tag{A.38}$$

Bessel Functions

Bessel functions of the first kind $J_n(x)$ are defined as solutions to the Bessel differential equation,

$$x^2 \frac{d^2 y}{dx^2} + x \frac{dy}{dx} + \left(x^2 - n^2\right) y = 0. \tag{A.39}$$

Derivatives of Bessel functions are related by

$$\frac{d J_n(x)}{dx} = \frac{1}{2}\left(J_{n-1}(x) - J_{n+1}(x)\right), \tag{A.40}$$

A useful definition in terms of a generating function is

$$\exp\{jy\sin x\} = \sum_{n=-\infty}^{\infty} J_n(y)\exp\{jnx\}. \tag{A.41}$$

For the special case of $n = 0$, the integral definition of $J_0(x)$ is

$$J_0(x) = \frac{1}{\pi} \int_0^\pi e^{jz\cos\theta} d\theta. \tag{A.42}$$

Constants

$$h = 6.626\,068 \times 10^{-34} \frac{m^2 kg}{s} \tag{A.43}$$

$$e = 1.602\,17646 \times 10^{-19}\,C \tag{A.44}$$

$$\varepsilon_0 = 8.854\,188 \times 10^{-12} \frac{As}{Vm} \tag{A.45}$$

$$\mu_0 = 1.256\,637 \times 10^{-6} \frac{Vs}{Am} \tag{A.46}$$

$$c = \frac{1}{\sqrt{\varepsilon_0 \mu_0}} = 299\,792\,458 \frac{m}{s} \tag{A.47}$$

$$Z_0 = \sqrt{\frac{\mu_0}{\varepsilon_0}} = 376.7303\,\Omega \tag{A.48}$$

A.4. Heterodyne Pump-Probe Setup Details

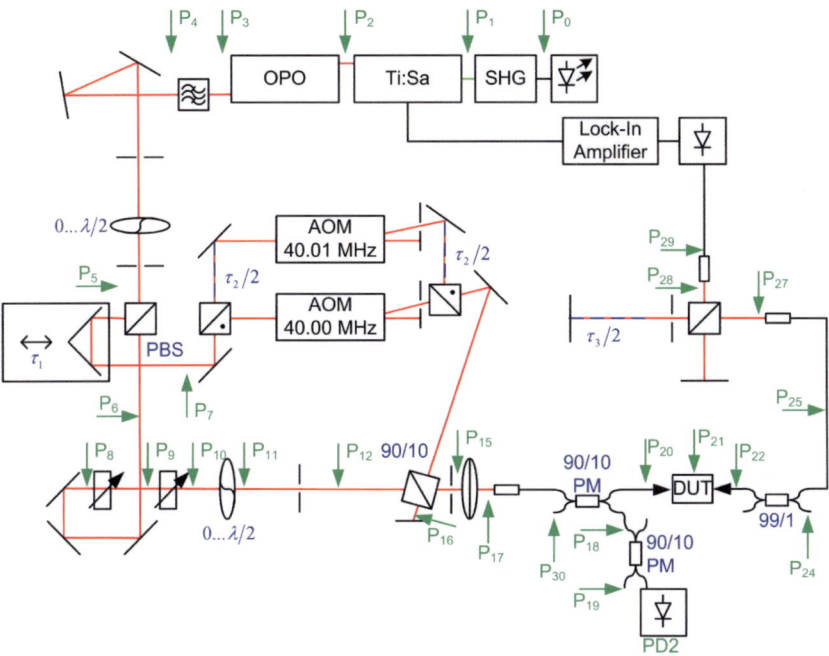

Fig. A 2 Heterodyne pump-probe setup details. SHG: second-harmonic generation; Ti:Sa: titanium-sapphire pulse laser; OPO: optical parametric oscillator; PBS: polarizing beam splitter; $0...\lambda/2$: half-wave plate, used to rotate polarization and create variable splitting ratio and variable attenuation; AOM: acousto-optical modulators; PD2: cross-correlation photodetector; 90/10: pellicle beam splitter; 90/10 PM: polarization maintaining 90/10 fiber couplers; DUT: device under test; At position P_4, multiple gray filters can be moved into the path to achive fixed attenuation over a 20 dB attenuation range.

Glossary

Calligraphic Symbols

$\mathcal{E}$ Vectorial electric waveguide mode field, unit V/m, Eq. (1.2.4)

$\mathcal{H}$ Vectorial magnetic waveguide mode field, unit A/m, Eq. (1.2.7)

$\mathcal{P}$ Power associated with numerical mode field, unit W, Eq. (1.2.8)

Greek Symbols

α_0 Power attenuation coefficient, unit m^{-1}, Eq. (1.2.29)

α_2 Two-photon absorption coefficient, unit m/W, Eq. (1.3.5)

α_{LE}, α_H Linewidth enhancement factor (Henry factor), Eq. (1.4.2)

β Modal propagation constant, unit m^{-1}, Eq. (1.2.4)

β_n n-th derivative of the propagation constant with respect to ω,

         $\beta_n = d^n\beta/(d\omega^n)$, unit s^n/m, Eq. (1.2.22)

$\Delta\beta$ Small perturbation to the propagation constant, unit m^{-1},

         Eq. (1.3.9)

Γ Confinement factor, Eq. (1.4.4)

Γ_{hom} FWHM of a Lorentzian function, Eq. (2.2.1)

γ Waveguide nonlinearity parameter, unit $(Wm)^{-1}$, Eq. (1.3.11)

ε_0 Electric permittivity of vacuum, $\varepsilon_0 = 8.854\,188 \times 10^{-12}\,As/(Vm)$,

         Eq. (1.1.6)

$\underline{\varepsilon}_r$ Dielectric permeability tensor, Eq. (1.1.12)

ε_r Scalar dielectric permeability, Eq. (1.1.13)

η Four-wave mixing efficiency, Eq. (1.3.18)

ϑ Waveguide sidewall angle, unit deg

λ Wavelength, unit m

$\Delta\lambda$ Wavelength detuning, unit m, Eq. (1.3.20)

μ_0 Magnetic permeability of vacuum, $\mu_0 = 1.256\,637 \times 10^{-6}\,Vs/(Am)$,

         Eq. (1.1.5)

$\mu_{e,h}$ Charge carrier mobility, unit $m^2/(Vs)$, Eq. (1.2.34)

$\xi_{e,h}$ Free-carrier effect ideality factor, Eq. (1.2.34)

σ Variance of Gaussian function, Eq. (2.2.2)

σ_α Free-carrier absorption cross-section, unit m^2, Eq. (1.2.36)

σ_n Free-carrier dispersion corss-section, unit m^3, Eq. (1.2.36)

$\tau_{1,2}$ Characteristic time constants of carrier dynamics, unit s, Eq. (2.3.1)

$\tau_{1,2,3,rep}$ Time delays in pump-probe setup, unit s, Fig. 1.6

ϕ Optical phase, Eq. (1.4.6)

ϕ_{NL} Nonlinear phase shift, Eq. (1.5.17)

$\Delta\phi$ Optical phase shift, Eq. (1.3.23)

$\underline{\chi}^{(n)}(t)$ n-th order time-domain Volterra kernel of polarization response, tensor of rank $n+1$, unit $s^{-n}(m/V)^{n-1}$, Eq. (1.1.7)

$\underline{\chi}^{(n)}(\omega)$ n-th order susceptibility, tensor of rank $n+1$, unit $(m/V)^{n-1}$, Eq. (1.3.12)

ω Angular frequency, unit rad/s, Eq. (1.2.2)

ω_c Carrier angular frequency, unit rad/s, Eq. (1.1.15)

Latin Symbols

1   Unity tensor, Eq. (1.1.12)

$\tilde{A}$ Slowly-varying envelope of a signal, unit $\sqrt{W}$, Eq. (1.2.4)

$A_{eff}^{(3)}$ Effective area of third-order nonlinear interaction, unit m^2, Eq. (1.3.12)

a_{cp} Coupling loss, Eq. (1.2.33)

$a_{ref,pump,prb}$ Amplitude of a pulse sequence, unit $\sqrt{W}$, Eq. (1.5.2)

B   Magnetic flux density, unit Vs/m^2, Eq. (1.1.2)

B Bandwidth, unit Hz, Eq. (1.4.18)

B_s Bit sequence, Eq. (1.3.25)

BER   Bit-error ratio

b_n Coefficient of Fourier series, Eq. (1.3.26)

CSR   Carrier-to-sideband ratio, Eq. (1.3.31)

c Speed of light in vacuum, $c = 1/\sqrt{\varepsilon_0\mu_0} = 299\,792\,458$ m/s

D   Displacement field, unit As/m^2, Eq. (1.1.1)

D Surface area, unit m^2

D_2 Dispersion coefficient, unit s/m^2, Eq. (1.2.25)

e Elementary charge, $e = 1.60217646 \times 10^{-19}\,\mathrm{C}$

$\mathbf{e}_z$ Unit vector along z-direction, Eq. (1.3.9)

$\mathbf{E}$ Electric field, unit V/m, Eq. (1.1.2)

E Energy, unit eV

$\mathrm{FOM_{TPA}}$ Two-photon absorption figure of merit, Eq. (1.3.37)

F Noise figure, Eq. (1.4.10)

f Frequency, unit Hz

G Gain, amplification factor, Eq. (1.4.9)

g Gain constant, unit m^{-1}, Eq. (1.4.2)

$g(x)$ Gaussian function, Eq. (2.2.2)

g_0 Small-signal gain constant, unit m^{-1}, Eq. (1.4.22)

Δg Small perturbation to the gain constant, unit m^{-1}, Eq. (1.4.1)

$\mathbf{H}$ Magnetic field, unit A/m, Eq. (1.1.1)

h Waveguide height, unit m

$\hbar$ Reduced Planck constant, $\hbar = 1.05457148 \times 10^{-34}\,\mathrm{m}^2\mathrm{kg}/\mathrm{s}$

I Optical field intensity, unit W/m^2, Eq. (1.1.17)

I Bias current, unit A

i Current density, unit A/m^2

J_n n-th order Bessel function, Eq. (1.3.28)

j Imaginary unit, $\mathrm{j}^2 = -1$

k_0 Free-space wavenumber, unit m^{-1}, Eq. (1.2.3)

L Length, unit m

L_{eff} Effective waveguide length, unit m, Eq. (1.3.18)

$l(x)$ Lorentzian function, Eq. (2.2.1)

$m^*_{\mathrm{e,h}}$ Effective mass of charge carriers, unit $m_0 = 9.11 \times 10^{-31}\,\mathrm{kg}$, Eq. (1.2.34)

$N_{1,2}$ Occupation numbers, Eq. (1.4.14)

$N_{\mathrm{e,h}}$ Carrier concentration, unit m^{-3}, Eq. (1.2.34)

NF   Noise figure, unit dB, Eq. (1.4.19)

$\mathbf{n}$ Vector of surface normale, unit m, Eq. (1.1.16)

n Refractive index, Eq. (1.2.3)

n_0 Unperturbed refractive index, Eq. (1.1.13)

n_2 Nonlinear refractive index, unit m^2/W, Eq. (1.3.4)

n_g Group refractive index, Eq. (1.2.23)

$n_{s,o,\mathrm{ASE}}$	Photon number, Eq. (1.4.11)
n_{sp}	Noise enhancement factor, Eq. (1.4.14)
Δn	Small perturbation to the refractive index, Eq. (1.2.28)
$\mathbf{P}$	Polarization, unit As/m^2, Eq. (1.1.6)
P	Power, unit W, Eq. (1.1.16)
P_{s}	Saturation power, unit W, Eq. (1.4.22)
Q^2	Eye quality factor
R	On-off ratio of two complex amplitudes, Eq. (1.5.14)
$\mathbf{r}$	Vector of Cartesian coordinates x, y, and z, unit m
$\mathbf{S}$	Poynting vector, unit W/m^2, Eq. (1.1.14)
S	Responsivity of a photodetector, unit A/W, Eq. (1.5.3)
SNR	Signal-to-noise ratio, Eq. (1.4.11)
s	Pulse shape, Eq. (1.3.25)
T	Pump-probe transmission factor, Eq. (1.5.8)
T_2	Dipole relaxation time, unit s, Eq. (1.4.22)
t	Time, unit s
U	Lock-in signal, unit V, Eq. (1.5.5)
u	Electrical signal, unit V, Eq. (1.5.3)
$u(t)$	Unit step function, Eq. (2.3.1)
v_g	Group velocity, unit m/s, Eq. (1.2.23)
w	Window function, Eq. (1.5.12)
$w_{\mathrm{strip,slot}}$	Waveguide strip or slot width, unit m
x	(Horizontal) spatial coordinate, unit m, Eq. (1.1.17)
y	(Vertical) spatial coordinate, unit m, Eq. (1.1.17)
z	(Longitudinal) spatial coordinate, unit m, Eq. (1.2.4)
Z_0	Free-space wave impedance, $Z_0 = \sqrt{\mu_0/\varepsilon_0} = 376.7303\,\Omega$

Acronyms

3R	Reamplification, reshaping, retiming
AMI	Alternate mark inversion (format)
AOM	Acousto-optic modulator
ASE	Amplified spontaneous emission
ASK	Amplitude-shift keying (format)

AWG   Arrayed waveguide grating
BEPR   Beam-equivalent pressure ratio
BER   Bit-error ratio
BERT   Bit-error ratio tester
BOX   Buried silicon oxide
CELFA Composition evaluation by lattice fringe analysis
CMOS Complementary metal oxide-semiconductor (technology)
COLC   Center of Laue circle
CSR   Carrier-to-sideband ratio
cw   Continuous-wave
CWDM Coarse wavelength-division multiplexing
DCA   Digital communications analyzer
DDMEBT   Organic molecule, (2-[4-(dimethylamino)phenyl]-3-{[4-(dimethylamino)phenyl]ethynyl}buta-1,3-diene-1,1,4,4-tetracarbonitrile))
DI   Delay interferometer
DOS   Density of states
DQPSK Differential quadrature phase-shift keying (format)
DUT   Device under test
DWDM Dense wavelength-division multiplexing
EDFA   Erbium-doped fiber amplifier
EPON   Ethernet PON, ethernet passive optical network
FCA   Free-carrier absorption
FCD   Free-carrier dispersion
FEC   Forward error correction
FEM   Finite-element simulation technique
FIT   Finite-integration simulation technique
FREAG Frequency-resolved electro-absorption gating (technique)
FWHM Full width at half maximum
FWM   Four-wave mixing
GI   Growth interruption
GPON   Gigabit PON, gigabit passive optical network
GRIN   Graded index
GSMBE Gas source MBE, gas source molecular beam epitaxy
GVD   Group velocity dispersion

HNLF   Highly-nonlinear fiber

HRTEM High-resolution TEM, high-resolution transmission electron microscopy

IPDR   Input power dynamic range

LEF   Linewidth enhancement factor (Henry factor, alpha factor)

MBE   Molecular beam epitaxy

ML   Monolayer

MLL   Mode-locked laser

MOS   Metal-oxide semiconductor

MZI   Mach-Zehnder interferometer

NF   Noise figure

NLSE   Nonlinear Schrödinger equation

NRZ-DQPSK Non-return-to-zero differential quadrature phase-shift keying (format)

NRZ-OOK   Non-return-to-zero on-off keying (format)

OBPF   Optical band-pass filter

ODL   Optical delay line

OOK   On-off keying (format)

OPO   Optical parametric oscillator

OSA   Optical spectrum analyzer

OSNR   Optical signal to noise ratio

OTDM   Optical time-division multiplexing

P2P   Peak to peak

PON   Passive optical network

PBS   Polarizing beam splitter

PDFA   Praseodymium-doped fiber amplifier

PhC   Photonic crystal

PL   Photoluminescence

PM   Power meter

PMF   Polarization-maintaining fiber

PPLN   Periodically-poled Lithium Niobate

PRBS   Pseudo-random bit sequence

PSK   Phase-shift keying (format)

PTS   Organic crystal, P-toluene sulphonate

QD   Quantum dot

QDash   Quantum dash

QD SOA Quantum dot semiconductor optical amplifier
QW   Quantum well
RHEED Reflection high energy electron diffraction
Rx   Receiver
RZ-OOK Return-to-zero on-off keying (format)
SHG   Second-harmonic generation
SK   Stranski-Krastanov (growth mode)
SMF   Single-mode fiber
SML   Sub-monolayer (growth technique)
SNR   Signal-to-noise ratio
SOA   Semiconductor optical amplifier
SOH   Silicon-organic hybrid
SOI   Silicon-on-insulator
SPM   Self-phase modulation
SVEA   Slowly-varying envelope approximation
TEM   Transmission electron microscopy
TE   Transverse electric (mode)
THG   Third-harmonic generation
TLS   Tunable laser source
TOD   Third-order dispersion
TM   Transverse magnetic (mode)
TPA   Two-photon absorption
TSFG   Third-order sum-frequency generation
Tx   Transmitter
UV   Ultra-violet
VCSEL Vertical cavity surface-emitting laser
VOA   Variable optical attenuator
WL   Wetting layer
XGM   Cross-gain modulation
XPM   Cross-phase modulation
XTPA   Cross-TPA, Cross-two-photon absorption

References

[1]   "Cisco visual networking index: Forecast and methodology, 2008–2013," Cisco Systems, Inc., San Jose, CA, USA, white paper, Jun. 2009. [Online]. Available: http://www.cisco.com/en/US/solutions/collateral/ns341/ns525/-ns537/ns705/ns827/white_paper_c11-481360.pdf

[2]   "Green IT initiative in Japan," Ministry of Economics Trade and Industry (METI), presentation, Oct. 2008. [Online]. Available: http://www.meti.go.jp/-english/policy/GreenITInitiativeInJapan.pdf

[3]   L. Stobbe,   N. Nissen,   M. Proske,   A. Middendorf,   B. Schlomann, M. Friedewald,   P. Georgieff,   and   T. Leimbach,   "Abschätzung   des Energiebedarfs   der   weiteren   Entwicklung   der   Informationsgesellschaft," Fraunhofer-Institut für Zuverlässigkeit und Mikrointegration (IZM) und Fraunhofer-Institut für System- und Innovationsforschung (ISI), Karlsruhe, Germany, Abschlussbericht an das Bundesministerium für Wirtschaft und Technologie, Mar. 2008. [Online]. Available: http://publica.fraunhofer.de/-dokumente/N-110231.html

[4]   "SMART 2020: Enabling the low carbon economy in the information age," The Climate Group, report on behalf of the Global eSustainability Initiative (GeSI), 2008. [Online]. Available: http://www.theclimategroup.org/_assets/-files/Smart2020Report.pdf

[5]   R. Tucker, "Petabit-per-second routers: optical vs. electronic implementations," in *Optical Fiber Communication Conference, 2006 and the 2006 National Fiber Optic Engineers Conference. OFC 2006*, Anaheim, CA, USA, Mar. 5–10 2006, doi: 10.1109/OFC.2006.215992.

[6]   S. Yoo and H. Yang, "Petabit-per-second routers: Case for all-optical over electronic implementation," in *Optical Fiber Communication and the National Fiber Optic Engineers Conference, 2007. OFC/NFOEC 2007. Conference on*, Anaheim,   CA,   USA,   Mar.   25–29   2007,   paper   OThF3,   doi: 10.1109/OFC.2007.4348668.

[7]   K. Hinton, G. Raskutti, P. Farrell, and R. Tucker, "Switching energy and device size limits on digital photonic signal processing technologies," *IEEE J. Sel. Top. Quantum Electron.*, vol. 14, no. 3, pp. 938–945, May 2008, doi: 10.1109/JSTQE.2008.916242.

[8]   G. Grasso, P. Galli, M. Romagnoli, E. Iannone, and A. Bogoni, "Role of integrated photonics technologies in the realization of terabit nodes [invited]," *J. Opt. Commun. Netw.*, vol. 1, no. 3, pp. B111–B119, 2009, doi: 10.1364/JOCN.1.00B111.

[9]   B. E. A. Saleh and M. C. Teich, *Fundementals of Photonics*, 1st ed. New York: John Wiley & Sons, 1991.

[10]   D. Marcuse, *Light Transmission Optics*. New York: Van Nostrand Reinhold, 1972.

[11]   ——, *Theory of Dielectric Optical Waveguides*. London: Academic Press, 1974.

[12]   K. Kawano and T. Kitoh, *Introduction to Optical Waveguide Analysis: Solving Maxwell's Equations and the Schrödinger Equation*. New York: John Wiley & Sons, 2001.

[13]   R. W. Boyd, *Nonlinear Optics*, second edition ed. Amsterdam: Academic Press, 2003.

[14]   G. P. Agrawal, *Applications of Nonlinear Fiber Optics*, ser. Optics and Photonics, P. L. Kelly, I. P. Kaminow, and G. P. Agrawal, Eds. San Diego: Academic Press, 2001.

[15]   ——, *Nonlinear Fiber Optics*, ser. Optics and Photonics, P. L. Kelley, I. P. Kaminov, and G. P. Agrawal, Eds. San Diego: Academic Press, 2001.

[16]   T. Kremp, "Split-step wavelet collocation methods for linear and nonlinear optical wave propagation," Dissertation, Universität Karlsruhe (TH), Cuvillier Verlag, Göttingen, 2002.

[17]   A. Sudbo, "Why are accurate computations of mode fields in rectangular dielectric waveguides difficult?" *J. Lightwave Technol.*, vol. 10, no. 4, pp. 418–419, Apr. 1992, doi: 10.1109/50.134193.

[18]   *BeamPROP 8.1 User Guide*, RSoft Design Group, Inc., Ossining, NY, 2008.
       [Online]. Available: www.rsoftdesign.com

[19]   *CST Microwave Studio 2009 User Guide*, CST – Computer Simulation
       Technology AG, Darmstadt, Germany, 2008. [Online]. Available:
       www.cst.com

[20]   *FemSIM 3.1 User Guide*, RSoft Design Group, Inc., Ossining, NY, 2008.
       [Online]. Available: www.rsoftdesign.com

[21]   L. Prkna, M. Hubalek, and J. Ctyroky, "Field modeling of circular
       microresonators by film mode matching," *IEEE J. Sel. Top. Quantum
       Electron.*, vol. 11, no. 1, pp. 217–223, Jan.–Feb. 2005, doi:
       10.1109/JSTQE.2004.841716.

[22]   R. Soref and B. Bennett, "Electrooptical effects in silicon," *IEEE J. Quantum
       Electron.*, vol. 23, no. 1, pp. 123–129, Jan. 1987. [Online]. Available: http://-
       ieeexplore.ieee.org/xpls/abs_all.jsp?arnumber=1073206

[23]   V. Passaro, F. De Leonardis, and G. Mashanovich, "Analysis of nonlinear
       effects in nanometer-scale silicon-on-insulator rib waveguides," in *Proc.25th
       International Conference on Microelectronics*, 2006, pp. 129–132, doi:
       10.1109/ICMEL.2006.1650913.

[24]   R. Claps, V. Raghunathan, D. Dimitropoulos, and B. Jalali, "Influence of
       nonlinear absorption on Raman amplification in silicon waveguides," *Opt.
       Express*, vol. 12, no. 12, pp. 2774–2780, 2004, doi: 10.1364/OPEX.12.002774.

[25]   A. C. Turner-Foster, M. A. Foster, J. S. Levy, C. B. Poitras, R. Salem, A. L.
       Gaeta, and M. Lipson, "Ultrashort free-carrier lifetime in low-loss silicon
       nanowaveguides," *Opt. Express*, vol. 18, no. 4, pp. 3582–3591, 2010, doi:
       10.1364/OE.18.003582.

[26]   M. Waldow, T. Plötzing, M. Gottheil, M. Först, J. Bolten, T. Wahlbrink, and
       H. Kurz, "25ps all-optical switching in oxygen implanted silicon-on-insulator
       microring resonator," *Opt. Express*, vol. 16, no. 11, pp. 7693–7702, 2008, doi:
       10.1364/OE.16.007693.

[27]   G. I. Stegeman, E. M. Wright, N. Finlayson, R. Zanoni, and C. T. Seaton,
       "Third order nonlinear integrated optics," *J. Lightw. Techn.*, vol. 6, no. 6, pp.
       953–970, Jun. 1988, doi: 10.1109/50.4087.

[28] H. Yamada, M. Shirane, T. Chu, H. Yokoyama, S. Ishida, and Y. Arakawa, "Nonlinear-optic silicon-nanowire waveguides," *Jpn. J. Appl. Phys.*, vol. 44, no. 9A, pp. 6541–6545, 2005, doi: 10.1143/JJAP.44.6541.

[29] O. Boyraz, P. Koonath, V. Raghunathan, and B. Jalali, "All optical switching via XPM in silicon waveguides," in *Lasers and Electro-Optics Society, 2004. LEOS 2004.*, vol. 2, Nov. 2004, paper ThBB1, doi: 10.1109/LEOS.2004.1363571.

[30] C. Koos, T. Vallaitis, B.-A. Bolles, R. Bonk, W. Freude, M. Laemmlin, C. Meuer, D. Bimberg, A. D. Ellis, and J. Leuthold, "Gain and phase dynamics in an InAs/GaAs quantum dot amplifier at 1300 nm," in *Proc. Conf. on Lasers and Electro-Optics (CLEO/IQEC 2007)*, Munich, Jun. 17–22 2007, paper CI3-1-TUE. [Online]. Available: http://www.opticsinfobase.org/-abstract.cfm?URI=CLEO_E-2007-CI3_1

[31] C. Koos, "Nanophotonic devices for linear and nonlinear optical signal processing," Ph.D. dissertation, Universität Karlsruhe (TH), Karlsruhe, Germany, 2007.

[32] R. S. Grant, "Effective non-linear coefficients of optical waveguides," *Optical and Quantum Electronics*, vol. 28, no. 9, pp. 1161–1173, Sep. 1996, doi: 10.1007/BF00347646.

[33] T.-T. Kung, C.-T. Chang, J.-C. Dung, and S. Chi, "Four-wave mixing between pump and signal in a distributed Raman amplifier," *J. Lightw. Techn.*, vol. 21, no. 5, pp. 1164–1170, May 2003, doi: 10.1109/JLT.2003.810929.

[34] M. Wu and W. I. Way, "Fiber nonlinearity limitations in ultra-dense WDM systems," *J. Lightw. Techn.*, vol. 22, no. 6, pp. 1483–1498, Jun. 2004, doi: 10.1109/JLT.2004.829222.

[35] G. I. Stegeman and W. E. Torruellas, "Nonlinear materials for information processing and communications," *Philosophical Transactions: Mathematical, Physical and Engineering Sciences*, vol. 354, no. 1708, pp. 745–756, Mar. 1996. [Online]. Available: http://www.jstor.org/stable/54556

[36]   G. Stegeman, E. Caglioti, S. Trillo, and S. Wabnitz, "Parameter trade-offs in nonlinear directional couplers: Two level saturable nonlinear media," *Opt. Commun.*, vol. 63, no. 5, pp. 281–284, 1987, doi: 10.1016/0030-4018(87)90175-1.

[37]   V. Mizrahi, K. W. DeLong, G. I. Stegeman, M. A. Saifi, and M. J. Andrejco, "Two-photon absorption as a limitation to all-optical switching," *Opt. Lett.*, vol. 14, no. 20, pp. 1140–1142, Oct. 1989, doi: 10.1364/OL.14.001140.

[38]   K. W. DeLong, K. B. Rochford, and G. I. Stegeman, "Effect of two-photon absorption on all-optical guided-wave devices," *Appl. Phys. Lett.*, vol. 55, no. 18, pp. 1823–1825, 1989, doi: 10.1063/1.102177.

[39]   C. Henry, "Theory of the linewidth of semiconductor lasers," *IEEE J. Quantum Electron.*, vol. 18, no. 2, pp. 259–264, Feb. 1982. [Online]. Available: http://ieeexplore.ieee.org/xpls/abs_all.jsp?arnumber=1071522&tag=1

[40]   H. Heffner, "The fundamental noise limit of linear amplifiers," *Proc. IRE*, vol. 50, no. 7, pp. 1604–1608, Jul. 1962, doi: 10.1109/JRPROC.1962.288130.

[41]   R. Tucker and D. M. Baney, "Optical noise figure: Theory and measurements," in *Optical Fiber Communication Conference, 2001. OFC 2001*, 2001, paper WI1. [Online]. Available: http://www.opticsinfobase.org/abstract.cfm?URI=OFC-2001-WI1

[42]   E. Desurvire, *Erbium-Doped Fiber Amplifiers*. New York: John Wiley & Sons, 1994.

[43]   G. Grau and W. Freude, *Optische Nachrichtentechnik*, 3rd ed. Berlin: Springer, 1991.

[44]   H. A. Haus, "The noise figure of optical amplifiers," *IEEE Photonics Technol. Lett.*, vol. 10, no. 11, pp. 1602–1604, 1998, doi: 10.1109/68.726763.

[45]   H. Haus, "Corrections to "the noise figure of optical amplifiers"," *IEEE Photonics Technol. Lett.*, vol. 11, no. 1, pp. 143–143, Jan. 1999, doi: 10.1109/LPT.1999.736424.

[46]   ——, "Noise figure definition valid from RF to optical frequencies," *IEEE J. Sel. Top. Quantum Electron.*, vol. 6, no. 2, pp. 240–247, Mar. 2000, doi: 10.1109/2944.847759.

[47]   H. A. Haus, "Optimum noise performance of optical amplifiers," *IEEE J. Quantum Electron.*, vol. 37, no. 6, pp. 813–823, Jun. 2001, doi: 10.1109/3.922780.

[48]   E. Desurvire, "Comments on "the noise figure of optical amplifiers"," *IEEE Photonics Technol. Lett.*, vol. 11, no. 5, pp. 620–621, May 1999, doi: 10.1109/68.759418.

[49]   T. Briant, P. Grangier, R. Tualle-Brouri, A. Bellemain, R. Brenot, and B. Thedrez, "Accurate determination of the noise figure of polarization-dependent optical amplifiers: theory and experiment," *J. Lightwave Technol.*, vol. 24, no. 3, pp. 1499–1503, Mar. 2006, doi: 10.1109/JLT.2005.864001.

[50]   G. P. Agrawal, *Fiber-Optic Communication Systems*, 3rd ed. John Wiley & Sons, 2002.

[51]   L. Occhi, "Semiconductor optical amplifiers made of ridge waveguide bulk InGaAsP/InP: Experimental characterization and numerical modelling of gain, phase and noise," Dissertation, ETH Zürich, Zürich, 2002.

[52]   K. E. Stubkjaer, "Semiconductor optical amplifier-based all-optical gates for high-speed optical processing," *IEEE J. Sel. Top. Quantum Electron.*, vol. 6, no. 6, pp. 1428–1434, Dec. 2000, doi: 10.1109/2944.902198.

[53]   M. Sugawara, H. Ebe, N. Hatori, M. Ishida, Y. Arakawa, T. Akiyama, K. Otsubo, and Y. Nakata, "Theory of optical signal amplification and processing by quantum-dot semiconductor optical amplifiers," *Phys. Rev. B: Condens. Matter*, vol. 69, no. 23, p. 235332, Jun. 2004, doi: 10.1103/PhysRevB.69.235332.

[54]   A. V. Uskov, E. P. O'Reilly, M. Laemmlin, N. N. Ledentsov, and D. Bimberg, "On gain saturation in quantum dot semiconductor optical amplifiers," *Opt. Commun.*, vol. 248, no. 1-3, pp. 211–219, Apr. 2004, doi: 10.1016/j.optcom.2004.12.001.

[55]   A. V. Uskov, T. W. Berg, and J. Mørk, "Theory of pulse-train amplification without patterning effects in quantum-dotsemiconductor optical amplifiers," *IEEE J. Quantum Electron.*, vol. 40, no. 3, pp. 306–320, Mar. 2004, doi: 10.1109/JQE.2003.823032.

[56] S. Sygletos, R. Bonk, T. Vallaitis, A. Marculescu, P. Vorreau, J. Li, R. Brenot, F. Lelarge, G. Duan, W. Freude, and J. Leuthold, "Filter assisted wavelength conversion with quantum-dot SOAs," *J. Lightwave Technol.*, vol. 28, no. 6, pp. 882–897, Mar. 2010, doi: 10.1109/JLT.2010.2040457.

[57] J. Leuthold, P.-A. Besse, E. Gamper, M. Dulk, S. Fischer, G. Guekos, and H. Melchior, "All-optical Mach-Zehnder interferometer wavelength converters and switches with integrated data- and control-signal separation scheme," *J. Lightwave Technol.*, vol. 17, no. 6, pp. 1056–1066, Jun. 1999, doi: 10.1109/50.769308.

[58] M. Spyropoulou, S. Sygletos, and I. Tomkos, "Simulation of multiwavelength regeneration based on QD semiconductor optical amplifiers," *IEEE Photonics Technol. Lett.*, vol. 19, no. 20, pp. 1577–1579, Oct. 2007, doi: 10.1109/LPT.2007.903879.

[59] J. Wang, A. Maitra, W. Freude, and J. Leuthold, "Regenerative properties of interferometric cross-gain and cross-phase modulation DPSK wavelength converters," in *2007 Nonlinear Photonics Topical Meeting and Tabletop Exhibit, Quebec city, Canada*, Sep. 2–6 2007, paper NTuB2.

[60] C. Dong, P. So, T. French, and E. Gratton, "Fluorescence lifetime imaging by asynchronous pump-probe microscopy," *Biophysical Journal*, vol. 69, no. 6, pp. 2234–2242, 1995, doi: 10.1016/S0006-3495(95)80148-7.

[61] N. E. Henriksen and V. Engel, "On the deconvolution of the temporal width of laser pulses from pump–probe signals," *J. Chem. Phys.*, vol. 111, no. 23, pp. 10469–10475, Dec. 1999, doi: 10.1063/1.480399.

[62] P. S. Spencer and K. A. Shore, "Pump-probe propagation in a passive Kerr nonlinear optical medium," *J. Opt. Soc. Am. B: Opt. Phys.*, vol. 12, no. 1, pp. 67–71, Jan. 1995, doi: 10.1364/JOSAB.12.000067.

[63] K. L. Hall, G. Lenz, E. P. Ippen, and G. Raybon, "Heterodyne pump-probe technique for time-domain studies of optical nonlinearities in waveguides," *Opt. Lett.*, vol. 17, no. 12, pp. 874–876, Jun. 1992, doi: 10.1364/OL.17.000874.

[64]   R. Bonk, S. Sygletos, R. Brenot, T. Vallaitis, A. Marculescu, P. Vorreau, J. Li,
       W. Freude, F. Lelarge, G.-H. Duan, and J. Leuthold, "Optimum filter for
       wavelength conversion with QD-SOA," in *Proc. Conf. on Lasers and Electro-
       Optics (CLEO/IQEC 2009)*, Baltimore, USA, May 31–Jun. 05 2009, paper
       CMC6.   [Online].   Available: http://www.opticsinfobase.org/-
       abstract.cfm?URI=CLEO-2009-CMC6

[65]   K.-P. Ho, *Phase-Modulated Optical Communication Systems*. New York:
       Springer, 2005.

[66]   A. Mecozzi and J. Mørk, "Theory of heterodyne pump-probe experiments with
       femtosecond pulses," *J. Opt. Soc. Am. B: Opt. Phys.*, vol. 13, no. 11, p. 2437,
       Nov. 1996, doi: 10.1364/JOSAB.13.002437.

[67]   P. Borri, W. Langbein, J. M, and J. M. Hvam, "Heterodyne pump-probe and
       four-wave mixing in semiconductor optical amplifiers using balanced lock-in
       detection," *Opt. Commun.*, vol. 169, no. 1–6, pp. 317–324, 1999, doi:
       10.1016/S0030-4018(99)00391-0.

[68]   A. J. Zilkie, J. Meier, P. W. E. Smith, M. Mojahedi, J. S. Aitchison, P. J. Poole,
       N. C. Allen, P. Barrios, and D. Poitras, "Characterization of the ultrafast carrier
       dynamics of an InAs/InGaAsP quantum dot semiconductor optical amplifier
       operating at 1.5μm," *Proc. SPIE. Int. Soc. Opt. Eng.*, vol. 5971, p. 59710G,
       Sep. 2005, doi: 10.1117/12.629698.

[69]   J. Mørk and A. Mecozzi, "Theory of the ultrafast optical response of active
       semiconductor waveguides," *J. Opt. Soc. Am. B: Opt. Phys.*, vol. 13, no. 8, pp.
       1803–1816, Aug. 1996, doi: 10.1364/JOSAB.13.001803.

[70]   U. Gubler and C. Bosshard, "Molecular design for third-order nonlinear
       optics," in *Polymers for Photonics Applications 1*, ser. Advances in Polymer
       Science. Berlin, Heidelberg: Springer, 2002, vol. 158, pp. 123–191.

[71]   J. Y. Marzin, J. M. Gérard, A. Izraël, D. Barrier, and G. Bastard,
       "Photoluminescence of single InAs quantum dots obtained by self-organized
       growth on GaAs," *Phys. Rev. Lett.*, vol. 73, no. 5, pp. 716–719, Aug. 1994, doi:
       10.1103/PhysRevLett.73.716.

[72]   D. Leonard, M. Krishnamurthy, C. M. Reaves, S. P. Denbaars, and P. M. Petroff, "Direct formation of quantum-sized dots from uniform coherent islands of ingaas on gaas surfaces," *Appl. Phys. Lett.*, vol. 63, no. 23, pp. 3203–3205, 1993, doi: 10.1063/1.110199.

[73]   Y. Arakawa and H. Sakaki, "Multidimensional quantum well laser and temperature dependence of its threshold current," *Appl. Phys. Lett.*, vol. 40, no. 11, pp. 939–941, 1982, doi: 10.1063/1.92959.

[74]   L. V. Asryan and R. A. Suris, "Inhomogeneous line broadening and the threshold current density of a semiconductor quantum dot laser," *Semicond. Sci. Technol.*, vol. 11, no. 4, pp. 554–567, 1996, doi: 10.1088/0268-1242/11/4/017.

[75]   N. Kirstaedter, N. Ledentsov, M. Grundmann, D. Bimberg, V. Ustinov, S. Ruvimov, M. Maximov, P. Kop'ev, Z. Alferov, U. Richter, P. Werner, U. Gosele, and J. Heydenreich, "Low threshold, large T_o injection laser emission from (In,Ga)As quantum dots," *Electron. Lett.*, vol. 30, no. 17, pp. 1416–1417, Aug. 1994. [Online]. Available: http://ieeexplore.ieee.org/search/-srchabstract.jsp?arnumber=326309

[76]   M. G. Thompson, A. R. Rae, R. V. Penty, I. H. White, A. R. Kovsh, S. S. Mikhrin, D. A. Livshits, and I. L. Krestnikov, "Absorber length optimisation for sub-picosecond pulse generation and ultra-low jitter performance in passively mode-locked 1.3μm quantum-dot laser diodes," in *Optical Fiber Communication Conference, 2006 and the 2006 National Fiber Optic Engineers Conference. OFC 2006*, Anaheim, California, USA, Mar. 5 2006, paper OThG3. [Online]. Available: http://www.opticsinfobase.org/-abstract.cfm?URI=OFC-2006-OThG3

[77]   M. Kuntz, G. Fiol, M. Laemmlin, C. Meuer, and D. Bimberg, "High-speed mode-locked quantum-dot lasers and optical amplifiers," *Proc. IEEE*, vol. 95, no. 9, pp. 1767–1778, Sep. 2007, doi: 10.1109/JPROC.2007.900949.

[78]   M. Hoffmann, Y. Barbarin, D. J. Maas, M. Golling, T. Südmeyer, U. Keller, I. L. Krestnikov, S. S. Mikhrin, and A. R. Kovsh, "First modelocked quantum dot vertical external cavity surface emitting laser," in *Advanced Solid-State Photonics (ASSP)*, Denver, Colorado, USA, Feb. 1 2009, paper ME5. [Online]. Available: http://www.opticsinfobase.org/abstract.cfm?URI=ASSP-2009-ME5

[79]   J. P. Reithmaier, G. Eisenstein, and A. Forchel, "InAs/InP quantum-dash lasers and amplifiers," *Proc. IEEE*, vol. 95, no. 9, pp. 1779–1790, Sep. 2007, doi: 10.1109/JPROC.2007.900950.

[80]   R. Brenot, F. Lelarge, O. Legouezigou, F. Pommereau, F. Poingt, L. Legouezigou, E. Derouin, O. Drisse, B. Rousseau, F. Martin, and G. Duan, "Quantum dots semiconductor optical amplifier with a -3dB bandwidth of up to 120 nm in semi-cooled operation," in *Optical Fiber communication/National Fiber Optic Engineers Conference, 2008. OFC/NFOEC 2008. Conference on*, San Diego, CA, USA, Feb. 24–28 2008, paper OTuC1, doi: 10.1109/OFC.2008.4528574.

[81]   T. Akiyama, M. Sugawara, and Y. Arakawa, "Quantum-dot semiconductor optical amplifiers," *Proc. IEEE*, vol. 95, no. 9, pp. 1757–1766, Sep. 2007, doi: 10.1109/JPROC.2007.900899.

[82]   P. Michler, A. Kiraz, C. Becher, W. V. Schoenfeld, P. M. Petroff, L. Zhang, E. Hu, and A. Imamoglu, "A Quantum Dot Single-Photon Turnstile Device," *Science*, vol. 290, no. 5500, pp. 2282–2285, 2000, doi: 10.1126/science.290.5500.2282.

[83]   K. Sebald, P. Michler, T. Passow, D. Hommel, G. Bacher, and A. Forchel, "Single-photon emission of CdSe quantum dots at temperatures up to 200 K," *Appl. Phys. Lett.*, vol. 81, no. 16, pp. 2920–2922, 2002, doi: 10.1063/1.1515364.

[84]   M. B. Ward, O. Z. Karimov, D. C. Unitt, Z. L. Yuan, P. See, D. G. Gevaux, A. J. Shields, P. Atkinson, and D. A. Ritchie, "On-demand single-photon source for 1.3μm telecom fiber," *Appl. Phys. Lett.*, vol. 86, no. 20, p. 201111, May 2005, doi: 10.1063/1.1922573.

[85]   W. Löffler, D. Tröndle, J. Fallert, H. Kalt, D. Litvinov, D. Gerthsen, J. Lupaca-Schomber, T. Passow, B. Daniel, J. Kvietkova, M. Grün, C. Klingshirn, and M. Hetterich, "Electrical spin injection from ZnMnSe into InGaAs quantum wells and quantum dots," *Appl. Phys. Lett.*, vol. 88, no. 6, p. 062105, 2006, doi: 10.1063/1.2172221.

[86] M. Hetterich, W. Löffler, J. Fallert, N. Höpcke, H. Burger, T. Passow, S. Li, B. Daniel, B. Ramadout, J. Lupaca-Schomber, J. Hetterich, D. Litvinov, D. Gerthsen, C. Klingshirn, and H. Kalt, "Electrical spin injection into InGa(N)As quantum structures and single InGaAs quantum dots," *Phys. Status Solidi B*, vol. 243, no. 14, pp. 3812–3824, Oct. 2006, doi: 10.1002/pssb.200672120.

[87] H. Wang, E. Aw, M. Xia, M. Thompson, R. Penty, I. White, and A. Kovsh, "Temperature independent optical amplification in uncooled quantum dot optical amplifiers," in *Optical Fiber communication/National Fiber Optic Engineers Conference, 2008. OFC/NFOEC 2008. Conference on*, San Diego, CA, USA, Feb. 24–28 2008, paper OTuC2, doi: 10.1109/OFC.2008.4528575.

[88] D. Bimberg, G. Fiol, M. Kuntz, C. Meuer, M. Laemmlin, N. N. Ledentsov, and A. R. Kovsh, "High speed nanophotonic devices based on quantum dots," *Phys. Status Solidi A*, vol. 203, pp. 3523–3532, Nov. 2006, doi: 10.1002/pssa.200622488.

[89] T. Akiyama, H. Kuwatsuka, T. Simoyama, Y. Nakata, K. Mukai, M. Sugawara, O. Wada, and H. Ishikawa, "Nonlinear gain dynamics in quantum-dot optical amplifiers and its application to optical communication devices," *IEEE J. Quantum Electron.*, vol. 37, no. 8, pp. 1059–1065, Aug. 2001, doi: 10.1109/3.937395.

[90] F. Lelarge, B. Dagens, J. Renaudier, R. Brenot, A. Accard, F. van Dijk, D. Make, O. L. Gouezigou, J.-G. Provost, F. Poingt, J. Landreau, O. Drisse, E. Derouin, B. Rousseau, F. Pommereau, and G.-H. Duan, "Recent advances on InAs/InP quantum dash based semiconductor lasers and optical amplifiers operating at 1.55μm," *IEEE J. Sel. Top. Quantum Electron.*, vol. 13, no. 1, pp. 111–124, Feb. 2007, doi: 10.1109/JSTQE.2006.887154.

[91] M. Asada, Y. Miyamoto, and Y. Suematsu, "Gain and the threshold of three-dimensional quantum-box lasers," *IEEE J. Quantum Electron.*, vol. 22, no. 9, pp. 1915–1921, Sep. 1986. [Online]. Available: http://ieeexplore.ieee.org/xpls/-abs_all.jsp?arnumber=1073149&tag=1

[92] Z. Xu, D. Birkedal, M. Juhl, and J. M. Hvam, "Submonolayer InGaAs/GaAs quantum-dot lasers with high modal gain and zero-linewidth enhancement factor," *Appl. Phys. Lett.*, vol. 85, no. 15, pp. 3259–3261, 2004, doi: 10.1063/1.1806564.

[93] D. Bimberg, N. Kirstaedter, N. Ledentsov, Z. Alferov, P. Kop'ev, and V. Ustinov, "InGaAs-GaAs quantum-dot lasers," *IEEE J. Sel. Top. Quantum Electron.*, vol. 3, no. 2, pp. 196–205, Apr. 1997, doi: 10.1109/2944.605656.

[94] P.-C. Peng, G. Lin, H.-C. Kuo, C.-E. Yeh, J.-N. Liu, C.-T. Lin, J. Chen, S. Chi, J. Chi, and S.-C. Wang, "Dynamic characteristics and linewidth enhancement factor of quantum-dot vertical-cavity surface-emitting lasers," *IEEE J. Sel. Top. Quantum Electron.*, vol. 15, no. 3, pp. 844–849, May 2009, doi: 10.1109/JSTQE.2008.2011375.

[95] A. Martinez, J.-G. Provost, A. Lemaître, O. Gauthier-Lafaye, B. Dagens, K. Merghem, L. Ferlazzo, C. Dupuis, O. L. Gouezigou, and A. Ramdane, "Static and dynamic measurements of the henry factor of 5 -quantum dot layer single mode lasers emitting at 1.3 µm on GaAs," in *Conference on Lasers and Electro-Optics/Quantum Electronics and Laser Science and Photonic Applications Systems Technologies*, 2005, paper CThH1. [Online]. Available: http://www.opticsinfobase.org/abstract.cfm?URI=CLEO-2005-CThH1

[96] M. van der Poel, E. Gehrig, O. Hess, D. Birkedal, and J. Hvam, "Ultrafast gain dynamics in quantum-dot amplifiers: Theoretical analysis and experimental investigations," *IEEE J. Quantum Electron.*, vol. 41, no. 9, pp. 1115–1123, Sep. 2005, doi: 10.1109/JQE.2005.852795.

[97] T. Vallaitis, C. Koos, R. Bonk, W. Freude, M. Laemmlin, C. Meuer, D. Bimberg, and J. Leuthold, "Slow and fast dynamics of gain and phase in a quantum dot semiconductor optical amplifier," *Opt. Express*, vol. 16, no. 1, pp. 170–178, Jan. 2008, doi: 10.1364/OE.16.000170.

[98] S. Schneider, P. Borri, W. Langbein, U. Woggon, R. L. Sellin, D. Ouyang, and D. Bimberg, "Linewidth enhancement factor in InGaAs quantum-dot amplifiers," *IEEE J. Quantum Electron.*, vol. 40, no. 10, pp. 1423–1429, Oct. 2004, doi: 10.1109/JQE.2004.834779.

[99] R. Alizon, D. Hadass, V. Mikhelashvili, G. Eisenstein, R. Schwertberger, A. Somers, J. Reithmaier, A. Forchel, M. Calligaro, S. Bansropun, and M. Krakowski, "Multiple wavelength amplification in wide band high power 1550 nm quantum dash optical amplifier," *Electron. Lett.*, vol. 40, no. 12, pp. 760–761, Jun. 2004, doi: 10.1049/el:20040531.

[100] T. B. Norris, K. Kim, J. Urayama, Z. K. Wu, J. Singh, and P. K. Bhattacharya, "Density and temperature dependence of carrier dynamics in self-organized InGaAs quantum dots," *J. Phys. D: Appl. Phys.*, vol. 38, no. 13, pp. 2077–2087, Jun. 2005, doi: 10.1088/0022-3727/38/13/003.

[101] P. Borri, W. Langbein, J. Hvam, F. Heinrichsdorff, M.-H. Mao, and D. Bimberg, "Spectral hole-burning and carrier-heating dynamics in InGaAs quantum-dot amplifiers," *IEEE J. Sel. Top. Quantum Electron.*, vol. 6, no. 3, pp. 544–551, 2000, doi: 10.1109/2944.865110.

[102] A. V. Uskov, J. Mørk, B. Tromborg, T. W. Berg, I. Magnusdottir, and E. P. O'Reilly, "On high-speed cross-gain modulation without pattern effects in quantum dot semiconductor optical amplifiers," *Opt. Commun.*, vol. 227, no. 4–6, pp. 363–369, 2003, doi: DOI: 10.1016/j.optcom.2003.09.052.

[103] G. Contestabile, A. Maruta, S. Sekiguchi, K. Morito, M. Sugawara, and K. Kitayama, "160 Gb/s cross gain modulation in quantum dot SOA at 1550 nm," in *Optical Communication, 2009. ECOC 2009. 35th European Conference on*, Vienna, Austria, Sep. 20–24 2009, postdeadline paper PD1.4.

[104] T. Akiyama, M. Ekawa, M. Sugawara, H. Sudo, K. Kawaguchi, A. Kuramata, H. Ebe, K. Morito, H. Imai, and Y. Arakawa, "An ultrawide-band (120 nm) semiconductor optical amplifier having an extremely-high penalty-free output power of 23 dBm realized with quantum-dot active layers," in *Optical Fiber Communication Conference, 2004. OFC 2004*, Los Angeles, CA, USA, Feb. 23–27 2004, postdeadline paper PDP12, doi: 10.1109/OFC.2004.1362282.

[105] N. Yasuoka, K. Kawaguchi, H. Ebe, T. Akiyama, M. Ekawa, K. Morito, M. Sugawara, and Y. Arakawa, "1.55-μm polarization-insensitive quantum dot semiconductoroptical amplifier," in *Optical Communication, 2008. ECOC 2008. 34th European Conference on*, Brussels, Belgium, Sep. 21–25 2008, paper Th.1.C.1.

[106] R. Bonk,   C. Meuer,   T. Vallaitis,   S. Sygletos,   P. Vorreau,   S. Ben-Ezra,
S. Tsadka, A. Kovsh, I. Krestnikov, M. Laemmlin, D. Bimberg, W. Freude, and
J. Leuthold, "Single and multiple channel operation dynamics of linear
quantum-dot semiconductor optical amplifier," in *Optical Communication,
2008. ECOC 2008. 34th European Conference on*, Brussels, Belgium, Sep. 21–
25 2008, paper Th.1.C.2, doi: 10.1109/ECOC.2008.4729375.

[107] T. Vallaitis,   R. Bonk,   J. Guetlein,   C. Meuer,   D. Hillerkuss,   W. Freude,
D. Bimberg, and J. Leuthold, "Optimizing SOA for large input power dynamic
range with respect to applications in extended GPON," in *OSA Topical
Meeting: Access Networks and In-house Communications (ANIC)*, 2010, paper
AThC4.

[108] H. Dery   and   G. Eisenstein,   "The   impact   of   energy   band   diagram   and
inhomogeneous broadening on the optical differential gain in nanostructure
lasers," *IEEE J. Quantum Electron.*, vol. 41, no. 1, pp. 26–35, 2005, doi:
10.1109/JQE.2004.837953.

[109] H. Benisty, C. M. Sotomayor-Torrès, and C. Weisbuch, "Intrinsic mechanism
for the poor luminescence properties of quantum-box systems," *Phys. Rev. B:
Condens. Matter*, vol. 44, no. 19, pp. 10945–10948, Nov. 1991, doi:
10.1103/PhysRevB.44.10945.

[110] V. A. Shchukin and D. Bimberg, "Spontaneous ordering of nanostructures on
crystal surfaces," *Rev. Mod. Phys.*, vol. 71, no. 4, pp. 1125–1171, Jul. 1999,
doi: 10.1103/RevModPhys.71.1125.

[111] J. H. Lee, Z. M. Wang, and G. J. Salamo, "The control on size and density of
inas qds by droplet epitaxy (april 2009)," *IEEE Trans. Nanotechnol.*, vol. 8,
no. 4, pp. 431–436, Jul. 2009, doi: 10.1109/TNANO.2009.2021654.

[112] I. L.   Krestnikov,   M. Straßburg,   M. Caesar,   A. Hoffmann,   U. W.   Pohl,
D. Bimberg, N. N. Ledentsov, P. S. Kop'ev, Z. I. Alferov, D. Litvinov,
A. Rosenauer, and D. Gerthsen, "Control of the electronic properties of CdSe
submonolayer superlattices via vertical correlation of quantum dots," *Phys.
Rev. B: Condens. Matter*, vol. 60, no. 12, pp. 8695–8703, Sep. 1999, doi:
10.1103/PhysRevB.60.8695.

[113] I. L. Krestnikov, N. N. Ledentsov, A. Hoffmann, and D. Bimberg, "Arrays of two-dimensional islands formed by submonolayer insertions: Growth, properties, devices," *Phys. Status Solidi A*, vol. 183, no. 2, pp. 207–233, Feb. 2001, doi: 10.1002/1521-396X(200102)183:2<207::AID-PSSA207>3.0.CO;2-2.

[114] F. Hopfer, A. Mutig, M. Kuntz, G. Fiol, D. Bimberg, N. N. Ledentsov, V. A. Shchukin, S. S. Mikhrin, D. L. Livshits, I. L. Krestnikov, A. R. Kovsh, N. D. Zakharov, and P. Werner, "Single-mode submonolayer quantum-dot vertical-cavity surface-emitting lasers with high modulation bandwidth," *Appl. Phys. Lett.*, vol. 89, no. 14, p. 141106, 2006, doi: 10.1063/1.2358114.

[115] D. Bimberg, M. Kuntz, and M. Laemmlin, "Quantum dot photonic devices for lightwave communication," *Appl. Phys. A*, vol. 80, no. 6, pp. 1179–1182, 2005, doi: 10.1007/s00339-004-3184-y.

[116] J. A. Lott, N. N. Ledentsov, V. M. Ustinov, N. A. Maleev, A. E. Zhukov, A. R. Kovsh, M. V. Maximov, B. V. Volovik, Z. I. Alferov, and D. Bimberg, "InAs-InGaAs quantum dot VCSELs on GaAs substrates emitting at 1.3 μm," *Electron. Lett.*, vol. 36, no. 16, pp. 1384–1385, Aug. 2000. [Online]. Available: http://ieeexplore.ieee.org/xpls/abs_all.jsp?arnumber=862159

[117] V. M. Ustinov, A. E. Zhukov, N. A. Maleev, A. R. Kovsh, S. S. Mikhrin, B. V. Volovik, Y. G. Musikhin, Y. M. Shernyakov, M. V. Maximov, A. F. Tsatsul'nikov, N. N. Ledentsov, Z. I. Alferov, J. A. Lott, and D. Bimberg, "1.3μm InAs/GaAs quantum dot lasers and VCSELs grown by molecular beam epitaxy," *J. Cryst. Growth*, vol. 227–228, pp. 1155–1161, 2001, doi: 10.1016/S0022-0248(01)01006-5.

[118] I. I. Novikov, N. Y. Gordeev, M. V. Maximov, Y. M. Shernyakov, A. E. Zhukov, A. P. Vasil'ev, E. S. Semenova, V. M. Ustinov, N. N. Ledentsov, D. Bimberg, N. D. Zakharov, and P. Werner, "Ultrahigh gain and non-radiative recombination channels in 1.5 μm range metamorphic InAs-InGaAs quantum dot lasers on gaas substrates," *Semiconductor Science and Technology*, vol. 20, no. 1, pp. 33–37, 2005, doi: 10.1088/0268-1242/20/1/005.

[119] J. P. Reithmaier, A. Somers, S. Deubert, R. Schwertberger, W. Kaiser, A. Forchel, M. Calligaro, P. Resneau, O. Parillaud, S. Bansropun, M. Krakowski, R. Alizon, D. Hadass, A. Bilenca, H. Dery, V. Mikhelashvili, G. Eisenstein, M. Gioannini, I. Montrosset, T. W. Berg, M. van der Poel, J. Mørk, and B. Tromborg, "InP based lasers and optical amplifiers with wire-/dot-like active regions," *J. Phys. D: Appl. Phys.*, vol. 38, no. 13, pp. 2088–2102, 2005, doi: 10.1088/0022-3727/38/13/004.

[120] H. Saito, K. Nishi, and S. Sugou, "Ground-state lasing at room temperature in long-wavelength InAs quantum-dot lasers on InP(311)B substrates," *Appl. Phys. Lett.*, vol. 78, no. 3, pp. 267–269, 2001, doi: 10.1063/1.1339846.

[121] O. Bierwagen and W. T. Masselink, "Self-organized growth of InAs quantum wires and dots on InP(001): The role of vicinal substrates," *Appl. Phys. Lett.*, vol. 86, no. 11, p. 113110, 2005, doi: 10.1063/1.1884762.

[122] F. Lelarge, B. Rousseau, B. Dagens, F. Poingt, F. Pommereau, and A. Accard, "Room temperature continuous-wave operation of buried ridge stripe lasers using InAs-InP (100) quantum dots as active core," *IEEE Photonics Technol. Lett.*, vol. 17, no. 7, pp. 1369–1371, Jul. 2005, doi: 10.1109/LPT.2005.848279.

[123] D. Franke, M. Moehrle, J. Boettcher, P. Harde, A. Sigmund, and H. Kuenzel, "Effect of metal organic vapor phase epitaxy growth conditions on emission wavelength stability of 1.55 μm quantum dot lasers," *Appl. Phys. Lett.*, vol. 91, no. 8, p. 081117, 2007, doi: 10.1063/1.2773971.

[124] T. Kita, O. Wada, H. Ebe, Y. Nakata, and M. Sugawara, "Polarization-independent photoluminescence from columnar InAs/GaAs self-assembled quantum dots," *Jpn. J. Appl. Phys.*, vol. 41, pp. L1143–L1145, 2002, doi: 10.1143/JJAP.41.L1143.

[125] P. Jayavel, H. Tanaka, T. Kita, O. Wada, H. Ebe, M. Sugawara, J. Tatebayashi, Y. Arakawa, Y. Nakata, and T. Akiyama, "Control of optical polarization anisotropy in edge emitting luminescence of InAs/GaAs self-assembled quantum dots," *Appl. Phys. Lett.*, vol. 84, no. 11, pp. 1820–1822, 2004, doi: 10.1063/1.1675923.

[126] T. Koonen, "Fiber to the home/fiber to the premises: What, where, and when?" *Proc. IEEE*, vol. 94, no. 5, pp. 911–934, May 2006, doi: 10.1109/JPROC.2006.873435.

[127] ITU, *Gigabit-capable passive optical networks (GPON): General characteristics (ITU Recommendation G.984.1)*, International Telecommunications Union, Mar. 2008. [Online]. Available: http://-www.itu.int/rec/T-REC-G.984.1-200803-I/en

[128] ——, *Gigabit-capable Passive Optical Networks (GPON): Physical Media Dependent (PMD) layer specification (ITU Recommendation G.984.2)*, International Telecommunications Union, Mar. 2003. [Online]. Available: http://www.itu.int/rec/T-REC-G.984.2-200303-I/en

[129] ——, *Gigabit-capable Passive Optical Networks (G-PON): Transmission convergence layer specification (ITU Recommendation G.984.3)*, International Telecommunications Union, Mar. 2008. [Online]. Available: http://-www.itu.int/rec/T-REC-G.984.3-200803-I/en

[130] ——, *Gigabit-capable passive optical networks (G-PON): ONT management and control interface specification (ITU Recommendation G.984.4)*, International Telecommunications Union, Feb. 2008. [Online]. Available: http://www.itu.int/rec/T-REC-G.984.4-200802-I/en

[131] IEEE, *Carrier sense multiple access with Collision Detection (CSMA/CD) Access Method and Physical Layer Specifications (IEEE Standard 802.3)*, Institute of Electrical and Electronics Engineers, Inc., Dec. 2008. [Online]. Available: http://standards.ieee.org/getieee802/802.3.html

[132] T. Akiyama, N. Hatori, Y. Nakata, H. Ebe, and M. Sugawara, "Pattern-effect-free semiconductor optical amplifier achieved using quantum dots," *Electron. Lett.*, vol. 38, no. 19, pp. 1139–1140, Sep. 2002, doi: 10.1049/el:20020716.

[133] M. Laemmlin, G. Fiol, C. Meuer, M. Kuntz, F. Hopfer, A. Kovsh, N. Ledentsov, and D. Bimberg, "Distortion-free optical amplification of 20-80 GHz modelocked laser pulses at 1.3 μm using quantum dots," *Electron. Lett.*, vol. 42, no. 12, pp. 697–699, Jun. 2006, doi: 10.1049/el:20061256.

[134] C. Schmidt-Langhorst, C. Meuer, R. Ludwig, D. Puris, R. Bonk, T. Vallaitis, D. Bimberg, K. Petermann, J. Leuthold, and C. Schubert, "Quantum-dot semiconductor optical booster amplifier with ultrafast gain recovery for pattern-effect free amplification of 80 Gb/s RZ-OOK data signals," in *Optical Communication, 2009. ECOC 2009. 35th European Conference on*, Vienna, Austria, Sep. 20–24 2009, paper We6.2.1.

[135] D. A. Francis, S. P. DiJaili, and J. D. Walker, "A single-chip linear optical amplifier," in *Optical Fiber Communication Conference, 2001. OFC 2001*, Anaheim, CA, USA, Mar. 17–22 2001, postdeadline paper PDP13.

[136] P. Iannane, K. Reichmann, and L. Spiekman, "In-service upgrade of an amplified 130-km metro CWDM transmission system using a single LOA with 140-nm bandwidth," in *Optical Fiber Communication Conference, 2003. OFC 2003*, Atlanta, GA, USA, Mar. 23–28 2003, paper ThQ3.

[137] R. Bonk, T. Vallaitis, J. Guetlein, D. Hillerkuss, J. Li, W. Freude, and J. Leuthold, "Quantum dot SOA dynamic range improvement for phase modulated signals," in *Proc. Optical Fiber Communication Conference (OFC'10)*, San Diego, CA, USA, Mar. 21–25 2010, paper OThK3.

[138] P. Borri, W. Langbein, J. Hvam, F. Heinrichsdorff, M.-H. Mao, and D. Bimberg, "Ultrafast gain dynamics in InAs-InGaAs quantum-dot amplifiers," *IEEE Photonics Technol. Lett.*, vol. 12, no. 6, pp. 594–596, 2000, doi: 10.1109/68.849054.

[139] M. van der Poel, J. Mørk, A. Somers, A. Forchel, J. P. Reithmaier, and G. Eisenstein, "Ultrafast gain and index dynamics of quantum dash structures emitting at 1.55μm," *Appl. Phys. Lett.*, vol. 89, no. 8, p. 081102, 2006, doi: 10.1063/1.2337881.

[140] A. J. Zilkie, J. Meier, P. W. E. Smith, M. Mojahedi, J. S. Aitchison, P. J. Poole, C. N. Allen, P. Barrios, and D. Poitras, "Femtosecond gain and index dynamics in an InAs/InGaAsP quantum dot amplifier operating at 1.5μm," *Opt. Express*, vol. 14, no. 23, pp. 11453–11459, Nov. 2006, doi: 10.1364/OE.14.011453.

[141] S. Dommers, V. V. Temnov, U. Woggon, J. Gomis, J. Martinez-Pastor, M. Laemmlin, and D. Bimberg, "Complete ground state gain recovery after ultrashort double pulses in quantum dot based semiconductor optical amplifier," *Appl. Phys. Lett.*, vol. 90, p. 033508, Jan. 2007, doi: 10.1063/1.2431789.

[142] V. Cesari, W. Langbein, P. Borri, M. Rossetti, A. Fiore, S. Mikhrin, I. Krestnikov, and A. Kovsh, "Ultrafast carrier dynamics in p-doped InGaAs quantum dot amplifiers," in *CLEO/Europe and IQEC 2007 Conference Digest*. Munich, Germany: Optical Society of America, Jun. 17 2007, paper CB9_1. [Online]. Available: http://www.opticsinfobase.org/- abstract.cfm?URI=CLEO_E-2007-CB9_1

[143] T. Akiyama, O. Wada, H. Kuwatsuka, T. Simoyama, Y. Nakata, K. Mukai, M. Sugawara, and H. Ishikawa, "Nonlinear processes responsible for nondegenerate four-wave mixing in quantum-dot optical amplifiers," *Appl. Phys. Lett.*, vol. 77, no. 12, pp. 1753–1755, 2000, doi: 10.1063/1.1311319.

[144] T. Akiyama, H. Kuwatsuka, N. Hatori, Y. Nakata, H. Ebe, and M. Sugawara, "Symmetric highly efficient (~0dB) wavelength conversion based on four-wave mixing in quantum dot optical amplifiers," *IEEE Photonics Technol. Lett.*, vol. 14, no. 8, pp. 1139–1141, Aug. 2002, doi: 10.1109/LPT.2002.1021995.

[145] O. Qasaimeh, "Theory of four-wave mixing wavelength conversion in quantum dot semiconductor optical amplifiers," *IEEE Photonics Technol. Lett.*, vol. 16, no. 4, pp. 993–995, 2004, doi: 10.1109/LPT.2004.824943.

[146] G. Contestabile, A. Maruta, S. Sekiguchi, K. Morito, M. S. Member, IEEE, and K. Kitayama, "Regenerative amplification by using self-phase modulation in a quantum-dot SOA," *IEEE Photonics Technol. Lett.*, vol. 22, no. 7, pp. 492– 494, Apr. 2010, doi: 10.1109/LPT.2010.2041222.

[147] C. Meuer, M. Laemmlin, S. Liebich, J. Kim, D. Bimberg, A. Capua, G. Eisenstein, R. Bonk, T. Vallaitis, and J. Leuthold, "High speed cross gain modulation using quantum dot semiconductor optical amplifiers at 1.3μm," in *Proc. Conf. on Lasers and Electro-Optics (CLEO/IQEC 2008)*, San Jose, CA, USA, May 4–9 2008, paper CTuH2. [Online]. Available: http://- www.opticsinfobase.org/abstract.cfm?URI=CLEO-2008-CTuH2

[148] C. Meuer, J. Kim, M. Laemmlin, S. Liebich, D. Bimberg, A. Capua, G. Eisenstein, R. Bonk, T. Vallaitis, J. Leuthold, A. R. Kovsh, and I. L. Krestnikov, "40 GHz small-signal cross-gain modulation in 1.3μm quantum dot semiconductor optical amplifiers," *Appl. Phys. Lett.*, vol. 93, no. 5, p. 051110, 2008, doi: 10.1063/1.2969060.

[149] T. Akiyama, N. Hatori, Y. Nakata, H. Ebe, and M. Sugawara, "Wavelength conversion based on ultrafast (<3 ps) cross-gain modulation in quantum-dot optical amplifiers," in _Optical Communication, 2002. ECOC 2002. 28th European Conference on_, vol. 2, Copenhagen, Denmark, Sep. 8–12 2002, paper Tu4.3.7.

[150] J. Wang, Y. Jiao, W. Freude, and J. Leuthold, "Regenerative properties of bulk and quantum dot SOA based all-optical Mach-Zehnder interferometer DPSK wavelength converters," in _Photonics in Switching, 2006. PS '06. International Conference on_, Heraklion, Crete, Oct. 16–18 2006, paper 04.5, doi: 10.1109/PS.2006.4350178.

[151] J. Leuthold, J. Wang, T. Vallaitis, C. Koos, R. Bonk, A. Marculescu, P. Vorreau, S. Sygletos, and W. Freude, "New approaches to perform all-optical signal regeneration," in _Transparent Optical Networks, 2007. ICTON '07. 9th International Conference on_, Rome, Italy, Jul. 1–5 2007, invited paper We.D2.1, doi: 10.1109/ICTON.2007.4296187.

[152] S. Sygletos, R. Bonk, P. Vorreau, T. Vallaitis, J. Wang, W. Freude, J. Leuthold, C. Meuer, D. Bimberg, R. Brenot, F. Lelarge, and G.-H. Duan, "A wavelength conversion scheme based on a quantum-dot semiconductor optical amplifier and a delay interferometer," in _Transparent Optical Networks, 2008. ICTON 2008. 10th Anniversary International Conference on_, Athens, Greece, Jun. 22–26 2008, invited paper We.B2.5, doi: 10.1109/ICTON.2008.4598617.

[153] S. Sygletos, R. Bonk, T. Vallaitis, A. Marculescu, P. Vorreau, J. Li, R. Brenot, F. Lelarge, G. Duan, W. Freude, and J. Leuthold, "Optimum filtering schemes for performing wavelength conversion with QD-SOA," in _Transparent Optical Networks, 2009. ICTON '09. 11th International Conference on_, Jun. 28–Jul. 2 2009, invited paper Mo.C1.3, doi: 10.1109/ICTON.2009.5185000.

[154] T. Sugaya, K. Komori, S. Yamauchi, and T. Amano, "1.3μm InAs quantum dots grown with an As_2 source using molecular-beam epitaxy," _J. Vac. Sci. Technol. B_, vol. 23, no. 3, pp. 1243–1246, Jun. 2005, doi: 10.1116/1.1913672.

[155] P. B. Joyce, T. J. Krzyzewski, G. R. Bell, T. S. Jones, S. Malik, D. Childs, and R. Murray, "Effect of growth rate on the size, composition, and optical properties of InAs/GaAs quantum dots grown by molecular-beam epitaxy," *Phys. Rev. B: Condens. Matter*, vol. 62, no. 16, pp. 10891–10895, Oct. 2000, doi: 10.1103/PhysRevB.62.10891.

[156] J. X. Chen, A. Markus, A. Fiore, U. Oesterle, R. P. Stanley, J. F. Carlin, R. Houdré, M. Ilegems, L. Lazzarini, L. Nasi, M. T. Todaro, E. Piscopiello, R. Cingolani, M. Catalano, J. Katcki, and J. Ratajczak, "Tuning InAs/GaAs quantum dot properties under Stranski-Krastanov growth mode for 1.3 µm applications," *J. Appl. Phys.*, vol. 91, no. 10, pp. 6710–6716, 2002, doi: 10.1063/1.1476069.

[157] B. Alloing, C. Zinoni, V. Zwiller, L. H. Li, C. Monat, M. Gobet, G. Buchs, A. Fiore, E. Pelucchi, and E. Kapon, "Growth and characterization of single quantum dots emitting at 1300 nm," *Appl. Phys. Lett.*, vol. 86, no. 10, p. 101908, Mar. 2005, doi: 10.1063/1.1872213.

[158] L. Chu, M. Arzberger, G. Böhm, and G. Abstreiter, "Influence of growth conditions on the photoluminescence of self-assembled InAs/GaAs quantum dots," *J. Appl. Phys.*, vol. 85, no. 4, pp. 2355–2362, 1999, doi: 10.1063/1.369549.

[159] K. Nishi, H. Saito, S. Sugou, and J.-S. Lee, "A narrow photoluminescence linewidth of 21 meV at 1.35µm from strain-reduced InAs quantum dots covered by In$_{0.2}$Ga$_{0.8}$As grown on GaAs substrates," *Appl. Phys. Lett.*, vol. 74, no. 8, pp. 1111–1113, Feb. 1999, doi: 10.1063/1.123459.

[160] G. S. Solomon, J. A. Trezza, and J. J. S. Harris, "Substrate temperature and monolayer coverage effects on epitaxial ordering of InAs and InGaAs islands on GaAs," *Appl. Phys. Lett.*, vol. 66, no. 8, pp. 991–993, 1995, doi: 10.1063/1.113822.

[161] ——, "Effects of monolayer coverage, flux ratio, and growth rate on the island density of InAs islands on GaAs," *Appl. Phys. Lett.*, vol. 66, no. 23, pp. 3161–3163, 1995, doi: 10.1063/1.113709.

[162] R. Songmuang, S. Kiravittaya, M. Sawadsaringkarn, S. Panyakeow, and O. G. Schmidt, "Photoluminescence investigation of low-temperature capped self-assembled InAs/GaAs quantum dots," *J. Cryst. Growth*, vol. 251, no. 1–4, pp. 166–171, 2003, doi: 10.1016/S0022-0248(02)02474-0.

[163] A. Madhukar, Q. Xie, P. Chen, and A. Konkar, "Nature of strained InAs three-dimensional island formation and distribution on GaAs(100)," *Appl. Phys. Lett.*, vol. 64, no. 20, pp. 2727–2729, 1994, doi: 10.1063/1.111456.

[164] K. Yamaguchi, K. Yujobo, and T. Kaizu, "Stranski-krastanov growth of InAs quantum dots with narrow size distribution," *Jpn. J. Appl. Phys.*, vol. 39, no. 2/12A, pp. L1245–L1248, Dec. 2000, doi: 10.1143/JJAP.39.L1245.

[165] B. J. Riel, K. Hinzer, S. Moisa, J. Fraser, P. Finnie, P. Piercy, S. Fafard, and Z. R. Wasilewski, "InAs/GaAs(100) self-assembled quantum dots: arsenic pressure and capping effects," *J. Cryst. Growth*, vol. 236, no. 1–3, pp. 145–154, 2002, doi: 10.1016/S0022-0248(01)02391-0.

[166] A. Ohtake and M. Ozeki, "In situ observation of surface processes in InAs/GaAs(001) heteroepitaxy: The role of As on the growth mode," *Appl. Phys. Lett.*, vol. 78, no. 4, pp. 431–433, Jan. 2001, doi: 10.1063/1.1342216.

[167] K.-i. Shiramine, T. Itoh, S. Muto, T. Kozaki, and S. Sato, "Adatom migration in Stranski-Krastanow growth of InAs quantum dots," *J. Cryst. Growth*, vol. 242, no. 3–4, pp. 332–338, 2002, doi: DOI: 10.1016/S0022-0248(02)01437-9.

[168] O. Suekane, S. Hasegawa, T. Okui, M. Takata, and H. Nakashima, "Growth temperature dependence of InAs islands grown on GaAs (001) substrates," *Jpn. J. Appl. Phys.*, vol. 41, no. 2B, pp. 1022–1025, 2002, doi: 10.1143/JJAP.41.1022.

[169] T. J. Krzyzewski, P. B. Joyce, G. R. Bell, and T. S. Jones, "Scaling behavior in InAs/GaAs(001) quantum-dot formation," *Phys. Rev. B: Condens. Matter*, vol. 66, no. 20, p. 201302, Nov. 2002, doi: 10.1103/PhysRevB.66.201302.

[170] V. G. Dubrovskii, G. E. Cirlin, Y. G. Musikhin, Y. B. Samsonenko, A. A. Tonkikh, N. K. Polyakov, V. A. Egorov, A. F. Tsatsul'nikov, N. A. Krizhanovskaya, V. M. Ustinov, and P. Werner, "Effect of growth kinetics on the structural and optical properties of quantum dot ensembles," *J. Cryst. Growth*, vol. 267, no. 1–2, pp. 47–59, 2004, doi: 10.1016/j.jcrysgro.2004.03.055.

[171] N. N. Ledentsov, V. A. Shchukin, D. Bimberg, V. M. Ustinov, N. A. Cherkashin, Y. G. Musikhin, B. V. Volovik, G. E. Cirlin, and Z. I. Alferov, "Reversibility of the island shape, volume and density in Stranski-Krastanow growth," *Semicond. Sci. Technol.*, vol. 16, no. 6, pp. 502–506, 2001, doi: 10.1088/0268-1242/16/6/316.

[172] S. Kiravittaya, Y. Nakamura, and O. G. Schmidt, "Photoluminescence linewidth narrowing of InAs/GaAs self-assembled quantum dots," *Physica E*, vol. 13, no. 2–4, pp. 224–228, 2002, doi: 10.1016/S1386-9477(01)00525-2.

[173] P. B. Joyce, T. J. Krzyzewski, G. R. Bell, T. S. Jones, E. C. Le Ru, and R. Murray, "Optimizing the growth of 1.3 μm InAs/GaAs quantum dots," *Phys. Rev. B: Condens. Matter*, vol. 64, no. 23, p. 235317, Nov. 2001, doi: 10.1103/PhysRevB.64.235317.

[174] T. J. Krzyzewski and T. S. Jones, "Ripening and annealing effects in InAs/GaAs(001) quantum dot formation," *J. Appl. Phys.*, vol. 96, no. 1, pp. 668–674, 2004, doi: 10.1063/1.1759788.

[175] N. Grandjean, J. Massies, and O. Tottereau, "Surface segregation in (Ga,In)As/GaAs quantum boxes," *Phys. Rev. B: Condens. Matter*, vol. 55, no. 16, pp. R10189–R10192, Apr. 1997, doi: 10.1103/PhysRevB.55.R10189.

[176] G. D. Lian, J. Yuan, L. M. Brown, G. H. Kim, and D. A. Ritchie, "Modification of InAs quantum dot structure by the growth of the capping layer," *Appl. Phys. Lett.*, vol. 73, no. 1, pp. 49–51, 1998, doi: 10.1063/1.121719.

[177] A. Rosenauer, W. Oberst, D. Litvinov, D. Gerthsen, A. Förster, and R. Schmidt, "Structural and chemical investigation of $In_{0.6}Ga_{0.4}As$ Stranski-Krastanow layers buried in GaAs by transmission electron microscopy," *Phys. Rev. B: Condens. Matter*, vol. 61, no. 12, pp. 8276–8288, Mar. 2000, doi: 10.1103/PhysRevB.61.8276.

[178] A. Ponchet, A. L. Corre, H. L'Haridon, B. Lambert, and S. Salaun, "Relationship between self-organization and size of InAs islands on InP(001) grown by gas-source molecular beam epitaxy," *Appl. Phys. Lett.*, vol. 67, no. 13, pp. 1850–1852, Sep. 1995, doi: 10.1063/1.114353.

[179] J. M. Moison, F. Houzay, F. Barthe, L. Leprince, E. Andre, and O. Vatel, "Self-organized growth of regular nanometer-scale InAs dots on GaAs," *Appl. Phys. Lett.*, vol. 64, no. 2, pp. 196–198, Jan. 1994, doi: 10.1063/1.111502.

[180] M. D. Kim, T. W. Kim, Y. D. Woo, S. G. Kim, and J. S. Hong, "Formation process of and lattice parameter variation in InAs/GaAs quantum dots dependent on the growth parameters," *J. Cryst. Growth*, vol. 278, no. 1–4, pp. 125–130, 2005, doi: 10.1016/j.jcrysgro.2004.12.121.

[181] P. Borri, W. Langbein, S. Schneider, U. Woggon, R. L. Sellin, D. Ouyang, and D. Bimberg, "Exciton relaxation and dephasing in quantum-dot amplifiers from room to cryogenic temperature," *IEEE J. Sel. Top. Quantum Electron.*, vol. 8, no. 5, pp. 984–991, Sep. 2002, doi: 10.1109/JSTQE.2002.804250.

[182] A. Strecker, J. Mayer, B. Baretzky, W. Eigenthaler, T. Gemming, R. Schweinfest, and M. Rühle, "Optimization of TEM specimen preparation by double-sided ion beam thinning under low angles," *J. Electron Microsc.*, vol. 48, no. 3, pp. 235–244, Feb. 1999. [Online]. Available: http://jmicro.oxfordjournals.org/cgi/content/abstract/48/3/235

[183] A. Rosenauer, U. Fischer, D. Gerthsen, and A. Förster, "Composition evaluation by lattice fringe analysis," *Ultramicroscopy*, vol. 72, no. 3–4, pp. 121–133, 1998, doi: 10.1016/S0304-3991(98)00002-3.

[184] S. Fafard, Z. R. Wasilewski, C. N. Allen, D. Picard, M. Spanner, J. P. McCaffrey, and P. G. Piva, "Manipulating the energy levels of semiconductor quantum dots," *Phys. Rev. B: Condens. Matter*, vol. 59, no. 23, pp. 15368–15373, Jun. 1999, doi: 10.1103/PhysRevB.59.15368.

[185] N. N. Ledentsov, M. Grundmann, N. Kirstaedter, O. Schmidt, R. Heitz, J. Böhrer, D. Bimberg, V. M. Ustinov, V. A. Shchukin, A. Y. Egorov, A. E. Zhukov, S. Zaitsev, P. S. Kop'ev, Z. I. Alferov, S. S. Ruvimov, A. O. Kosogov, P. Werner, U. Gösele, and J. Heydenreich, "Ordered arrays of quantum dots: Formation, electronic spectra, relaxation phenomena, lasing," *Solid-State Electron.*, vol. 40, no. 1–8, pp. 785–798, 1996, doi: 10.1016/0038-1101(95)00364-9.

[186] K. Muraki, S. Fukatsu, Y. Shiraki, and R. Ito, "Surface segregation of In atoms during molecular beam epitaxy and its influence on the energy levels in InGaAs/GaAs quantum wells," *Appl. Phys. Lett.*, vol. 61, no. 5, pp. 557–559, 1992, doi: 10.1063/1.107835.

[187] D. Litvinov, D. Gerthsen, A. Rosenauer, M. Schowalter, T. Passow, P. Feinäugle, and M. Hetterich, "Transmission electron microscopy investigation of segregation and critical floating-layer content of indium for island formation in $In_xGa_{1-x}As$," *Phys. Rev. B: Condens. Matter*, vol. 74, no. 16, p. 165306, Oct. 2006, doi: 10.1103/PhysRevB.74.165306.

[188] V. A. Shchukin, N. N. Ledentsov, P. S. Kop'ev, and D. Bimberg, "Spontaneous ordering of arrays of coherent strained islands," *Phys. Rev. Lett.*, vol. 75, no. 16, pp. 2968–2971, Oct. 1995, doi: 10.1103/PhysRevLett.75.2968.

[189] I. Daruka and A.-L. Barabási, "Dislocation-free island formation in heteroepitaxial growth: A study at equilibrium," *Phys. Rev. Lett.*, vol. 79, no. 19, pp. 3708–3711, Nov. 1997, doi: 10.1103/PhysRevLett.79.3708.

[190] I. Kegel, T. H. Metzger, A. Lorke, J. Peisl, J. Stangl, G. Bauer, K. Nordlund, W. V. Schoenfeld, and P. M. Petroff, "Determination of strain fields and composition of self-organized quantum dots using x-ray diffraction," *Phys. Rev. B: Condens. Matter*, vol. 63, no. 3, p. 035318, Jan. 2001, doi: 10.1103/PhysRevB.63.035318.

[191] D. M. Bruls, J. W. A. M. Vugs, P. M. Koenraad, H. W. M. Salemink, J. H. Wolter, M. Hopkinson, M. S. Skolnick, F. Long, and S. P. A. Gill, "Determination of the shape and indium distribution of low-growth-rate InAs quantum dots by cross-sectional scanning tunneling microscopy," *Appl. Phys. Lett.*, vol. 81, no. 9, pp. 1708–1710, 2002, doi: 10.1063/1.1504162.

[192] P. D. Quinn, N. R. Wilson, S. A. Hatfield, C. F. McConville, G. R. Bell, T. C. Q. Noakes, P. Bailey, S. Al-Harthi, and F. Gard, "Composition profiles of InAs–GaAs quantum dots determined by medium-energy ion scattering," *Appl. Phys. Lett.*, vol. 87, no. 15, p. 153110, 2005, doi: 10.1063/1.2099533.

[193] N. Liu, J. Tersoff, O. Baklenov, A. L. Holmes, and C. K. Shih, "Nonuniform composition profile in $In_{0.5}Ga_{0.5}As$ alloy quantum dots," *Phys. Rev. Lett.*, vol. 84, no. 2, pp. 334–337, Jan. 2000, doi: 10.1103/PhysRevLett.84.334.

[194] A. Lenz, R. Timm, H. Eisele, C. Hennig, S. K. Becker, R. L. Sellin, U. W. Pohl, D. Bimberg, and M. Dähne, "Reversed truncated cone composition distribution of $In_{0.8}Ga_{0.2}As$ quantum dots overgrown by an $In_{0.1}Ga_{0.9}As$ layer in a GaAs matrix," *Appl. Phys. Lett.*, vol. 81, no. 27, pp. 5150–5152, Dec. 2002, doi: 10.1063/1.1533109.

[195] M. A. Migliorato, A. G. Cullis, M. Fearn, and J. H. Jefferson, "Atomistic simulation of strain relaxation in $In_xGa_{1-x}As$/GaAs quantum dots with nonuniform composition," *Phys. Rev. B: Condens. Matter*, vol. 65, no. 11, p. 115316, Feb. 2002, doi: 10.1103/PhysRevB.65.115316.

[196] P. Offermans, P. M. Koenraad, J. H. Wolter, K. Pierz, M. Roy, and P. A. Maksym, "Atomic-scale structure and photoluminescence of InAs quantum dots in GaAs and AlAs," *Phys. Rev. B: Condens. Matter*, vol. 72, no. 16, p. 165332, Oct. 2005, doi: 10.1103/PhysRevB.72.165332.

[197] C. Heyn, D. Endler, K. Zhang, and W. Hansen, "Formation and dissolution of InAs quantum dots on GaAs," *J. Cryst. Growth*, vol. 210, no. 4, pp. 421–428, 2000, doi: 10.1016/S0022-0248(99)00901-X.

[198] C. Heyn, A. Bolz, T. Maltezopoulos, R. Johnson, and W. Hansen, "Intermixing in self-assembled InAs quantum dot formation," *J. Cryst. Growth*, vol. 278, no. 1–4, pp. 46–50, 2005, doi: 10.1016/j.jcrysgro.2004.12.055.

[199] A. Rosenauer and D. Gerthsen, "Composition evaluation by the lattice fringe analysis method using defocus series," *Ultramicroscopy*, vol. 76, no. 1–2, pp. 49–60, 1999, doi: 10.1016/S0304-3991(98)00067-9.

[200] A. Rosenauer, M. Schowalter, F. Glas, and D. Lamoen, "First-principles calculations of 002 structure factors for electron scattering in strained $In_xGa_{1-x}As$," *Phys. Rev. B: Condens. Matter*, vol. 72, no. 8, p. 085326, Aug. 2005, doi: 10.1103/PhysRevB.72.085326.

[201] T. Passow, S. Li, P. Feinäugle, T. Vallaitis, J. Leuthold, D. Litvinov, D. Gerthsen, and M. Hetterich, "Systematic investigation into the influence of growth conditions on InAs/GaAs quantum dot properties," *J. Appl. Phys.*, vol. 102, no. 7, p. 073511, 2007, doi: 10.1063/1.2779270.

[202] D. Litvinov, H. Blank, R. Schneider, D. Gerthsen, T. Vallaitis, J. Leuthold, T. Passow, A. Grau, H. Kalt, C. Klingshirn, and M. Hetterich, "Influence of InGaAs cap layers with different In concentration on the properties of InGaAs quantum dots," *J. Appl. Phys.*, vol. 103, p. 083532, 2008, doi: 10.1063/1.2903143.

[203] E. Piscopiello, A. Rosenauer, A. Passaseo, E. H. M. Rossi, and G. V. Tendeloo, "Segregation in $In_xGa_{1-x}As$/GaAs Stranski-Krastanow layers grown by metal-organic chemical vapour deposition," *Philos. Mag.*, vol. 85, no. 32, pp. 3857–3870, Nov. 2005, doi: 10.1080/147830500269402.

[204] F. Guffarth, R. Heitz, A. Schliwa, O. Stier, N. N. Ledentsov, A. R. Kovsh, V. M. Ustinov, and D. Bimberg, "Strain engineering of self-organized InAs quantum dots," *Phys. Rev. B: Condens. Matter*, vol. 64, no. 8, p. 085305, Aug. 2001, doi: 10.1103/PhysRevB.64.085305.

[205] M. V. Maximov, A. F. Tsatsul'nikov, B. V. Volovik, D. S. Sizov, Y. M. Shernyakov, I. N. Kaiander, A. E. Zhukov, A. R. Kovsh, S. S. Mikhrin, V. M. Ustinov, Z. I. Alferov, R. Heitz, V. A. Shchukin, N. N. Ledentsov, D. Bimberg, Y. G. Musikhin, and W. Neumann, "Tuning quantum dot properties by activated phase separation of an InGa(Al)As alloy grown on InAs stressors," *Phys. Rev. B: Condens. Matter*, vol. 62, no. 24, pp. 16671–16680, Dec. 2000, doi: 10.1103/PhysRevB.62.16671.

[206] G. A. Narvaez, G. Bester, and A. Zunger, "Dependence of the electronic structure of self-assembled (In,Ga)As/GaAs quantum dots on height and composition," *J. Appl. Phys.*, vol. 98, no. 4, p. 043708, 2005, doi: 10.1063/1.1980534.

[207] O. Stier, M. Grundmann, and D. Bimberg, "Electronic and optical properties of strained quantum dots modeled by 8-band k·p theory," *Phys. Rev. B: Condens. Matter*, vol. 59, no. 8, pp. 5688–5701, Feb. 1999, doi: 10.1103/PhysRevB.59.5688.

[208] C. Pryor, "Geometry and material parameter dependence of InAs/GaAs quantum dot electronic structure," *Phys. Rev. B: Condens. Matter*, vol. 60, no. 4, pp. 2869–2874s, Jul. 1999, doi: 10.1103/PhysRevB.60.2869.

[209] Z. Z. Sun, S. F. Yoon, W. K. Loke, and C. Y. Liu, "Mechanism of emission-energy tuning in InAs quantum dots using a thin upper confinement layer," *Appl. Phys. Lett.*, vol. 88, no. 20, p. 203114, 2006, doi: 10.1063/1.2206248.

[210] H. Shin, J.-B. Kim, Y.-H. Yoo, W. Lee, E. Yoon, and Y.-M. Yu, "Enhanced strain of InAs quantum dots by an InGaAs ternary layer in a GaAs matrix," *J. Appl. Phys.*, vol. 99, no. 2, p. 023521, 2006, doi: 10.1063/1.2137880.

[211] T. Piwonski, I. O'Driscoll, J. Houlihan, G. Huyet, R. J. Manning, and A. V. Uskov, "Carrier capture dynamics of InAs/GaAs quantum dots," *Appl. Phys. Lett.*, vol. 90, p. 122108, Mar. 2007, doi: 10.1063/1.2715115.

[212] K. L. Hall, G. Lenz, A. M. Darwish, and E. P. Ippen, "Subpicosecond gain and index nonlinearities in InGaAsP diode lasers," *Opt. Commun.*, vol. 111, no. 5, pp. 589–612, Oct. 1994, doi: 10.1016/0030-4018(94)90538-X.

[213] A. Uskov, E. O'Reilly, R. Manning, R. Webb, D. Cotter, M. Laemmlin, N. Ledentsov, and D. Bimberg, "On ultrafast optical switching based on quantum-dot semiconductor optical amplifiers in nonlinear interferometers," *IEEE Photonics Technol. Lett.*, vol. 16, no. 5, pp. 1265–1267, 2004, doi: 10.1109/LPT.2004.826260.

[214] J. Wang, A. Maitra, C. G. Poulton, W. Freude, and J. Leuthold, "Temporal dynamics of the alpha factor in semiconductor optical amplifiers," *J. Lightwave Technol.*, vol. 25, no. 3, pp. 891–900, Mar. 2007, doi: 10.1109/JLT.2006.890439.

[215] T. Akiyama, H. Kuwatsuka, T. Simoyama, Y. Nakata, K. Mukai, and M. Sugawara, "Application of spectral-hole burning in the inhomogeneously broadened gain of self-assembled quantum dots to a multiwavelength-channel nonlinear optical device," *IEEE Photonics Technol. Lett.*, vol. 12, no. 10, pp. 1301–1303, Oct. 2000, doi: 10.1109/68.883810.

[216] M. Sugawara, N. Hatori, T. Akiyama, Y. Nakata, and H. Ishikawa, "Quantum-dot semiconductor optical amplifiers for high bit-rate signal processing over 40 Gbit/s," *Jpn. J. Appl. Phys.*, vol. 40, no. 5B, pp. L488–L491, May 2001, doi: 10.1143/JJAP.40.L488.

[217] T. Vallaitis, R. Bonk, J. Guetlein, D. Hillerkuss, J. Li, R. Brenot, F. Lelarge, G. H. Duan, W. Freude, and J. Leuthold, "Quantum dot SOA input power dynamic range improvement for differential-phase encoded signals," *Opt. Express*, vol. 18, no. 6, pp. 6270–6276, Mar. 2010, doi: 10.1364/OE.18.006270.

[218] A. Högele, S. Seidl, M. Kroner, K. Karrai, R. J. Warburton, B. D. Gerardot, and P. M. Petroff, "Voltage-controlled optics of a quantum dot," *Phys. Rev. Lett.*, vol. 93, no. 21, p. 217401, Nov. 2004, doi: 10.1103/PhysRevLett.93.217401.

[219] T. Yang, J. Tatebayashi, S. Tsukamoto, M. Nishioka, and Y. Arakawa, "Narrow photoluminescence linewidth (<17 meV) from highly uniform self-assembled InAs/GaAs quantum dots grown by low-pressure metalorganic chemical vapor deposition," *Appl. Phys. Lett.*, vol. 84, no. 15, pp. 2817–2819, 2004, doi: 10.1063/1.1711163.

[220] C. Meuer, J. Kim, M. Laemmlin, S. Liebich, G. Eisenstein, R. Bonk, T. Vallaitis, J. Leuthold, A. Kovsh, I. Krestnikov, and D. Bimberg, "High-speed small-signal cross-gain modulation in quantum-dot semiconductor optical amplifiers at 1.3µm," *IEEE J. Sel. Top. Quantum Electron.*, vol. 15, no. 3, pp. 749–756, May 2009, doi: 10.1109/JSTQE.2009.2012395.

[221] J. Tatebayashi, M. Nishioka, and Y. Arakawa, "Luminescence in excess of 1.5 µm at room-temperature of InAs quantum dots capped by a thin InGaAs strain-reducing layer," *J. Cryst. Growth*, vol. 237–239, no. 2, pp. 1296–1300, 2002, doi: 10.1016/S0022-0248(01)02048-6.

[222] K. Matsuda, K. Ikeda, T. Saiki, H. Saito, and K. Nishi, "Carrier–carrier interaction in single $In_{0.5}Ga_{0.5}As$ quantum dots at room temperature investigated by near-field scanning optical microscope," *Appl. Phys. Lett.*, vol. 83, no. 11, pp. 2250–2252, 2003, doi: 10.1063/1.1609662.

[223] X. Mei, M. Blumin, M. Sun, D. Kim, Z. H. Wu, H. E. Ruda, and Q. X. Guo, "Highly-ordered GaAs/AlGaAs quantum-dot arrays on GaAs (001) substrates grown by molecular-beam epitaxy using nanochannel alumina masks," *Appl. Phys. Lett.*, vol. 82, no. 6, pp. 967–969, 2003, doi: 10.1063/1.1544065.

[224] E. C. Le Ru, P. Howe, T. S. Jones, and R. Murray, "Strain-engineered InAs/GaAs quantum dots for long-wavelength emission," *Phys. Rev. B: Condens. Matter*, vol. 67, no. 16, p. 165303, Apr. 2003, doi: 10.1103/PhysRevB.67.165303.

[225] D. J. Mowbray and M. S. Skolnick, "New physics and devices based on self-assembled semiconductor quantum dots," *J. Phys. D: Appl. Phys.*, vol. 38, no. 13, pp. 2059–2076, Jul. 2005, doi: 10.1088/0022-3727/38/13/002. [Online]. Available: http://stacks.iop.org/0022-3727/38/2059

[226] Z. Mi and P. Bhattacharya, "Molecular-beam epitaxial growth and characteristics of highly uniform InAs/GaAs quantum dot layers," *J. Appl. Phys.*, vol. 98, no. 2, p. 023510, 2005, doi: 10.1063/1.1985969.

[227] A. Surrente, P. Gallo, M. Felici, B. Dwir, A. Rudra, and E. Kapon, "Dense arrays of ordered pyramidal quantum dots with narrow linewidth photoluminescence spectra," *Nanotechnology*, vol. 20, no. 41, p. 415205, 2009, doi: 10.1088/0957-4484/20/41/415205.

[228] R. Murray, D. Childs, S. Malik, P. Siverns, C. Roberts, J.-M. Hartmann, and P. Stavrinou, "1.3 μm room temperature emission from InAs/GaAs self-assembled quantum dots," *Jpn. J. Appl. Phys.*, vol. 38, no. 1B, pp. 528–530, 1999, doi: 10.1143/JJAP.38.528.

[229] M. Sugawara, K. Mukai, and Y. Nakata, "Light emission spectra of columnar-shaped self-assembled InGaAs/GaAs quantum-dot lasers: Effect of homogeneous broadening of the optical gain on lasing characteristics," *Appl. Phys. Lett.*, vol. 74, no. 11, pp. 1561–1563, 1999, doi: 10.1063/1.123616.

[230] P. Borri, W. Langbein, J. M. Hvam, F. Heinrichsdorff, M.-H. Mao, and D. Bimberg, "Time-resolved four-wave mixing in inas/ingaas quantum-dot amplifiers under electrical injection," *Appl. Phys. Lett.*, vol. 76, no. 11, pp. 1380–1382, 2000, doi: 10.1063/1.126038.

[231] M. Sugawara, N. Hatori, M. Ishida, H. Ebe, Y. Arakawa, T. Akiyama, K. Otsubo, T. Yamamoto, and Y. Nakata, "Recent progress in self-assembled quantum-dot optical devices for optical telecommunication: temperature-insensitive 10 Gbs^{-1} directly modulated lasers and 40 Gbs^{-1} signal-regenerative amplifiers," *J. Phys. D: Appl. Phys.*, vol. 38, no. 13, pp. 2126–2134, Jun. 2005, doi: 10.1088/0022-3727/38/13/008.

[232] M. Sugawara, N. Hatori, H. Ebe, M. Ishida, Y. Arakawa, T. Akiyama, K. Otsubo, and Y. Nakata, "Modeling room-temperature lasing spectra of 1.3-μm self-assembled InAs/GaAs quantum-dot lasers: Homogeneous broadening of optical gain under current injection," *Appl. Phys. Lett.*, vol. 97, no. 4, p. 043523, Jan. 2005, doi: 10.1063/1.1849426.

[233] D. Hadass, A. Bilenca, R. Alizon, H. Dery, V. Mikhelashvili, G. Eisenstein, R. Schwertberger, A. Somers, J. P. Reithmaier, A. Forchel, M. Calligaro, S. Bansropun, and M. Krakowski, "Gain and noise saturation of wide-band InAs-InP quantum dash optical amplifiers: model and experiments," *IEEE J. Sel. Top. Quantum Electron.*, vol. 11, no. 5, pp. 1015–1026, Sep.–Oct. 2005, doi: 10.1109/JSTQE.2005.853740.

[234] T. Akiyama, N. Hatori, Y. Nakata, H. Ebe, and M. Sugawara, "Pattern-effect-free amplification and cross-gain modulation achieved by using ultrafast gain nonlinearity in quantum-dot semiconductor optical amplifiers," *Phys. Status Solidi B*, vol. 238, no. 2, pp. 301–304, Jul. 2003, doi: 10.1002/pssb.200303048.

[235] A. V. Uskov, A.-P. Jauho, B. Tromborg, J. Mørk, and R. Lang, "Dephasing times in quantum dots due to elastic LO phonon-carrier collisions," *Phys. Rev. Lett.*, vol. 85, no. 7, pp. 1516–1519, Aug. 2000, doi: 10.1103/PhysRevLett.85.1516.

[236] A. Sakamoto and M. Sugawara, "Theoretical calculation of lasing spectra of quantum-dot lasers: effect of homogeneous broadening of optical gain," *IEEE Photonics Technol. Lett.*, vol. 12, no. 2, pp. 107–109, Feb. 2000, doi: 10.1109/68.823485.

[237] M. Sugawara, K. Mukai, Y. Nakata, H. Ishikawa, and A. Sakamoto, "Effect of homogeneous broadening of optical gain on lasing spectra in self-assembled $In_xGa_{1-x}As$/GaAs quantum dot lasers," *Phys. Rev. B: Condens. Matter*, vol. 61, no. 11, pp. 7595–7603, Mar. 2000, doi: 10.1103/PhysRevB.61.7595.

[238] H. Dery, E. Benisty, A. Epstein, R. Alizon, V. Mikhelashvili, G. Eisenstein, R. Schwertberger, D. Gold, J. P. Reithmaier, and A. Forchel, "On the nature of quantum dash structures," *J. Appl. Phys.*, vol. 95, no. 11, pp. 6103–6111, 2004, doi: 10.1063/1.1715135.

[239] P. P. Iannone, H. H. Lee, K. C. Reichmann, X. Zhou, M. Du, B. Pálsdóttir, K. Feder, P. Westbrook, K. Brar, J. Mann, , and L. Spiekman, "Hybrid CWDM amplifier shared by multiple TDM PONs," in *Optical Fiber Communication and the National Fiber Optic Engineers Conference, 2007. OFC/NFOEC 2007. Conference on*, Anaheim, CA, USA, Mar. 25–29 2007, postdeadline paper PDP13.

[240] D. Nesset, T. Kelly, S. Appathurai, and R. Davey, "High gain semiconductor optical amplifiers for extended reach GPON systems," in *Optical Communication, 2007. ECOC 2007. 33th European Conference on*, Berlin, Germany, Sep. 16–20 2007, postdeadline paper PDS3.5.

[241] L. Spiekman, D. Piehler, P. Iannone, K. Reichmann, and H.-H. Lee, "Semiconductor optical amplifiers for FTTx," in *Transparent Optical Networks, 2007. ICTON '07. 9th International Conference on*, vol. 2, Jul. 2007, paper Mo.D2.4, pp. 48–50, doi: 10.1109/ICTON.2007.4296137.

[242] D. Zimmerman and L. Spiekman, "Amplifiers for the masses: EDFA, EDWA, and SOA amplets for metro and access applications," *J. Lightwave Technol.*, vol. 22, no. 1, pp. 63–70, Jan. 2004, doi: 10.1109/JLT.2003.822144.

[243] M. Sauer and J. Hurley, "Experimental 43 Gb/s NRZ and DPSK performance comparison for systems with up to 8 concatenated SOAs," in *Lasers and Electro-Optics, 2006 and 2006 Quantum Electronics and Laser Science Conference. CLEO/QELS 2006. Conference on*, Long Beach, CA, USA, May 21 2006, paper CThY2, doi: 10.1109/CLEO.2006.4628112.

[244] E. Ciaramella, A. D'Errico, and V. Donzella, "Using semiconductor-optical amplifiers with constant envelope WDM signals," *IEEE J. Quantum Electron.*, vol. 44, no. 5, pp. 403–409, May 2008, doi: 10.1109/JQE.2007.914883.

[245] J. D. Downie and J. Hurley, "Effects of dispersion on SOA nonlinear impairments with DPSK signals," in *Lasers and Electro-Optics Society, 2008. LEOS 2008.*, Newport Beach, CA, USA, Nov. 9–13 2008, paper WX3, doi: 10.1109/LEOS.2008.4688766.

[246] C. Dorrer and I. Kang, "Real-time implementation of linear spectrograms for the characterization of high bit-rate optical pulse trains," *IEEE Photonics Technol. Lett.*, vol. 16, no. 3, pp. 858–860, Mar. 2004, doi: 10.1109/LPT.2004.823692.

[247] T. Mizuochi, K. Kubo, H. Yoshida, H. Fujita, H. Tagami, M. Akita, and K. Motoshima, "Next generation FEC for optical transmission systems," in *Optical Fiber Communication Conference*, 2003, paper ThN1. [Online]. Available: http://www.opticsinfobase.org/abstract.cfm?URI=OFC-2003-ThN1

[248] T. Mizuochi, "Next generation FEC for optical communication," in *Optical Fiber communication/National Fiber Optic Engineers Conference, 2008. OFC/NFOEC 2008. Conference on*, San Diego, CA, USA, Feb. 24–28 2008, tutorial OTuE5, doi: 10.1109/OFC.2008.4528593.

[249] F. Ginovart, J. C. Simon, and I. Valiente, "Gain recovery dynamics in semiconductor optical amplifier," *Optics Communications*, vol. 199, no. 1-4, pp. 111–115, 2001, doi: 10.1016/S0030-4018(01)01574-7.

[250] A. Saleh and I. Habbab, "Effects of semiconductor-optical-amplifier nonlinearity on the performance of high-speed intensity-modulation lightwave systems," *IEEE Trans. Commun.*, vol. 38, no. 6, pp. 839–846, Jun. 1990, doi: 10.1109/26.57476.

[251] K.-P. Ho, "The effect of interferometer phase error on direct-detection DPSK and DQPSK signals," *IEEE Photonics Technol. Lett.*, vol. 16, no. 1, pp. 308–310, Jan. 2004, doi: 10.1109/LPT.2003.819359.

[252] H. Kim and P. J. Winzer, "Robustness to laser frequency offset in direct-detection DPSK and DQPSK systems," *J. Lightwave Technol.*, vol. 21, no. 9, pp. 1887–1891, Sep. 2003, doi: 10.1109/JLT.2003.816816.

[253] P. Winzer and R.-J. Essiambre, "Advanced optical modulation formats," *Proc. IEEE*, vol. 94, no. 5, pp. 952–985, May 2006, doi: 10.1109/JPROC.2006.873438.

[254] X. Wei and L. Zhang, "Analysis of the phase noise in saturated SOAs for DPSK applications," *IEEE J. Quantum Electron.*, vol. 41, no. 4, pp. 554–561, Apr. 2005, doi: 10.1109/JQE.2005.843943.

[255] M. Lipson, "Guiding, modulating, and emitting light on silicon—challenges and opportunities," *J. Lightw. Techn.*, vol. 23, no. 12, pp. 4222–4238, Dec. 2005, doi: 10.1109/JLT.2005.858225.

[256] T. Tsuchizawa, K. Yamada, H. Fukuda, T. Watanabe, J.-i. Takahashi, M. Takahashi, T. Shoji, E. Tamechika, S.-i. Itabashi, and H. Morita, "Microphotonics devices based on silicon microfabrication technology," *IEEE J. Sel. Top. Quantum Electron.*, vol. 11, no. 1, pp. 232–240, Jan. 2005, doi: 10.1109/JSTQE.2004.841479.

[257] W. Bogaerts, R. Baets, P. Dumon, V. Wiaux, S. Beckx, D. Taillaert, B. Luyssaert, J. V. Campenhout, P. Bienstman, and D. V. Thourhout, "Nanophotonic waveguides in silicon-on-insulator fabricated with CMOS technology," *J. Lightw. Technol.*, vol. 23, no. 1, pp. 401–412, Jan. 2005, doi: 10.1109/JLT.2004.834471.

[258] M. A. Popovic, T. Barwicz, M. S. Dahlem, F. Gan, C. W. Holzwarth, P. T. Rakich, M. R. Watts, H. I. Smith, F. X. Kärtner, and E. P. Ippen, "Hitless-reconfigurable and bandwidth-scalable silicon photonic circuits for telecom and interconnect applications," in *Optical Fiber communication/National Fiber Optic Engineers Conference, 2008. OFC/NFOEC 2008. Conference on*, San Diego, CA, USA, Feb. 24–28 2008, paper OTuF4, doi: 10.1109/OFC.2008.4528597.

[259] W. Bogaerts, P. Dumon, D. V. Thourhout, D. Taillaert, P. Jaenen, J. Wouters, S. Beckx, V. Wiaux, and R. G. Baets, "Compact wavelength-selective functions in silicon-on-insulator photonic wires," *IEEE J. Sel. Top. Quantum Electron.*, vol. 12, no. 6, pp. 1394–1401, Nov.–Dec. 2006, doi: 10.1109/JSTQE.2006.884088.

[260] T. Fukazawa, F. Ohno, and T. Baba, "Very compact arrayed-waveguide-grating demultiplexer using Si photonic wire waveguides," *Jpn. J. Appl. Phys.*, vol. 43, no. 5B, pp. L673–L675, Apr. 2004, doi: 10.1143/JJAP.43.L673.

[261] Y. A. Vlasov, M. O'Boyle, H. F. Hamann, and S. J. McNab, "Active control of slow light on a chip with photonic crystal waveguides," *Nature*, vol. 438, pp. 65–69, Nov. 2005, doi: 10.1038/nature04210.

[262] H. Rong, A. Liu, R. Jones, O. Cohen, D. Hak, R. Nicolaescu, A. Fang, and M. Paniccia, "An all-silicon Raman laser," *Nature*, vol. 433, pp. 292–294, Jan. 2005, doi: 10.1038/nature03273.

[263] L. Liao, A. Liu, D. Rubin, J. Basak, Y. Chetrit, H. Nguyen, R. Cohen, N. Izhaky, and M. Paniccia, "40 Gbit/s silicon optical modulator for high-speed applications," *Electron. Lett.*, vol. 43, no. 22, pp. 1196—1197, Oct. 2007, doi: 10.1049/el:20072253.

[264] R. Salem, M. A. Foster, A. C. Turner, D. F. Geraghty, M. Lipson, and A. L. Gaeta, "Signal regeneration using low-power four-wave mixing on silicon chip," *Nat. Photonics*, vol. 2, pp. 35–38, Jan. 2008, doi: 10.1038/nphoton.2007.249.

[265] Y.-H. Kuo, H. Rong, V. Sih, S. Xu, and M. Paniccia, "Demonstration of wavelength conversion at 40 Gb/s data rate in silicon waveguides," *Opt. Express*, vol. 14, no. 24, pp. 11721–11726, Nov. 2006, doi: 10.1364/OE.14.011721.

[266] M. Hochberg, T. Baehr-Jones, G. Wang, M. Shearn, K. Harvard, J. Luo, B. Chen, Z. Shi, R. Lawson, P. Sullivan, A. K. Y. Jen, L. Dalton, and A. Scherer, "Terahertz all-optical modulation in a silicon-polymer hybrid system," *Nat. Mater.*, vol. 5, no. 9, pp. 703–709, Sep. 2006, doi: 10.1038/nmat1719.

[267] R. A. Soref and J. P. Lorenzo, "Single-crystal silicon: a new material for 1.3 and 1.6 μm integrated-optical components," *Electron. Lett.*, vol. 21, no. 21, pp. 953–954, 1985, doi: 10.1049/el:19850673.

[268] Z. Li, J. Yu, S. Chen, J. Liu, and J. Xia, "Paired interference 3-dB coupler based on SOI rib waveguides with anisotropic chemical wet etching," *Chin. Opt. Lett.*, vol. 5, no. 4, pp. 215–217, Apr. 2007. [Online]. Available: http://www.opticsinfobase.org/col/abstract.cfm?URI=col-5-4-215

[269] [Online]. Available: http://www.epixfab.eu

[270] L. Vivien, J. Osmond, J.-M. Fédéli, D. Marris-Morini, P. Crozat, J.-F. Damlencourt, E. Cassan, Y. Lecunff, and S. Laval, "42 GHz p.i.n germanium photodetector integrated in a silicon-on-insulator waveguide," *Opt. Express*, vol. 17, no. 8, pp. 6252–6257, 2009, doi: 10.1364/OE.17.006252.

[271] S. Selvaraja, P. Jaenen, W. Bogaerts, D. Van Thourhout, P. Dumon, and R. Baets, "Fabrication of photonic wire and crystal circuits in silicon-on-insulator using 193-nm optical lithography," *J. Lightwave Technol.*, vol. 27, no. 18, pp. 4076–4083, Sep. 2009, doi: 10.1109/JLT.2009.2022282.

[272] G. Masini, G. Capellini, J. Witzens, and C. Gunn, "A four-channel, 10 Gbps monolithic optical receiver in 130nm CMOS with integrated Ge waveguide photodetectors," in *Optical Fiber Communication and the National Fiber Optic Engineers Conference, 2007. OFC/NFOEC 2007. Conference on*, Anaheim, California, USA, Mar. 25–29 2007, postdeadline paper PDP31.

[273] M. S. Rasras, K.-Y. Tu, D. M. Gill, Y.-K. Chen, A. White, S. Patel, A. Pomerene, D. Carothers, J. Beattie, M. Beals, J. Michel, and L. Kimerling, "Demonstration of a tunable microwave-photonic notch filter using low-loss silicon ring resonators," *J. Lightwave Technol.*, vol. 27, no. 12, pp. 2105–2110, Jun. 2009, doi: 10.1109/JLT.2008.2007748.

[274] J. Orcutt, A. Khilo, M. A. Popovic, C. Holzwarth, H. Li, J. Sun, B. Moss, M. Dahlem, E. Ippen, J. Hoyt, V. Stojanovic, F. Kärtner, H. Smith, and R. Ram, "Photonic integration in a commercial scaled bulk-CMOS process," in *Proc. Photonics in Switching, 2009 (PS 2009). International Conference on*, Pisa, Italy, Sep. 15–19 2009, paper ThI3-3, doi: 10.1109/PS.2009.5307769.

[275] J. Song and N. Zhu, "Design and fabrication of compact etched diffraction grating demultiplexers based on α-Si nanowire technology," *Electron. Lett.*, vol. 44, no. 13, pp. 816–818, Jun. 2008, doi: 10.1049/el:20081038.

[276] K. Preston, S. Manipatruni, A. Gondarenko, C. B. Poitras, and M. Lipson, "Deposited silicon high-speed integrated electro-optic modulator," *Opt. Express*, vol. 17, no. 7, pp. 5118–5124, 2009, doi: 10.1364/OE.17.005118.

[277] R. S. Jacobsen, K. N. Andersen, P. I. Borel, J. Fage-Pedersen, L. H. Frandsen, O. Hansen, M. Kristensen, A. V. Lavrinenko, G. Moulin, H. Ou, C. Peucheret, B. Zsigri, and A. Bjarklev, "Strained silicon as a new electro-optic material," *Nature*, vol. 441, pp. 199–202, May 2006, doi: 10.1038/nature04706.

[278] J. Liu, X. Sun, R. Camacho-Aguilera, L. C. Kimerling, and J. Michel, "Ge-on-Si laser operating at room temperature," *Opt. Lett.*, vol. 35, no. 5, pp. 679–681, Mar. 2010, doi: 10.1364/OL.35.000679.

[279] J. Liu, D. Pan, S. Jongthammanurak, K. Wada, L. C. Kimerling, and J. Michel, "Design of monolithically integrated GeSi electro-absorption modulators and photodetectors on a SOI platform," *Opt. Express*, vol. 15, no. 2, pp. 623–628, Jan. 2007, doi: 10.1364/OE.15.000623.

[280] Y. Kang, H.-D. Liu, M. Morse, M. J. Paniccia, M. Zadka, S. Litski, G. Sarid, A. Pauchard, Y.-H. Kuo, H.-W. Chen, W. S. Zaoui, J. E. Bowers, A. Beling, D. C. McIntosh, X. Zheng, and J. C. Campbell, "Monolithic germanium/silicon avalanche photodiodes with 340 GHz gain-bandwidth product," *Nat. Photonics*, vol. 3, no. 1, pp. 59–63, Jan. 2009, doi: 10.1038/nphoton.2008.247.

[281] L. Chen and M. Lipson, "Ultra-low capacitance and high speed germanium photodetectors on silicon," *Opt. Express*, vol. 17, no. 10, pp. 7901–7906, 2009, doi: 10.1364/OE.17.007901.

[282] S. Assefa, F. Xia, S. Bedell, Y. Zhang, T. Topuria, P. Rice, and Y. Vlasov, "CMOS-integrated 40GHz germanium waveguide photodetector for on-chip optical interconnects," in *Optical Fiber Communication 2009. OFC 2009. Conference on*, Mar. 22–26 2009, paper OMR4.

[283] T. Maruyama, T. Okumura, S. Sakamoto, K. Miura, Y. Nishimoto, and S. Arai, "GaInAsP/InP membrane BH-DFB lasers directly bonded on SOI substrate," *Opt. Express*, vol. 14, no. 18, pp. 8184–8188, 2006, doi: 10.1364/OE.14.008184.

[284] J. V. Campenhout, P. R. Romeo, P. Regreny, C. Seassal, D. V. Thourhout, S. Verstuyft, L. D. Cioccio, J.-M. Fedeli, C. Lagahe, and R. Baets, "Electrically pumped InP-based microdisk lasers integrated with a nanophotonic silicon-on-insulator waveguide circuit," *Opt. Express*, vol. 15, no. 11, pp. 6744–6749, 2007, doi: 10.1364/OE.15.006744.

[285] F. Bordas, G. Roelkens, R. Zhang, E. J. Geluk, F. Karouta, J. J. G. M. van der Tol, P. J. van Veldhoven, R. Nötzel, D. Van Thourhout, R. Baets, and M. K. Smit, "Compact passive devices in InP membrane on silicon," in *Optical Communication, 2009. ECOC 2009. 35th European Conference on*, Vienna, Austria, Sep. 20–24 2009, paper 4.2.4.

[286] A. W. Fang, H. Park, O. Cohen, R. Jones, M. J. Paniccia, and J. E. Bowers, "Electrically pumped hybrid algainas-silicon evanescent laser," *Opt. Express*, vol. 14, no. 20, pp. 9203–9210, Oct. 2006, doi: 10.1364/OE.14.009203.

[287] A. W. Fang, E. Lively, Y.-H. Kuo, D. Liang, and J. E. Bowers, "Distributed feedback silicon evanescent laser," in *Optical Fiber communication/National Fiber Optic Engineers Conference, 2008. OFC/NFOEC 2008. Conference on*, San Diego, CA, USA, Feb. 24–28 2008, postdeadline paper PDP15.

[288] A. Fang, B. Koch, R. Jones, E. Lively, D. Liang, Y.-H. Kuo, and J. Bowers, "A distributed Bragg reflector silicon evanescent laser," *IEEE Photonics Technol. Lett.*, vol. 20, no. 20, pp. 1667 –1669, Oct. 2008, doi: 10.1109/LPT.2008.2003382.

[289] A. Fang, M. Sysak, B. Koch, R. Jones, E. Lively, Y.-H. Kuo, D. Liang, O. Raday, and J. Bowers, "Single-wavelength silicon evanescent lasers," *IEEE J. Sel. Top. Quantum Electron.*, vol. 15, no. 3, pp. 535–544, May 2009, doi: 10.1109/JSTQE.2009.2014251.

[290] M. N. Sysak, J. O. Anthes, J. E. Bowers, O. Raday, and R. Jones, "Integration of hybrid silicon lasers and electroabsorption modulators," *Opt. Express*, vol. 16, no. 17, pp. 12478–12486, Aug. 2008, doi: 10.1364/OE.16.012478.

[291] H.-W. Chen, Y.-h. Kuo, and J. E. Bowers, "25Gb/s hybrid silicon switch using a capacitively loaded traveling wave electrode," *Opt. Express*, vol. 18, no. 2, pp. 1070–1075, 2010, doi: 10.1364/OE.18.001070.

[292] H. Park, A. W. Fang, R. J. Oded Cohen, M. J. Paniccia, and J. E. Bowers, "A hybrid AlGaInAs-silicon evanescent amplifier," *IEEE Photonics Technol. Lett.*, vol. 19, no. 4, pp. 230–232, Feb. 2007, doi: 10.1109/LPT.2007.891188.

[293] H. Park, A. W. Fang, R. Jones, O. Cohen, O. Raday, M. N. Sysak, M. J. Paniccia, and J. E. Bowers, "A hybrid AlGaInAs-silicon evanescent waveguide photodetector," *Opt. Express*, vol. 15, no. 10, pp. 6044–6052, May 2007, doi: 10.1364/OE.15.006044.

[294] T. Baehr-Jones and M. Hochberg, "Silicon photonics: slot machine," *Nat. Photonics*, vol. 3, pp. 193–194, Apr. 2009, doi: 10.1038/nphoton.2009.37.

[295] B. Esembeson, M. L. Scimeca, T. Michinobu, F. Diederich, and I. Biaggio, "A high optical quality supramolecular assembly for third-order integrated nonlinear optics," *Adv. Mater.*, vol. 20, pp. 4584–4587, 2008, doi: 10.1002/adma.200801552.

[296] L. Alloatti, D. Korn, D. Hillerkuss, T. Vallaitis, J. Li, R. Bonk, R. Palmer, T. Schellinger, A. Barklund, R. Dinu, J. Wieland, J.-M. Fedeli, C. Koos, W. Freude, and J. Leuthold, "40 Gbit/s silicon-organic hybrid (SOH) phase modulator," in *Optical Communication, 2010. ECOC 2010. 36th European Conference on*, Torino, Italy, Sep. 19–23 2010, paper Tu.5.C.4.

[297] C. Koos, P. Vorreau, T. Vallaitis, P. Dumon, W. Bogaerts, R. Baets, B. Esembeson, I. Biaggio, T. Michinobu, F. Diederich, W. Freude, and J. Leuthold, "All-optical high-speed signal processing with silicon-organic hybrid slot waveguides," *Nat. Photonics*, vol. 3, pp. 216–219, Mar. 2009, doi: 10.1038/nphoton.2009.25.

[298] T. Vallaitis, C. Koos, B. Esembeson, I. Biaggio, T. Michinobu, F. Diederich, P. Dumon, R. Baets, W. Freude, and J. Leuthold, "Highly nonlinear silicon photonics slot waveguides without free carrier absorption related speed-limitations," in *Optical Communication, 2008. ECOC 2008. 34th European Conference on*, Brussels, Belgium, Sep. 21–25 2008, paper Th.2.D.6, doi: 10.1109/ECOC.2008.4729411.

[299] S. McNab, N. Moll, and Y. Vlasov, "Ultra-low loss photonic integrated circuit with membrane-type photonic crystal waveguides," *Opt. Express*, vol. 11, no. 22, pp. 2927–2939, Nov. 2003, doi: 10.1364/OE.11.002927.

[300] R. Sun, V. Nguyen, A. Agarwal, C.-y. Hong, J. Yasaitis, L. Kimerling, and J. Michel, "High performance asymmetric graded index coupler with integrated lens for high index waveguides," *Appl. Phys. Lett.*, vol. 90, no. 20, p. 201116, May 2007, doi: 10.1063/1.2740589.

[301] G. Roelkens, D. Vermeulen, F. Van Laere, S. Selvaraja, S. Scheerlinck, D. Taillaert, W. Bogaerts, P. Dumon, D. Van Thourhout, and R. a. Baets, "Bridging the gap between nanophotonic waveguide circuits and single mode optical fibers using diffractive grating structures," *J. Nanosci. Nanotechnol.*, vol. 10, no. 3, pp. 1551–1562, Mar. 2010, doi: 10.1166/jnn.2010.2031.

[302] D. Taillaert, F. V. Laere, M. Ayre, W. Bogaerts, D. V. Thourhout, P. Bienstman, and R. Baets, "Grating couplers for coupling between optical fibers and nanophotonic waveguides," *Jpn. J. Appl. Phys.*, vol. 45, no. 8A, pp. 6071–6077, Aug. 2006, doi: 10.1143/JJAP.45.6071.

[303] F. Van Laere, G. Roelkens, M. Ayre, J. Schrauwen, D. Taillaert, D. Van Thourhout, T. Krauss, and R. Baets, "Compact and highly efficient grating couplers between optical fiber and nanophotonic waveguides," *J. Lightwave Technol.*, vol. 25, no. 1, pp. 151–156, Jan. 2007, doi: 10.1109/JLT.2006.888164.

[304] S. Selvaraja, D. Vermeulen, M. Schaekers, E. Sleeckx, W. Bogaerts, G. Roelkens, P. Dumon, D. Van Thourhout, and R. Baets, "Highly efficient grating coupler between optical fiber and silicon photonic circuit," in *Proc. Conf. on Lasers and Electro-Optics (CLEO/IQEC 2009)*, Baltimore, MD, USA, Jun. 2–4 2009, paper CTuC6. [Online]. Available: http://-ieeexplore.ieee.org/search/srchabstract.jsp?tp=&arnumber=5225319

[305] D. Taillaert, H. Chong, P. Borel, L. Frandsen, R. D. L. Rue, and R. Baets, "A compact two-dimensional grating coupler used as a polarization splitter," *IEEE Photonics Technol. Lett.*, vol. 15, no. 9, pp. 1249–1251, Sep. 2003, doi: 10.1109/LPT.2003.816671.

[306] F. Van Laere, W. Bogaerts, P. Dumon, G. Roelkens, D. Van Thourhout, and R. Baets, "Focusing polarization diversity grating couplers in silicon-on-insulator," *J. Lightwave Technol.*, vol. 27, no. 5, pp. 612–618, Mar. 2009, doi: 10.1109/JLT.2008.2004946.

[307] C. R. Doerr, P. J. Winzer, Y.-K. Chen, S. Chandrasekhar, M. S. Rasras, L. Chen, T.-Y. Liow, K.-W. Ang, and G.-Q. Lo, "Monolithic polarization and phase diversity coherent receiver in silicon," *J. Lightwave Technol.*, vol. 28, no. 4, pp. 520–525, Feb. 2010, doi: 10.1109/JLT.2009.2028656.

[308] U. Fischer, T. Zinke, J.-R. Kropp, F. Arndt, and K. Petermann, "0.1 dB/cm waveguide losses in single-mode SOI rib waveguides," *IEEE Photonics Technol. Lett.*, vol. 8, no. 5, pp. 647–648, May 1996, doi: 10.1109/68.491567.

[309] S. Lardenois, D. Pascal, L. Vivien, E. Cassan, S. Laval, R. Orobtchouk, M. Heitzmann, N. Bouzaida, and L. Mollard, "Low-loss submicrometer silicon-on-insulator rib waveguides and corner mirrors," *Opt. Lett.*, vol. 28, no. 13, pp. 1150–1152, Jul. 2003, doi: 10.1364/OL.28.001150.

[310] P. Dumon, W. Bogaerts, V. Wiaux, J. Wouters, S. Beckx, J. V. Campenhout, D. Taillaert, B. Luyssaert, P. Bienstman, D. V. Thourhout, and R. Baets, "Low-loss SOI photonic wires and ring resonators fabricated with deep UV lithography," *IEEE Photonics Technol. Lett.*, vol. 16, no. 5, pp. 1328–1330, May 2004, doi: 10.1109/LPT.2004.826025.

[311] T. Tsuchizawa, K. Yamada, H. Fukuda, T. Watanabe, S. Uchiyama, and S. Itabashi, "Low-loss Si wire waveguides and their application to thermooptic switches," *Jpn. J. Appl. Phys.*, vol. 45, no. 8B, pp. 6658–6662, Aug. 2006, doi: 10.1143/JJAP.45.6658.

[312] M. Gnan, S. Thorns, D. Macintyre, R. De La Rue, and M. Sorel, "Fabrication of low-loss photonic wires in silicon-on-insulator using hydrogen silsesquioxane electron-beam resist," *Electron. Lett.*, vol. 44, no. 2, pp. 115–116, Jan. 2008, doi: 10.1049/el:20082985.

[313] D. Sparacin, S. Spector, and L. Kimerling, "Silicon waveguide sidewall smoothing by wet chemical oxidation," *J. Lightwave Technol.*, vol. 23, no. 8, pp. 2455–2461, Aug. 2005, doi: 10.1109/JLT.2005.851328.

[314] K. K. Lee, D. R. Lim, L. C. Kimerling, J. Shin, and F. Cerrina, "Fabrication of ultralow-loss Si/SiO$_2$ waveguides by roughness reduction," *Opt. Lett.*, vol. 26, no. 23, pp. 1888–1890, Dec. 2001, doi: 10.1364/OL.26.001888.

[315] L. Rowe, M. Elsey, N. Tarr, A. Knights, and E. Post, "CMOS-compatible optical rib waveguides defined by local oxidation of silicon," *Electron. Lett.*, vol. 43, no. 7, pp. 392–393, Mar. 2007, doi: 10.1049/el:20073680.

[316] J. Cardenas, C. B. Poitras, J. T. Robinson, K. Preston, L. Chen, and M. Lipson, "Low loss etchless silicon photonic waveguides," *Opt. Express*, vol. 17, no. 6, pp. 4752–4757, 2009, doi: 10.1364/OE.17.004752.

[317] Y. Vlasov and S. McNab, "Losses in single-mode silicon-on-insulator strip waveguides and bends," *Opt. Express*, vol. 12, no. 8, pp. 1622–1631, Apr. 2004, doi: 10.1364/OPEX.12.001622.

[318] Z. Sheng, D. Dai, and S. He, "Comparative study of losses in ultrasharp silicon-on-insulator nanowire bends," *IEEE J. Sel. Top. Quantum Electron.*, vol. 15, no. 5, pp. 1406–1412, 2009, doi: 10.1109/JSTQE.2009.2013360.

[319] C. Koos, C. G. Poulton, L. Zimmermann, L. Jacome, J. Leuthold, and W. Freude, "Ideal bend contour trajectories for single-mode operation of low-loss overmoded waveguides," *IEEE Photonics Technol. Lett.*, vol. 19, no. 11, pp. 819–821, Jun. 2007, doi: 10.1109/LPT.2007.897294.

[320] F. Xia, L. Sekaric, and Y. Vlasov, "Ultracompact optical buffers on a silicon chip," *Nat. Photonics*, vol. 1, no. 1, pp. 65–71, Jan. 2007, doi: 10.1038/nphoton.2006.42.

[321] M. Tokushima, J. Vegas Olmos, and K.-I. Kitayama, "Multimode Si-wire waveguides for integrated optical delay lines," *Electron. Lett.*, vol. 45, no. 10, pp. 500 –501, Jul. 2009, doi: 10.1049/el.2009.0168.

[322] J. Brouckaert, W. Bogaerts, P. Dumon, D. Van Thourhout, and R. Baets, "Planar concave grating demultiplexer fabricated on a nanophotonic silicon-on-insulator platform," *J. Lightwave Technol.*, vol. 25, no. 5, pp. 1269–1275, May 2007, doi: 10.1109/JLT.2007.893025.

[323] J. Brouckaert, W. Bogaerts, S. Selvaraja, P. Dumon, R. Baets, and D. Van Thourhout, "Planar concave grating demultiplexer with high reflective Bragg reflector facets," *IEEE Photonics Technol. Lett.*, vol. 20, no. 4, pp. 309–311, Feb. 2008, doi: 10.1109/LPT.2007.915585.

[324] A. Kazmierczak, W. Bogaerts, E. Drouard, F. Dortu, P. Rojo-Romeo, F. Gaffiot, D. Van Thourhout, and D. Giannone, "Highly integrated optical 4×4 crossbar in silicon-on-insulator technology," *J. Lightwave Technol.*, vol. 27, no. 16, pp. 3317–3323, Aug. 2009, doi: 10.1109/JLT.2008.2010462.

[325] B. Lee, A. Biberman, N. Sherwood-Droz, C. Poitras, M. Lipson, and K. Bergman, "High-speed 2×2 switch for multiwavelength silicon-photonic networks-on-chip," *J. Lightwave Technol.*, vol. 27, no. 14, pp. 2900–2907, Jul. 2009, doi: 10.1109/JLT.2009.2019256.

[326] J.-M. Brosi, "Slow-light photonic crystal devices for high-speed optical signal processing," Ph.D. dissertation, Universität Karlsruhe (TH), Karlsruhe, Germany, Jul. 2008.

[327] Y. Jiang, W. Jiang, L. Gu, X. Chen, and R. T. Chen, "80-micron interaction length silicon photonic crystal waveguide modulator," *Appl. Phys. Lett.*, vol. 87, no. 22, p. 221105, 2005, doi: 10.1063/1.2138367.

[328] X. Chen, A. X. Wang, S. Chakravarty, and R. T. Chen, "Electrooptically-active slow-light-enhanced silicon slot photonic crystal waveguides," *IEEE J. Sel. Top. Quantum Electron.*, vol. 15, no. 5, pp. 1506–1509, Sep. 2009, doi: 10.1109/JSTQE.2009.2016980.

[329] J.-M. Brosi, C. Koos, L. C. Andreani, M. Waldow, J. Leuthold, and W. Freude, "High-speed low-voltage electro-optic modulator with a polymer-infiltrated silicon photonic crystal waveguide," *Opt. Express*, vol. 16, no. 6, pp. 4177–4191, Mar. 2008, doi: 10.1364/OE.16.004177.

[330] J. H. Wülbern, J. Hampe, A. Petrov, M. Eich, J. Luo, A. K.-Y. Jen, A. D. Falco, T. F. Krauss, and J. Bruns, "Electro-optic modulation in slotted resonant photonic crystal heterostructures," *Appl. Phys. Lett.*, vol. 94, p. 241107, Jun. 2009, doi: 10.1063/1.3156033.

[331] M. Ebnali-Heidari, C. Monat, C. Grillet, and M. K. Moravvej-Farshi, "A proposal for enhancing four-wave mixing in slow light engineered photonic crystal waveguides and its application to optical regeneration," *Opt. Express*, vol. 17, no. 20, pp. 18340–18353, 2009, doi: 10.1364/OE.17.018340.

[332] C. Monat, B. Corcoran, M. Ebnali-Heidari, C. Grillet, B. J. Eggleton, T. P. White, L. O'Faolain, and T. F. Krauss, "Slow light enhancement of nonlinear effects in silicon engineered photonic crystal waveguides," *Opt. Express*, vol. 17, no. 4, pp. 2944–2953, Feb. 2009, doi: 10.1364/OE.17.002944.

[333] H.-H. Chang, A. W. Fang, M. N. Sysak, H. Park, R. Jones, O. Cohen, O. Raday, M. J. Paniccia, and J. E. Bowers, "1310nm silicon evanescent laser," *Opt. Express*, vol. 15, no. 18, pp. 11466–11471, Sep. 2007, doi: 10.1364/OE.15.011466.

[334] A. Liu, R. Jones, L. Liao, D. Samara-Rubio, D. Rubin, O. Cohen, R. Nicolaescu, and M. Paniccia, "A high-speed silicon optical modulator based on a metal–oxide–semiconductor capacitor," *Nature*, vol. 427, pp. 615–618, Feb. 2004, doi: 10.1038/nature02310.

[335] L. Liao, D. Samara-Rubio, M. Morse, A. Liu, D. Hodge, D. Rubin, U. Keil, and T. Franck, "High speed silicon Mach-Zehnder modulator," _Opt. Express_, vol. 13, no. 8, pp. 3129–3135, 2005, doi: 10.1364/OPEX.13.003129.

[336] D. Marris-Morini, X. L. Roux, L. Vivien, E. Cassan, D. Pascal, M. Halbwax, S. Maine, S. Laval, J. M. Fédéli, and J. F. Damlencourt, "Optical modulation by carrier depletion in a silicon PIN diode," _Opt. Express_, vol. 14, no. 22, pp. 10838–10843, 2006, doi: 10.1364/OE.14.010838.

[337] A. Mao, J. Liu, D. Gao, and Z. Zhou, "High efficient silicon phase modulator based on n-p-n configuration," _Electron. Lett._, vol. 44, no. 6, pp. 438 –439, Mar. 2008, doi: 10.1049/el:20083503.

[338] A. Liu, L. Liao, D. Rubin, H. Nguyen, B. Ciftcioglu, Y. Chetrit, N. Izhaky, and M. Paniccia, "High-speed optical modulation based on carrier depletion in a silicon waveguide," _Opt. Express_, vol. 15, no. 2, pp. 660–668, Jan. 2007, doi: 10.1364/OE.15.000660.

[339] Q. Xu, S. Manipatruni, B. Schmidt, J. Shakya, and M. Lipson, "12.5 Gbit/s carrier-injection-based silicon micro-ring silicon modulators," _Opt. Express_, vol. 15, no. 2, pp. 430–436, 2007, doi: 10.1364/OE.15.000430.

[340] J. E. Roth, O. Fidaner, R. K. Schaevitz, Y.-H. Kuo, T. I. Kamins, J. S. Harris, and D. A. B. Miller, "Optical modulator on silicon employing germanium quantum wells," _Opt. Express_, vol. 15, no. 9, pp. 5851–5859, 2007, doi: 10.1364/OE.15.005851.

[341] M. W. Geis, S. J. Spector, M. E. Grein, R. T. Schulein, J. U. Yoon, D. M. Lennon, S. Deneault, F. Gan, F. X. Kaertner, and T. M. Lyszczarz, "CMOS-compatible all-Si high-speed waveguide photodiodes with high responsivity in near-infrared communication band," _IEEE Photonics Technol. Lett._, vol. 19, no. 3, pp. 152–154, Feb. 2007, doi: 10.1109/LPT.2006.890109.

[342] D. Ahn, C.-y. Hong, J. Liu, W. Giziewicz, M. Beals, L. C. Kimerling, J. Michel, J. Chen, and F. X. Kärtner, "High performance, waveguide integrated Ge photodetectors," _Opt. Express_, vol. 15, no. 7, pp. 3916–3921, 2007, doi: 10.1364/OE.15.003916.

[343] H. Park, Y.-h. Kuo, A. W. Fang, R. Jones, O. Cohen, M. J. Paniccia, and J. E. Bowers, "A hybrid AlGaInAs-silicon evanescent preamplifier and photodetector," *Opt. Express*, vol. 15, no. 21, pp. 13539–13546, Oct. 2007, doi: 10.1364/OE.15.013539.

[344] A. W. Fang, R. Jones, H. Park, O. Cohen, O. Raday, M. J. Paniccia, and J. E. Bowers, "Integrated AlGaInAs-silicon evanescent race track laser and photodetector," *Opt. Express*, vol. 15, no. 5, pp. 2315–2322, Mar. 2007, doi: 10.1364/OE.15.002315.

[345] H. K. Tsang and Y. Liu, "Nonlinear optical properties of silicon waveguides," *Semiconductor Science and Technology*, vol. 23, no. 6, p. 064007, May 2008, doi: 10.1088/0268-1242/23/6/064007.

[346] V. R. Almeida, Q. Xu, C. A. Barrios, and M. Lipson, "Guiding and confining light in void nanostructure," *Opt. Lett.*, vol. 29, no. 11, pp. 1209–1211, 2004, doi: 10.1364/OL.29.001209.

[347] Q. Xu, V. R. Almeida, R. R. Panepucci, and M. Lipson, "Experimental demonstration of guiding and confining light in nanometer-size low-refractive-index material," *Opt. Lett.*, vol. 29, no. 14, pp. 1626–1628, 2004, doi: 10.1364/OL.29.001626.

[348] P. Muellner, M. Wellenzohn, and R. Hainberger, "Nonlinearity of optimized silicon photonic slot waveguides," *Opt. Express*, vol. 17, no. 11, pp. 9282–9287, 2009, doi: 10.1364/OE.17.009282.

[349] P. Sanchis, J. Blasco, A. Martinez, and J. Marti, "Design of silicon-based slot waveguide configurations for optimum nonlinear performance," *J. Lightwave Technol.*, vol. 25, no. 5, pp. 1298–1305, May 2007, doi: 10.1109/JLT.2007.893909.

[350] F. Dell'Olio and V. M. Passaro, "Optical sensing by optimized silicon slot waveguides," *Opt. Express*, vol. 15, no. 8, pp. 4977–4993, 2007, doi: 10.1364/OE.15.004977.

[351] C. Koos, L. Jacome, C. Poulton, J. Leuthold, and W. Freude, "Nonlinear silicon-on-insulator waveguides for all-optical signal processing," *Opt. Express*, vol. 15, no. 10, pp. 5976–5990, May 2007, doi: 10.1364/OE.15.005976.

[352] K. R. Hiremath, "Analytical modal analysis of bent slot waveguides," _J. Opt. Soc. Am. A_, vol. 26, no. 11, pp. 2321–2326, 2009, doi: 10.1364/JOSAA.26.002321.

[353] C. Ma, Q. Zhang, and E. V. Keuren, "Right-angle slot waveguide bends with high bending efficiency," _Opt. Express_, vol. 16, no. 19, pp. 14330–14334, 2008, doi: 10.1364/OE.16.014330.

[354] L. Zhang, Y. Yue, Y. Xiao-Li, R. G. Beausoleil, and A. E. Willner, "Slot waveguides with a flattened near-zero dispersion and a small effective mode area," in _Integrated Photonics and Nanophotonics Research and Applications._ Optical Society of America, 2009, paper IWD6. [Online]. Available: http://-www.opticsinfobase.org/abstract.cfm?URI=IPNRA-2009-IWD6

[355] ———, "Highly dispersive slot waveguides," _Opt. Express_, vol. 17, no. 9, pp. 7095–7101, 2009, doi: 10.1364/OE.17.007095.

[356] H. Sun, A. Chen, and L. R. Dalton, "Enhanced evanescent confinement in multiple-slot waveguides and its application in biochemical sensing," _IEEE Photonics J._, vol. 1, no. 1, pp. 48 –57, Jun. 2009, doi: 10.1109/JPHOT.2009.2025602.

[357] T. Baehr-Jones, M. Hochberg, C. Walker, and A. Scherer, "High-Q optical resonators in silicon-on-insulator-based slot waveguides," _Appl. Phys. Lett._, vol. 86, no. 8, p. 081101, Feb. 2005, doi: 10.1063/1.1871360.

[358] C. A. Barrios, M. J. Bañuls, V. González-Pedro, K. B. Gylfason, B. Sánchez, A. Griol, A. Maquieira, H. Sohlström, M. Holgado, and R. Casquel, "Label-free optical biosensing with slot-waveguides," _Opt. Lett._, vol. 33, no. 7, pp. 708–710, Apr. 2008, doi: 10.1364/OL.33.000708.

[359] M. Hochberg, T. Baehr-Jones, G. Wang, J. Huang, P. Sullivan, L. Dalton, and A. Scherer, "Towards a millivolt optical modulator with nano-slot waveguides," _Opt. Express_, vol. 15, no. 13, pp. 8401–8410, 2007, doi: 10.1364/OE.15.008401.

[360] T. W. Baehr-Jones and M. J. Hochberg, "Polymer silicon hybrid systems: A platform for practical nonlinear optics," _J. Phys. Chem. C_, vol. 112, no. 21, pp. 8085–8090, Apr. 2008, doi: 10.1021/jp7118444.

[361] C. Koos, J. Brosi, M. Waldow, W. Freude, and J. Leuthold, "Silicon-on-insulator modulators for next-generation 100 Gbit/s-ethernet," in *Optical Communication, 2007. ECOC 2007. 33th European Conference on*, Berlin, Germany, Sep. 16–20 2007, poster P056.

[362] A. Säynätjoki, T. Alasaarela, A. Khanna, L. Karvonen, P. Stenberg, M. Kuittinen, A. Tervonen, and S. Honkanen, "Angled sidewalls in silicon slot waveguides: conformal filling and mode properties," *Opt. Express*, vol. 17, no. 23, pp. 21066–21076, 2009, doi: 10.1364/OE.17.021066.

[363] R. Sun, P. Dong, N.-n. Feng, C.-y. Hong, J. Michel, M. Lipson, and L. Kimerling, "Horizontal single and multiple slot waveguides: optical transmission at λ = 1550 nm," *Opt. Express*, vol. 15, no. 26, pp. 17967–17972, 2007, doi: 10.1364/OE.15.017967.

[364] R. Guider, N. Daldosso, A. Pitanti, E. Jordana, J.-M. Fedeli, and L. Pavesi, "NanoSi low loss horizontal slot waveguides coupled to high Q ring resonators," *Opt. Express*, vol. 17, no. 23, pp. 20762–20770, Nov. 2009, doi: 10.1364/OE.17.020762.

[365] J. T. Robinson, K. Preston, O. Painter, and M. Lipson, "First-principle derivation of gain in high-index-contrast waveguides," *Opt. Express*, vol. 16, no. 21, pp. 16659–16669, 2008, doi: 10.1364/OE.16.016659.

[366] K. Preston and M. Lipson, "Slot waveguides with polycrystalline silicon for electrical injection," *Opt. Express*, vol. 17, no. 3, pp. 1527–1534, 2009, doi: 10.1364/OE.17.001527.

[367] B. L. Lawrence, M. Cha, J. U. Kang, W. Toruellas, G. Stegeman, G. Baker, J. Meth, and S. Etemad, "Large purely refractive nonlinear index of single crystal P-toluene sulphonate (PTS) at 1600 nm," *Electron. Lett.*, vol. 30, no. 5, pp. 447–448, Mar. 1994. [Online]. Available: http://ieeexplore.ieee.org/xpls/-abs_all.jsp?arnumber=273240

[368] C. Koos, P. Vorreau, P. Dumon, R. Baets, B. Esembeson, I. Biaggio, T. Michinobu, F. Diederich, W. Freude, and J. Leuthold, "Highly-nonlinear silicon photonics slot waveguide," in *Optical Fiber communication/National Fiber Optic Engineers Conference, 2008. OFC/NFOEC 2008. Conference on*, San Diego, CA, USA, Feb. 24–28 2008, postdeadline paper PDP25.

[369] T. Vallaitis, S. Bogatscher, L. Alloatti, P. Dumon, R. Baets, M. L. Scimeca, I. Biaggio, F. Diederich, C. Koos, W. Freude, and J. Leuthold, "Optical properties of highly nonlinear silicon-organic hybrid (SOH) waveguide geometries," *Opt. Express*, vol. 17, no. 20, pp. 17357–17368, Sep. 2009, doi: 10.1364/OE.17.017357.

[370] T. Vallaitis, C. Heine, R. Bonk, W. Freude, J. Leuthold, C. Koos, B. Esembeson, I. Biaggio, T. Michinobu, F. Diederich, P. Dumon, and R. Baets, "All-optical wavelength conversion at 42.7 Gbit/s in a 4 mm long silicon-organic hybrid waveguide," in *Optical Fiber Communication 2009. OFC 2009. Conference on*, San Diego, CA, USA, Mar. 22–26 2009, paper OWS3. [Online]. Available: http://www.opticsinfobase.org/-abstract.cfm?URI=OFC-2009-OWS3

[371] T. Vallaitis, R. Bonk, J. Guetlein, D. Hillerkuss, J. Li, W. Freude, J. Leuthold, C. Koos, M. L. Scimeca, I. Biaggio, F. Diederich, B. Breiten, P. Dumon, and R. Baets, "All-optical wavelength conversion of 56 Gbit/s NRZ-DQPSK signals in silicon-organic hybrid strip waveguides," in *Proc. Optical Fiber Communication Conference (OFC'10)*, San Diego, CA, USA, Mar. 21–25 2010, paper OTuN1.

[372] T. Vallaitis, D. Hillerkuss, J.-S. Li, R. Bonk, N. Lindenmann, P. Dumon, R. Baets, M. L. Scimeca, I. Biaggio, F. Diederich, C. Koos, W. Freude, and J. Leuthold, "All-optical wavelength conversion using cross-phase modulation at 42.7 Gbit/s in silicon-organic hybrid (SOH) waveguides," in *Proc. Photonics in Switching, 2009 (PS 2009). International Conference on*, Pisa, Italy, Sep. 15–19 2009, postdeadline paper PD3, doi: 10.1109/PS.2009.5307823.

[373] H. Garcia and R. Kalyanaraman, "Phonon-assisted two-photon absorption in the presence of a dc-field: the nonlinear Franz–Keldysh effect in indirect gap semiconductors," *J. Phys. B: At. Mol. Opt. Phys.*, vol. 39, no. 12, p. 2737, 2006, doi: 10.1088/0953-4075/39/12/009.

[374] M. Sheik-Bahae, A. Said, T.-H. Wei, D. Hagan, and E. Van Stryland, "Sensitive measurement of optical nonlinearities using a single beam," *IEEE J. Quantum Electron.*, vol. 26, no. 4, pp. 760–769, Apr. 1990, doi: 10.1109/3.53394.

[375] H. K. Tsang, C. S. Wong, T. K. Liang, I. E. Day, S. W. Roberts, A. Harpin, J. Drake, and M. Asghari, "Optical dispersion, two-photon absorption and self-phase modulation in silicon waveguides at 1.5μm wavelength," *Appl. Phys. Lett.*, vol. 80, no. 3, pp. 416–418, Jan. 2002, doi: 10.1063/1.1435801.

[376] R. Claps, D. Dimitropoulos, V. Raghunathan, Y. Han, and B. Jalali, "Observation of stimulated Raman amplification in silicon waveguides," *Opt. Express*, vol. 11, no. 15, pp. 1731–1739, Jul. 2003, doi: 10.1364/OE.11.001731.

[377] M. Dinu, F. Quochi, and H. Garcia, "Third-order nonlinearities in silicon at telecom wavelengths," *Appl. Phys. Lett.*, vol. 82, no. 18, pp. 2954–2956, May 2003, doi: 10.1063/1.1571665.

[378] G. W. Rieger, K. S. Virk, and J. F. Young, "Nonlinear propagation of ultrafast 1.5μm pulses in high-index-contrast silicon-on-insulator waveguides," *Appl. Phys. Lett.*, vol. 84, no. 6, pp. 900–902, Feb. 2004, doi: 10.1063/1.1645991.

[379] H. Rong, A. Liu, R. Nicolaescu, M. Paniccia, O. Cohen, and D. Hak, "Raman gain and nonlinear optical absorption measurements in a low-loss silicon waveguide," *Appl. Phys. Lett.*, vol. 85, no. 12, pp. 2196–2198, 2004, doi: 10.1063/1.1794862.

[380] T.-K. Liang and H.-K. Tsang, "Nonlinear absorption and Raman scattering in silicon-on-insulator optical waveguides," *IEEE J. Sel. Top. Quantum Electron.*, vol. 10, no. 5, pp. 1149–1153, Sep.–Oct. 2004, doi: 10.1109/JSTQE.2004.835290(410) 1.

[381] O. Boyraz, T. Indukuri, and B. Jalali, "Self-phase-modulation induced spectral broadening in silicon waveguides," *Opt. Express*, vol. 12, no. 5, pp. 829–834, 2004, doi: 10.1364/OPEX.12.000829.

[382] H. Fukuda, K. Yamada, T. Shoji, M. Takahashi, T. Tsuchizawa, T. Watanabe, J.-i. Takahashi, and S.-i. Itabashi, "Four-wave mixing in silicon wire waveguides," *Opt. Express*, vol. 13, no. 12, pp. 4629–4637, Jun. 2005, doi: 10.1364/OPEX.13.004629.

[383] R. L. Espinola, J. I. Dadap, R. M. Osgood, Jr., S. J. McNab, and Y. A. Vlasov, "C-band wavelength conversion in silicon photonic wire waveguides," *Opt. Express*, vol. 13, no. 11, pp. 4341–4349, May 2005, doi: 10.1364/OPEX.13.004341.

[384] E. Dulkeith, Y. A. Vlasov, X. Chen, N. C. Panoiu, and R. M. Osgood, Jr., "Self-phase-modulation in submicron silicon-on-insulator photonic wires," *Opt. Express*, vol. 14, no. 12, pp. 5524–5534, Jun. 2006, doi: 10.1364/OE.14.005524.

[385] A. D. Bristow, N. Rotenberg, and H. M. van Driel, "Two-photon absorption and Kerr coefficients of silicon for 850–2200 nm," *Appl. Phys. Lett.*, vol. 90, no. 19, p. 191104, 2007, doi: 10.1063/1.2737359.

[386] Q. Lin, J. Zhang, G. Piredda, R. W. Boyd, P. M. Fauchet, and G. P. Agrawal, "Dispersion of silicon nonlinearities in the near infrared region," *Appl. Phys. Lett.*, vol. 91, no. 2, p. 021111, 2007, doi: 10.1063/1.2750523.

[387] K. Ikeda, Y. Shen, and Y. Fainman, "Enhanced optical nonlinearity in amorphous silicon and its application to waveguide devices," *Opt. Express*, vol. 15, no. 26, pp. 17761–17771, Dec. 2007, doi: 10.1364/OE.15.017761.

[388] P. Apiratikul, A. M. Rossi, and T. E. Murphy, "Nonlinearities in porous silicon optical waveguides at 1550 nm," *Opt. Express*, vol. 17, no. 5, pp. 3396–3406, Feb. 2009, doi: 10.1364/OE.17.003396.

[389] T. Michinobu, J. C. May, J. H. Lim, C. Boudon, J.-P. Gisselbrecht, P. Seiler, M. Gross, I. Biaggio, and F. Diederich, "A new class of organic donor–acceptor molecules with large third-order optical nonlinearities," *Chem. Commun.*, pp. 737–739, Jan. 2005, doi: 10.1039/b417393g.

[390] D. Marcuse, *Principles of optical fiber measurements*. New York: Academic Press, 1981.

[391] M. A. Foster, A. C. Turner, R. Salem, M. Lipson, and A. L. Gaeta, "Broadband continuous-wave parametric wavelength conversion in silicon nanowaveguides," *Opt. Express*, vol. 15, no. 20, pp. 12949–12958, 2007, doi: 10.1364/OE.15.012949.

[392] E. Ciaramella, G. Contestabile, F. Curti, and A. D'ottavi, "Fast tunable wavelength conversion for all-optical packet switching," *IEEE Photonics Technol. Lett.*, vol. 12, no. 10, pp. 1361–1363, Oct. 2000, doi: 10.1109/68.883830.

[393] W. Mathlouthi, H. Rong, and M. Paniccia, "Characterization of efficient wavelength conversion by four-wave mixing in sub-micron silicon waveguides," *Opt. Express*, vol. 16, no. 21, pp. 16735–16745, Oct. 2008/10/13, doi: 10.1364/OE.16.016735.

[394] I.-W. Hsieh, X. Chen, J. I. Dadap, N. C. Panoiu, R. M. Richard Osgood, Jr., S. J. McNab, and Y. A. Vlasov, "Cross-phase modulation-induced spectral and temporal effects on co-propagating femtosecond pulses in silicon photonic wires," *Opt. Express*, vol. 15, no. 3, pp. 1135–1146, 2007, doi: 10.1364/OE.15.001135.

[395] R. Dekker, A. Driessen, T. Wahlbrink, C. Moormann, J. Niehusmann, and M. Först, "Ultrafast Kerr-induced all-optical wavelength conversion in silicon waveguides using 1.55µm femtosecond pulses," *Opt. Express*, vol. 14, no. 18, pp. 8336–8346, Sep. 2006, doi: 10.1364/OE.14.008336.

[396] W. Astar, J. B. Driscoll, X. Liu, J. I. Dadap, W. M. J. Green, Y. A. Vlasov, G. M. Carter, and R. M. Osgood, "Conversion of 10 Gb/s NRZ-OOK to RZ-OOK utilizing XPM in a Si nanowire," *Opt. Express*, vol. 17, no. 15, pp. 12987–12999, Jul. 2009, doi: 10.1364/OE.17.012987.

[397] F. Luan, M. D. Pelusi, M. R. E. Lamont, D.-Y. Choi, S. Madden, B. Luther-Davies, and B. J. Eggleton, "Dispersion engineered As_2S_3 planar waveguides for broadband four-wave mixing based wavelength conversion of 40 Gb/s signals," *Opt. Express*, vol. 17, no. 5, pp. 3514–3520, Feb. 2009, doi: 10.1364/OE.17.003514.

[398] A. Tychopoulos, O. Koufopavlou, and I. Tomkos, "FEC in optical communications - a tutorial overview on the evolution of architectures and the future prospects of outband and inband FEC for optical communications," *IEEE Circuits Devices Mag.*, vol. 22, no. 6, pp. 79–86, Nov.–Dec. 2006, doi: 10.1109/MCD.2006.307281.

Acknowledgements

At this point, I would like to acknowledge the valuable support provided by others in in the last years and during the preparation of this thesis.

First of all, I want to thank my supervisors Prof. Jürg Leuthold and Prof. Wolfgang Freude for providing vision, guidance and funding for my work. Prof. Leuthold I thank for his inexhaustible stock of ideas and challenges, which always spurred my interest and effort. Prof. Freude I thank for his thoroughness, his love for precision, and his attention to details, a combination which in good conscience guaranteed a high scientific level. I also want to thank him for the time and large effort he always put into working on our manuscripts.

I want to thank my referee Prof. Michael Siegel, head of the Institut für Mikro- und Nanoelektronische Systeme for his continuous support of our work on silicon photonics with equipment and technology. Alexander Stassen I want to thank for his precision-dicing of our first SOI wafers, which was essential for our first experimental results.

Prof. Dr. Dagmar Gerthsen of the Laboratory for Electron Microscopy (LEM) and Dr. Christian Röthig of the Center for Functional Nanostructures (CFN) I thank for their support and funding of the joint quantum dot research project.

I thank Dr. Michael Grün, Dr. Michael Hetterich, and Dr. Thorsten Passow of the Institute of Applied physics for introducing me to the MBE growth of III-V materials and their confidence in my abilities to operate the MBE system on my own. Dr. Dimitri Litvinov of the LEM I thank for sharing his insight into quantum dot formation processes and the immediate sample analysis even on short notice.

Dr. Martin Walther, Dr. Michael Mikulla, and Dr. Gudrun Kaufel of the Fraunhofer-Institut für Angewandte Festkörperphysik (IAF) in Freiburg I thank for giving me access to the IAF facilities and for the processing of several quantum dot wafers into devices.

Prof. Dieter Bimberg and Christian Meuer of the Institute of Solid State Physics, Technische Universität Berlin I thank for our harmonious and fruitful collaboration, especially the supply of samples and our common experiments. Dr. Carsten Schmidt-Langhorst of Fraunhofer Institute for Telecommunications, Heinrich-Hertz-Institut (HHI) I thank for our discussions and experiments on the performance of quantum dot semiconductor optical amplifiers.

Prof. Guang-Hua Duan, Dr. François Lelarge, and Dr. Romain Brenot of Alcatel-Thalès III-V Lab I thank for the cooperation and the supplied samples.

Prof. Roel Baets and Dr. Pieter Dumon of the Photonics Research Group at Ghent University-IMEC I thank for the fabrication of the SOI waveguides and their immediate and encouraging reviews of our paper drafts.

Prof. Ivan Biaggio, Dr. Bweh Esembeson, and Michelle L. Scimeca of the Department of Physics at Lehigh University I thank for the countless number of deposited samples and their general support.

Prof. François Diederich and Benjamin Breiten of Laboratorium für Organische Chemie at ETH Zürich and Prof. Tsuyoshi Michinobu of the Tokyo Institute of Technology I thank for supplying the nonlinear material DDMEBT and the encouraging comments on our paper drafts.

Prof. Jiří Čtyroký and Dr. Tomáš Lauerman I thank for the discussion on dispersion in slot waveguides and for the collaboration on simulation of pulse propagation in nonlinear waveguides.

The mechanical workshop, Hans Bürger, Manfred Hirsch, Werner Höhne, and the apprentices I thank for their great support for the construction of the femtosecond characterization lab. Oswald Speck of the packaging lab I thank for the great support in wafer cleaving, fiber splicing, and the difficult packaging of prototype devices. Johann Hartwig Hauschild I thank for his support in maintaining the free-space laser system.

My former colleagues taught me a lot that I am grateful for. I thank Dr. Christian Koos for introducing me into the world of engineering and his unconditional help with all experimental problems. Dr. Jan-Michael Brosi I thank for being my 'golden reference' on semiconductor physics and silicon waveguides. Dr. Stelios Sygletos I thank for sharing his insight into the inner workings of all popular models of quantum dot semiconductor optical amplifiers. Dr. Philipp Vorreau I thank for teaching me the hard way about communication systems. Dr. Gunnar Böttger I thank for helping me steer clear of pitfalls in my simulations. Dr. Shunfeng Li I thank for his help in optimizing the quantum dot growth parameters.

For the great collaboration I want to thank all my colleagues at IPQ. My teammate Rene Bonk I thank for always pulling together. Thanks for the unconditional trust, that made our successful work possible. David Hillerkuß I thank for his wholehearted support of all system-level experiments. Jingshi Li I thank for providing the indispensable tunable delay interferometers. Swen König and Moritz Röger I thank for teaching me about electronics from DC to RF. Argishti Melikyan and Nicole Lindenmann I thank for our cooperation on realizing the dream of a plasmonic modulator. Luca Alloatti, Dietmar Korn, and Martin Moch I thank for the discussions on silicon photonics and hybrid integration of organic materials. Andrej Marculescu, René Schmogrow, Marcus Winter I thank for their support in tutoring the semiconductor devices lecture.

Many thanks to all my students who have contributed to our work: Boris-Alexander Bolles, Akhmed Tussupov, Siegwart Bogatscher, Johann Christian Rode, Christoph Heine, Thomas Schellinger, Johanna Guetlein, Gregor Huber, and Jörg Pfeifle.

I thank our secretaries Bernadette Lehmann, Ilse Kober, and Eva-Maria Schubart for their caring personalities and the help in administrative matters.

Last but not least, I thank my love Evelyn Schmich for her unconditional support over all these years. Thank you for always showing sympathy and understanding. Without you, this work would not have been possible.

This work was supported by the Center for Functional Nanostructures (CFN) of the Deutsche Forschungsgemeinschaft (DFG) within Project A4.4, the European project TRIUMPH (grant IST-027638 STP), the European FP6 Network of Excellence ePIXnet, and the European Project SOFI (grant 248609).

List of Publications

Journal Papers

[J1]   **T. Vallaitis**, R. Bonk, J. Guetlein, D. Hillerkuss, J. Li, R. Brenot, F. Lelarge, G. H. Duan, W. Freude, and J. Leuthold, "Quantum dot SOA input power dynamic range improvement for differential-phase encoded signals," Opt. Express, vol. 18, no. 6, pp. 6270–6276, Mar. 2010, doi: 10.1364/OE.18.006270.

[J2]   S. Sygletos, R. Bonk, **T. Vallaitis**, A. Marculescu, P. Vorreau, J. Li, R. Brenot, F. Lelarge, G. Duan, W. Freude, and J. Leuthold, "Filter assisted wavelength conversion with quantum-dot SOAs," J. Lightwave Technol., vol. 28, no. 6, pp. 882–897, Mar. 2010, doi: 10.1109/JLT.2010.2040457.

[J3]   M. L. Scimeca, I. Biaggio, B. Breiten, F. Diederich, **T. Vallaitis**, W. Freude, and J. Leuthold, "Vapor deposition of small organic molecules with large nonlinearities for ultrafast all-optical switching on the silicon photonics platform." Optics and Photonics News, vol. 20, no. 12, p. 39, Dec. 2009.

[J4]   **T. Vallaitis**, S. Bogatscher, L. Alloatti, P. Dumon, R. Baets, M. L. Scimeca, I. Biaggio, F. Diederich, C. Koos, W. Freude, and J. Leuthold, "Optical properties of highly nonlinear silicon-organic hybrid (SOH) waveguide geometries," Opt. Express, vol. 17, no. 20, pp. 17357–17368, Sep. 2009, doi: 10.1364/OE.17.017357.

[J5]   C. Koos, P. Vorreau, **T. Vallaitis**, P. Dumon, W. Bogaerts, R. Baets, B. Esembeson, I. Biaggio, T. Michinobu, F. Diederich, W. Freude, and J. Leuthold, "All-optical high-speed signal processing with silicon-organic hybrid slot waveguides," Nat. Photonics, vol. 3, pp. 216–219, Mar. 2009, doi: 10.1038/nphoton.2009.25.

[J6]   C. Meuer,   J. Kim,   M. Laemmlin,   S. Liebich,   G. Eisenstein,   R. Bonk,
T. Vallaitis, J. Leuthold, A. Kovsh, I. Krestnikov, and D. Bimberg, "High-
speed small-signal cross-gain modulation in quantum-dot semiconductor
optical amplifiers at 1.3µm," IEEE J. Sel. Top. Quantum Electron., vol. 15,
no. 3, pp. 749–756, May 2009, doi: 10.1109/JSTQE.2009.2012395.

[J7]   **T. Vallaitis**,   C. Koos,   R. Bonk,   W. Freude,   M. Laemmlin,   C. Meuer,
D. Bimberg, and J. Leuthold, "Slow and fast dynamics of gain and phase in a
quantum dot semiconductor optical amplifier," Opt. Express, vol. 16, no. 1, pp.
170–178, Jan. 2008, doi: 10.1364/OE.16.000170.

[J8]   D. Litvinov,   H. Blank,   R. Schneider,   D. Gerthsen,   **T. Vallaitis**,   J. Leuthold,
T. Passow, A. Grau, H. Kalt, C. Klingshirn, and M. Hetterich, "Influence of
InGaAs cap layers with different In concentration on the properties of InGaAs
quantum dots," J. Appl. Phys., vol. 103, p. 083532, 2008, doi:
10.1063/1.2903143.

[J9]   C. Meuer,   J. Kim,   M. Laemmlin,   S. Liebich,   D. Bimberg,   A. Capua,
G. Eisenstein, R. Bonk, **T. Vallaitis**, J. Leuthold, A. R. Kovsh, and I. L.
Krestnikov, "40 GHz small-signal cross-gain modulation in 1.3µm quantum
dot semiconductor optical amplifiers," Appl. Phys. Lett., vol. 93, no. 5, p.
051110, 2008, doi: 10.1063/1.2969060.

[J10]   T. Passow,   S. Li,   P. Feinäugle,   **T. Vallaitis**,   J. Leuthold,   D. Litvinov,
D. Gerthsen, and M. Hetterich, "Systematic investigation into the influence of
growth conditions on InAs/GaAs quantum dot properties," J. Appl. Phys., vol.
102, no. 7, p. 073511, 2007, doi: 10.1063/1.2779270.

Conference Contributions

[C1]   **T. Vallaitis**,   R. Bonk,   J. Guetlein,   C. Meuer,   D. Hillerkuss,   W. Freude,
D. Bimberg, and J. Leuthold, "Optimizing SOA for large input power dynamic
range with respect to applications in extended GPON," in OSA Topical
Meeting: Access Networks and In-house Communications (ANIC), 2010, paper
AThC4.

[C2] M. Spyropoulou, R. Bonk, D. Hillerkuss, N. Pleros, **T. Vallaitis**, W. Freude, I. Tomkos, and J. Leuthold, "Experimental investigation of multi-wavelength clock recovery based on a quantum-dot SOA at 40 Gb/s," in OSA Topical Meeting: Signal Processing in Photonic Communications (SPPCom), Karlsruhe, Germany, Jun. 21—24 2010, paper SPTuB4.

[C3] W. Freude, J. Leuthold, L. Alloatti, **T. Vallaitis**, D. Korn, R. Palmer, C. Koos, J.-M. Brosi, P. Dumon, R. Baets, M. L. Scimeca, I. Biaggio, B. Breiten, F. Diederich, A. Barklund, R. Dinu, and J. Wieland, "100 Gbit/s electro-optic modulator and 56 Gbit/s all-optical wavelength converter in silicon-organic hybrid (SOH) technology," in IEEE Summer Topicals 2010, Playa del Carmen, Riviera Maya, Mexico, Jul. 19–21 2010, invited paper.

[C4] W. Freude, R. Bonk, **T. Vallaitis**, A. Marculescu, A. Kapoor, E. K. Sharma, C. Meuer, D. Bimberg, R. Brenot, F. Lelarge, G.-H. Duan, and J. Leuthold, "Linear and nonlinear semiconductor optical amplifiers," in Transparent Optical Networks, 2010. ICTON 2010. 12th International Conference on, Munich, Germany, Jun. 27–Jul. 1 2010, invited paper.

[C5] D. Hillerkuss, T. Schellinger, R. Schmogrow, M. Winter, **T. Vallaitis**, R. Bonk, A. Marculescu, J. Li, M. Dreschmann, J. Meyer, S. B. Ezra, N. Narkiss, B. Nebendahl, F. Parmigiani, P. Petropoulos, B. Resan, K. Weingarten, T. Ellermeyer, J. Lutz, M. Möller, M. Huebner, J. Becker, C. Koos, W. Freude, and J. Leuthold, "Single source optical OFDM transmitter and optical FFT receiver demonstrated at line rates of 5.4 and 10.8 Tbit/s," in Proc. Optical Fiber Communication Conference (OFC'10), San Diego, CA, USA, Mar. 21–25 2010, postdeadline paper PDPC1.

[C6] A. Melikyan, **T. Vallaitis**, N. Lindenmann, T. Schimmel, W. Freude, and J. Leuthold, "A surface plasmon polariton absorption modulator," in Proc. Conf. on Lasers and Electro-Optics (CLEO/IQEC'10), San Jose, CA, USA, May 16–21 2010, poster JThE77.

[C7] W. Freude, **T. Vallaitis**, C. Koos, J.-M. Brosi, L. Alloatti, P. Dumon, R. Baets, M. L. Scimeca, I. Biaggio, B. Breiten, F. Diederich, and J. Leuthold, "Ultrafast silicon-organic hybrid (SOH) photonics," in Proc. Conf. on Lasers and Electro-Optics (CLEO/IQEC'10), San Jose, CA, USA, May 16–21 2010, invited paper.

[C8] J. Leuthold, R. Bonk, **T. Vallaitis**, A. Marculescu, W. Freude, C. Meuer, D. Bimberg, R. Brenot, F. Lelarge, and G.-H. Duan, "Linear and nonlinear semiconductor optical amplifiers," in Proc. Optical Fiber Communication Conference (OFC'10), San Diego, CA, USA, Mar. 21–25 2010, invited paper.

[C9] **T. Vallaitis**, R. Bonk, J. Guetlein, D. Hillerkuss, J. Li, W. Freude, J. Leuthold, C. Koos, M. L. Scimeca, I. Biaggio, F. Diederich, B. Breiten, P. Dumon, and R. Baets, "All-optical wavelength conversion of 56 Gbit/s NRZ-DQPSK signals in silicon-organic hybrid strip waveguides," in Proc. Optical Fiber Communication Conference (OFC'10), San Diego, CA, USA, Mar. 21–25 2010, paper OTuN1.

[C10] R. Bonk, **T. Vallaitis**, J. Guetlein, D. Hillerkuss, J. Li, W. Freude, and J. Leuthold, "Quantum dot SOA dynamic range improvement for phase modulated signals," in Proc. Optical Fiber Communication Conference (OFC'10), San Diego, CA, USA, Mar. 21–25 2010, paper OThK3.

[C11] W. Freude, R. Bonk, **T. Vallaitis**, A. Marculescu, A. Kapoor, C. Meuer, D. Bimberg, R. Brenot, F. Lelarge, G.-h. Duan, and J. Leuthold, "Semiconductor optical amplifiers (SOA) for linear and nonlinear applications," in DPG Spring Meeting 2010, Regensburg, Germany, Mar. 2010, Topical Talk DS2.3. [Online]. Available: http://www.dpg-verhandlungen.de/2010/regensburg/ds2.pdf

[C12] S. König, J. Pfeifle, R. Bonk, **T. Vallaitis**, C. Meuer, D. Bimberg, C. Koos, W. Freude, and J. Leuthold, "Optical and electrical power dynamic range of semiconductor optical amplifiers in radio-over-fiber networks," in Optical Communication, 2010. ECOC 2010. 36th European Conference on, Torino, Italy, Sep. 19–23 2010, paper Th.10.B.6.

[C13] L. Alloatti, D. Korn, D. Hillerkuss, **T. Vallaitis**, J. Li, R. Bonk, R. Palmer, T. Schellinger, A. Barklund, R. Dinu, J. Wieland, J.-M. Fedeli, C. Koos, W. Freude, and J. Leuthold, "40 Gbit/s silicon-organic hybrid (SOH) phase modulator," in Optical Communication, 2010. ECOC 2010. 36th European Conference on, Torino, Italy, Sep. 19–23 2010, paper Tu.5.C.4.

[C14] W. Freude, C. Koos, **T. Vallaitis**, J.-M. Brosi, L. Alloatti, S. Bogatscher, P. Dumon, R. Baets, M. L. Scimeca, I. Biaggio, F. Diederich, and J. Leuthold, "Silicon-organic hybrid (SOH) photonics for ultra-fast optical signal processing," in LEOS Annual Meeting Conference Proceedings, 2009. LEOS '09. IEEE, Belek-Antalya, Turkey, Oct. 4–8 2009, invited paper WI 2.

[C15] S. Sygletos, R. Bonk, **T. Vallaitis**, A. Marculescu, P. Vorreau, J. Li, R. Brenot, F. Lelarge, G. Duan, W. Freude, and J. Leuthold, "Optimum filtering schemes for performing wavelength conversion with QD-SOA," in Transparent Optical Networks, 2009. ICTON '09. 11th International Conference on, Jun. 28–Jul. 2 2009, invited paper Mo.C1.3, doi: 10.1109/ICTON.2009.5185000.

[C16] **T. Vallaitis**, D. Hillerkuss, J.-S. Li, R. Bonk, N. Lindenmann, P. Dumon, R. Baets, M. L. Scimeca, I. Biaggio, F. Diederich, C. Koos, W. Freude, and J. Leuthold, "All-optical wavelength conversion using cross-phase modulation at 42.7 Gbit/s in silicon-organic hybrid (SOH) waveguides," in Proc. Photonics in Switching, 2009 (PS 2009). International Conference on, Pisa, Italy, Sep. 15–19 2009, postdeadline paper PD3, doi: 10.1109/PS.2009.5307823.

[C17] **T. Vallaitis**, C. Heine, R. Bonk, W. Freude, J. Leuthold, C. Koos, B. Esembeson, I. Biaggio, T. Michinobu, F. Diederich, P. Dumon, and R. Baets, "All-optical wavelength conversion at 42.7 Gbit/s in a 4 mm long silicon-organic hybrid waveguide," in Optical Fiber Communication 2009. OFC 2009. Conference on, San Diego, CA, USA, Mar. 22–26 2009, paper OWS3. [Online]. Available: http://www.opticsinfobase.org/-abstract.cfm?URI=OFC-2009-OWS3

[C18] R. Bonk, R. Brenot, C. Meuer, **T. Vallaitis**, A. Tussupov, J. C. Rode, S. Sygletos, P. Vorreau, F. Lelarge, G.-H. Duan, H.-G. Krimmel, T. Pfeiffer, D. Bimberg, W. Freude, and J. Leuthold, "1.3 / 1.5 μm QD-SOAs for WDM/TDM GPON with extended reach and large upstream / downstream dynamic range," in Optical Fiber Communication 2009. OFC 2009. Conference on, San Diego, CA, USA, Mar. 22–26 2009, paper OWQ1. [Online]. Available: http://www.opticsinfobase.org/abstract.cfm?URI=OFC-2009-OWQ1

[C19] C. Schmidt-Langhorst, C. Meuer, R. Ludwig, D. Puris, R. Bonk, **T. Vallaitis**, D. Bimberg, K. Petermann, J. Leuthold, and C. Schubert, "Quantum-dot semiconductor optical booster amplifier with ultrafast gain recovery for pattern-effect free amplification of 80 Gb/s RZ-OOK data signals," in Optical Communication, 2009. ECOC 2009. 35th European Conference on, Vienna, Austria, Sep. 20–24 2009, paper We6.2.1.

[C20] J. Leuthold, W. Freude, C. Koos, **T. Vallaitis**, J.-M. Brosi, S. Bogatscher, P. Dumon, R. Baets, M. L. Scimeca, I. Biaggio, and F. Diederich, "Silicon-organic hybrid (SOH) — a platform for ultrafast optics," in Optical Communication, 2009. ECOC 2009. 35th European Conference on, Vienna, Austria, Sep. 20–24 2009, invited paper Tu5.2.4.

[C21] R. Bonk, S. Sygletos, R. Brenot, **T. Vallaitis**, A. Marculescu, P. Vorreau, J. Li, W. Freude, F. Lelarge, G.-H. Duan, and J. Leuthold, "Optimum filter for wavelength conversion with QD-SOA," in Proc. Conf. on Lasers and Electro-Optics (CLEO/IQEC 2009), Baltimore, USA, May 31–Jun. 05 2009, paper CMC6. [Online]. Available: http://www.opticsinfobase.org/-abstract.cfm?URI=CLEO-2009-CMC6

[C22] J. Leuthold, W. Freude, S. Sygletos, R. Bonk, **T. Vallaitis**, and A. Marculescu, "All-optical regeneration," in Asia Communications and Photonics Conference and Exhibition, Shanghai, China, Nov. 2–6 2009, invited paper TuK1.

[C23] N. Lindenmann, **T. Vallaitis**, R. Bonk, C. Koos, W. Freude, and J. Leuthold, "Amplitude and phase dynamics in silicon compatible waveguides with highest Kerr-nonlinearities," in AMOP Spring Meeting, Deutsche Physikalische Gesellschaft, DPG Quantum Optics and Photonics Section, Hamburg, Germany, Mar. 2–6 2009, paper Q 57.4.

[C24] S. Sygletos, R. Bonk, P. Vorreau, **T. Vallaitis**, J. Wang, W. Freude, J. Leuthold, C. Meuer, D. Bimberg, R. Brenot, F. Lelarge, and G.-H. Duan, "A wavelength conversion scheme based on a quantum-dot semiconductor optical amplifier and a delay interferometer," in Transparent Optical Networks, 2008. ICTON 2008. 10th Anniversary International Conference on, Athens, Greece, Jun. 22–26 2008, invited paper We.B2.5, doi: 10.1109/ICTON.2008.4598617.

[C25] **T. Vallaitis**, C. Koos, J.-M. Brosi, B. Esembeson, I. Biaggio, T. Michinobu, F. Diederich, P. Dumon, R. Baets, W. Freude, and J. Leuthold, "Silicon-organic hybrid (SOH) modulators and nonlinear waveguides for 100 GbE signal processing," in Epixnet Annual Meeting, Eindhoven, Jun. 9–10 2008, Poster JRA-NL.

[C26] R. Bonk, P. Vorreau, S. Sygletos, **T. Vallaitis**, J. Wang, W. Freude, J. Leuthold, R. Brenot, F. Lelarge, G.-H. Duan, C. Meuer, S. Liebich, M. Laemmlin, and D. Bimberg, "An interferometric configuration for performing cross-gain modulation with improved signal quality," in Optical Fiber communication/National Fiber Optic Engineers Conference, 2008. OFC/NFOEC 2008. Conference on, San Diego, CA, USA, Feb. 24–28 2008, Poster JWA70, doi: 10.1109/OFC.2008.4528227.

[C27] C. Koos, J.-M. Brosi, P. Vorreau, **T. Vallaitis**, P. Dumon, R. Baets, B. Esembeson, I. Biaggio, T. Michinobu, F. Diederich, W. Freude, and J. Leuthold, "Silicon-organic hybrid (SOH) devices for optical signal processing," in Frontiers in Optics. Optical Society of America, 2008, invited paper FMG6. [Online]. Available: http://www.opticsinfobase.org/-abstract.cfm?URI=URI=FiO-2008-FMG6

[C28] **T. Vallaitis**, C. Koos, B. Esembeson, I. Biaggio, T. Michinobu, F. Diederich, P. Dumon, R. Baets, W. Freude, and J. Leuthold, "Highly nonlinear silicon photonics slot waveguides without free carrier absorption related speed-limitations," in Optical Communication, 2008. ECOC 2008. 34th European Conference on, Brussels, Belgium, Sep. 21–25 2008, paper Th.2.D.6, doi: 10.1109/ECOC.2008.4729411.

[C29] R. Bonk, C. Meuer, **T. Vallaitis**, S. Sygletos, P. Vorreau, S. Ben-Ezra, S. Tsadka, A. Kovsh, I. Krestnikov, M. Laemmlin, D. Bimberg, W. Freude, and J. Leuthold, "Single and multiple channel operation dynamics of linear quantum-dot semiconductor optical amplifier," in Optical Communication, 2008. ECOC 2008. 34th European Conference on, Brussels, Belgium, Sep. 21–25 2008, paper Th.1.C.2, doi: 10.1109/ECOC.2008.4729375.

[C30] R. Bonk, S. Sygletos, P. Vorreau, **T. Vallaitis**, J. Wang, W. Freude, J. Leuthold, R. Brenot, F. Lelarge, and G.-H. Duan, "Performance analysis of an interferometric scheme for media with limited cross-phase modulation nonlinearity," in Proc. 6th Intern. Symp. on Communication Systems, Networks and Digital Signal Processing (CNSDSP'08), Graz, Austria, Jul. 25–25 2008, pp. 487–491, doi: 10.1109/CSNDSP.2008.4610832.

[C31] C. Meuer, M. Laemmlin, S. Liebich, J. Kim, D. Bimberg, A. Capua, G. Eisenstein, R. Bonk, **T. Vallaitis**, and J. Leuthold, "High speed cross gain modulation using quantum dot semiconductor optical amplifiers at 1.3μm," in Proc. Conf. on Lasers and Electro-Optics (CLEO/IQEC 2008), San Jose, CA, USA, May 4–9 2008, paper CTuH2. [Online]. Available: http://-www.opticsinfobase.org/abstract.cfm?URI=CLEO-2008-CTuH2

[C32] J. Leuthold, J. Wang, **T. Vallaitis**, C. Koos, R. Bonk, A. Marculescu, P. Vorreau, S. Sygletos, and W. Freude, "New approaches to perform all-optical signal regeneration," in Transparent Optical Networks, 2007. ICTON '07. 9th International Conference on, Rome, Italy, Jul. 1–5 2007, invited paper We.D2.1, doi: 10.1109/ICTON.2007.4296187.

[C33] **T. Vallaitis**, C. Koos, B.-A. Bolles, R. Bonk, W. Freude, M. Laemmlin, C. Meuer, D. Bimberg, and J. Leuthold, "Quantum dot semiconductor optical amplifier at 1.3μm for ultra-fast cross-gain modulation," in Optical Communication, 2007. ECOC 2007. 33th European Conference on, Berlin, Germany, Sep. 16–20 2007, paper We8.6.5.

[C34] C. Koos, **T. Vallaitis**, B.-A. Bolles, R. Bonk, W. Freude, M. Laemmlin, C. Meuer, D. Bimberg, A. D. Ellis, and J. Leuthold, "Gain and phase dynamics in an InAs/GaAs quantum dot amplifier at 1300 nm," in Proc. Conf. on Lasers and Electro-Optics (CLEO/IQEC 2007), Munich, Jun. 17–22 2007, paper CI3-1-TUE. [Online]. Available: http://www.opticsinfobase.org/-abstract.cfm?URI=CLEO_E-2007-CI3_1

Curriculum Vitae

Thomas Vallaitis

thomas.vallaitis@gmail.com

Work Experience

06/2005–04/2010	**Karlsruhe Institute of Technology (KIT), Institute of Photonics and Quantum Electronics (IPQ)** PhD studies - Fabrication of quantum dot devices (epitaxy, device design) - Construction of a characterization lab for sub-picosecond device dynamics (pump-probe) - Experimental demonstration of ultrafast all-optical signal processing in a communication system context (fastest wavelength conversion on Si) - Contribution to work packages and deliverables of several European and national research projects - Tutorial lectures on optical communications (fiber optics and waveguides, lasers, detectors, communication systems, nonlinear optics) - Supervision of student projects and master theses
01/2004–03/2004	**Technische Universität München (TUM)**
03/2003–04/2003	Student trainee - Construction of a gas handling system for a ^{3}He/^{4}He dilution refrigerator
03/2002–04/2002	**DaimlerCrysler** Factory worker
03/1999–04/2001	**University of Stuttgart, Institute of Geophysics** Student trainee - Y2K proofing of a seismograph data acquisition system - Administration of a heterogeneous UNIX network
12/1998–02/1999	**Hagen Stanek, Sindelfingen** Programmer - Development of a Win/CE driver's log application
07/1998–09/1998	**Daimler-Benz** Factory worker

Education

06/2005–present	**Universität Karlsruhe (TH) / Karlsruhe Institute of Technology (KIT), Institut für Photonik und Quantenelektronik (IPQ)** PhD thesis on "Ultrafast Nonlinear Silicon Waveguides and Quantum Dot Semiconductor Optical Amplifiers: Characterization and Applications." Grade "very good" ("magna cum laude")
03/2005	**Technische Universität München** Physics major, "Dipl.-Phys." Grade 1.9 (gut, "good")
11/2003–12/2004	**Technische Universität München E25** Final thesis "Growth and characterization of manganese-doped germanium" Grade: 1.0 (sehr gut, "very good")
09/2001–12/2004	**Technische Universität München** Physics major: - Semiconductor physics - Nuclear physical methods of analysis
09/1998–08/2001	**University of Stuttgart** Undergraduate studies: - nanostructures and nanotechnology - semiconductor physics
09/1997–06/1998	**Military service**
08/1988–06/1997	**Gymnasium Unterrieden Sindelfingen (secondary school)** Allgemeine Hochschulreife (general qualification for university entrance) Grade: 1,4 (sehr gut, "very good")
04/1984–06/1988	**Grundschule Sindelfingen Hinterweil (elementary school)**

Karlsruhe Series in Photonics & Communications
KIT, Institute of Photonics and Quantum Electronics (IPQ) (ISSN 1865-1100)

Die Bände sind unter www.ksp.kit.edu als PDF frei verfügbar
oder als Druckausgabe bestellbar.